THE
OLD
TESTAMENT
TEXT *and* CONTEXT

THIRD EDITION

THE
OLD
TESTAMENT

TEXT *and* CONTEXT

VICTOR H. MATTHEWS

AND JAMES C. MOYER

Baker Academic
a division of Baker Publishing Group
Grand Rapids, Michigan

© 1997, 2005, 2012 by Victor H. Matthews and James C. Moyer

Published by Baker Academic
a division of Baker Publishing Group
P.O. Box 6287, Grand Rapids, MI 49516-6287
www.bakeracademic.com

Printed in the United States of America

Library of Congress Cataloging-in-Publication Data

Matthews, Victor Harold.
    The Old Testament : text and context / Victor H. Matthews and James C. Moyer. — 3rd ed.
      p. cm.
    Includes bibliographical references and index.
    ISBN 978-0-8010-4835-7 (pbk.)
    1. Bible. O.T.—Criticism, interpretation, etc. 2. Bible. O.T.—History of Biblical events. I. Moyer, James C.
  II. Title.
  BS1171.52.M38 2012
  221.6′1—dc23
                                                    2011043237

The internet addresses, email addresses, and phone numbers in this book are accurate at the time of publication. They are provided as a resource. Baker Publishing Group does not endorse them or vouch for their content or permanence.

12 13 14 15 16 17 18   7 6 5 4 3 2 1

Contents

Figures and Maps

Figures

Maps

PREFACE TO THIRD EDITION

It has now been well over a decade since the first edition of *The Old Testament: Text and Context* first appeared in 1997. In looking back and also taking into account the changes that were made in the second edition (2005), we remain pleased with the volume, but there are always ways to improve any textbook. In this third edition, we have worked to improve its readability and added new features (Key Points) that are designed to assist students who are coming to the material for the first time. We have also injected new ideas, such as geographic reiteration, that help to clarify some of the strategies employed by the ancient authors. As always, we are grateful to those scholars who reviewed the second edition and made helpful suggestions. We are also indebted to our students who each semester provide us with feedback in our classes. They have always been the ultimate arbiters of whether the textbook accomplishes its goals.

Here is a basic list of what you will find in this newly revised third edition:

1. The entire textbook has been rewritten and significantly expanded. Special attention has been given to highlighting the four major themes of covenant, universalism, wisdom, and remnant.

2. More aids have been added to provide a better sense of chronology, historical events, and literary devices.

3. The study questions at the end of each section or chapter have been revised so that they are a catalyst for class discussion and for personal reflection.

4. Additional examples and insets have been provided from ancient Near Eastern texts so that students have a better understanding of the social and literary milieu of the ancient world.

5. Attention is given to new archaeological discoveries and the continuing debate among scholars over some interpretations of these data.

6. Some sections of the textbook have been relocated to provide a smoother transition from one chapter to another.

7. The glossary entries have been revised and rewritten and are indicated in text when introduced by boldface type.

It is our hope that these changes will make this textbook even more useful to students and their teachers. And, as we always do in our classes, we invite you to contact us with your comments and suggestions. You can consult an online syllabus for our course at http://courses.missouristate.edu/VictorMatthews/courses/101syl.htm and can write to us by email at VictorMatthews@missouristate.edu or JamesMoyer@missouristate.edu.

ABBREVIATIONS

General

A.	Tablet signature of texts from Mari
ANET	*Ancient Near Eastern Texts Relating to the Old Testament.* Edited by J. B. Pritchard. 3rd ed. Princeton University Press, 1969.
BCE	before the Common Era (= BC)
ca.	circa
CE	Common Era (= AD)
cf.	*confer*, compare
CH	Code of Hammurabi
ch./chs.	chapter/chapters
COS	*Context of Scripture.* Edited by W. W. Hallo and K. L. Younger Jr. 3 vols. Leiden, 1997–2003.
HB	Hebrew Bible
KJV	King James Version
KUB	Keilschrifturkunden aus Boghazköi
LXX	Septuagint
MAL	Middle Assyrian Law Code
NAB	New American Bible
NIV	New International Version
NJPS	*Tanakh: The Holy Scriptures: The New JPS Translation according to the Traditional Hebrew Text*
NRSV	New Revised Standard Version
NT	New Testament
OT/HB	Old Testament/Hebrew Bible
OTPar[3]	Victor H. Matthews and Don C. Benjamin, *Old Testament Parallels: Laws and Stories from the Ancient Near East.* 3rd ed. Mahwah, NJ: Paulist Press, 2006.
REB	Revised English Bible
SBL	Society of Biblical Literature
v./vv.	verse/verses

Hebrew Bible

Gen.	Genesis
Exod.	Exodus
Lev.	Leviticus
Num.	Numbers
Deut.	Deuteronomy
Josh.	Joshua
Judg.	Judges
Ruth	Ruth
1–2 Sam.	1–2 Samuel
1–2 Kings	1–2 Kings
1–2 Chron.	1–2 Chronicles
Ezra	Ezra
Neh.	Nehemiah
Esther	Esther
Job	Job
Ps./Pss.	Psalms
Prov.	Proverbs
Eccles. (or Qoh.)	Ecclesiastes (or Qoheleth)
Song (or Cant.)	Song of Songs (Song of Solomon, or Canticles)
Isa.	Isaiah
Jer.	Jeremiah
Lam.	Lamentations
Ezek.	Ezekiel
Dan.	Daniel
Hosea	Hosea

Joel	Joel
Amos	Amos
Obad.	Obadiah
Jonah	Jonah
Mic.	Micah
Nah.	Nahum
Hab.	Habakkuk
Zeph.	Zephaniah
Hag.	Haggai
Zech.	Zechariah
Mal.	Malachi

New Testament

Matt.	Matthew
Mark	Mark
Luke	Luke
John	John
Acts	Acts
Rom.	Romans
1–2 Cor.	1–2 Corinthians
Gal.	Galatians
Eph.	Ephesians
Phil.	Philippians
Col.	Colossians
1–2 Thess.	1–2 Thessalonians
1–2 Timothy	1–2 Timothy

Titus	Titus
Philem.	Philemon
Heb.	Hebrews
Jas.	James
1–2 Pet.	1–2 Peter
1–3 John	1–3 John
Jude	Jude
Rev.	Revelation

Apocrypha

Bar.	Baruch
Add. Dan.	Additions to Daniel
Pr. Azar.	Prayer of Azariah
Sg. Three	Song of the Three Young Men
Bel	Bel and the Dragon
Sus.	Susanna
1–2 Esd.	1–2 Esdras
Add. Esth.	Additions to Esther
Ep. Jer.	Epistle of Jeremiah
Jdt.	Judith
Let. Jer.	Letter of Jeremiah
1–2 Macc.	1–2 Maccabees
Pr. Man.	Prayer of Manasseh
Sir.	Sirach/Ecclesiasticus
Tob.	Tobit
Wis.	Wisdom of Solomon

·1·

INTRODUCTION

The Purpose of This Book

The Old Testament: Text and Context provides an introduction for beginning students to the literature, history, and social context of the Old Testament/Hebrew Bible (OT/HB). Our effort is to attract and to keep the student's interest with lively prose and a variety of study aids. In addition, we wish to explain why studying the literature of ancient Israel is relevant and why it is still relevant today. One only needs to consider our value system, our understanding of religion, our basic reaction to injustice, and our sense of appropriate behavior to see how profound these writing have been to the development of Western culture. A cursory review of our literature and even the plots of television dramas demonstrate the debt we owe to the peoples of the ancient Near East. The Bible cannot be dismissed as ancient, dead, or boring. It remains an integral part of our culture and will continue to provide guidance into the future.

The Bible's general impact on modern society is reason enough for educated persons to study it whether they have a faith commitment or not. For those who revere the Bible as sacred literature and the God of the Bible as their own God, the text holds even greater significance. In either case, the richness of the stories, the vivid human emotions found in many episodes, and the practical advice that forms the heart of much of this literature makes it a remarkable literary achievement.

Student aids as well as teaching and discussion suggestions are found in each chapter of this textbook. The writing style and interactive textboxes are designed to draw students into the text without overwhelming them with too much information. Our aim is to tell the ancient stories and provide a variety of methods to explore their meaning and place them within their historical and social context. To achieve that goal, we have included information boxes, brief insets on aspects of daily life, and comparisons with extrabiblical texts. Each of these supplementary insets can be used for part of class discussion as cultural enrichment opportunities.

One key to learning any material is to grasp the ways in which diverse biblical materials interrelate. What we mean by this is that a single fact may be important in and of itself. However, it becomes infinitely more valuable when it is seen as a part of the whole picture of the biblical story. For instance, we know from the Bible's many references that David is portrayed as a shepherd while he was a boy. That creates one picture in our mind, but it does not give us the larger picture. As the youngest member of his household, David is given the task of shepherding his father's flock. The practical aspects of protecting his flock from danger are then applied when David, the warrior, struggles to win battles to make his people safe. David the shepherd manages his animals to ensure that their numbers increase and thereby contribute to the livelihood for his family. David the king administers the affairs of state in order to build up the economy and bring a greater prosperity to his country. And finally, David the shepherd, alone with his flock, examines God's creation and builds a foundation of faith and a sense of God's protection of the faithful (see Ps. 23). That experience then helps shape his policies when he establishes **Yahweh** as the God of Israel and brings the **ark of the covenant** to Jerusalem.

Making connections such as these helps to increase a basic familiarity with the stories. At the same time, these connections open the mind to a range of possibilities, including how choices are made and relationships are built. If characters remain only characters in a story, they will never become real to the reader. The persons mentioned in the Bible are too often idealized as a body of saints and sinners, not as real people. Once it becomes clear that many of the episodes involve normal human activities in a traditional society, then the social setting can be explored more fully. An approach such as this, which stresses the social world of ancient Israel, differs from that found in

most devotional or religious contexts. However, what we are doing here is essential for understanding the Bible on any level. With that in mind, this textbook can benefit students in a variety of educational and religious contexts.

It is a simple reality that a textbook that does not follow a logical order will not be widely used by teachers or students. Some textbooks arrange the material based on literary categories or an attempt to place the material in the chronological order in which it was composed. For instance, it is accepted by many scholars that much of the Genesis material was composed or compiled during the monarchic (ca. 1000–600 BCE) and postexilic (ca. 500–300 BCE) periods of Israelite history. Therefore, some introductions begin their discussion with the monarchy and discuss the creation and flood epics and the ancestral narratives only as they relate to and are reflections of the monarchic or postexilic periods. Such an arrangement can be extremely confusing to students. We believe a better way is to present the material in the order of the books as they are arranged in most English translations of the Bible, starting with Genesis and running through much of 2 Kings. The only exception to this will be when dealing with the prophets, whose **canonical** order has little relation to their chronological order. They are divided in the Bible into major and minor prophets based on their length.

Because we both are historians, we place a great deal of emphasis on the historical narrative presented in the biblical text. As a result, a great deal of effort has gone into re-creating the social setting of basic institutions, including marriage, debt slavery, kinship ties, and business practices. Obviously it is necessary to be cautious so that we do not impose a solution or a rigid interpretation on these narratives. It is understood that there are always new data surfacing from archaeological and social-scientific research that will have an effect on biblical interpretation.

To provide a general focus throughout the book, we have chosen to emphasize four basic concepts: **covenant**, **universalism**, **wisdom**, and **remnant**. These concepts provide general themes for much of biblical narrative, plot, and dialogue. Here is a brief sketch of each.

Covenant. A covenant is a contractual arrangement between two parties. In the biblical text it is used in the context of the following:

1. The promise of "land and children" made to Abraham by Yahweh in exchange for Abraham's sole allegiance and obedience to Yahweh's word or law (Gen. 15:5–21). This is a *conditional* covenant that requires both sides to fulfill all the stipulations of the agreement. There are periodic *renewals* of this covenant as the people or their leaders believe a fresh start is necessary (Exod. 24:3–8; Josh. 24:1–28; Neh. 8:1–12).

2. The **Law** (**Torah**) grew out of the Abrahamic covenant. As the Israelite community becomes larger and requires more guidance, the covenant is expanded upon in the **Decalogue** (Ten Commandments), which is given to Moses (Exod. 20:1–17). Subsequent legal codes such as the **Covenant Code** (Exod. 21–23), **Deuteronomic Code** (Deut. 12–26), and **Holiness Code** (Lev. 17–26) reflect the growing complexity of the nation as it shifted from a village culture to one dominated, at least politically, by urban centers like Jerusalem. However, each of these legal codes retains the covenant as its central principle.

3. The "**everlasting covenant**" is made between King David and Yahweh (2 Sam. 7:4–16). According to this agreement, Yahweh promises that there will always be a king of the "line of David" ruling in Jerusalem. It is an *unconditional* covenant, which means that no matter how bad a particular descendant of David may be, that does not terminate the agreement. After the monarchy ends (587 BCE), this covenant is transformed into a *messianic expectation*, which assumes that Yahweh will provide a **Messiah** figure that will restore the nation to its former independence and proper relationship with Yahweh.

Universalism. This term is used in the sense of the presence, the power, and the concern of Yahweh extending over the entire creation (see Isa. 40:12–26). In their attempt to portray Yahweh as supreme among the gods, the biblical writers periodically inject this element into narratives. It generally involves the use of a non-Israelite character who, because of her or his knowledge of what Yahweh has done for the Israelites (e.g., crossing the Red Sea; see Rahab's speech in Josh. 2:8–10) or because of a personal experience (e.g., cure from disease), makes a statement of faith that Yahweh is the most powerful or the only true God (see Naaman's speech in 2 Kings 5:15). Eventually this will be expanded into an exclusive belief in Yahweh as the only true God, but this **monotheistic** belief will not take its full form or be widely accepted until late (after 400 BCE) in Israelite history.

Wisdom. While a specific section of the Bible is recognized as **Wisdom literature** (primarily Job, Proverbs, Ecclesiastes), examples of Wisdom speech or admonition are found throughout the biblical text. Wisdom embodies both common sense and basic social values in antiquity. Ultimately all wisdom comes from God (see Prov. 3:5–8). The Wisdom theme includes such ideas as wise behavior: no action taken hastily or without thinking (see 14:29); wise speech: no word spoken that may injure someone else (16:13); wise person: one who walks in the "way" or "path" of Yahweh and who recognizes that wisdom may be acquired from persons of all ages, genders, and occupations (see Prov. 12:15; Eccles. 8:1).

Remnant. Because the people were unable to keep the covenant, recognize the universal character of Yahweh, or act wisely, Yahweh periodically punished them. The **theodicy** (an explanation for God's actions) that the prophets use to explain why the nation is conquered by non-Yahweh-worshiping peoples includes the idea that God is required under the covenant to provide a warning (see Isa. 10:5–11). It is assumed that the righteous (always a minority or remnant) will heed this warning, take appropriate action to come back into compliance with the covenant, and, after the punishment has occurred, become the people—a righteous remnant—who will restore the nation (see Ezek. 9).

How to Use This Book

The intent of this textbook is to be as objective as possible in providing a presentation of the materials found in the OT/HB. No denominational viewpoint will be espoused, and a variety of significant theories and interpretations of the text will be presented. The translation of the Bible that we have used is the New Revised Standard Version (NRSV). We have chosen it because of its literal translation of the Hebrew and Aramaic text and because of its use of **inclusive language**, which applies the correct pronoun based on the context. A number of features in this volume are designed to aid the student in dealing most effectively with the material. These include:

Insets. These boxes provide a variety of information for the student. They may have a

translation of an ancient text that parallels the biblical narrative. There may be a chart outlining the structure of a biblical passage, or there may be examples of a particular issue addressed in the biblical text. In every case, the box will be referred to and attention drawn to it for specific purposes by the authors.

Key Points. At the beginning of each section or chapter, a box will be provided that includes several short statements intended to provide keys to understanding the information found here.

Maps. Maps are included to provide a visual and spatial sense of direction, distance, and topography for the student.

Glossary. Throughout the pages of the text, technical terms associated with biblical studies have been set in **bold**. They are often defined in the text at that point, but a complete glossary of these technical terms is also found at the end of the volume. Students are encouraged to consult the glossary whenever they need additional information on a technical term.

Study Questions. We have provided study questions at the end of each chapter. These are intended to promote student learning and class discussion and to reiterate major points in the chapter.

Indexes. At the end of the volume the following information is indexed: subjects, personal and place names, and Scripture citations. These will help the student find particular topics more easily in the text.

Abbreviations. Certain abbreviations and conventions will be used by the authors in this textbook. A key is found after the Table of Contents. Among the most important are:

Old Testament/Hebrew Bible (OT/HB). Since the material found in Scripture belongs to more than one religious tradition, we have chosen to use this longer title throughout the volume. It also identifies the portion of Scripture that has been recognized by Jews and Protestants as their canon. The expanded canon of the **Septuagint** and the Catholic Bible, which includes the **Apocrypha**, or **Deuterocanonical books**, will be discussed in a separate section of the chapter on the Hellenistic period.

BCE and CE. These abbreviations stand for "before the Common Era" and "Common Era." They correspond precisely to BC and AD dates, but they are more religiously neutral designations than "before Christ" (BC) and "in the year of our Lord" (*anno Domini* = AD).

Geography and Climate of the Ancient Near East

KEY POINTS

- Riverine cultures are shaped by the predictability and availability of resources.
- Topography and climate are key factors in ancient Near Eastern cultural development.
- Rival superpower empires created in Egypt and Mesopotamia will influence the history and culture of ancient Israel.
- Israel's diverse geographic zones and placement between the two great empires influence its history and cultural development.

Topography and climate are major factors in the development and interaction of cultures in the ancient world. Given the difficulties associated with travel on foot or with pack animals, the dangers of contact with new peoples, and the physical challenges presented by mountains, rivers, and arid regions, it is amazing how much interaction took place. Of course, commerce and warfare are primary catalysts for travel, and a great deal can be overcome with the right motivation. In this portion of our textbook, we will provide a brief overview of the major regions of the ancient Near East, including their primary topographical features, climatic conditions, and cultural developments.

The ancient Near East can be divided into three primary geographic areas: Mesopotamia (primarily modern Iraq), Egypt, and Syria-Palestine. Adjacent to these regions are Anatolia (modern Turkey), Persia (modern Iran), Arabia (modern Saudi Arabia), and the island of Cyprus. They also figure in the history and the development of advanced cultures during this period but are less important than the others in terms of the story of the ancient Israelites.

Mesopotamia

The region of ancient Mesopotamia, which today comprises the area of Iraq and portions of northern Syria and eastern Turkey, is dominated by the twin river system of the Tigris and Euphrates. These rivers are fed by melting snows in the mountains of eastern Anatolia. They flow southeastward into the Persian Gulf and provide a ready link between the various cities that grew up along their banks. Because of the unpredictable amount of snow available in any given year, it was impossible to rely on standardized flood levels. Since much of southern Mesopotamia is flat and featureless, there are periodic, devastating floods, especially along the Euphrates River. These floods can cover miles on either side of the rivers and occasionally even wash over whole cities, as in the case of ancient Ur. Normally, however, the floods tend to change the course of the Euphrates River. That, in turn, could isolate the cities located on its banks from easy access

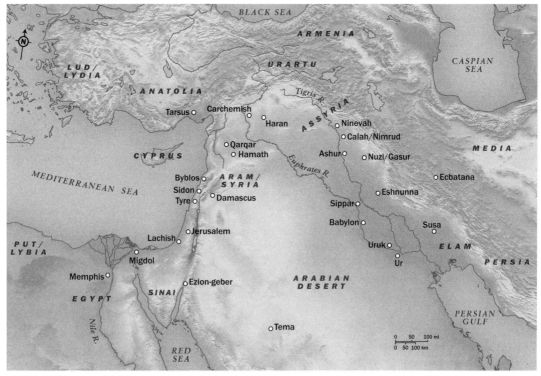

Map 1.1. Old Testament World

to the waters needed to irrigate their fields and sometimes resulted in the abandonment of a site. These periodic, devastating floods may be the origin of the flood epics that appear in some of the earliest literature from ancient Mesopotamia.

The southeasternmost reaches of the Tigris and Euphrates system form a marshy region that was the home of the earliest human settlements in this area. In more modern times, they served as the dwelling place for the marsh Arabs of Iraq until that region was drained by the Iraqi government in the twentieth century. The rivers become widely separated as they traverse the hilly area of the southern Caucasus Mountains, but at one point in their southern march, near the site of ancient Babylon, they are only a few miles apart.

The land that the Tigris and Euphrates travel through is quite arid, and thus it is their waters that make life and travel possible here. Initially the marshy area in the south provided the inhabitants with fish and wild game as well as protection from outsiders. As the population grew, however, settlements moved northward, and by 4000 BCE several **city-states** developed in what is later known as the land of Sumer. This region extended from the narrow confluence of the two rivers south to the Persian Gulf. Cities like Ur, Nippur, Kish, Uruk, and Lagash were founded here, and they shaped their culture around life on the rivers. The people also learned to accept the constant threat of invasion by their neighbors or raids by marauding bands from the steppe areas to the east that periodically disrupted their lives. Because rainfall is minimal throughout this region, irrigation is the principal means of growing crops. A network of irrigation canals allowed people to extend their plots of farmland, create a surplus for trade, and expand their populations. These monumental construction projects also promoted a bureaucratic, stratified society dominated by kings and a temple-based priesthood. The elements of their cultures, including the **cuneiform** writing system, political organization, and **polytheistic** religion, will be discussed in the chapter on the history of these regions.

In this section we will examine the other geographic areas of Mesopotamia. The region north of Sumer eventually developed another major population center, Babylonia. Over time, this section of the country was able to dominate all of Mesopotamia during the period from 2000 to 1500 BCE. The kings of Babylonia were the first to unite the majority of Mesopotamia under a single ruler. The Amorite culture of the Babylonians and their vassal city-states borrowed many of the cultural advances that first developed in Sumer. Although international diplomatic and economic contacts increased during this period, bringing new peoples and products to the region, the land's basic existence was still dominated by dependence on managing the waters taken from the Tigris and Euphrates.

The third major region of Mesopotamia lies in the northern reaches of the Tigris River and is known as Assyria. Here, from their capitals at Ashur and Nineveh, emerged some of the most aggressive and warlike people of the ancient world. Because of their northern position, they had a harsher climate, with greater temperature extremes, a shorter growing season, and more mountainous terrain. When they began to push out of their own area in about 1000 BCE, the Assyrian war machine

Map 1.2. Mesopotamia

quickly took control over the more temperate regions to the south and eventually (by ca. 660) extended its empire as far as Egypt. The Assyrians were the first to control all the regions of the ancient Near East and the first people to have to cope with the environmental as well as social and political demands of each of its geographic areas. They were also despised by the people whom they conquered and exploited (see Nahum's rejoicing over their destruction, especially in 3:18–19). Assyria eventually succumbed to internal disputes and the pressure from emerging powers in Babylonia and Persia.

Egypt

Egypt is also dominated by a river system, the Nile. Since its territory otherwise consists of arid wastes and desert, nearly all of Egypt's culture and history developed within a very narrow band along the Nile River valley.

Map 1.3. Egypt

The Nile flows north from the mountains of Kenya to the Mediterranean, where it forms a fan-shaped estuary much like that near New Orleans on the Mississippi River. It is broken periodically in its flow by cataracts (rapids and waterfalls) that prevent easy passage to its source. Thus travel routes, guiding merchants carrying frankincense from Arabia and other exotic products, followed the Nile. However, due to a series of cataracts along its southern stretch, travelers seldom sailed its full length. Caravaneers would portage their goods and small vessels over short stretches or take short voyages northward along the Red Sea to where they could make an easy overland connection with the Nile boatmen.

Due to its more isolated position, Egypt developed much of its culture independently. It is cut off from the west by the Sahara, from the south by the Nilotic cataracts, and from the east by the waters of the Red Sea and the desert of the Sinai peninsula. Of course, there were contacts with other peoples early in Egyptian history, but the Egyptians always considered their culture superior to all others and became quite **xenophobic** (fearful of foreigners) in their attitudes.

Unlike the unpredictable character of the Tigris and Euphrates rivers, the Nile has an established cycle of flooding, which brings new layers of rich soil to the irrigated fields of the Egyptians. By building canals and dikes, farmers are able to reinvigorate their fields each year, making Egypt the breadbasket of the ancient world (see Gen. 12:10; 41:53–57). The very constancy of their existence also contributes to the Egyptians' development of a well-defined, positive concept of the afterlife, the only ancient Near Eastern culture to do this.

The climate in this region is very dry, having only small annual rainfall amounts. Temperatures are hot nearly year round, although they do moderate in the evening, and in the desert it can become quite cold at night. Throughout its history, Egyptian culture has been attuned to the rise and fall of the Nile. The Egyptians acclimated themselves, through clothing and architectural styles, to the extremes in temperature. The rhythm of their lives took on a cyclic flow that for much of their history contributed to long periods of stability. It is only when Egypt began being threatened by outside invaders (starting in about 1750 BCE) that they became more aggressive and emerged as a superpower rivaling the Hittites of Anatolia and the various empires that arise in Mesopotamia.

Syria-Palestine

Because there are more geographical references in the Bible than in most sacred

8

literature, no one can effectively follow the biblical narrative without studying the geography and climate of Syria-Palestine. The events of the Bible occur in a relatively small area, but this region contains a tremendous degree of geographical and climatic diversity. Ideally we should charter a jet and take a trip to the Middle East to see and experience this for ourselves. Better yet, we could take a whole year to live and study abroad. Since these options are not always available, we will settle for a brief description based on the authors' experiences.

The areas to the north and east of Palestine include most of the traditional rivals and allies of ancient Israel. Immediately north is the region of Phoenicia (modern Lebanon), which dominated the trade on the Mediterranean Sea from approximately 1100 BCE until its absorption into the Persian Empire after 540 BCE. Its climate is tempered by the sea breezes off the Mediterranean, but the mountain range that runs north-south through the country

Map 1.4. Palestine during Ancient Times

enjoys abundant rainfall during the fall and winter (36–40 inches/year), supporting the cedar forests so prized in antiquity. The area has chilling temperatures during the winter months, and the mountains are capped with snow. The principal cities of Tyre and Sidon were situated on the only deep water ports along the coast, and the inhabitants were quick to take advantage of such a resource for

their shipping industry. They are the second people in this area to control the trade in the Mediterranean. From 1600 to 1200 BCE, the northern Syrian seaport city of Ugarit served the merchants who traveled throughout the Mediterranean. But Ugarit was conquered and destroyed in about 1200 by the **Sea Peoples**, and its commercial activities eventually were inherited by the Phoenicians.

Syria, or Aram, comprised the land between northern Mesopotamia and Phoenicia. Its capital city at Damascus was a way station for caravans as far back as 2500 BCE, and it served as the chief rival to the kingdoms of Israel and Judah during much of the biblical monarchic period. This city, located on the only perennial river, the Barada, in an otherwise arid region, created an oasis with enough irrigated land to support a fairly large population. A land of mountains, plains, and deserts, Syria was able to maintain itself through trade and agriculture. Due to the variations in elevation, its temperature ranges are quite extreme. In Damascus, it is hot and dry much of the year, but a few miles north, in the mountains, winter can have bitingly cold temperatures. Because of its strategic location on the trade routes, it was in constant conflict with the Mesopotamian empires.

Turning south to Canaan, what may be emphasized are the contrasts in terrain and climate. For instance, it is possible on a December day in Jerusalem to need heavy overcoats. The atmosphere will be damp, and the wind will chill a person to the bone. That same day, you can travel twenty miles in about thirty-five to forty minutes to the Dead Sea. There the temperature will be in the balmy seventies, and it is possible to go swimming. How could this be? Though Jerusalem is only about twenty miles from the Dead Sea, it sits at almost 2,700 feet above sea level, while the Dead Sea is more than 1,300 feet below sea level. The result is a 4,000-foot drop that contributes to a temperature change of about forty degrees. This kind of diversity is one excellent reason for studying the climate and geography of Israel. Another significant reason is the fact that Israel is situated on a centrally located land bridge between the two ancient superpowers: Egypt to the south (in Africa), and Mesopotamia to the north. There were no direct routes between the two on the Mediterranean Sea or through the Arabian desert. Instead, people traveled the coastal highway in Canaan or along the plateau in Transjordan (the King's Highway). Israel's central location gave it a significance and prominence far exceeding the size of the country or its political power. Furthermore, it was impossible for ancient Israel to isolate itself from the superpowers. Consequently, throughout much of its history, Israel was dominated by the political and economic ambitions of either Egypt or Mesopotamia.

How large was ancient Israel? The best estimates suggest a total land area of approximately 8,000 square miles. This is slightly less than one of the small New England states (e.g., Vermont or New Hampshire). From the northern extremity to the southern extremity, from Dan to Beersheba (Judg. 20:1; 1 Sam. 3:20), the distance is about 145 miles. An average east-west distance would be from the coast to Jerusalem (about 30 miles) and from Jerusalem to the northern tip of the Dead Sea (about 20 miles); thus the east-west dimensions total about 50 miles. A helpful way to understand the geography and climate of the country is to think of the country as divided into four north-south strips of land.

Coastal Plain. Starting on the west is the coastal plain, which is characterized by flat, low lands with white sand dunes right on the Mediterranean coast. A little farther inland in ancient times were fertile areas, as well as forested or marshy regions. Lacking natural deepwater harbors, the ancient Israelites never developed into a seafaring state, unlike their Phoenician neighbors to the north.

The coastal zone includes three very fertile plains: Acre, Sharon, and Philistia. The Plain of Acre stretches to the north from Mount Carmel about twenty-five miles and extends inland anywhere from five to eight miles. It never figures prominently as a significant geographical feature during biblical times. Probably it was controlled much of the time by Phoenicia. To the south of Mount Carmel for about fifty miles lies the Plain of Sharon. It extends inland about ten miles. Because in biblical times it was generally a marshy wasteland, it did not figure as a prominent region either. Still farther to the south is the Plain of Philistia, named after the Philistines, another of Israel's rivals. It is one of the most fertile areas in the country. The Philistines settled here after the invasion of the Sea Peoples weakened Egyptian control (after 1200 BCE). They built several cities (Ashdod, Ashkelon, Ekron, Gaza, Gezer), from which they dominated this area until the reign of David.

An international route or highway named the *Via Maris* stretched through this coastal plain. It ran a few miles inland from the sea, and near the northern part of the Plain of Sharon it cut inland through a mountain pass in the Carmel range. Armies and traders usually did not continue farther north along the coast from where the road to this inland pass branched away from the coast because some miles north along the coast the Carmel range of hills extends to within 150 yards of the sea. That narrow strip of land between the sea and the Carmel range proved to be a hazard to travelers, who could fall easy prey to bandits. Megiddo, guarding the inland mountain pass and the entrance to the Jezreel Valley, became the focal point for merchants and invading armies as they traveled the *Via Maris* eastward.

The climate on the coastal plain is extremely hot in the summer. During the day the temperatures register at about one hundred degrees Fahrenheit. A sea breeze at night makes the temperature more tolerable. Many modern inhabitants of Israel living in Tel Aviv have balconies on their apartments so they can enjoy these night breezes. In the winter the temperatures go down into the forties and fifties, warm enough to keep frost at bay because of the moderating influence of the Mediterranean Sea. This allows all kinds of citrus and other fruits to be grown in the coastal plain, including the famous Jaffa orange, as well as grapefruits, lemons, limes, and avocados. A large portion of the coast has inviting sandy beaches, where many Israelis head on weekends.

Central Hill Country. The second north-south strip is called the central hill country. As one moves from the coastal plain up into this hilly region there is a transitional area referred to as the **Shephelah**. The Shephelah region is characterized by gently rolling hills as one goes farther and farther inland toward the east and up into the central hill country. The hills are really just low, ranging slopes. They extend up to 3,300 feet high in the area around Hebron, but they certainly are not high enough to be called mountains.

The central hill country was the chief center of ancient Israel's population. In antiquity, these hills were heavily wooded. Only sparsely populated before the emergence of the Israelites in the twelfth century BCE, the hill country was the easiest region for ancient Israel to capture and hold. The Canaanites inhabiting the plains were unable to use their advanced weaponry (chariotry) here, a fact that provides the Israelites with a foothold in the land (Judg. 1:19). The area can be conveniently divided into three sections: to the north is the Galilee, in the center is Samaria,

Figure 1.1. The transitional area between the coastal plain and the central hill country looks like this and is called the Shephelah.
(Baker Photo Archive)

and in the south is Judah. The most important geographical features in the Galilee are the Valley of Jezreel and the Sea of Galilee. This was an important and fertile region. The cities of Megiddo, Beth-shan, Jezreel, and Hazor are located here. In the center are the hills of Samaria. The most famous of these hills are Mount Ebal and Mount Gerizim, near the city of Shechem. To the south are the hills of Judah, and in the most southern sections of Judah is the Negev desert.

A limited amount of grain could be grown in the central hill country, but agricultural work was difficult and labor-intensive. The hillsides had to be terraced and then could serve as excellent locations for the planting of vineyards (Isa. 5:1–2) and fig and olive trees.

These trees do well because their deep root system enables them to survive the hot, dry summers. The grazing of goats and sheep is also more typical here than in the coastal plain.

During the summer the climate is hot and dry with temperatures ranging around ninety degrees. Because of the wind that comes up in the evening, it can get chilly at night. However, during the winter this is a difficult place to live. The temperatures are in the thirties and forties, and it is rainy, damp, and blustery. There is even some frost, though the average temperature does not often go below thirty-two degrees, and snow is uncommon.

Jordan River Valley. The third north-south strip is the Jordan River Valley. This is a gigantic rift or geological fault starting in the north in Syria and extending southward all the way into Africa. Much of it lies below sea level. Lake Hulah in the north is 230 feet above sea level. However, in the twentieth century it was drained and so does not appear on modern maps. Only ten miles to the south is the Sea of Galilee, which is 700 feet below sea level. The Jordan River flows out of the Sea of Galilee and winds its way south, eventually emptying into the Dead Sea. The Jordan River covers a distance of only about seventy miles, but it travels such a circuitous route that the banks of the Jordan River cover close to two hundred miles. The Dead Sea is well known as the lowest water surface on earth. It is more than 1,300 feet below sea level, with the lowest depth of the sea at the northern end somewhere around 2,600 feet below sea level. It is so warm in this region that no outlet is needed since the water evaporates. The salt content is so high that no large life forms can live in the Dead Sea. Around Jericho, just north of the Dead Sea, the average annual rainfall is only two inches per year.

Since the Jordan River cuts such a deep path into the soil, it is not very valuable for irrigation purposes. In biblical times it was too difficult to raise the water up to the surrounding land to water fields. The result is that very limited amounts of land were tilled in this region in ancient times except around Jericho, where there is a spring that today allows farmers to grow citrus fruits, bananas, and vegetables in abundance. During the summer, the temperature averages about one hundred degrees with very low humidity levels. At night the temperature cools down into the sixties. In winter, the high temperature is in the seventies, which helps to explain why later rulers like Herod built winter palaces in the Jericho region.

Transjordan Plateau. The fourth of the north-south strips is the Transjordan Plateau. The climate is similar to the central hill country, but the terrain is flat and ranges from about 2,000 feet high in the north to about 5,000 feet high in the extreme south. The region is fairly fertile, but there is not enough rain to produce extensive crops or support a large population. Again, as in the central hill country, sheep and goats are common livestock, and they help balance the risks of famine and economic ruin for the farmers. This north-south plateau or strip is divided by four streams: the Yarmuk, Jabbok, Arnon, and Zered. Each flows to the west, and together they divide the Transjordan Plateau into five areas: to the north of the Yarmuk is the land of Bashan; between the Yarmuk and Jabbok is Gilead; between the Jabbok and the Arnon rivers is the kingdom of Ammon; south of the Arnon lies Moab; and to the south of the Zered is Edom. Running along this plateau from the Gulf of Aqaba in the south to Damascus in the north is the King's Highway, a major trade link for both the Sinai and the Red Sea. Living in this area were Israel's neighbors and sometime rivals, the Ammonites, Moabites, and Edomites.

It is important to understand that in the Mediterranean climate of Syria-Palestine there is a dry season in the summer that extends from much of May into most of September. As a result, for four to five months each year one can plan each day without ever having to worry about rain. There is also a rainy season that is concentrated between December and March. Of course, the total rainfall varies dramatically from about two inches in the desert regions to more than forty-five inches in parts of Galilee. Still, the conditions make it necessary to conserve and channel water sources, to develop dry farming techniques, and to divide the year into rainy and dry seasons between planting and harvesting activity.

Conclusions

Ancient Israel was primarily rural with a mixed economy based on agriculture and **pastoralism**. Throughout the biblical period the majority of the people lived in small villages and had limited contact with the urban centers of Jerusalem and Samaria. The hills and valleys of this region made transportation difficult and hazardous. Therefore, the people developed various sections of the land in their own distinctive ways and attempted to preserve those distinctions as part of their cultural heritage. The hills and valleys also kept people isolated from one another and slowed political unification until the tribes were faced with the necessity of organizing under a single ruler. When we read the book of Judges, for example, it is obvious why the tribes could not unify. They were people with regional differences who did not easily mingle with one another or join together as political entities.

■■■■■■■■ **STUDY QUESTIONS** ■■■■■■■■

1. What questions should be asked about the topography of a region, and how has topography helped to define the development of culture in the ancient Near East?
2. Why are the worldviews of the two major riverine cultures in the ancient Near East completely different?
3. Why is Syria-Palestine so important geographically for the cultures in Mesopotamia and Egypt?
4. How do the four areas or north-south strips of ancient Israel differ with respect to climate, geography, and resources?
5. What aspects of geography are evident when reading a biblical narrative (e.g.,

Gen. 12:4–9; Josh. 22:1–6; Judg. 1:8–21)? How do geographical descriptions in such passages affect the stories being told?

Outline of Israelite History

What follows is a brief outline of the major time periods and events in Israelite history. The dates for all premonarchic events are of necessity approximations since we currently lack any archaeological or extrabiblical evidence to corroborate them. The dates and historicity of the early monarchic period are also subject to question and have been the basis for a great deal of scholarly debate.

A. *Premonarchic* periods portrayed in the biblical text in Genesis through Judges
   1. *Primeval* period: Adam and Eve, Noah and the flood (date uncertain).
   2. *Ancestral* period: Abraham and Sarah, Isaac and Rebekah, Jacob and Rachel and Leah (possible dates range from 2000 to 1300 BCE, with a preference for 2000 to 1750 BCE by many scholars); covenant established.
   3. Movement of Jacob/Israel's family into Goshen (Egypt) with Joseph's assistance (possibly dated to Hyksos period, ca. 1750–1570 BCE).
   4. *Exodus* from Egypt: Moses and Aaron (perhaps in the reign of Ramses II, ca. 1290–1226 BCE).
   5. *Settlement* period: Joshua (dating to ca. 1250–1100 BCE) with possible links to the Merneptah **Stele**, the incursions of the Sea Peoples, including the Philistines.
   6. *Judges* period: Ehud, Deborah, Gideon, Jephthah, Samson (ca. 1200–1020 BCE).

B. *Monarchic* period

   1. *Early monarchy:* Samuel and Saul (ca. 1020–1000 BCE).
   2. *United kingdom:* David and Solomon (ca. 1000–922 BCE); Jerusalem; "everlasting covenant" established.
   3. *Divided monarchy:* Secession of northern tribes under Jeroboam (ca. 922 BCE); Israel survives until 721 BCE (Assyrian deportation in 720 BCE) and Judah until 587 BCE (exiled by Nebuchadnezzar).

C. Exile and Persian period

   1. *Babylonian exile* (596–539 BCE): Jewish identity movement begins; Ezekiel, Isaiah of exile.
   2. *Persian* period (539–332 BCE): Cyrus, Darius, Xerxes, Artaxerxes; temple rebuilt (515 BCE), Zerubbabel, Haggai; Jerusalem's walls rebuilt (ca. 445 BCE), Nehemiah; renewal of covenant by Ezra (ca. 400 BCE).

D. Hellenistic and Roman period

   1. Conquests of Alexander of Macedonia (336–323 BCE) end Persian control over Judah. All of Palestine becomes part of the Hellenistic Empire. Palestine is ruled first by the Ptolemies and after 198 BCE by the **Seleucids**. The **Maccabees'** revolt against Seleucid king Antiochus IV in 167 BCE brought brief period of independence led by the **Hasmoneans.**
   2. Roman general Pompey captures Jerusalem in 63 BCE. First unsuccessful revolt against Roman rule occurs in 66–73 CE, Herod's temple is destroyed in 70 CE, and the Bar Kokhba revolt occurs in 132–135 CE.

Archaeology and the Bible

KEY POINTS

- Archaeology is a team effort with meticulous standards and a scientific base of operations.
- Archaeology is not designed and is not equipped to prove the Bible is true.
- Archaeology assists in the study and reconstruction of aspects of life in the ancient world.

Archaeology's ability to enhance our understanding of the Bible and its world affords it a special status for many scholars. In particular, archaeology enhances our understanding of the written text with physical evidence. During the past century, archaeology has revolutionized the study of the text of the Bible. In this section we will briefly discuss how archaeological methods and artifactual evidence help us to re-create the world of the Bible.

Archaeological evidence provides some of the best information on everyday living conditions, architecture, industry and agriculture, religious practices, and social customs in ancient times. When careful methods are applied to the excavation of a large artificial mound created by accumulated occupation levels of an ancient city (**tell**) and much smaller village (**khirbet**) sites, information slowly emerges from the ground that can aid our understanding of the people of the past and in some cases clarify historical events. These methods include:

Systematic Recording of Finds. Photographic and written records are made of each level of occupation (**stratum**) within the dig, special finds are noted and drawn to scale, and a clear sense of the location and dimensions of the excavation is maintained with the use of ground-penetrating radar and surveying equipment. In some cases the images of artifacts are digitized and placed on websites to share with students and scholars and create a virtual comparative collection for future study. All this record keeping is necessary because once one level of a site has been cleared, it is removed in order to discover the levels that lie beneath it and cannot be reexcavated. Although the work of recording is slow and costly, archaeology would be nothing but treasure hunting without it.

Careful Attention to Excavation Methods. Much of what comes out of the ground is grimy, broken, or corroded. Therefore it takes care and experience to recognize a coin, a particular ceramic style, an inscription on a wall, or an **ostracon** (broken piece of pottery used to record a message). Field supervisors spend a great deal of their time training the volunteer workers to use the proper tools, exacting excavation techniques, and the correct manner in which to carefully remove and identify artifacts as they appear in the dig. In this way they prepare the next generation of archaeologists, and they ensure more meticulous work by these volunteers.

Artifactual Material Is Shared with a Wide Range of Experts. In order to gain the most information and to draw a more complete conclusion on life in the biblical period than the archaeologists can obtain alone, what comes out of the ground must be made public. For instance, the carbonized remains found in storage jars, grain silos, and on the floors of excavated threshing floors, when examined by teams of microbiologists, botanists, and paleobotanists, can provide information on the diet of ancient humans. Their general level of health can be surmised, and the sophistication of their methods of agriculture and animal husbandry can be at least partially ascertained.

Figure 1.2. A carved ivory panel of a woman looking out a window. This decoration from a piece of furniture was originally made in Phoenicia in about the beginning of the eighth century BCE and imported to the then-capital of Assyria, Calah, in what is today northern Iraq. (Baker Photo Archive, courtesy of the British Museum)

Advantages and Limitations of Archaeology

We can summarize the advantages of archaeology as follows:

- It adds new evidence to help reconstruct the biblical world (e.g., inscriptions, objects from daily life).
- It helps us to visualize objects and places mentioned in the biblical narrative.
- It helps to illuminate some poorly understood sections of the Bible.
- It makes biblical people come alive as real people who used tools, weapons, and other items.
- It creates interest, excitement, and enthusiasm by making new discoveries.

- It supplements ancient written records. Written records tend to depict upper classes; archaeological discoveries tend to add to this the artifacts of the common people.

We can summarize the limitations of archaeology as follows:

- The evidence (physical remains) is fragmentary and often damaged.
- The evidence requires interpretation, which is based on subjective judgment.
- It deals with physical remains but not the abstract. Therefore, it cannot prove or disprove theological statements such as "There is [not] a God."
- It is one consideration within scholarly debate, but literary evidence (the Bible) often takes priority over archaeological evidence among biblical scholars.

Archaeological techniques are constantly changing and improving. Reports from older excavations usually have limitations and should be used with care.

Geologists and chemists can determine the origin of the clay used to make an ancient pottery jar by examining its microscopic components, including shells and minerals distinctive to particular areas. That data, in turn, can suggest trade between areas and the changes in ceramic technology.

Results of Each Year's Excavation Must Be Presented and Published. This includes the site plans (detailed drawings of the architectural remains and other finds discovered at each level of occupation) prepared by the archaeologist in consultation with an architect, the photographs and drawings of the individual artifacts, quantified data of the entire scientific team, and the reconstructive analysis of the site director and the other scholars associated with the project. Presentation of each season's finds at scholarly meetings provides other researchers with new data and alerts them to new ideas and conclusions that may change current thinking or suggest new hypotheses. Publication in print and digital form enables other archaeologists to interpret their own finds from other sites. The

archaeologist who does not present and publish the results of an excavation deprives other scholars and students of the benefit of his or her work.

Advantages and Limitations of Archaeology for Understanding the Bible

To expect archaeological discoveries to prove the truth of the Bible conclusively is unreasonable. The findings of archaeologists are only mute evidence of life in the ancient past. In other words, to say, as the archaeologist John Garstang did in the 1930s, that a particular wall found in the excavations at Jericho was the one that fell to the trumpet blasts of Joshua, without examining all the surrounding evidence (pottery, building styles, depth within the excavated site's **stratigraphy**), is unfair to the student and to the biblical text as well. Improved methods of excavation later proved Garstang to be incorrect even in his identification of the stratigraphic level of Joshua's Jericho, and this mistake led to controversy and a misunderstanding of the proper role of

Siloam Tunnel

The excavation of a tunnel dug from inside the walls of Jerusalem out to the spring of Gihon provided a secure link to water during the Assyrian siege of the city in 701 BCE. A record of this tunnel is found in 2 Kings 20:20 as part of the "deeds of Hezekiah." Excavators discovered the tunnel in 1880 and found an inscription carved into the wall describing its construction. Unfortunately, there is no mention of the king responsible for ordering this work to be done. Examination of the style of the script dates it to the eighth century BCE, and recent **carbon 14** (C^{14}) testing of carbonized remains from the tunnel further certify this date. In this instance, the biblical account is at least partially verified by both textual and chemical evidence.

archaeological research in relation to the study of the Bible.

For archaeological evidence to be useful, artifacts (everything from architectural remains to pottery) must first be examined within the context of the occupation sites where they are found. Then they must be treated as part of a general archaeological survey of the region as a whole. The sites, or **tells,** of ancient Canaanite and Israelite cities are layered. Each level or stratum represents a different phase in the history of the site. Since objects found within the lower levels of the tell can generally be assumed to be older than those found closer to the surface, a chronology of the various levels or strata can be developed. On the rare occasions when inscriptions are discovered, they must be examined by linguistic experts and then analyzed to see if they can throw any light on the biblical narrative.

The work of developing a reliable stratigraphy of the tell is made more difficult in that some confusion of the strata does occur due to earthquake activity and the digging of pits (for storage or refuse) and foundations by later inhabitants. To overcome this obstacle and to establish a relative chronology for each city site, archaeologists examine pottery types

and other artifacts from each layer. The findings are then compared with finds from the same levels in several similar sites. Carbon 14 dating of organic remains, as well as other scientific methods, also aid in the process.

Due to the limitations of time and money, archaeologists seldom excavate an entire mound. They carefully map out squares for excavation or dig exploratory shafts in those portions of the mound that surveys or ground-penetrating radar have shown to contain the most important structures (temples, palaces, gates) or the most representative objects of interest. Walls of earth called **baulks** are left

Figure 1.3. Hezekiah's tunnel (Siloam tunnel) was dug through rock late in the eighth century BCE. It connected the Gihon spring concealed just outside the walls of the city of Jerusalem with pools constructed within the walls. This enabled the residents of the city to draw water during any military siege without exposure to the enemy. (Baker Photo Archive)

Archaeological and Historical Periods in Palestine	
Paleolithic prior to 10,000 BCE	**Iron Age I** ca. 1200–1000 BCE
Mesolithic ca. 10,000–8500 BCE	**Iron Age II-A** ca. 1000–925 BCE
Neolithic ca. 8500–4300 BCE	**Iron Age II-B/C** ca. 925–586 BCE
Chalcolithic ca. 4300–3300 BCE	**Assyrian Period** 732–604 BCE
Early Bronze ca. 3300–2300 BCE	**Neo-Babylonian Period** 604–539 BCE
Early Bronze IV/Middle Bronze I ca. 2300–2000 BCE	**Persian Period** 539–332 BCE
Middle Bronze II-A ca. 2000–1800 BCE	**Hellenistic Period** 332–63 BCE
Middle Bronze II-B/C ca. 1800–1550 BCE	**Roman Period** 63 BCE–324 CE
Late Bronze ca. 1550–1200 BCE	**Byzantine Period** 324–640 CE

standing. They divide the excavated squares and allow a clear record of the stratigraphy as well as convenient walkways around the dig site.

Recently developed archaeological techniques do try to obtain a broader perspective on the entire mound, but it is unlikely that every shovelful of dirt will be turned or every object uncovered. The fact that many sites were excavated before the development of modern methods magnifies the difficulties of obtaining a complete picture of how a site was occupied. In some cases, time is lost when new teams are forced to reexamine the dumps of previous excavations or have to reconstruct architectural features from what is left behind by too-eager excavators. This means that a great deal of valuable information has been lost forever. Archaeology is a destructive process (each level must be recorded and then removed to get to the level below it), and what has been removed can never be replaced. As a result, it is impossible to learn all there is to know about life in these ancient cities through archaeology. Thus, responsible archaeologists today intentionally leave some portions of the mound untouched for later generations and their more advanced excavation methods.

Chronological Periods of Biblical History

For convenience's sake, the various periods of biblical history have been divided into chronological periods. This can be somewhat misleading in the earliest periods since there is no extrabiblical evidence for the existence of the characters described in the Bible prior to the monarchy (ca. tenth century BCE). Archaeology, however, has provided us with chronological divisions based on technology levels, and these will be used to identify the uncertain periods of Israelite history.

The earliest historical period associated with the Israelites is the *Middle Bronze Age* (ca. 2000–1550 BCE). Its name is based on the use of bronze (an alloy of copper and tin) as the chief metal for making tools, utensils, and implements. It is also defined by styles and techniques of producing pottery. Tradition places the ancestral narratives in this period, but there are no existing extrabiblical written materials that mention Abraham and Sarah, Isaac and Rebekah, or Jacob and Rachel and Leah by name. Texts written in the cuneiform (wedge-shaped) script from ancient Mesopotamian cities such as Mari, Nuzi, and Alalakh and hieroglyphic **execration** texts from Egypt (see geography section for the location of these sites) have helped to illuminate the world described in these narratives, but, like all archaeological artifacts, they cannot prove the historicity of these characters.

advent of the *Iron Age* (ca. 1200–586 BCE). *Iron I* (ca. 1200–1000 BCE) is associated with the early monarchy in Israel. There is some dispute among scholars about the archaeological evidence for the early monarchy period due to a lack of inscriptional data and the somewhat inconclusive results of excavations at Jerusalem and elsewhere.

During *Iron II* (ca. 1000–586 BCE) Israel divided into two nations: Judah in the south, with its capital at Jerusalem; and Israel in the north, with its eventual capital at Samaria. This

Figure 1.4. Merneptah, son of Ramses II, reigned in Egypt during the latter part of the thirteenth century BCE. He describes his victories over the Libyans in this granite stele. Toward the bottom of the inscription it says, "Israel is crushed, it has no more seed." (Baker Photo Archive, courtesy of the Museum of Egyptian Antiquities, Cairo)

The *Late Bronze Age* (ca. 1550–1200 BCE) is generally associated with the periods of the exodus, conquest, and settlement in Israelite history. Archaeological evidence can be used to note population shifts, the establishment of new settlements, and the destruction of existing towns and villages. Nevertheless, the only piece of extrabiblical evidence during this period that points to the existence of the Israelites is the Merneptah Stele from Egypt, a royal inscription that mentions Israel as a people conquered by the pharaoh and dating to about 1208 BCE.

The introduction of new peoples and new technologies into Canaan contributed to the

Figure 1.5. Standing a bit over one foot in height, this Assyrian foundation record (Taylor Prism) mentions the Assyrian ruler Sennacherib's victory over the Israelite king Hezekiah (ca. 701 BCE). (Baker Photo Archive, courtesy of the British Museum)

Figure 1.6. The tell of ancient Beth-shan located in the lower Jezreel Valley three miles west of the Jordan River. In the foreground are some of the remains of Scythopolis, a NT city. (Baker Photo Archive)

is a time of considerable contact with other nations, and as a result archaeology reveals the construction and fortification of many walled cities (Hazor, Megiddo, Gezer, Jerusalem; see map for these sites), and the presence of trade goods from all over the Mediterranean world (pottery, jewelry, metals, incense). The first inscriptional evidence mentioning biblical characters by name comes from this period (**Mesha Stele** from Moab, House of David Stele from Dan, Assyrian Annals). There is also a much larger number of inscriptions mentioning biblical characters and events that date to this period. Some of these, like the annals of the Assyrian kings (Sargon II, Sennacherib) and King Nebuchadnezzar of Babylon, reflect the dangers presented by empire-building superpowers. A few Israelite inscriptions, such as the Arad ostraca and the Lachish letters, afford a glimpse of Israelite scribal and writing style and the concerns of individuals in these troubled times.

The final historical period we will consider in this volume is the postexilic era. During this time, some of the exiles return to Judah (known as Yehud at that time) and live under Persian rule (539–332 BCE). The temple in Jerusalem is rebuilt in about 515 BCE. Relations with the Persian government can be seen in the minting of coins and in written materials such as the Cyrus Cylinder.

This era ended with the conquests by Alexander the Great of Macedonia and the initiation of the Hellenistic period (332–63 BCE). The blending of cultures that resulted from the infusion of Greek philosophy, religion, art, and literature into the Near East transformed that region and led Judaism to further define itself within a broader cultural context.

A brief period of Jewish independence does occur during the Hasmonean period (167–63 BCE). The **Maccabean** Revolt, sparked by the repressive decrees of Antiochus IV, had driven the Seleucid Greek rulers out of Palestine. The Jews were able to rule themselves for several generations. Eventually the corruption of their kings and fighting among the various religious factions made them easy prey for Pompey and the Romans in 63 BCE.

Roman rule invigorated Palestine's economy and saw the construction of monumental buildings, roads, and water systems. The New Testament (NT) and the works of the first-century-CE Jewish historian Flavius Josephus contain a wealth of information on the social world of the Jews under the Romans. These documents describe the various factions (**Sadducees, Pharisees, Essenes,** and **Zealots**) that existed at that time, as well as the currents of discontent among the people. The basis for their anger was the imposition of Roman custom and law as well as the tyrannical and economy-draining policies of the Herods. The desire of the Jews to be free of foreign rule and to worship as they pleased led to numerous uprisings. In response the Romans in 70 CE destroyed Jerusalem and the temple, which had been built by Herod. This, plus the expulsion of most of the Jews from Palestine following the Bar Kokhba Revolt (135), was the final step in pushing the Jews into a religion of the book—one not tied to temple, priesthood, or land.

STUDY QUESTIONS

1. What resources are used by an archaeologist to determine where to dig?

2. Why are there occasional differences between the biblical narrative and the archaeological record?
3. What are some of the disciplines that analyze the artifacts and other remains discovered by the excavators?
4. Describe how ceramics and C^{14} are used to determine the relative chronology of a tell.
5. What can we learn about daily life from the examination of ancient architecture?

Oral Tradition and the Development of the Canon

KEY POINTS
- Writing systems develop to assist business and to provide governments with records and propaganda.
- Though the story of ancient Israel began orally, it was shaped in the editing process after the rise of the monarchy.
- The Hebrew canon is a product of centuries of editing and was not closed and standardized until the period after the destruction of Jerusalem by the Romans.
- Translation into Greek, Latin, and vernacular languages led to the development of new canons and new levels of interpretation.

In the beginning was the spoken word. The biblical stories as we read them today began as orally transmitted episodes, told by elders, parents, and itinerant storytellers. Except for a small scribal class, the nearly universal illiteracy among the earliest people of the ancient Near East made oral transmission of information, history, and poetry necessary. Although the ancient cultures of Egypt and Mesopotamia invented writing systems as early as 3500 BCE, they are very difficult to learn. These ancient languages are written syllabically. Every sound is represented by a different symbol. As many as nine hundred different characters are found in these writing systems, while English is written in twenty-six different letters. As a result, only trained scribes, who had devoted many years to study, knew how to read and write. Elite members of society employed scribes to read and write for them. But in everyday situations, people relied on spoken communication, not written texts.

A cuneiform variant using a linear alphabetic system was developed at Ugarit, a seaport city at the extreme northern edge of Syria's Mediterranean coastline and fifty miles east of the island of Cyprus during the period between 1600 and 1200 BCE. Because merchants found it inconvenient and expensive to employ scribes to maintain their business records, a simplified script, using only thirty cuneiform signs, was developed. This easy-to-learn system allowed anyone,

with a minimal amount of study, to prepare documents and examine those of customers and suppliers. It also contributed to the development of cursive, alphabetic scripts throughout Syria-Palestine and eventually to a rise in literacy among the people.

Another alphabetic system of writing was invented in about 1600 BCE by West Semitic people in Canaan and the Sinai area. The first examples of a linear alphabetic script, using an **acrophonic** style (shaping the letters based on sound and meaning) were found at Shechem, Gezer, and Lachish, and it is probable that this script was developed under the influence of Egyptian administrators in that region. This alphabetic system was quickly adapted for use by the scribes throughout the region and was further perfected by the Phoenicians after 1100 BCE.

Governments and religious institutions use oral tradition for their own purposes. Their scribes edited ancient stories and events from their own time for publication. The result is court histories, religious literature and drama, and a large body of folk stories woven into narrative form. It is likely that the first sections of written biblical narrative originated in a wave of nationalism created by the establishment of the monarchy after 1000 BCE. Over time the body of literature continued to grow, but not all of it became a part of the official version of events. Volumes of histories, such as the Book of Jashar (Josh. 10:13b), presumably provided detailed accounts of battles and leaders, but these enticing reference works no longer exist. When those in authority came to realize that a single voice is necessary to standardize the people's understanding and knowledge of events, editors were put to the task of shaping the narratives.

Figure 1.7. The Babylonian Chronicle, written in wedge-shaped writing called cuneiform on a clay tablet shown in approximately actual size, records Nebuchadnezzar's victory over Jerusalem in 587 BCE. (Baker Photo Archive, courtesy of the British Museum)

Development of the Canon

This editorial process continued throughout the period prior to about 200 BCE. By that time a large number of books had been identified as belonging to a **canon** (i.e., sacred Scripture) by the Jewish community. Evidence of this is found in the Prologue to the Apocryphal or Deuterocanonical (see p. 271) book of Sirach that mentions the "Law and the Prophets." Although these books continue to exist in various versions for centuries, the basic form of the **Hebrew canon** had taken shape.

Pentateuch, Law, or Torah: The five books at the beginning of all recognized biblical canons deal with beginnings and ancestral stories and contain instructions (law) for living. They are Genesis, Exodus, Leviticus, Numbers, and Deuteronomy.

Historical books: These books tell the story of Israel as a nation before its destruction and exile and then continue the story following its exile. Their major divisions are as follows:

Wisdom, **Liturgy**, and Songs: Six works are concerned with worship and wisdom. They are Job, Psalms, Proverbs, Ecclesiastes (also known as Qoheleth), Song of Songs (also known as Song of Solomon or Canticles), and Lamentations.

Deuteronomic Histories: These six books are concerned with the history of the Israelites from the conquest to the end of their independence as a nation. They are Joshua, Judges, 1–2 Samuel, and 1–2 Kings.

Postexilic Histories: Four books tell Israel's story from the viewpoint of those who returned from the exile. These are 1–2 Chronicles, Ezra, and Nehemiah.

Popular Histories: Three books tell the stories of heroes who are intended to serve as role models of courage and faithfulness in the midst of difficult social situations. They are Ruth, Daniel, and Esther.

Prophets: There are fifteen books associated with named prophets. They range in time from the eighth century BCE, during the divided monarchy, to the postexilic period (after 500 BCE). The prophetic books are arranged in the canon with the books of the three Major Prophets coming first and being followed by the books of the Minor Prophets. They are not in chronological order.

Major Prophets: Isaiah, Jeremiah, and Ezekiel.

Minor Prophets or *The Twelve*: The twelve shorter books as they appear in the canon are Hosea, Joel, Amos, Obadiah, Jonah, Micah, Nahum, Habakkuk, Zephaniah, Haggai, Zechariah, and Malachi.

Apocrypha (Deuterocanon)

Additional books were composed during the **Second Temple** period (500–100 BCE) that were not included in the HB canon. These volumes, largely written in Greek and known as the Deuterocanonical books (the term used by Roman Catholics) or the Apocrypha (the term used by Protestants), include histories such as 1–2 Maccabees, as well as continuations of some of the canonical books (Additions to Esther [Esther]; Bel and the Dragon [Daniel]). Although these books ultimately were not chosen for inclusion in the final order and composition of the Hebrew canon, they are important for understanding the history and traditions of the Second Temple period. In particular, they provide insight into the period of early Judaism leading up to the birth of Christianity.

The intent of the canonization process was to standardize the text for use by Jews wherever they had been scattered after the destruction of Jerusalem in 70 CE. In this textbook we will include a discussion of the books of the HB recognized by both Jewish and all Christian people as canonical while noting that the canon of the OT within much of the Christian church, particularly the Roman Catholic and Eastern Orthodox churches, includes the additional books of the Deuterocanon/Apocrypha (see ch. 6).

The Move toward and the Trouble with Translations

At approximately the same time that some of the earliest of the Apocryphal/Deuterocanonical books were being written (mid-third century BCE), the first translation of the Hebrew text was produced in Greek. This project, initiated by the large Jewish community in Alexandria, Egypt, was necessitated by the decline of Hebrew as a spoken language, especially in the scattered settlements of the **Diaspora**. Jews wished to read and study their **holy** texts in the language that they used every day. The translation that they produced is known as the Septuagint (LXX, based on the tradition that seventy-two or **seventy elders** created the translation). In the process they also created a separate (Alexandrian) canon that includes the books of the Deuterocanon/Apocrypha.

Any translation, ancient or modern, will have its problems due to cultural and linguistic differences. Language is a reflection of individual culture. As a result, some words, phrases, and colloquialisms do not translate precisely from one language to another. The translators of the Septuagint therefore had to make judgment calls in order to interpret the meaning of some key words and passages. An example of this may be found in the dilemma over the word "love." Hebrew has several words for love, *'ahab*, **khesed**, and *hashaq*, which are

used in a variety of contexts, from human love to the love expressed in God's covenant with the people of Israel. Greek also has three: *eros*, *agapē*, and *philia*. Being able to match the correct linguistic equivalent to the social or legal context of the text is the task and the trial of the translator.

The Septuagint is only the first of the biblical translations. It was followed by many others, including the Latin translation, the **Vulgate**. This work was the monumental effort of a leading scholar of the fourth century CE, Jerome, who translated both the OT and the NT from Hebrew and Greek manuscripts available at the time. He chose to include the books of the Apocrypha in this new Bible and in the process created the Catholic canon of the Bible. Jerome's Vulgate was produced under the patronage of Pope Damasus in the early 380s, and he continued to work on it after 387 in Bethlehem. The Vulgate was made the official Bible of the Roman Catholic Church at the Council of Trent in 1546.

From the fourteenth century onward, the officials of the Roman Catholic Church persecuted anyone who attempted to translate the biblical text into the common languages of Europe. The emerging political powers of northern Europe supported people's desire to read the Bible in the vernacular. Under the protection of local kings and princes, the leaders of the Protestant Reformation—Martin Luther, Thomas Cranmer, John Calvin, and William Tyndale—chose to translate the Bible into their own national languages as a part of their attempt to break with the Roman church and to make the Bible available for study and reflection by the masses. Luther changed the canon once again in his translation by excluding the Apocrypha, or Deuterocanonical books, and thus created a Protestant canon.

In England, as part of the general wave of translations being produced, James I commissioned a group of thirty scholars to create a standard or authorized version for use in his kingdom. The result is the King James Version (KJV), published in 1611. This work represents the efforts of the finest scholars of the time and, along with the works of William Shakespeare, is a chief contributor to the development of modern English. While the KJV continued to include the books of the Apocrypha until 1825, the majority of the Protestant movement adopted a canon of thirty-nine books for the Hebrew canon, which differed from the Catholic canon containing forty-six books.

Modern translations of the Bible have continued to be produced and in recent years, from time to time, have become a source of theological contention with various religious groups.

The discovery (1947) of the **Dead Sea Scrolls** in caves near the settlement of **Qumran** created an explosion of new scholarship and new translations. These scrolls, which were produced between 100 BCE and 70 CE, contain portions from thirty-eight books of the Hebrew canon (minus Esther) in versions older than any other Hebrew manuscript available to us. They are approximately one thousand years older than the existing **codices** (book manuscripts) of the Hebrew text produced in the Middle Ages. While they do demonstrate that several versions of the biblical books existed prior to the final setting of the canon, they have not revealed any major contradictions or provided materials that would require a radical rethinking of the biblical message.

The Hebrew writing system as it existed in the time of the Qumran community did not contain vowel signs or punctuation. When Hebrew ceased to be a living language, difficulties arose over pronunciation and translation. These problems were addressed by a group of Jewish scholars known as the **Masoretes**. They developed a system of counting the number of letters in each manuscript and then, when they made a fresh copy, counting them once again to be sure nothing had been added or deleted. They also invented a system of vowel and punctuation marks that were placed above and below the now-sacred letters as an aid in reading the text. Their task was designed to prevent any further changes from creeping into the text. The variations in manuscripts had proved to them that this had happened in the past due to errors by copyists. Among the most common errors that they were able to prevent by their system were **dittography** (accidently writing the same word twice), **haplography** (accidentally deleting a word or a phrase), and scribal **glosses** (marginal notes or explanations that were later incorporated into the text).

The biblical text as we have it today is a product of a long process and the work of many writers, editors, and copyists. Its revelatory character is based on the belief system of its own day and must be understood within that social and historical context. Applications of the biblical material to later periods and cultures come most easily from the wisdom (such as Proverbs) and poetic (Psalms) materials. Genealogies, histories, and political propaganda have more interest to historians than to theologians.

Modern Methods in Studying the Bible

Today students and scholars rely on a variety of methods to study the Bible. This is because ancient documents, like the Bible, are often subject to uninformed interpretation, based on

Figure 1.8. A reproduction of three columns from the Isaiah Scroll. Found in Qumran Cave 1, it was the first of the Dead Sea Scrolls to be identified and has been dated to the second century BCE. (Dr. James C. Martin. Collection of the Israel Museum, Jerusalem, and courtesy of the Israel Antiquities Authority, exhibited at the Shrine of the Book, Jerusalem)

modern misconceptions or biases. Devotional or doctrinal interpretations may also slant the meaning of the text or harmonize stories to eliminate inconsistencies or contradictions. The inset below that deals with "How to Read and Interpret the Bible: Some Cautions" attempts to describe some of these issues.

A scientific or analytical examination of the biblical text is known as **exegesis**. It attempts to establish the original meaning and purpose of the narrative using the original languages of the text. The competent exegete attempts to determine no more and no less than what the text can tell us, and this process should not be influenced by speculation or creative interpretation (i.e., **eisegesis**). We will briefly examine several of the scientific methods employed by exegetes. Each will be referred to as a form of biblical criticism. This should not be understood as a negative term but as a means of describing and analyzing the biblical text. If the term "criticism" is too negative for some

students, they should use "analysis" in all the examples below.

Textual Criticism. We do not possess a single **autograph** (original manuscript) of any biblical book. Therefore scholars are forced to study those ancient manuscripts of the biblical text that have survived. The discovery of the Dead Sea Scrolls at Qumran greatly advanced the work of text critics. In particular, these manuscripts cast light on the history of the transmission of the Hebrew text. The multiple copies of the books of the OT/HB (except Esther) found at Qumran are more than a thousand years older than any previously known texts.

Throughout ancient times, manuscripts were copied by hand. As a result, each varies slightly from the others due to copyist errors and sometimes because the scribe chose for theological or other reasons to alter the text. Therefore careful comparisons must be made between scrolls, codices, and fragments in all the original biblical languages (Hebrew, Greek, and Aramaic) and in early translations of the Bible in Syriac, Latin, and other languages. Through these comparisons scholars known as text critics are able to reconstruct the original words of the text to the best of their ability. Text critics also do comparative work with other languages from the ancient Near East, such as Akkadian, Phoenician, Ugaritic, Hittite, Egyptian, and Canaanite dialects (Moabite and Edomite). In some cases this has made it possible to translate Hebrew words that had previously been considered a misspelling or were unknown (see the discussion of the translation of technical terms in the Psalms in ch. 5).

Historical Criticism. This method attempts to determine the historical context out of which the text emerged and eventually took its shape. Items of importance to the historical critic are the original audience, the intent of the writer in addressing specific historical events, and the influence of the place and time (context) in which a document was written. Archaeological data, textual clues on dating the text (e.g., Isa. 6:1 or Jer. 1:1–3), and extrabiblical evidence are utilized. Historical critics concern themselves with matters of authorship, date of composition, literary genre, style of writing, and vocabulary.

Source Criticism. Since none of the biblical material still exists in original manuscripts and none has been proved to be written by any single individual, the determination of authorship or source has become a separate category. Much of modern scholarship is influenced by the work of the nineteenth-century German scholar Julius Wellhausen. He developed what came to be known as the **documentary hypothesis,** a theory that originally divided the Pentateuch (Genesis through Deuteronomy)

into historical periods and ascribed authorship to a succession of four editors, now termed J, E, D, and P. His methodology of source criticism was extended by later scholars to the study of other biblical books.

While it is a matter of debate among modern scholars—ranging from those referred to as maximalists, who accept the biblical account as mostly straightforward and accurate; to minimalists, who see the majority of the biblical text as a fictional creation of the late postexilic or Hellenistic era (after 400 BCE)—the actual dating and events surrounding the compilation and editing of the biblical narratives is still unknown. A centrist or middle-of-the-road position suggests that it began to take shape after the establishment of the monarchy (after 950 BCE).

In his documentary hypothesis, Wellhausen's source-critical method identified the earliest source or editor of the Pentateuch as J (standing for *Jahweh,* the German spelling of Yahweh), the most commonly used name for God in this portion of the text. His **J-source** included most of Genesis and is considered the oldest story told by the Israelites about themselves. According to his scheme, because this source was compiled during the early monarchy (tenth century BCE), Jerusalem and the claim to the promised land are very prominent in these stories. It is also less polished than later stories, allowing the ancestors to display human errors and uncertainties. For instance, Abraham lies to and cheats the pharaoh (Gen. 12), telling him that Sarah is his sister rather than his wife. More recent evaluation of the J-source suggests that it may be a later (post-700 BCE), pro-Judah compilation whose intent is to solidify the importance of the Davidic monarchy and the events and places associated with the southern kingdom.

The Deuteronomistic Historian and the Archaeological Record of the Ninth to Seventh Centuries BCE

- Ahab, king of Israel, is chronicled in great detail in 1 Kings 17–22, but only his failures, his idolatry, and his domination by his Phoenician wife, Jezebel, are emphasized by the Deuteronomistic Historian. However, Assyrian records (Shalmaneser III) describe him as the head of a coalition of twelve kings and the contributor of the largest contingent of war chariots at the Battle of Qarqar in 853 BCE. The Mesha Stele from Moab includes the admission that Omri, Ahab's father, had imposed his political control over that Transjordanian kingdom. Archaeological excavations have shown monumental construction projects by both Omri and Ahab at Samaria, Jezreel, Hazor, and Megiddo. All this evidence points to a much more powerful king than the biblical editors chose to portray in their version of the story.

- Ahaz, a late eighth-century king of Judah, is described in the biblical narrative (2 Kings 16; Isa. 7) as a vacillating monarch who submits to the Assyrians and carries out idolatrous worship practices in Jerusalem. The archaeological record, however, indicates dramatic population growth and an increase in the Arabian trade, which sparked a flourishing of the Beersheba region during the period of his reign. For the biblical editors, however, his failure to listen to the prophet Isaiah outweighs any accomplishments by his government.

- Hezekiah, king of Judah and son of Ahaz, is celebrated as a righteous successor to David, defying the Assyrians, cleansing the temple of foreign gods and idols, and miraculously surviving a crippling siege of Jerusalem by the rapacious Assyrian king Sennacherib (2 Kings 18–20; Isa. 36–37). The archaeological record demonstrates that Hezekiah's decision leads to a general devastation of Judah by the invading Assyrian army. Nearly every site excavated in the Shephelah plateau of western Judah and the Beersheba valley had been conquered and burned. The Assyrian Annals also describe their success and graphically depict the siege of Judah's principal border settlement at Lachish and the deportation of its surviving people.

- Manasseh, a seventh-century king of Judah and son of Hezekiah, is pointedly described by the Deuteronomistic Historian as the worst king of Judah. He is defined as the monarch who contributed the most to introducing foreign worship and cultural practices. His policy of cooperation with Assyria during that empire's strongest period benefited the economy of Judah and allowed many of its abandoned or destroyed cities to be rebuilt. The olive groves in the Shephelah supplied the massive olive-oil industry in Assyrian-controlled Ekron, and inscriptions, seals, and inscribed weights indicate that in Manasseh's time Judah reached its fullest level of statehood, while existing as a vassal of the Assyrians.

The second source identified by Wellhausen is called the **E-source**. Dating it to the period of the divided monarchy (about 850–750 BCE), he saw this as a development of the political changes caused by the division of Israel. This material was blended with the J-source, adding a greater emphasis on northern cities like Shechem and using the Hebrew word **Elohim** for "God." In this source there is also a greater emphasis on the use of angelic messengers rather than direct communication with God.

Perhaps the most influential of these editors is the **D-source**, also known as the **Deuteronomistic Historian**. While Wellhausen identified this source in the material from Deuteronomy (technically Deut. 12–26, but generally referred to as all of Deuteronomy), it is also identified by scholars with the books of Joshua through 2 Kings. Thus its editorial agenda uses the retelling of the history of Sinai and the wilderness and the renewal of the covenantal relationship with Yahweh to set a theological tone for the historical survey found in these later books. It has been identified primarily by vocabulary and the use of a clear-cut morality. Because it is a historical chronicle composed in hindsight (written and edited after the end of the monarchy in 587 BCE), it is able to look back at the mistakes made by kings and other leaders, highlight them, and then ideologically explain the consequences as based on a failure to uphold the covenant. For example, the term **"Jeroboam's sin"** refers to the policies of an Israelite king who promoted the use of worship centers other than Jerusalem (1 Kings 12:25–33). This label then is used as the basis for determining whether subsequent kings of Israel and Judah are good or bad (see 1 Kings 16:2, 26; 2 Kings 3:3). The efforts of the Deuteronomistic Historian also demonstrate that the ideological emphasis of the biblical editors sometimes disregards political and social realities in order to present a theological position designed to glorify some rulers (Hezekiah and Josiah especially) and vilify (Ahaz, Manasseh) or ignore the actions of others (Omri, Ahab).

Wellhausen's fourth source and the final attempt at editing the biblical narrative is the **P-source**. He dates it to the postexilic period (after 500 BCE), when the monarchy had been eliminated by the Babylonians and a portion of the priestly community led a minority of the exiles, with the assistance of the Persian government, back to Jerusalem. This source is identified by its interest in priestly matters: liturgy, genealogy, ritual, and sacrifice. Because it is believed to be the last of the editing efforts, it puts a final stamp on the contents of the stories and the sequence of events. One example of the P-source is the creation story in Gen. 1:1–2:4a, which is more of an outline than a narrative and stands in contrast with the episodic creation story in Gen. 2:4b–24.

Although Wellhausen's hypothesis is no longer accepted in its original form, it has been the method against which all others are tested. The conspicuous editing of some narratives, especially in terms of the elimination or shortening of stories (e.g., chronicles of the kings), can be seen by any careful reader. The shades of authorial enhancement or theological agenda, however, are not always that obvious, and many interpretations are possible. The student should also note that source criticism is sometimes called literary criticism.

But the latter term we reserve for the following method of analysis.

Literary Criticism. The literary critic concentrates on the final form of the received biblical text as a piece of literature. The interpretation of the text becomes an end in itself and is not a means for reconstructing history or a former version of the text. Using the tools of language study, **philology**, and lexicography, the literary critic analyzes the words of the text in terms of syntax, grammar, and vocabulary. Comment is made on the use of parallelism, metaphor, and other stylistic and poetic devices, as well as on the choice of words or phrases. The task of the literary critic is to determine and categorize genres, such as poetry, law, and wisdom literature. This then aids in the interpretation of a text because literary classification of a story as **myth**, **legend**, allegory, history, or other genre informs the interpreter and provides a guide for approaching a given text.

Narrative Criticism. Through a close reading, this method identifies formal and conventional structures of the narrative, determines plot, develops characterization, distinguishes point of view, exposes language play, and relates it all to some overarching theme. Narrative critics focus on information related to the story world. They ask: What is the significance of the setting of the story? What is the narrator's purpose? What is the plot? Is the sequence of events important? What is the point of view of the narrative? Among the methods employed by narrative critics is discourse analysis, which attempts to examine the writer's use of characters, conversation, and choice of vocabulary. Narrative criticism of the NT has tended to note the mechanics or artistry of literary construction but has also remained committed to historical criticism's desire to determine the author's intention and the text's original readers. Studies of the HB have gone further in the direction of a purely literary approach.

Form Criticism. The form critic is primarily concerned with the structure of the text (its meter, number of stanzas, voice) and the different genres of literature that it contains (e.g., hymn, lament, thanksgiving in the Psalms). This means that an attempt is made to determine the original form of each portion of the narrative and the reason it was eventually set in its final form. Comparison is often made between different versions of the same episode or narrative item. For example, the wording of the Ten Commandments in Exod. 20:1–17 differs from the set of laws listed in Exod. 34:17–26. The form critic attempts to determine the tradition history and the social background of the text by examining structure, vocabulary, and style. For example, the customary beginning and concluding formulas for prophetic books include the phrase "The word of the LORD that came to . . ." (Ezek. 1:3; Hosea 1:1).

Redaction Criticism. Because the text shows signs of **redaction**, or editing, the redaction critic attempts to identify where such edits occur—the rough edges of combined narratives, the presence of **anachronisms**, and references to outside sources. Redaction criticism studies the different pieces as they are assembled into the text and tries to understand the reasoning behind the redactor's order or composition of the final text. For example, the redaction critic would be interested in editorial insertions (e.g., Hosea 14:9) or asides addressed to the reader (e.g., 2 Kings 17:7–41). Redaction critics are also interested in the arrangement of the text (see the placement of **oracles** in Isa. 1–5 prior to the prophet's call narrative in Isa. 6), since placement or evidence of reorganization can be significant for interpretation. The redaction critic also looks for links between texts as a way to determine how the editor has created a seam or link between otherwise unrelated passages (see the use of "God also said to Moses" in Exod. 3:15a).

Canonical Criticism. Canonical critics are less interested in the process of the development of the text and more interested in the final form of the text within the larger context of the canon. Their primary interest is in the perspective of the text as sacred or canonical and in the process of asking questions about the ways in which the text is used to address the faith concerns of the communities that read it. The books of the Bible are also read as part of an overall story, not just as individual texts, and no single passage may then be taken in isolation as the basis for study. It is more important to look at where the text has been placed within the canon than to speculate on why it has been placed there. Thus, for the canonical critic the Torah, placed in the canon prior to the conquest of the promised land, serves as a promise of covenantal relationship for the later exilic community in Babylon (after 587 BCE). That faith community did not need to concern itself solely with questions of original historical or social setting, but instead sought the benefit it provided of communal identity and social structure.

Social Scientific Criticism. With the advent of the social sciences in the late nineteenth century, it has become increasingly clear that the biblical text can be illuminated by close attention to the context of its social world. The text contains presuppositions about social situations that may have been understandable to the original audience but have now lost a portion of their meaning for modern readers. Social-science critics take this to mean that the social world of ancient Israel is very different from modern Western culture and that the reader should suspend judgment on the behavior or words of the characters found in the biblical narrative. They utilize methods developed by psychologists, anthropologists, and sociologists as an aid to re-creating the biblical world and to gain insights into the reasoning behind such things as ritual performance, shame as a social control device, and the religious and social implications of **purity** concepts. One example would be analysis of the social process in which Boaz and the elders devise a settlement of the legal dispute over the status of Ruth and Naomi and the disposition of Elimelech's property near Bethlehem (Ruth 4:1–12). In this story, issues of marriage, inheritance rights (both for offspring and the widow), and the role of redeemer in Israelite society can be evaluated by using legal and social methods of analysis.

Feminist Criticism. The feminist movement, as it developed in the latter half of the twentieth century, took the position that a patriarchal or androcentric interpretation of the biblical text was no longer socially acceptable, nor was it correct in terms of the world of the biblical writers. Feminist critics attempt to show the intrinsic importance of women in the ancient world, their interaction with men, and the influence they had in shaping its culture as well as the biblical narrative. For instance, the actions of the wives of the ancestors in Genesis are closely examined and they become more than shadowy companions. Using this method, female characters take on the strong narrative roles given to them by the authors and push aside the chauvinistic biases applied by later interpreters and editors. Feminist critics are also interested in showing the limits of the biblical text in terms of theology, due to

its overwhelming male gender bias. Closely related to feminist criticism is womanist criticism, which is utilized by African American scholars. This method focuses particularly on oppressed women such as Hagar and her mistreatment by Sarah.

Reader-Response Criticism. This method assumes that a text gains its meaning through the purposeful act of a reader reading and interpreting it. Of course, not every interpretation is equally valid. The reader-response critic takes into account the work of other interpretative communities (i.e., scholars using other forms of analysis) and those features of the text that have been determined to be particularly important. For example, historical critics tend to focus more on the historical setting, events described in the text, and the probabilities of whether the story is an actual historical account. The reader-response critic might also look at the way particular interpretative communities value a text (e.g., see it as of particular importance to a theological or ideological position) or the propositions advanced by interpretative communities for best reading a text. The basic assumption is that every text presupposes a specific reader and that reader's interests, whether this is a concrete person or only a hypothetical receiver. Every reader influences the way in which the text is structured and framed, and the author of the text assumes that every reader has the ability required to decode and understand what is written.

Rhetorical Criticism. This method first began with an interest in the study of the stylistics of Hebrew prose and poetry (see in Judg. 9:24–57 the repeated use of the preposition "upon/on" [9:24, 57a] in relation to the term "head" and the pattern of alternating the numbers 1 and 70). It has evolved into a method that focuses on close readings of

How to Read and Interpret the Bible: Some Cautions

1. Even those who claim to take the text literally do not do so in every case. It becomes an issue of how much or how little one interprets the text literally. Consider these passages:
   (a) Isa. 55:12—mountains singing and trees clapping their hands—is likely intended to be figurative language to express the joy of creation at God's act of power in releasing the Israelites from the exile in Mesopotamia.
   (b) 2 Chron. 16:9, "The eyes of the LORD range throughout the entire earth," describes God's omniscient ability to see events throughout creation and is clearly **anthropomorphism** (describing God with human characteristics).
2. How is the story a reflection of the cultural attitudes and legal procedures of its time period? Only by answering this question can we hope to understand the biblical writer. *Example:* In Gen. 16:1–4, Abram impregnates Hagar, his wife's slave, in order to produce a son. Why does he do this?
   (a) Abram's wife, Sarai, had not been able to provide her husband with a child.

   (b) Hagar was Sarai's property, and any child she produced belonged to Sarai. Thus Hagar could serve as a surrogate mother, and the child could be declared Abram's heir.
   (c) A son carried on the family name, was the inheritor of property, and could take care of his elderly parents.
   (d) Sons were needed in war and for the work of farming and herding.
3. The Bible is not the product of a scientific age and therefore should not be pressed to make scientific statements about creation or be used as a scientific textbook.
4. Numbers or statistics are not necessarily used with a scientific or statistical precision. *Examples:* Moses's life is divided into three periods of forty years. Joseph and Joshua both die at age 110, and they both have connections with ancient Egypt, where 110 was considered to be the ideal age.
5. Ancient literature was not written like most modern Western literature. Rarely is an author listed, and copyrights did not exist. Most of the earliest works are the product

   of oral tradition and thus are the property of the community that produced them, not of a particular person.
6. One must determine the type of literature one is reading before trying to interpret it. For instance, worshipful and hymnic literature (e.g., Ps. 84:1–2) has a much different purpose than does adventurous, heroic literature (e.g., Judg. 4:12–22).
7. For nearly all of ancient literature, we do not have the author's original version. Thus we depend on whatever copies have survived. Of course, copies may contain errors made in the process of copying them by hand. Numbers are especially hard to transcribe accurately. *Example:* 1 Sam. 13:1 reads, "Saul was [? or one] year old when he began to reign and he reigned for two [?] years over Israel." Probably a number has dropped out in both cases.
8. We are too far removed in time to expect to clear up every problem or discrepancy. Therefore we should honestly admit problems and work to resolve them with any new evidence that becomes available.

singular texts, which are often studied in isolation. Of particular interest are those literary or poetic devices that are clearly rhetorical in form and usage, such as repetition, parallelism, analogy, and inclusio. Recent discussion has moved to expand its scope beyond stylistics in order to probe the persuasive power of texts to influence action or practice. Thus the texts can no longer be viewed as isolated objects of study. Rather, they are examined within their historical context in order to see how cultural preconceptions inevitably influence the writers and the readers. The aim is to describe the ideology embedded in the text in order to see

how its construction preconditions experience for both the writer and the reader.

Tradition Criticism. This method seeks to inquire about the community or group responsible for the shaping and transmission of a particular text. By using this method, it is possible to find deposits of tradition in the text, such as information about sacrifice, **rubrics** for cultic practices, and details of priestly equipment and activity. The narrative sections of the Pentateuch are frequently interrupted by blocks of information injected into the narrative by priestly circles (Exod. 35–40; Num. 1:1–10:10). A second area of importance is the particular geographical location with which a tradition was associated. Examination of stories centering on a particular site (Bethel, Shechem, or Jerusalem) helps to develop an understanding of their political, economic, or cultic significance. Tradition criticism also emphasizes searching for the way particular themes of the OT/HB came to be formulated and the role they continued to play as they were brought into different contexts. Thus each theme is viewed as having its own history before it became a part of the larger literary complex of the Pentateuch.

Each of these methodologies described above has value to students of the Bible, and often different methods are used in conjunction with other methods. While it is not our intent to force students into one of these molds, it is important that students understand each approach and how it helps us obtain a better understanding of the Bible.

▬▬▬ STUDY QUESTIONS ▬▬▬

1. What were the factors that led to the creation of ancient writing systems?

2. How does oral tradition differ from written versions of stories, and what factors contributed to writing down the stories?

3. What are the various genres of literature represented in the Bible? Give an example of each.

4. What led to the translation of the Hebrew Bible into Greek, and what problems resulted from this translation?

5. How did the beginning of the Christian movement and the destruction of Jerusalem in 70 CE contribute to the finalization of the Hebrew canon?

6. What were the major contributions of the Masoretes?

7. How has the discovery of the Dead Sea Scrolls contributed to the modern study of the Bible?

8. After reading through each of the methods that scholars use to study the Bible, consider which methods you would find most useful in interpreting the text. What are the advantages of each approach? Explain your answer.

·2·

THE PREMONARCHIC PERIOD

The Book of Genesis

KEY POINTS

- The stories of creation in Genesis contain similarities to and differences from the other ancient Near Eastern epic accounts.
- The Genesis creation stories contain etiologies designed to explain such things as death, birth, and the necessity of work.
- There is a clear contrast between the Mesopotamian flood epics and the story of Noah in Genesis. The latter provides precedents for Yahweh's supremacy, consistency, and the concept of the remnant.

We have chosen to begin our survey of the OT/HB with Genesis because we find that students respond best to an approach based on the current order of the biblical canon. Since Genesis purports to describe the beginnings of the universe, it is a natural beginning for us as well. It should be understood, however, that the majority of the material in Genesis is intended to describe the political and religious foundations of the nation of Israel. In the first eleven chapters, the primeval history, the stories provide an **etiology**, or explanation for the origins of the earth and the human race,

rather than a scientific depiction of events. It is likely that the material found in the book of Genesis was not compiled and edited until the latter part of the monarchy or the early Persian period (ca. 500 BCE). The resulting anachronisms (terms or events in the text that do not fit the time period being described) will be pointed out and explained based on our current understanding of the data.

Primeval History: Genesis 1–11

Like many of the nations and cultures of the ancient Near East, the Israelites formulated their own history of the "beginning time." The Israelites had two main goals in their primeval epics: to portray their God as sovereign, without challenge, and **transcendent** over all of creation; and to present the origin of a relationship with their God that led to the covenant with Abram (Gen. 15). The establishment of a more defined covenantal relationship with the Israelite people as a result of the exodus and the giving of the Ten Commandments is predicated on these earlier events. These goals were accomplished through a series of etiologies (stories explaining origin and causation) and **genealogies** (family histories).

The Israelites shared much of the worldview of ancient Mesopotamia. As a result, a great deal of the material contained in the primeval epics in Genesis is borrowed and adapted from the ancient cultures of that region. This is what makes the study of nonbiblical epics so valuable. By making comparisons and by seeing the general religious and literary environment of the ancient Near East, it is possible to understand more fully how the Israelites perceived their world and their place in it.

What is particularly interesting about the Israelite use of foreign epic material is their ability to transform foreign religious dramas and the epic **motifs** and structures into a distinctive model that is uniquely their own. The exact time period in which this process began is unknown. Most likely it started after 900 BCE as part of the efforts of the monarchy to solidify its power more fully and to demonstrate a longstanding claim to the land of Canaan. Form critics point out that some of this material is structured into a liturgical drama (patterned sequences in worship or ritual; see

pages 38–39 on Gen. 1:1–2:4a). Source critics emphasize that the material's descriptions of a monotheistic religion suggest a strong priestly influence (Wellhausen's P-source). The union of political and priestly elements in the primeval epics may be the result of a partnership between the powers represented in the palace and temple communities. By blending their versions of the stories, giving both the chance to include what they felt was most important to emphasize, they could create a form of unity for the nation. It could also reflect a later reworking of the stories shortly after the exile, when the Jews in the **diasporic** communities in Mesopotamia, as well as those who chose to return to Jerusalem, wished to solidify their cultural identity and origins as a people (ca. 500 BCE).

Perhaps the best way to demonstrate the use of ancient Near Eastern material in biblical epics is by comparison. Later we will sketch the close ties between Mesopotamian creation epics and those in Genesis. Both are products of a shared literary and cultural climate; the points where they diverge indicate distinct theological perspectives.

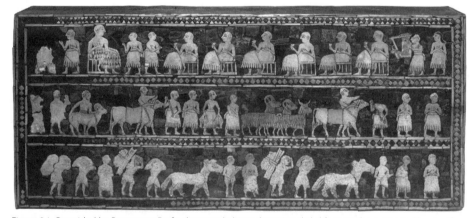

Figure 2.1. One side (the Peace panel) of a decorated object depicting daily life in Ur, the purported home of the famous ancestor Abraham. It was found in a royal grave (ca. twenty-fifth century BCE). (Baker Photo Archive, courtesy of the British Museum)

Polytheism Compared with Monotheism

Polytheism	Monotheism
many gods	one God
immanent gods	transcendent God
capricious gods	consistent God
cosmic combat between gods	absence of divine challengers to the one God
different gods associated with each human political entity	a universal God operating outside human political systems
gods dependent on humanity or human beings	God independent of humanity or human beings

The chart above sketches out the differences between the polytheistic system of ancient Mesopotamia and the Israelite monotheistic system that developed by the time of the exile. It uses the stories in Gen. 1–4 and 6–9 and the Babylonian *Enuma Elish* epic for its comparisons. In ancient Mesopotamia and Egypt, the gods were personifications of the forces of nature. They represented the wind, the storm, the sea, and the forces of fertility, all of which could harm as well as benefit human communities. Like the forces of nature, these gods could at times appear to be at odds with one another. For example, rain is needed for crops, but too much rain is transformed into a flood that carries away people, houses, animals, and crops. The sun can ripen grain or burn it to shriveled stocks. The sea provides a bounty, but it also erodes the land, can become a raging monster when driven by the winds, and can take a voyager's life all too easily.

Because these mighty forces could not easily be addressed or visualized, they were portrayed as nearly human and given anthropomorphic qualities. They spoke, walked, ate, and engaged in sexual activity. The epics also depict the gods with human emotions and failings, such as jealousy, anger, and ambition.

The authors of the creation and flood epics of ancient Mesopotamia used these human characteristics and combined them with their observation of the tensions that they found in nature to create their descriptions of primeval events. As a result, the narratives describe the primordial history in terms of cosmic combat, with the gods continually battling for supremacy. Thus in the Babylonian creation epic *Enuma Elish*, Apsu, the primordial god of watery chaos, decides to destroy all the younger gods in order to restore the peacefulness of original chaos. Ea, the god of the channeled (ordered) waters, assassinates his father and becomes the ruler of all the gods. In this way political change takes place (one god kills another/one city defeats another), and order symbolically triumphs over chaos.

This drama also illustrates how early farmers managed their water resources with irrigation canals and how such precious resources in an arid region figured in the politics of that day. It was believed that each god was the patron of one of the ancient city-states of Mesopotamia. When the city-states went to war against each other, the gods also fought. The winning city-state would not only loot the towns and villages of the loser but also would collect the images of the losing gods and hold them hostage in the temple of their victorious patron god. Ea's defeat of Apsu thus represents a political change of fortunes as well as the triumph of ordered civilization over chaos and anarchy.

A transfer of political power is also the basis for the second stage of the *Enuma Elish*. The version used by scholars dates to the Old Babylonian period (2000–1500 BCE) and is obviously intended to serve as both religious and political propaganda. Babylon and its chief god, Marduk, are able to gain supremacy through a cosmic battle and a reordering of the universe. Again, the principal danger to the gods is a primordial deity of watery chaos—Tiamat, the female counterpart to Apsu. With the help of an army of dragons, she prepares to seize control and take revenge for the murder of her consort, Apsu. To meet this threat, the gods turn to a new champion, Marduk, the god of storms and the patron of Babylon. Ea's withdrawal from this struggle and his replacement by Marduk serve as a political statement of change in regimes from southern to central Mesopotamia during the Old Babylonian period.

Eventually Marduk challenges Tiamat to single combat, and with the aid of the winds that he commands, he kills her. Her army of dragons and rebellious gods is rounded up, and her new lover and coconspirator, Kingu, is executed. Tiamat's body is cut in half, with the upper portion becoming the heavens and the lower becoming the earth. Her blood becomes the oceans, rivers, and streams. To promote order in this newly created universe, the gods are each given tasks to perform, but the real work is assigned to humans, who are created from the blood of the slain rebel Kingu. It will be the task of humanity to manage the resources of the earth and pay homage to the gods through prayer and sacrifice.

The epic concludes with the construction of a massive stepped pyramid in Babylon, known as the Esagila temple. This structure, probably the model for the story of the Tower of Babel in Gen. 11:1–9, provided the physical symbol of power for Marduk and Babylon, marking them as the chief powers in Mesopotamia. The political aspect of the epic is emphasized by the ascent of Marduk to the position of king of the gods and the placement of Babylon and

the dynasty of the human king Hammurabi (1792–1750 BCE) at the center of a Mesopotamian Empire.

Genesis Creation Accounts. The two Genesis accounts of the creation utilize some of this Mesopotamian material as well as other epics composed in ancient Egypt. However, they contain unique reorientations of the material that make them distinctively Israelite. The first of these accounts, Gen. 1:1–2:4a, is composed in the form of a simple outline, giving only the bare minimum of information needed to provide sequence and order to the story of the creation of the universe. This matches what would be expected in a literary **framework story**, a device common in biblical narrative (see Exod. 7–12 for another example). A framework story is a narrative with an outline that can be used to provide structure for other narratives. It offers a fill-in-the-blank format that can be utilized for different stories. The inset on the liturgical framework of 1:1–2:4a presents the elements of the creation according to this literary scheme. If we can assume that the role of creation stories in other ancient traditions has relevance, the Gen. 1:1–2:4a creation story may have served as the outline for a religious drama performed as part of the New Year's celebration. It could also have functioned as a set of steps in a liturgy or sacrificial ritual designed to celebrate the **Sabbath**, the day of rest established to commemorate Yahweh's creative act.

There are some similarities between the versions of the creation story found in Gen. 1:1–2:4a and that found in the Egyptian Hymn to Ptah from ancient Memphis. For instance, a sense of majesty and complete control over creation is shared by the Memphite version and the Genesis account. In both epics, creation takes place when the divine word is spoken.

> **The Liturgical Framework of Gen. 1:1–2:4a**
>
> - Creation by the word ("And God said, 'Let there be . . .'")
> - Certification ("God saw that it was good")
> - Manipulation of the newly created item ("God separated the light from the darkness")
> - Naming ("God called the light day")
> - Transition ("And there was evening and there was morning, the _____ day")

This contrasts with the picture of the secondary creation of humankind from the substance of the creation in Gen. 2:7 (dust) and in Marduk's creation of humanity in the *Enuma Elish* from the blood of a rebellious god.

The second creation story, found in Gen. 2:4b–25, is composed as a narrative with a distinct story line, expressed emotions, a growing crisis, and an instructive character. In this account, initially only a single human is created, rather than the pair called into being as the final act of creation in the first version (1:26–27). Why this first human is created is not made clear in the story until a second human is formed as his "partner" (2:18–22). Together they are given charge of the garden of Eden and its nonhuman inhabitants. The story then concerns itself with the etiology of why humans are no longer living in the garden and why death came into the world. The expulsion of Adam and Eve from the garden marks one of many turning points in the human story, in this case from an existence of deathless leisure to a world of work, pain, and strife.

In both Genesis stories, only one supreme deity is named, although Gen. 1:26 mentions the **divine assembly**: God says, "Let us make humankind"; and 3:22 reads, "See, the man has become like one of us." Like other ancient Near Eastern cultures, the Israelites projected into the divine realm their own use of an assembly of advisers who assisted royal decision making. The use of the plural pronoun here therefore reflects a heavenly court over which Yahweh presides (see also 1 Kings 22:19–23).

Separating it from the polytheistic epics, the biblical creation accounts in Genesis assume no cosmic battle with other gods. Yahweh is completely transcendent over the creation, untouched by the power of nature. However, the use of the word *tehom* in the Hebrew text for the "formless void" (Gen. 1:2) may be a reference to Tiamat of the Babylonian epic. If this is the case, then it is a clear attempt to **demythologize** the story by turning a divine being into an unpersonified state of nature. The principal interaction in the Genesis narrative is between Yahweh and the newly created humans. Only in the story of Eve and the serpent is there any sense that humans might have the power to contravene the Creator's intentions, but this wisdom story simply introduces the theme of freedom of action that will dominate the relationship between God and the Israelites.

Genesis Flood Accounts. Other points of contrast between the Genesis accounts and those from Mesopotamia are clearer in the flood epics. The various ancient Near Eastern accounts of the flood, including those in Genesis, provide many close parallels with one another. They all follow the same basic sequence of events: a decision is made to destroy all life on earth with a flood; a god warns a human and instructs him to build an ark, or boat, that will allow the survival of a small group of humans and animals; the floodwaters are unleashed on the earth, and all life outside the ark is exterminated; the ark comes to rest on a mountaintop, and a series of birds are sent out to determine when the waters have receded;

a sacrifice is made after the ark is emptied; a sign is placed in the heavens marking the end of the flood. Differences that occur between the stories are based in large part on the contrast between polytheism and monotheism religious systems (see the inset, p. 37).

The comparisons and contrasts listed below attempt to show that Noah, unlike Utnapishtim in the Gilgamesh epic of Sumerian and Akkadian literature, is never left to his own resources during the flood. His survival is due to God's direct intervention. Utnapishtim's survival reflects the triumph of humanity over the destructiveness of nature and the capriciousness of the gods.

1. The decision to destroy all life on earth is made by the divine assembly in the Gilgamesh and Atrahasis epics (also in Sumerian and Akkadian literature). In the Gilgamesh epic, no reason is given for the flood. In the Atrahasis epic, the flood is designed to eliminate the noisy nuisance of humanity without any concern for a moral judgment.

2. When Utnapishtim is warned by the god Ea in the Gilgamesh epic, it seems almost accidental that he is on the other side of a wall when Ea speaks. The god thereby maintains a level of plausible deniability by not directly seeking out Utnapishtim. He apparently picks a spot at random in which to speak a warning.

3. It takes the collective efforts of all the gods in both the Gilgamesh and Atrahasis epics to bring the destructive elements of the flood into being. Each god contributes his or her particular attribute of power (wind, rain, lightning). In the Gilgamesh epic, Utnapishtim is forced to lock himself within the ark after it has begun to rain. In Genesis, Yahweh closes the ark for Noah before it began to rain, showing a divine concern for human welfare that is lacking in the Gilgamesh epic.

4. During the height of the storm in the Mesopotamian epics, the gods are forced to cower like frightened dogs behind a wall while some scream in terror. Only when the powers that have been unleashed by the gods subside do the floodwaters begin to recede. The arks of the Mesopotamian heroes come to rest without the guidance or help of the gods. The Mesopotamian gods never demonstrate any desire to help the survivors of the flood.

5. Once they exit the ark, Utnapishtim and Noah both build sacrificial altars. Noah's altar is designed to express his thanks, but Utnapishtim's altar simply forms the basis for reviving the old symbiotic relationship between humanity and the gods. Utnapishtim's sacrifice serves as a bribe in the hope that no further calamity will occur. The ravenous Mesopotamian gods respond to Utnapishtim's offering "like flies" that have been starved. They flock to the sacrifice to feed. Ironically, the gods apparently had overlooked their dependence on the sacrifices of humankind to maintain their well-being.

6. In the Gilgamesh epic, the goddess Ishtar completes the flood sequence by placing her necklace in the heavens. Ishtar's necklace serves as a memorial of the flood, but unlike Yahweh's rainbow (Gen. 9:13–17), Ishtar's necklace does not function as a covenantal guarantee that floodwaters will never again be used to "destroy all flesh" (9:15). To allow the gods to save face and hide the evidence of their actions, Utnapishtim and his wife are taken away to the Eden-like land of Dilmun, where they become immortals. In contrast, Noah is faced with the task of rebuilding human culture. He and his family are given the same command to "be fruitful and multiply" (Gen. 9:1) that had been given to humankind (1:28) in the first version of creation.

The similarities between the stories suggest that literary borrowing and adaptation may have occurred between the Israelites and Mesopotamian culture. Since the Gilgamesh and Atrahasis epics predate the composition of the Genesis account by many centuries, it is most likely that they served as the literary model for the Noah story. It is possible that the Mesopotamian epics and the Genesis account are all based on an earlier version, but there is no proof of its existence. In any case, once the Israelites had reshaped their story, it took on the elements of their own understanding of Yahweh, the transcendent creator God, who deals justly with the creation.

This latter attribute will become a favorite theme throughout the Bible. In the flood story it is assumed that Yahweh is just and therefore by definition will not destroy righteous human beings without first warning them of the approaching doom. Thus Noah, who is recognized as the only righteous man of his time, is warned of the coming flood, is given the chance to take action, and survives as a remnant of earth's population. His family benefits from his righteousness based on the legal principle of **corporate identity**: because the head of the household is the legal representative for the entire family, what he does can bring reward or punishment on them all. This legal idea dominated much of Israelite thought and history until the time of Jeremiah and Ezekiel (sixth century BCE), when the crisis of the destruction of Jerusalem and the exile transformed Israel's understanding of redemption and individual responsibility—eliminating punishment based on the "sins of the father" while maintaining the concept of a communal society (see Ezek. 18:5–32).

Ancestral Narratives: Genesis 12–50

KEY POINTS

- The ancestral narratives center on the establishment of the covenant and the search-for-the-heir theme.
- The ancestors are often portrayed as trickster figures.
- The social customs of the ancestors (marriage, inheritance, burial) set precedents for later generations of Israelites.

The primeval history concludes with a section that lists the generations following the flood and a few etiological stories explaining the dispersal of the earth's peoples and the diversity of languages (Tower of Babel, Gen.

Principal Themes in the Ancestral Narratives

- Covenant Promise: God promises Abraham and his descendants "land and children" in exchange for absolute obedience and exclusive worship (Gen. 15:5–6, 18–21; 17:3–8).
- Covenant Endangered: Tension is created in the stories by events or conditions that threaten the fulfillment of the covenant promise.

  Barren-Wife Motif: Wife of the ancestor is barren for many years (Gen. 11:30; 25:21; 29:31).

  Search-for-Heir Motif: Ancestors employ various strategies to ensure that an heir is born and designated with a formal blessing (Gen. 15:2–4; 16:1–4).

  Wife-Sister Motif: Ancestor deceives foreign ruler, claiming his wife is his sister and allowing her to enter ruler's harem. God must step in to correct this (Gen. 12:10–20; 20:1–13; 26:6–11).

  Disqualification Story: A story is shaped to disqualify the unacceptable heirs and to highlight the rise of the true heir (often a younger son; Gen. 21:8–20; 25:29–34).

- Trickster Theme: Because of their immigrant and politically weak status, the ancestors employ trickster strategies that add ironic and comic twists to the stories (Gen. 27:1–29; 29:21–30; 30:27–43).
- Supremacy of Yahweh: Through contests between Yahweh and the gods of other nations, it is demonstrated "who really is God" (Gen. 14:1–20; 41:1–39).

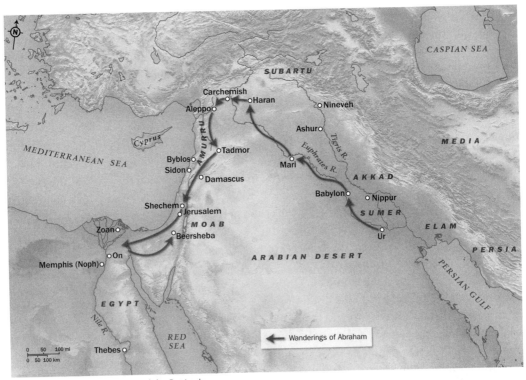

Map 2.1. The World of Genesis and the Patriarchs

11:1–9). At the conclusion of the primeval history, a quasi-historical narrative begins whose principal value for scholars is found in its description of cultural ideas, social customs, and the various aspects of life for a mixed economy of village agriculture and **pastoral nomadism**. The individuals described in these stories may have been composites of numerous tribal leaders, so-called **eponymous** heroes (founding fathers), but to this point no evidence has come to light of the historicity of the ancestral narratives. Our discussion of these stories will therefore concentrate on their literary and social aspects, especially with regard to precedents that these characters establish for later custom and law among the Israelites.

Genesis 12–50 describes several generations of a family founded by a couple originally named Abram (meaning in Hebrew "father of a multitude") and Sarai ("princess"). During the course of the story, God changes the names of this couple to Abraham and Sarah to signify that the Deity has chosen them to be the ancestors of the great nation of people who would later be known as Israel. The story is set first in Mesopotamia, in the ancient city of Ur of the Chaldees. The use of "Chaldees" is an anachronism because it is an ethnic term that applies to the Neo-Babylonian people who dominated Mesopotamia from about 625 BCE until 540 BCE. This gives us a clue as to when this material might have been edited into its final form. Certainly some of it may date back to the second millennium BCE, but in many cases the events and places of the story are more important to the political history of the

Israelite monarchy or even the exilic period (after 600 BCE) than to the time ascribed to the ancestors (ca. 1800–1600 BCE).

The principal theme throughout the ancestral narratives is the establishment of the covenant and the trials associated with determining who would become the heir of that covenantal promise. A motif, a repeated story line, appears in which the selection of the potential or the proper heir is endangered. Among the ways in which this promise is endangered are the barren-wife theme and the search-for-heir motif. Each of the primary ancestral wives is barren for long periods of time (Sarah for 90 years, Rebekah for 20 years, Rachel for an unspecified period). The disastrous social concerns over a wife's inability to produce an heir are combined with numerous attempts on the part of the ancestral couple to create and identify the heir themselves. Abraham does this three times (with his nephew Lot, his servant Eliezer, and with his son Ishmael) before Yahweh provides a son for the elderly couple. In the next generation, Isaac chooses the wrong twin son as his heir (Esau), and Rebekah and Yahweh have to join forces to straighten out the problem. During the third generation, Jacob, who has twelve sons, eventually has to acknowledge as his heir one of the youngest, Joseph. In each case, the tension created by the search for the heir leads to a climax when the heir is identified or born. The movement of the narrative toward this climax underscores the heir's importance. Perhaps the ultimate example of the endangerment theme is found in God's command to Abraham that he sacrifice his long-awaited son Isaac (Gen. 22:1–19). While this appears to be illogical given the lengths to which Abraham and Sarah have gone to obtain an heir, this troubling story serves two purposes: it demonstrates that Abraham

must be willing to give up everything and trust God, and it provides a precedent that, unlike their Canaanite neighbors, the Israelites will not engage in human sacrifice.

Another of the curiosities associated with the ancestral narratives is the limited details contained in the stories. The historicity of the characters currently cannot be established with any certainty, and the storyteller does not seem to be concerned with fleshing out aspects of the story that would be of interest to modern readers. For instance, Abram is called by Yahweh to leave Haran and journey to Canaan, but there is no mention of the events of the journey. In one verse he and his household are in Mesopotamia, and in the next they are in Canaan, near the city of Shechem, hundreds of miles away. Such a monumental trek surely could have generated an epic tale, but for reasons known only to the editors of this text, the story is not included here. Speculation is possible, of course. For some features of Abram's journey, a fairly full picture can be drawn based on our knowledge of caravan routes and the movements of peoples during the second millennium BCE, as well as the practical needs of travelers at that time.

Route of Travel. After leaving Haran, located near the northern headwaters of the Euphrates River, Abram's household most likely traveled the international trade route that curved southwest from the northern Euphrates region to Tadmor (Palmyra). From Tadmor the route continued west to Damascus and Hazor, then turned south and passed through the Jezreel valley to Megiddo. The trade route then headed southwest along the coast of ancient Canaan and ended at the border of Egypt. This well-traveled road was used by merchant caravans, messengers from various governments, and pastoral nomadic groups with their livestock. Pastoral nomads probably used the highway more as a marker than a route of travel. They would have taken the opportunity to graze their flocks and herds along the way. However, they would not, as stateless persons, have wished to have frequent contact with persons or potentially hostile groups outside their own company. A generic term applied to these stateless groups in ancient Near Eastern texts is *khabiru* (in Mesopotamia; *'apiru* in Egypt). They sometimes served as hired laborers and mercenaries, but their loyalty was always considered suspect, and therefore they were regarded as a necessary evil.

Since the biblical text does not explicitly mention any of the probable stops along Abram's route, one can only surmise brief detours to places to obtain supplies, perhaps bartered in exchange for a surplus lamb or goat. The only indication of one of these stops is the mention of Eliezer of Damascus in Gen. 15:2–3. He is described as Abram's heir, a "slave born in my house." Adoption of a servant as an heir is certainly not unknown in the ancient Near East. What may be particularly important here is that the young (?) man had apparently been picked up by Abram during a stop in Damascus, just as Hagar, Sarai's Egyptian slave woman, was apparently added to the group during their stay in Egypt.

Retribalization. Preparations for Abram's departure from Haran include only the statement "Abram took his wife Sarai, and his brother's son Lot, and all the possessions that they had gathered, and the persons whom they had acquired in Haran; and they set forth to go to the land of Canaan" (Gen. 12:5a).

A basic household group (referred to as a *beit 'ab* in Hebrew) is described here: the head of the household, his wife, his heir, their servants, animals, and baggage. This is the bare minimum of detail needed by the ancient audience, who were familiar with both the social concept and nomadic groups. Surely any household group undertaking a journey of several hundred miles through potentially hostile regions would make some provision to protect the family and provide for its needs along the way.

Later in the narrative we are told that Abram and his descendants had flocks and herds. These animals would have served as a form of capital on the hoof, a combination of a ready food supply and a portable bank account. We are not told whether Abram had any previous experience handling animals. But most persons of that time and place would have had some familiarity with them, and his servants would have functioned as herdsmen.

But how does a person hitherto associated only with village living make the transition to life as a pastoral nomad? One possible way of answering this is by referring to the process of adaptation known as **retribalization**. This phenomenon, noted among Middle Eastern peoples in modern times, involves the movement back and forth between sedentary village life and seminomadic pastoralism. The transition away from a sedentary life sometimes occurs because of economic exigency (such as a business failure), a war, too much political pressure from the local or national government, or a famine or epidemic that requires families to move away from the village. Abandonment of a nomadic existence and return to the village may be the result of a disaster that decimates the herd, growing economic prosperity that allows for the purchase of land, or the growing influence of government agencies to control the movement of herdsmen.

In Genesis, Abram is portrayed as an inhabitant of the village of Haran who becomes at God's command a pastoral nomad. The description of Abram's initial transition to pastoral nomadism is not intended to represent a shift in permanent occupation. The story line of the narrative is designed to provide an explanation for his departure from a settled existence, his shift to immigrant status, and his interaction with the peoples of the land in which he traveled. For the purposes of the journey and until he can acquire a holding in the new land, he must maintain flocks and herds as his livelihood (see the map 2.1 for major sites associated with the ancestral narratives).

Immigrant Psychology. Abram's change of social condition brings with it a change in social attitude as well. Abram, on the death of his father, Terah, had assumed the role of head of the household. His responsibilities and powers within the village life would have differed from those in the encampment of a nomadic group. There would have been elders in the village to consult, friends and neighbors with whom to socialize and share concerns. From the moment that his household leaves Haran, Abram is faced with the opportunities and the dangers of being a "stranger" in a strange land.

The traveling company associated with Abram would have had to rely on each other completely. They could not have expected to receive more than simple hospitality from strangers, and quite often they could anticipate being treated as undesirables or enemies. They would have immediately been recognized as strangers by their manner of dress, their speech, and their general appearance. Because they were not citizens of the places that they visited, they would not have been protected by local laws. Their unfamiliarity with local custom could have drawn them into hostile encounters (see the dispute over the use of wells in Gen. 26:17–22).

They would not have been welcomed in every village or city. When a famine strikes Canaan (Gen. 12:10), Abram's household is forced to leave like other stateless people before him and seek food and perhaps employment in Egypt. Here again, however, the writers fail to add the one detail that would have tied Abram to a particular time in history. The pharaoh Abram encounters when they journey to Egypt is unnamed (12:10–20). Historians have compiled a list of dates for each of the pharaohs, but that fact is no concern of the authors. They are more concerned to show Yahweh's supremacy over the "god-king" of Egypt.

Even when immigrants had gained a certain measure of respect, such as Lot's right to sit and do business in the gate area at Sodom

---

Hospitality Customs in the Ancestral Narratives

In the midst of these narratives are often episodes that portray the ancestors as strict adherents to social custom. For example, in Gen. 18:1–15 Abraham carefully follows proper protocol in extending the hospitality of his household to three strangers. When they enter his sphere of responsibility, he rushes out to invite them to stop and refresh themselves before traveling on their way. Their acceptance of his invitation obligates Abraham to feed them, wash their feet, and engage in friendly conversation. The visitors would reciprocate with news of where they had been, and in the case of this narrative provide Abraham with the happy announcement that he and Sarah would soon become parents. Hospitality functioned as a means of at least temporarily setting aside hostility between strangers and required both parties to respect and protect each other during the time they were together. It is this latter obligation that Lot cites in defending his guests and maintaining the honor of his household when confronted by the assembled citizens of Sodom in Gen. 19:4–8.

Figure 2.2. Tamarisk tree and well outside the walls of ancient Beersheba. Although the remains here are later than the time of Abraham, Beersheba is mentioned several times in the patriarchal narratives (Gen. 21, 22, 26, 28, and 46). (Baker Photo Archive)

(Gen. 19:1), their status as resident aliens (Hebrew *ger*) sometimes was used against them by the local population (see 19:9). Abraham is called "a prince among us" by the elders of Hebron (23:6), but they then take advantage of him when he bargains with Ephron for a burial place for his wife (23:12–16).

The result among these tribal peoples is the development of defense mechanisms, including trickster characteristics, designed to either camouflage or protect the members of the group. For example, the narrator has Abram demonstrate very canny diplomatic abilities in his encounters with the pharaoh of Egypt (Gen. 12:10–20) and Abimelech of Gerar (Gen. 20). He shows a willingness to deceive both kings, lying about his marital status and accepting their proffered bride price for his wife and half-sister, Sarai. In addition, Abram performs a series of acts designed to lay claim to the land of Canaan. Thus his first official act upon entering Canaan is to build an altar near Shechem (Gen. 12:6–7). He repeats this ritual performance east of Bethel (12:8), near Hebron (13:18), and on Mount Moriah (22:9). His planting of a tamarisk tree at Beersheba has a similar ritual function (21:33). All of these places (if the tradition that equates Moriah with Jerusalem is correct) become major cultic or historical sites in later Israelite history. Abraham's association with these places, rather than the many others his group visited, shows the selective editing process (based on source-critical principles) once again and sets precedents for worship practices and political claims in later periods.

Abraham's two final steps in laying claim to the land suggest the intent of the authors to establish a legal title to this area. In the first case, Abraham negotiates a covenant treaty with Abimelech of Gerar that substantiates the pastoralist's right to dig and use wells in that region (Gen. 21:25–34). The narrative also includes the statement that "Abraham resided as an alien many days in the land of the Philistines" (21:34). While the term "Philistine" is anachronistic, because the Philistines were not present until after 1200 BCE, one of the elements of the text indicates that gaining access to water rights allows a nomadic group to settle for a time and legitimizes their continued presence in that area (cf. Isaac's similar experience in 26:12–22).

The second episode that functions as a legal claim to the land is found in the story of the purchase of the cave of Machpelah (Gen. 23). Abraham, who has apparently dwelled with his household near the settlement of Hebron for a fairly long period, follows the proper legal protocol when attempting to purchase a burial cave for his family. He speaks first to the city elders, asks for their help as witnesses and intermediaries, and then negotiates with the owner of the cave. Since he is obviously in a weakened position, needing a burial site for his recently deceased wife, Abraham is forced to pay an exorbitant price and include as part of the transaction some adjoining property. Clearly, the elements of the narrative expose yet again the reality of immigrant life: strangers are most often at the mercy of the local inhabitants. Despite the social implications of this transactional dialogue, the intent to demonstrate how the Israelites first gained legal title to the promised land is fulfilled. The story also increases the importance of Hebron, a city where David rules prior to becoming king over all Israel (2 Sam. 2:1–4a, 11).

Trickster Themes. The tenuous position in which the ancestors often find themselves requires inventive responses. As a result, each of the ancestral figures functions as a **trickster** at some point in the narrative. Both male and female characters will take advantage of the weaknesses or even the strengths of their antagonists.

One of the most important trickster stories uses the wife-sister motif. This narrative device is found twice in the Abraham-Sarah cycle (Gen. 12:10–20; 20) and once again in the Isaac narrative (26:1–11). In each case a framework story is employed that includes the following elements: the husband's instruction to lie about his wife's status in order to save his life when they enter a new country, payment of the bride price by the local ruler, Yahweh's infliction of a plague on the local ruler, and recrimination and return of the wife. The story also highlights a recurring theme designed to demonstrate to the Israelites and to their neighbors who really is God. In this case, the story includes a contest between Yahweh and the local deities (i.e., pharaoh and the other gods of Egypt), demonstrating who is the most powerful (cf. the similar story of the ten plagues in Exod. 7–12). In the end the ancestral household is enriched by the deception, and the audience is provided with comic relief in a story in which the weak defeat the strong. Finally, the episode fits into the search-for-heir motif in which the wife (and thus the potential heir) is in danger when she is taken into the pharaoh's household and must be rescued by Yahweh.

The Jacob cycle contains a continuous series of trickster stories in which Jacob successively tricks his brother Esau out of his birthright (Gen. 25:29–34); his father, Isaac, into giving him a blessing (27:5–29); and his uncle and father-in-law, Laban, on several occasions (see 30:35–43). Jacob, like most trickster figures, in turn is tricked by Laban on his wedding night (29:22–28) and by Yahweh's angel during a wrestling match (32:24–31). Many of the intricate maneuvers in these episodes revolve around the search-for-heir motif, attempting to ascertain first who will receive the blessing of the covenant and then showing how Jacob, later renamed Israel, eventually achieves the status of heir of the covenant, which in this case involves obtaining a household and possessions.

The narrator guides the audience to see who the rightful heir will be by employing disqualification stories, narratives that portray the other candidate(s) as unworthy. Thus Esau is portrayed as a man who does not adhere to family custom when he marries foreign wives (Gen. 26:34–35). Jacob, by contrast, obediently follows his parents' instructions to return to Haran for a proper bride (28:1–10). Jacob's correct action is further certified by a **theophany** (a human's meeting with God) at Bethel in which God assures him that he will be the heir of the covenant (28:10–15). For additional examples of this literary form, see the disqualification of Lot (13:8–17) and of Ishmael (17:15–22), as well as the anti-Saul stories that are designed to disqualify Saul's family from retaining the kingship (1 Sam. 10:17–27; 13:1–15:35).

The ancestral narratives conclude with the Joseph cycle of stories (Gen. 37; 39–50), which include his extraordinary abilities as an interpreter of dreams while noting that he is one of Jacob's younger sons. These elements provide the backdrop to another contest with pharaoh and another example of a younger son being named the heir of the covenant. The episodes

are also tied together with a garment motif that has Joseph first receiving clothing that marks his high status (Gen. 37:3) and then has it being stripped from him as he sinks to slave status (37:23–28). Subsequently Joseph rises to a position of trust and then is thrown into prison before his interpretative gift allows him once again to rise to great power and authority in the unnamed pharaoh's court. His life functions as a microcosm for the past and future history of the Israelites during the monarchy and exilic period. They saw themselves as rising from slavery to new heights. Joseph's abilities to interpret dreams merely provide him with the edge needed to convince the pharaoh of his worth as an adviser and eventually to gain supremacy over his own brothers. It also demonstrates Yahweh's supremacy and will be the catalyst for the move of Jacob's clan to Egypt. Joseph's rise to prominence, even though he is not the oldest son of Jacob, is the political model for David to become king, even though he is the youngest son of Jesse (1 Sam. 16:1–13).

In spite of the sketchy character of much of the ancestral narratives, they provide a basis for inferences about the social world of ancient Israel that is the setting for these and later episodes. This is not to say that the ancestors are historical characters. Even composite creations must follow established social patterns to maintain a modicum of reality in the stories. Otherwise the ancient audience would have considered them little more than amusing pieces of fiction. Certain actions would have to be taken to make the journey from Haran plausible. Certain recognized social attitudes, including suspicion and near paranoia, would be generated by both the immigrant group and the people of the lands the group visited. By reading the text in light of the elements of retribalization and immigrant psychology, we can uncover some of the text's ancient context.

STUDY QUESTIONS

Primeval Stories

1. Compare and contrast the various ancient Near Eastern creation epics and the manner in which they portray their god(s).
2. Compare the methods of creation as described in the *Enuma Elish* with those employed in Genesis.
3. Identify the etiologies contained in the Genesis creation accounts.
4. Is the story of Eve and the serpent a wisdom tale?
5. Why would the ancient Israelites choose to borrow or adapt elements of the Mesopotamian creation epics in their stories of the creation?
6. Why are there two creation accounts in Genesis (1–2:4a and 2:4b–25)? How do these accounts differ, and how are they similar?

Flood Stories

1. Why and how do the gods create the flood in the Gilgamesh epic, and how does this differ from the Genesis account?
2. As a source critic, explain the differences between the instructions given to Noah in Gen. 6:19–20 and 7:2–3.

Ancestral Narratives

1. What are the basic elements of the covenant between Abram and Yahweh, and why is this a revolutionary agreement (Gen. 15:5–6, 18–21)?
2. Why do Abram and Sarai attempt to obtain a son through so many different means? Consider why each of their attempts fail (see Lot in Gen. 13; Eliezer in Gen. 15:1–6; Ishmael in Gen. 16–17).
3. How does the wife-sister motif fit in with the theme in the narrative that Abram and Sarai are too old to have children (Gen. 12:10–20; Gen. 20)?
4. What cultural precedents are set by Abraham as he travels throughout Canaan (see Gen. 12:6–8; 14:17–24; 17:9–14; 18:1–8; 21:22–34; 22:9–19; 23; 24:1–9)?
5. What is the purpose for the ritual of circumcision (Gen. 17:9–14)?
6. What are the basic elements of Middle Eastern hospitality as described in Gen. 18:1–8 and then applied in the story of Lot in Sodom (Gen. 19)?
7. Why should Abraham be concerned about the fate of Sodom and Gomorrah (Gen. 18:16–33)?
8. What are the various purposes for the story of Abraham's near sacrifice of Isaac? What would the original audience conclude about human sacrifice based on this story (Gen. 22)?
9. Why does Abraham go to the elders of Hebron to get their help when he wants to buy a burial cave? What kind of precedent is set in the purchase of Machpelah (Gen. 23)?
10. Why does the younger brother (both Jacob and Joseph) emerge as heir of the covenant (Gen. 25:29–34; 27:1–28:9)?
11. Note the conflict theme that ties together the Jacob cycle of stories. Why would a people celebrate such a character?
12. Trace the appearance and disappearance of clothing in the story of Joseph. What is the significance (Gen. 37; 39–45)?

The Exodus-Settlement Period

Historical Background

KEY POINTS

- While the exodus is a key to Israel as a covenant community, its historicity is uncertain.
- Moses functions as a prototype prophetic figure, lawgiver, and arbitrator between God and the people.
- The giving of the Ten Commandments provides a legal foundation of the development of law in ancient Israel.

The exodus-settlement period forms the second major stage in the history of ancient Israel. In this chapter we will discuss the escape from Egypt, the wilderness wanderings, the conquest of Canaan, and the era of the judges (Exodus–Judges). In these narratives the Israelites undergo several shifts in lifestyle, from slaves quartered in Egyptian villages, to pastoral nomadic tribes wandering in the wilderness after the flight from Egypt, to a sedentary existence in the village culture of Canaan. The tribes were forced to adjust to new patterns of living and accommodate themselves to life within Canaan. Lacking the weapons or military strength to capture walled cities along the coastal plains, the people who would eventually become the Israelites settled primarily in the hill country of central Canaan.

Establishing a definite chronology and a clear historical setting for this period is not easy. The biblical writers are more interested in showing God's power on behalf of the Israelites than in providing concrete chronological and historical aids for future readers. The biblical account in 1 Kings 6:1 places the traditional date for the exodus in the fifteenth century BCE. However, the strength of the Egyptian presence in Canaan during this period, the lack of archaeological evidence for a systematic conquest during this time, and

Biblical Date of the Exodus

In the four hundred eightieth year after the Israelites came out of the land of Egypt, in the fourth year of Solomon's reign over Israel, ... he began to build the house of the LORD. (1 Kings 6:1)

other chronological difficulties make the date problematic. Any firm date for the exodus remains uncertain at present.

Extrabiblical sources that help to date the exodus-settlement period are very scarce. The evidence of archaeology is also incomplete and in some cases contradictory. Egyptian sources do not mention the exodus, quite likely because it would be considered a defeat. Yet, there is evidence of the use of forced labor gangs to construct the Egyptian storehouse cities of Pithom and Pi-Ramses in the inscriptions of pharaohs Seti I and Ramses II (ca. 1300–1250 BCE). This fits the description of the Israelite slaves who are put to the task of building these cities or others with similar names as recorded in Exod. 1:11.

The settlement of so-called 'apiru tribes in the delta region of Egypt is also mentioned in Egyptian texts. The name 'apiru or khabiru appears to be a generic term for stateless persons or tribal groups who lived on the fringes of the settled areas of the ancient Near East. They sometimes served as surplus labor or as mercenaries, but they appear as brigands and raiders in texts from several different historical periods (from 2000 to 1200 BCE) and in several different areas. While there is no direct linguistic connection between khabiru and Hebrew, the description of a people without roots who live on the fringes of society and who sometimes infiltrate poorly defended areas does fit the biblical description of the Israelites.

The only documentary evidence from Egypt of Israel as a people is found in a victory stele prepared for Pharaoh Merneptah dated at about 1208 BCE. This inscription lists the regions and cities that the pharaoh conquered during an expedition into Canaan. The only line in the inscription that mentions a specific people states that Israel has been "decimated." The language of the inscription is typical of many other similar victory announcements, and the inclusion of Israel may reflect knowledge of their existence but not necessarily direct contact with them. The pharaoh may just be boasting that he has subdued all the peoples in the area. Still, it is the first known extrabiblical mention of the ethnic name Israel and the best available evidence for this people's existence in the thirteenth century BCE. Additional discussion of the settlement period and the conquest narrative will appear later in this chapter when we deal with the book of Joshua.

The Figure of Moses

Moses, whose Egyptian name is based on their word for "to give birth," dominates the exodus narrative and ultimately becomes a prototypical Israelite leader and prophetic figure. His life story is divided into three periods of exactly forty years each and begins with a story of a miraculous survival, a form often used in the ancient world to signify that an individual is to become a significant person. For instance, there are great similarities between Moses's birth story and those of Sargon of Akkad, a great ruler of ancient Mesopotamia (ca. 2500 BCE), and Jesus in the NT (Matt. 1:18–2:23). In each case the child survives a potential death threat, is raised in a foreign land or foster household, and eventually becomes an influential leader of his people.

The career for which Moses has been spared premature death begins after the age of forty. He is forced to flee Egypt after killing an Egyptian taskmaster and joins the company of a pastoral nomadic tribe living in Midian (in the area of Sinai and eastern Arabia). Moses marries one of the daughters of Jethro, a local tribal leader, and it appears that he will spend the remainder of his life in obscurity. However, that tranquil existence ends with a theophany on Mount Sinai (exact location unknown; traditional site is in the southern part of the Sinai peninsula). Moses is called to lead his people out of Egypt (Exod. 3:1–4:17). His **call narrative** provides a model for the call narratives in the later prophetic tradition (see Isa. 6; Jer. 1). Prophetic call narratives generally include the following steps: a theophany, the appearance of a divine being to a human; a demur or excuse made by the frightened or intimidated person who is called to serve; an empowering event and reassurance that puts aside all such excuses; and a charge that provides explicit instructions for the newly called prophet.

Moses is accompanied by his brother Aaron in this mission, which provides a classic example of the contest-between-gods theme. In this case it is the pharaoh, considered to be a god-king in Egypt, who serves as Yahweh's overmatched opponent. The plague sequence that forms the staged events for this contest is designed to demonstrate that Yahweh, the God of creation, is superior to all other gods and is in command of the forces of nature. All but the last plague contains elements of an environmental disaster (polluted river, plagues of insects, diseased animals, hail, and darkness), and in every case the pharaoh is unable to deal effectively with the challenge.

Perhaps the most important element in this framework story is Moses's ability to predict a plague, have it occur on cue, and then, on request, predict the end of the plague and have this occur on cue as well. The question

---

Plague-Sequence Pattern

- Moses and Aaron ask the pharaoh to allow the Israelites to worship for three days in the desert.
- When the pharaoh refuses, Moses predicts that Yahweh will inflict a plague on Egypt.
- The pharaoh, unable to stop the plague, asks Moses to intercede with Yahweh and promises to allow the Israelites to go into the desert to make their sacrifices.
- Moses prays, and Yahweh ends the plague.
- Yahweh "hardens pharaoh's heart," and the Israelites are not allowed to leave.
- Moses once again approaches the pharaoh.

---

might be asked, "Why are there ten plagues?" (Seven or eight plagues are mentioned in Pss. 78:44–51; 105:28–36.) Among the possible answers to this question are that repetition serves a didactic purpose or the number ten has some connection with the Ten Commandments, which form a significant part of a later portion of the Moses narrative.

The most important of the plagues is the last one, the death of the firstborn son (Exod. 11:4–8). This final plague, which decisively convinces the pharaoh that he must allow the Israelites to depart, has a much more important ritual purpose. The sequence of actions described in 12:1–32 forms the basis for later reenactments of the Passover festival as part of a ritual meal and becomes the most important sacred event in the Israelite religious calendar.

The Route of the Exodus

After departing from their villages in Egypt, the Israelites travel southward (Exod. 12:37). This is done to avoid the Egyptian military posts that had been built along the more direct Way of the Philistines, which ran along the coastal plain (13:17). (The name of this road in the narrative is an anachronism because the Philistines did not settle in Canaan until after

1200 BCE.) The Israelites are guided in their journey by a pillar of cloud during the day and a pillar of fire at night. These are designed to reassure the Israelites with divine manifestations of Yahweh's power (13:20–22). However, very early in their journey a motif appears that will dominate the story of the Israelite wanderings—the **murmuring motif**, in which the Israelites grumble about the lack of food or water or about Moses's leadership style (Exod. 14:10–12; 15:23–25). This motif is followed, in most instances, by divine punishment of the Israelites and by Moses's quick intercession on their behalf. In the narrative of their departure from Egypt, the murmuring motif also serves as a prelude to the Red Sea crossing.

The events described in the biblical narrative of the Red Sea crossing (Exod. 14) are difficult for the modern student and scholar alike. While the ancient audience would not have been disturbed by a tale that included miraculous happenings and a rearrangement of the laws of nature, modern readers can seldom set aside their scientific worldview. Of course, this is not the only miracle story in the OT/HB. Others are found in Josh. 3–4 (another water crossing at the Jordan River) and 2 Kings 4:8–44 (a series of miracles performed by the prophet Elisha). In each case the miracle is designed to suspend the rules and demonstrate that Yahweh has complete control over nature.

Scholars attempt to interpret this story in essentially two ways: they search for natural explanations (volcanic eruptions, earthquakes), or they investigate the possible symbolic/mythic themes that provide the context for these events. For example, many scholars point to the words *yam suph* in the Hebrew text (Exod. 13:18) and translate them as "Reed Sea." The assumption is that "Reed Sea" refers to a freshwater marsh that existed in the area of northern Egypt where the Suez Canal now connects the Mediterranean Sea with the Red Sea. It is easier to imagine a group of Israelites escaping through a marsh while the heavy chariots of the pharaoh become bogged down (14:22–25). Other scholars translate this phrase as "Sea of the South," a legendary region where watery chaos threatened to overwhelm the ordered universe. Yahweh's ability to hold these waters in check thus represents God's protective attitude toward the Israelites. Certainly the poetic version of the story, the Song of the Sea (15:1–18), provides explicit imagery of the power of Yahweh as the **Divine Warrior** who has "triumphed gloriously" by drowning pharaoh's charioteers.

Once they have at last escaped Egyptian territory, Moses leads the Israelites through the Sinai wilderness toward Mount Sinai. Along the way two important events take place. First, the people's continual murmuring leads Moses to ask Yahweh for help, and God provides "manna and quail" (Exod. 16:1–21). The quail are migratory birds that regularly fly over the Sinai, and thus their presence can be explained quite easily. The manna, a breadlike substance that melts in the sunlight, is more difficult to identify. Among the suggestions that have been advanced for it is the excrement of a kind of locust that taps the moisture of porous desert plant life. The resulting residue can be gathered and consumed. Yahweh's provision of food in the wilderness also serves as the occasion for the first mention of the Sabbath holiday. The people were instructed not to gather manna on the Sabbath because it is "a day of solemn rest" (16:22–30).

The other major event during their Sinai trek is the confrontation with the Amalekites (Exod. 17:8–16). These pastoral nomadic tribal groups did not appreciate having a new people enter their territory and use up their meager water sources and pasturage. The conflict between the Amalekites and the Israelites furnishes an opportunity once again to present the Divine-Warrior theme. In this case Yahweh weighs in against a human enemy. What makes this necessary is the fact that the Israelites were not well armed or trained as warriors. Therefore, in order to defeat the Amalekites, Moses is instructed to raise his arms over his head. As long as he remains in this position overlooking the battle, the Israelites are victorious. Of course, it is because Yahweh fights for them, and that is the point of the story (17:14–16). The underdog Israelites are shown to have the divine favor of a powerful deity and will be feared by other peoples.

The Giving of the Law

The events at Mount Sinai center on a renewal of the covenant that Yahweh originally made with Abraham. The giving of the law is an extension of that agreement in the form of a treaty with the Israelites, and it will be referred to as the Decalogue, or the Ten Commandments. During the course of these events, Moses's role as the supreme leader of the people is highlighted and enhanced. He alone speaks directly with God. Interestingly, his brother Aaron, who serves as the first high priest for the people, is portrayed as a weak leader when Moses is absent (see Exod. 32:1–24).

Just prior to the giving of the Ten Commandments, as the people arrive at Mount Sinai, they are provided with God's reason for bringing them to this place (Exod. 19:4–6). Yahweh explains that divine intervention on their behalf in Egypt is designed to convince the Israelites of the power of their God. Now they are presented with the terms upon which their future relationship with Yahweh will be

> ### Eagles' Wings Catechism
>
> You have seen what I did to the Egyptians, and how I bore you on eagles' wings and brought you to myself. Now therefore, if you obey my voice and keep my covenant, you shall be my treasured possession out of all the peoples. Indeed, the whole earth is mine, but you shall be for me a priestly kingdom and a holy nation. (Exod. 19:4–6)

based. Yahweh's explanation, along with the **Shema**, "Hear, O Israel: the LORD is our God, the LORD alone" (Deut. 6:4), forms the basic creedal statements for the Israelites. The strict monotheism of the Shema, however, reflects the theology of the postexilic era and the development of the **Jewish Identity Movement** (see pp. 200–202). The words of the Eagles' Wings Catechism set a tone of obedience and obligation on the people if they choose to be a part of the covenant community.

With that understanding in place, Moses is presented with a foundational set of laws in Exod. 20:1–17. The Decalogue is set forth in **apodictic** style (note the repetition of the Decalogue in Deut. 5:6–21 with some variation in emphasis [see especially Exod. 20:11 and Deut. 5:15 regarding the institution of Sabbath worship]). These are command laws that do not require much explanation and do not contain the "if . . . then" sequence more common in **casuistic**, or case, law (see Exod. 21:1–11 for this form). The Ten Commandments can be divided into two segments:

Communal statutes apply to the conduct of the entire nation.

(a) Israelites are commanded to worship only one God. There is to be no other god set before Yahweh. A careful reading indicates that this is not a statement of monotheistic belief. Rather, it is **henotheism**, the idea that there are many gods, but the worshiper chooses to place greater emphasis on a particular one.

(b) They are forbidden to construct or worship idols. Idol worship is a common practice in the ancient Near East. To restrict the people from the use of images made them unique and increased the mysterious character of Yahweh. It also prevents the identification of an image made by humans with the actual person of the god (see Isa. 44:9–20).

(c) They, like other peoples, are to be cautious in invoking the name of God since that made the Deity a party to their oath. Names had power and were not to be used lightly.

(d) The setting aside of a day of rest each week is unique to ancient Israel. Sabbath (seven) is a sacrifice of precious time and recognition of Yahweh as the sole author of creation.

(e) The command to "honor your father and your mother" ensures that the aged would be taken care of and that the wisdom of elders would be respected. Note the gender equality here.

Personal statutes set the code of conduct for each person in the final five laws. These statutes commonly were found in the legal collections of other cultures (as in Hammurabi's Code from ancient Babylon). Laws such as "Do not steal" or "Do not commit adultery" are designed to maintain order and to protect the rights of property owners.

Law Codes

The remainder of the laws in Exodus and those found in Numbers, Leviticus, and Deuteronomy are primarily case laws. In nearly every instance, they are reflections of the legal formulas presented in the Ten Commandments and are the result of judges or individuals asking, "But what if . . . ?" about a particular legal phrase. For instance, the command that the people not steal (Exod. 20:15) is expanded on in Exod. 22:1. Here specific fines are imposed for the theft of an ox or a sheep, depending on whether the animal is found alive or dead. In another example, the group of laws that relate to caring for the poor (including widows, orphans, and resident aliens; Deut. 26:12–13) can be traced back to the commandments to honor one's parents, the prohibition against theft, and the injunction against coveting. They each speak to a particular legal situation that required an expansion of the law so that it dealt more directly with current concerns. At the heart of this expansion is an exhortation to remember "where you came from." The period of slavery in Egypt is continually cited as the basis for legal restraint or legal guarantees (Deut. 5:15; 15:15; 16:12; 24:18).

Since the laws are designed to regulate the life of the people, it is necessary for these statutes to evolve as the social situation of the people changes. They could not be governed by laws meant only for nomadic herders once they had become village-based farmers and urban dwellers ruled by a king. As a result, the collection of laws in Deuteronomy contains numerous references to towns and cities (19:1–13; 21:1–9) and the role of village elders in settling disputes (see 22:13–19; 25:5–10). There is also evidence of the shift in focus from an older law code to one developed in a later period. Thus, in the law that governs the treatment of those who have sold themselves into slavery to pay a debt, the version in Exod. 21:2–6 says the man must work six years and is set free in the seventh year. But the later version in Deut. 15:12–17 adds the provision that the former slave is to be given animals from the flock as a means of starting over.

There are many similarities between these law codes and those found elsewhere in the ancient Near East. The Code of Hammurabi

Seven Major Bodies of Law
• Decalogue: Exod. 20:1–17; Deut. 5:6–21
• Covenant Code: Exod. 20:18–23:33
• Ritual Decalogue: Exod. 34:11–26
• Deuteronomic Code: Deut. 12–26
• Holiness Code: Lev. 17–26
• Priestly Code: Lev. 1–16; 27; Num. 1–10
• Curses Code: Deut. 27:14–26

(CH; eighteenth century BCE) and the Middle Assyrian Law Code (MAL; eighth–seventh centuries BCE) contain so many laws that are similar to those in the Bible that it seems quite likely that legal formulas often are transmitted between cultures, just as other ideas, customs, technologies, and styles are. For instance, both Hammurabi's code and biblical law contain the principle of **lex talionis**, "an eye for an eye" (see Deut. 19:21). This legal concept is based on the idea of complete reciprocity for loss or injury.

Even here, however, the primary difference between other ancient Near Eastern codes and biblical law can be found. The legal codes of the Israelites demand full equality for all the people, with no exceptions even for the king. In ancient Babylon, there is a multitiered social system in which citizens do not receive the same punishment that is imposed on slaves for similar injuries.

Another difference is found in the apparent harshness of Israelite law. There are many crimes for which capital punishment is prescribed, and in no case is there a loophole that allows the convicted parties to be released or to pay a fine, as is the case in laws from Mesopotamia. Such a strict interpretation is based on the concept of purity that is inherent to biblical law. If the society wishes to remain pure, or in the state necessary for proper worship of Yahweh, it cannot take half measures in

Israelite Laws Relating to the Poor

- Debts were to be canceled every seventh year (Deut. 15:1–2).
- Loans to the poor should be made without interest (Lev. 25:35–37).
- Debt slaves were to be freed after six years of labor (Exod. 21:2).
- The edges of fields were not to be harvested so that the poor could glean in them (Lev. 19:9).
- The poor were entitled to the same legal rights as the rich (Deut. 16:19).

dealing with criminal behavior. To do so would eventually contaminate the entire nation. For this reason a rebellious son is to be stoned to death (Deut. 21:18–21) in order to "purge the evil from your midst."

The inset below illustrates some of the similarities and differences between other ancient Near Eastern codes and biblical law. What is particularly striking in these examples is the more objective character of Mesopotamian law. For instance, there is a sense of poetic justice in requiring the amputation of the hand

of a son who strikes his father (CH 195). In Israelite law, however, both father and mother are mentioned, and the death penalty is imposed to prevent this action from becoming acceptable in their society (Exod. 21:15).

The **covenant-renewal ceremony** staged at Mount Sinai completes the picture of the rededication of the people to their covenant obligations (Exod. 24:3–8). It also provides the model for a similar ceremony that marks three later major shifts in the history of the Israelite people. The purpose in Exodus is to reestablish the covenantal relationship with Yahweh's chosen people and set them on a course that will once again bring them to the promised land. Moses's orchestration of a communal renewal of the people's vow of obedience to the covenant also provides an example of the ideology contained in the commandment about using God's name (Exod. 20:7). By accepting their position as people of the covenant, they invoke Yahweh as their judge. This will later be the principle on which God will punish their

Crime and Punishment in Mesopotamia and Ancient Israel

False Witness

CH 1: If the father of one household charges another with murder, but has no evidence, then the sentence is death. (OTPar[3], 106)

Deut. 19:16–19: If a malicious witness comes forward to accuse someone of wrongdoing, then both parties to the dispute shall appear before the LORD, before the priests and the judges who are in office in those days, and the judges shall make a thorough inquiry. If the witness is a false witness, . . . then you shall do to the false witness just as the false witness had meant to do to the other. So you shall purge the evil from your midst.

Adultery

CH 129: If a wife of a father of a household is arrested in the act of committing adultery, then she and her partner are to be tied up and tried by ordeal in a river. If, however, the woman's husband pardons her, then the monarch can pardon his subject. (OTPar[3], 109)

Deut. 22:22: If a man is caught lying with the wife of another man, both of them shall die, the man who lay with the woman as well as the woman. So you shall purge the evil from Israel.

Parental Abuse

CH 195: If the son of a household strikes his father, then his hand is to be cut off. (OTPar[3], 111)

Exod. 21:15: Whoever strikes father or mother shall be put to death.

Sorcery

MAL 47: If the father of a household or the mother of a household is discovered working magic, then, following due process, the defendants are sentenced to death. (OTPar[3], 128)

Lev. 20:27: A man or a woman who is a medium or a wizard shall be put to death; they shall be stoned to death, their blood is upon them.

disobedience as they begin their trek from Sinai to the promised land.

The Wilderness Period

Shortly before leaving Mount Sinai, Aaron and his sons are instructed to construct a portable shrine known as the ark of the covenant. The ark is a lidded box that contained the tablets of the law as well as other sacred objects. It is carried by members of Moses's tribe, the Levites, and it is housed, while the people were encamped, in an elaborate tent. The tabernacle, or tent of meeting, is structured so that the ark is placed in a special enclosed area in the tent (the **holy of holies**). The tent is surrounded on all sides by a high screen that forms a rectangular courtyard around the sacred structure. In the courtyard, Aaron and his sons perform animal sacrifices on behalf of the people. The very detailed description of the construction of the portable shrine and the installation of its priesthood are designed to provide a traditional foundation and pattern for religious activity in later periods (Exod. 25–30). For instance, the priestly hierarchy is established giving control of the high priesthood to the descendants of Aaron (Exod. 29:1–9).

With these objects accompanying the people as symbols of God, the trek from Sinai begins. Their journey will be prolonged due to the people's failure to keep the covenantal agreement (they worshiped a golden calf in Exod. 32:1–10) and their initial refusal to attempt

an immediate invasion of the promised land (Num. 13:17–14:12). Also embedded in these narratives is the recurrent murmuring motif, which includes general complaints and periodic rebellions against Moses's leadership (12:1–3; 16:1–35). Ultimately all of those who were adults at the time of the departure from Egypt, except for Joshua and Caleb, are condemned to die during this forty-year period. These two men were the only ones among the twelve spies sent by Moses into Canaan who reported that the Israelites could successfully take the land (13:25–33). Even Moses and Aaron died before entry into the land because they also failed to obey Yahweh's commands on at least one occasion (Num. 20:2–13). In this way the wilderness serves as a period of purification and punishment, preparing the Israelites for their conquest of the promised land.

In addition to the **culling process** that gradually diminished the Israelites' numbers (Num. 21:4–9), the wilderness period is characterized by the emergence of Joshua as a military leader, a role he continues to play in the conquest of Canaan. As the wilderness period comes to an end, the Israelites engage in a series of military encounters in Transjordan that highlight Joshua as the new leader of the people. At this point Moses dies. He is instructed by God to scale Mount Nebo. He is allowed to view the land that he can never enter. The dimensions of the promised land are provided, as well as a reiteration of God's covenant promise (Deut. 34:1–8). With Moses's death, the people, under their new leader, are brought to a new stage in their history. Now their task is to conquer and settle the land.

A postscript to this narrative must include the warning that there is no extrabiblical evidence for these stories or any others prior to

Arguments for an Exodus Event

- The negative depiction of Israel in Egypt is not likely to be a total invention. People seldom tell such stories about themselves unless they have some basis in history.
- The detailed description of the events again points to a strong tradition based on the story of the exodus.

the monarchy. Moses is never mentioned in contemporary Egyptian records and neither is the exodus itself. Assuming that the exodus did take place, it is possible that only a portion of the Israelites, perhaps only the Levites, were involved. The importance of the Levites within the temple community during the monarchy could then explain the magnification of the role of Moses and Aaron in this narrative.

The exodus event is extremely important in the theology of the prophets. Many times Yahweh used the exodus as the basis for recriminations against Israelites who did not appreciate what had been done for them.

■ STUDY QUESTIONS ■

1. What are the arguments for the various chronologies of the exodus? Which do you consider most plausible (see Exod. 1; 1 Kings 6:1)?

Exodus Referenced in Prophetic Literature

Hosea 11:1: "When Israel was a child, I loved him, and out of Egypt I called my son."

Amos 3:1: "Hear this word that the LORD has spoken against you, O people of Israel, against the whole family that I brought up out of the land of Egypt."

Mic. 6:4: "For I brought you up from the land of Egypt, and redeemed you from the house of slavery."

Jer. 2:6: Your ancestors "did not say, 'Where is the LORD who brought us up from the land of Egypt, who led us in the wilderness?'"

2. How does the birth narrative of Sargon of Akkad compare with that of Moses?
3. What are the basic features of Moses's call narrative at Mount Sinai? Why does Moses appear to be so reluctant to serve (Exod. 3:1–4:17)?
4. Why is the story of the ten plagues contained in a framework narrative?
5. What are the various explanations for what happens at the Red/Reed Sea (Exod. 14)?
6. Why do the Israelites "murmur" so much (Exod. 14:10–12; 16:2–3; 17:2–3)?
7. Describe and explain the examples of the Divine-Warrior theme in these narratives (Exod. 17:8–16).
8. What is the Eagles' Wings Catechism? How does this covenant statement in Exod. 19:4–6 differ from that given to Abraham?
9. How do biblical law codes compare with other ancient Near Eastern law codes? Why are there so many similarities?

The Book of Joshua

KEY POINTS

- The Joshua conquest narrative has more to do with ideology than history.
- Archaeological data do not support a general conquest of Canaan.
- The peoples who settled in the central hill country faced environmental challenges.

The book of Joshua provides an idealized version of the conquest of Canaan based on the Deuteronomist's principle of Yahweh's rewarding the faithfully obedient. The narrative in the first twelve chapters contains a series of victories (often miraculously won) by Yahweh, the Divine Warrior, and the people of Israel. It is in these stories that Joshua emerges

Moses and Joshua Compared

- Yahweh tells Joshua he will be with him "just as I was with Moses" (Josh. 1:5; cf. Exod. 3:12 and Deut. 31:6–8).
- Both Moses and Joshua send spies into Canaan (Num. 13:1–3; Josh. 2:1).
- Both Moses and Joshua direct the Israelites to cross a body of water that miraculously opens before them (Exod. 14; Josh. 3:7–17).
- Both Moses and Joshua hold out their hands until a military victory is complete (Exod. 17:8–12; Josh. 8:18–26).
- Moses brings Israel into the covenant and performs a covenant-renewal ceremony; Joshua also performs a covenant-renewal ceremony (Exod. 24:3–11; Deut. 29:2–30:20; Josh. 24:1–28).

as a new Moses, and on many occasions his career directly parallels that of Moses. Such a portrayal is necessary to ensure that Joshua is accepted as the new leader of the people (see his ceremonial installation in Num. 27:12–23). It also ensures continuity of leadership and commitment to the covenant with Yahweh.

Joshua's task as Moses's successor is not easy. He has to shoulder the responsibilities of leadership and conduct a multipronged military campaign. The biblical writers portray him as an obedient servant of Yahweh, but there are at least two instances where his personality comes through in the narrative. The first is found when he is surprised by the Israelites' failure to capture the city of Ai (Josh. 7:6–15). He discovers that God holds a commander responsible for the actions of his soldiers as well as his own. The conquest is stalled until the man who has violated the rules of holy war is found and executed. In the other example, Joshua's ego is inflated by the false claims of the disguised Gibeonites who are trying to save themselves from defeat by the Israelites. Joshua takes an oath that he cannot break and finds himself defending a portion of his sworn enemies because of this personal mistake (Josh. 9:3–27).

The Conquest Account

Evidence for the conquest, as it is described in the book of Joshua, is problematic. The only account of this holy war occurs in the biblical text. Archaeological investigations at the major sites that are said to have been destroyed by the Israelites have provided mixed results. Jericho,

Figure 2.3. Remains of an ancient wall found during excavations at Jericho, the reputed site of Joshua's first victory in the Israelites' conquest of Canaan.
(Kim Walton)

the first city listed as conquered by the Israelites (Josh. 6), was extensively excavated three times in the twentieth century. Despite some early claims that the remains of Joshua's Jericho had been found, it has generally been accepted that in the period between 2000 and 1100 BCE the city was much smaller and was not defended by a major wall system. In a previous period, Jericho had been a major site with monumental walls, but that city was destroyed in about 2200 BCE.

Ai, the second city mentioned in the conquest (Josh. 7:2–6), has also proved to be a puzzle. Excavations at this site (1965–1975) by Joseph Callaway demonstrated that the mound was not a significant population center between 2400 and 1200 BCE. It is possible that it was used as a military outpost by the nearby city of Bethel, which does show evidence of destruction in the thirteenth century BCE. However, there was no major settlement at Ai during the thirteenth century. The name of Ai, which means "the ruin," may have contributed to its being added to Joshua's list of conquests, but there is no way to prove this.

Other cities, including Hazor, Lachish, and Tell Beit Mirsim, do have destruction levels that date to the thirteenth century. However, it is unclear whether their destruction can be attributed to the efforts of the Israelites. The destruction levels at these sites could just as easily have been the result of the devastation of the area by Pharaoh Merneptah. It is also possible that internal disputes such as those described in the fourteenth-century-BCE El Amarna texts were the cause, or these cities may have been the victims of the invading Sea Peoples. This latter group raided much of the ancient Near East in about 1200 BCE. Their attacks significantly weakened the Hittite kingdom in Anatolia, destroyed the seaport city of Ugarit in northern Syria, and nearly defeated the Egyptians. Pharaoh Ramses III describes a desperate struggle in which Egyptian forces beat off the invaders. Following their initial incursion, portions of the Sea Peoples split off, settling in Canaan and becoming known as the Philistines.

With so many conflicting pieces of information, it is best to take a cautious view of the Israelite conquest of Canaan. Several theories have been proposed to explain the disparities between the archaeological evidence and the description of sweeping campaigns in which the Israelites achieved a nearly total victory over the Canaanites (Josh. 1–12). The authors and editors of the book of Joshua are not as interested in historical details as they are in making the theological point that the victory is engineered by Yahweh, the Divine Warrior. Each battle is won because of the direct intervention of God. For instance, the fall of Jericho is not based on a conventional siege or strategy, but rather on the opening given to the Israelites when Yahweh miraculously destroys the city's walls (Josh. 6).

There is also a certain selectivity in the conquest account. For instance, there is no clear indication of how long the conquest took to complete. It seems that some cities immediately fell to the wave of immigrants while others succumbed to later attacks. The possibility exists that the Israelite tribes entered Canaan over a fairly long period of time, with each successive wave adding to their numbers and their ability to achieve victories. Other migrating groups or even displaced Canaanites (e.g., the Gibeonites in Josh. 9:3–15) may have joined forces with the Israelite tribes as they settled in the hill country. Such defections could have undermined the authority and strength of the Canaanite culture, which was already

Figure 2.4. Remains of the foundation of a large ancient building found during excavations at Hazor in northern Israel. Joshua is said to have destroyed this strategic city during his northern campaign (Josh. 11). (Baker Photo Archive)

weakened or was under fire from both the Egyptians and the Sea Peoples. Under these circumstances it is possible to conclude that the Israelites would have been able to establish a bridgehead in the hill country and eventually to expand their holdings. More than a century after the beginning of the settlement period, the Israelites were able to control larger areas and some cities. The Philistine city-states in the south central plains of Palestine continued to provide the major opposition to Israelite expansion until the time of King David (ca. 1000 BCE).

Joshua's Account of the Conquest. The conquest of Canaan is depicted in the book of Joshua as a swiftly moving, three-pronged campaign. The initial thrust into the midst of the country just north of the Dead Sea is aimed at the important site of Jericho. Following the miraculous victory there, the Israelites turn northwest and continue their foray into the hill country, targeting the city of Ai. After dealing with the consequences of disobedience and divine anger, the second attack on Ai is successful (Josh. 7:1–8:29). The subsequent battle of Gibeon (Josh. 9–10), with its victory over the king of Jerusalem and his allies, solidifies the Israelites' control of the central hill country and the major trade routes leading into the southern Shephelah. This phase of the narrative also contains an example of universalism. The Gibeonites save themselves through disguise, flattery, and a statement similar to Rahab's, acknowledging that they "have heard a report of [your God], of all that he did in Egypt, and . . . to the two kings of the Amorites" (9:3–13). Joshua makes a treaty with these tricksters, and they, like Rahab, are spared the destruction rained on the other Canaanite peoples (9:15–26). The final phase of the campaign matches Joshua's forces against Jabin, king of Hazor, and another coalition of Canaanite rulers (Josh. 11). No details of this campaign are provided other than the capture of some chariots and the hamstringing of the enemy horses. Only Hazor is burned by the Israelites, but the text does mention an effort to systematically strike down "all the people" and loot their towns (11:10–14).

Once again caution must be taken when reading these accounts. The archaeological records from the twelfth century BCE indicate that Egypt's pharaoh Ramses III continued to maintain a presence in Canaan at least until the midpoint of the century. In addition, while Hazor may have been attacked, it continued to serve as a major Canaanite settlement throughout this period. Perhaps these facts are an indication that the Israelites did more to disrupt commercial activity than to annex territory in the northern region of Canaan.

Conquest Themes. According to Joshua 1–12, the Israelites gain almost immediate access to this promised territory because of two things: the obedience of the people to Yahweh's commands and the repeated intervention of the Divine Warrior. That is why the walls of Jericho fall flat. Joshua obediently follows Yahweh's instructions to stage a series of religious processions around the city for a seven-day period (a number commonly associated with Yahweh's creative act in Gen. 1). The shout of the Israelites on the seventh day invokes the presence of Yahweh and ensures their victory (Josh. 6:1–21). Similarly, in the battle against

---

Obedience Theme

Joshua's success in leading the Israelites to victory is the result of his adherence to the principle of total obedience to God's command (Josh. 11:15, 23). Such an unquestioning attitude is in line with the Deuteronomist's theology of obedience as the basis for the fulfillment of the covenant promise. It is also found in the admonitions of the prophets:

"If you obey the commandments of the LORD your God . . . by loving the LORD your God, walking in his ways, and observing his commandments, decrees, and ordinances, then you shall live and become numerous, and the LORD your God will bless you in the land that you are entering to possess. But if your heart turns away and you do not hear, but are led astray to bow down to other gods and serve them, I declare to you today that you will perish. . . . Choose life so that you and your descendants may live." (Deut. 30:16–19)
"Seek the LORD and live." (Amos 5:6)
"See, I am setting before you the way of life and the way of death." (Jer. 21:8; during the siege of Jerusalem by Nebuchadnezzar's Babylonian army)
"Incline your ear, and come to me; listen, so that you may live." (Isa. 55:3)

---

the combined forces of the five Amorite kings (Josh. 10), Joshua follows Yahweh's instructions to attack after an all-night march from Gilgal. Because of this unfailing obedience, Yahweh joins the battle, casting hailstones on the enemy to confuse them and then miraculously extending the daylight so that the slaughter could be completed (10:12–13).

Besides episodes in which obedience is the key to success, the biblical text also reports an example of what happens when the Israelites fail to follow instructions. In Josh. 7:2–5, Joshua's forces fail to capture the city of Ai. After praying to Yahweh to determine why they have been defeated, it is revealed that a man named Achan has taken loot from the city of Jericho (7:6–15). His action violates the divine *kherem* command. According to the principle of *kherem* (holy war), all the inhabitants of

Jericho and all their property are to be sacrificed to God in a massive conflagration of the city. In essence, this means that Achan has stolen from God.

The punishment of all the people for the sin of one man is an example of corporate identity. Lots are cast to determine the guilty person, and Achan is implicated. Then he and his entire family as well as their animals are stoned to death. In this way Achan is cast out of the covenant community, and he and his household share the fate of the people of Jericho. Their punishment serves as an example to all the Israelites (Josh. 7:16–26). As for the value of such extreme measures, they are consistent with other forms of psychological warfare and are designed to ensure strict obedience on the part of the Israelites. They are also a way of demonstrating to the enemy Israel's determination to capture the land.

Another theme evident in Joshua's conquest narrative is universalism. The editors of the narrative inject this theme in order to show that even non-Israelites can recognize the power and majesty of Yahweh. Applying this theme, Rahab, the prostitute in Jericho, is portrayed as helping Joshua's spies escape because of her genuine conversion to Israel's God. As a result of her courage and statement of faith, she is able to save her family while all other inhabitants of the city are put to the sword. The key to the universalism theme in this story is Rahab's statement: "The LORD your God is indeed God in heaven above and on earth below" (Josh. 2:9–11). Her acceptance of Yahweh's power to command events is far stronger than that of the Israelites who besiege her city.

Alternative Conquest Theories

One of the primary difficulties with the account of the conquest in Josh. 1–12 is that there is insufficient supportive physical evidence (either artifactual or textual) supplied

The Universalism Theme

- The universalism theme pervades the biblical text from the book of Numbers through the later prophetic writings of Isaiah, Jonah, and the postexilic book of Ruth. The first clear expression of the theme appears during the story of the Transjordanian trek by the Israelites prior to their entrance into Canaan. There a non-Israelite prophet is introduced, who performs a task that shows Yahweh's power (Balaam, Num. 22–24). In a later example, a Syrian general personally experiences a work of power and is cured of leprosy (Naaman, 2 Kings 5). What makes this theme so effective is that these actions or the characters' statements often show a greater faith in Yahweh than that demonstrated by the chosen people of God.

- A later usage of the universalism theme attempts to show that it is the job of the chosen people to share their knowledge of Yahweh's power with non-Israelite people. Thus, Second Isaiah (ca. 540 BCE, found in Isa. 40–55), in his Servant Songs, says that once the returning exiles have restored Zion, their mission is to be a "light to the nations" (49:6). Like a lighthouse, the Israelites are to demonstrate to the gentiles the light of the Torah and the universal power of Yahweh. Similarly, in Third Isaiah (Isa. 56–66), the prophet argues against restrictions on those who may worship in the newly rebuilt temple in Jerusalem (ca. 515 BCE). He says that only an acknowledgment of and an adherence to Sabbath worship is required to become a worshiper of Yahweh (58:13–14).

- Perhaps the most powerful of the later universalistic stories is found in Jonah. In this book, set in the period of Assyrian domination (eighth century BCE) but most likely written after the exile (after 500 BCE), God directs the prophet to preach repentance to the city of Nineveh. The Assyrians were hated by the peoples that they had conquered, and that included the Israelites. Nineveh's inhabitants were the target of many curses and cries for justice (e.g., see Nah. 2–3 for a depiction of Nineveh's fall). Thus it is not surprising that Jonah refuses. However, the prophetic commission cannot be resisted, and ultimately Jonah carries out his task and saves the city. In this way the story demonstrates Yahweh's concern for the entire creation, even the most onerous to Israel.

by archaeological excavation or extrabiblical documents. From what has been discovered, Jericho in the twelfth century BCE was apparently only partially occupied. The massive wall systems uncovered by archaeologists have been proved to date to the period around 2200 BCE, long before the time assigned for the conquest period. Similarly, Ai was an abandoned ruin during much of the twelfth century BCE and was reoccupied when a small village site was established there in the latter part of that century, perhaps by Israelite settlers. It too had once been a large, fortified city, but this earlier occupation also dated to the third millennium BCE.

While there are other sites (Bethel, Lachish, Hazor) that do have evidence of destruction dating to the twelfth century BCE, there is no way to assign these attacks with certainty to the Israelites. Given what we know of that period, it is possible to ascribe them to the Sea Peoples, the Egyptians, or some other people.

Because of the failure to discover corroborating archaeological evidence that matches the account in the book of Joshua, scholars have attempted to provide alternative theories about the conquest. These theories are based on our current understanding of historical events and economic pressures during the time generally associated with the conquest (i.e., the twelfth century BCE). In no case is a particular theory accepted by all scholars, and in any case, without clear archaeological and epigraphic evidence, it will be difficult to establish the historicity of the conquest account in Joshua.

Infiltration/Migration Theory. According to this theory, a series of migrations took place in which Israelites or peoples who eventually became identified as Israelites gradually moved into the region of the central hill country in Canaan. This theory is bolstered somewhat by archaeological surveys in the area, which have shown the establishment of well over one hundred new, unfortified village sites (most housing 75 to 125 people) during this time. There is no conclusive explanation given for why this occurred. One explanation put forward is that the settlements are a response to the invasion of the Near East by the Sea Peoples after 1200 BCE. Under pressure from these invaders, refugees from conquered Canaanite cities may have fled to the hill country. Subsequently the settlement of the Philistines along the southern coast of Canaan and in the Shephelah would have prevented these people from returning to their homes. Even in forced exile, these indigenous Canaanites would have retained a portion of their previous culture and technology. However, the hardships of life in the marginal region of the hill country would have caused them to evolve socially and adapt to a lifestyle based more on a subsistence economy. A variation on this theory is espoused by the archaeologist Lawrence Stager, who has surmised that once the political base in the Canaanite city-states was weakened or broken, much of their subject peasant population chose to shift into the hill country and out of the effective control of their former masters. This ruralization could help account for the establishment of many new villages in the hill country and a growth of population in previously uninhabited or underinhabited areas. Under these conditions, the indigenous hill-country inhabitants may have welcomed the addition of new people. They would be seen as a boon to the stretched labor force allowing villages to open up additional acreage, build terraces on hillsides, and assist with the herds. In this way a synthesis of Canaanite and "Israelite" forces would have created a new culture in the hill country. Based on this scenario, no systematic

Map 2.2. Palestine under Joshua and the Judges

appeared, people from the Canaanite peasant classes chose to withdraw their support
from their own leaders and join the Israelites.
According to this theory, they were attracted
by the **egalitarian** spirit of the Israelites and
the chance to advance themselves among a new
people. One story used to support this view
is the tale of Rahab. As a prostitute, she is a
member of the lower class, and thus her willingness to help Joshua's spies is based more on
the survival of her family and the likelihood of
a better life among the Israelites than on the
strength of their god. Therefore her statement
of faith in Josh. 2:9–11, while typical of the
belief that victorious peoples have powerful
gods, is designed to ingratiate and explain her
actions to the spies.

The actual explanation for the conquest
narrative in Joshua may share elements from
the ancient narrative and from both modern
theories. It is impossible to prove whether the
exodus occurred and whether ex-slaves forced
their way into Canaan and eventually established a people known as Israel. It may be that
the Joshua account, written during the later
monarchic period, is based on folk traditions
and idealized because its purpose was to bolster public support for the monarchy and the
state. The narrative in Judges, which is probably compiled in the period shortly after the establishment of the monarchy, and which speaks
of the failure of the Israelites to capture portions of the land, may have a different purpose.
The book of Judges is a strong argument for
the existence of the monarchy, as opposed to
the weak, anarchic tribal period that preceded
it. By promising strong centralized leadership,
David and his successors can use the Judges
material to their political advantage.

conquest would have ever taken place (thus
explaining the lack of archaeological data).
Instead, the situation as described in the book
of Judges, in which the Israelites are oppressed
by their neighbors, would be closer to the real
picture of the early settlement period.

Withdrawal/Peasant-Revolt Theory. According to the withdrawal theory, the rigid
social structure that existed in the cities of
Canaan prevented movement between social
classes or political and economic advancement.
The result was major discontent among the
lower classes. The monumental construction
projects, heavy taxes, forced labor, and military service of these Canaanite states further
contributed to a climate of unrest among
the lower classes. When the Israelite tribes

Division of the Land and Covenant Renewal

The latter part of the book of Joshua contains detailed accounts of the formal division of the land among the Israelite tribes. Not all tribes will settle in Canaan. Reuben, Gad, and the half-tribe of Manasseh are given territory east of the Jordan River in Gilead (Josh. 13:8–32). One tribe, the Levites, does not receive a portion of the promised land (13:33). The Levites were set aside to serve as the priestly class for all the Israelites. Therefore, to prevent them from becoming territorial or corrupted by a conflict of interest between their priestly duties and their tribal holdings, the Levites owned no land. Instead, they receive a portion of the tithe for their services (Num. 18:21–26).

Once the job of distribution is complete, the narrative concludes with a reiteration of the covenant-renewal ceremony first performed by Moses at Mount Sinai (Exod. 24). Like Moses, Joshua calls the people to assemble (Josh. 24:1). He details God's covenantal promise and the succession of saving events that have brought them successfully to that day (24:13). The people are then challenged to acknowledge their indebtedness to Yahweh and to recommit themselves to the covenant (24:14–15). Once they do so, Joshua reiterates their obligations and the risks they are taking should they fail to uphold their promise to put aside all other gods (24:16–24). At that point, the ceremony ends with the erection of a stone monument to commemorate the event and to serve as a perpetual reminder of their covenantal obligations (24:25–27). A parallel version of the story in 8:30–35 adds some details to the scene, including the presence of the ark of the covenant and the construction of the altar on Mount Ebal.

Joshua stages his ceremony at Shechem, which is an interesting choice. While Shechem

Geographic Reiteration and Shechem

The reuse of particular sites as the location for significant events is based in part on the relatively small size of Canaan and the limited number of major towns. Scribes, however, seem to repeatedly draw attention to these places by staging major events there.

Shechem is the first place where the ancestral narrative states that Abram stopped and built an altar to give thanks to Yahweh (Gen. 12:6–7).

Jacob purchases a plot of land near Shechem. His daughter Dinah is raped by the king's son, and the city's population is massacred in revenge by Jacob's sons (Gen. 33:18–34:31).

Joshua stages his covenant-renewal ceremony at Shechem (Josh. 24:1–28).

Solomon's successor, Rehoboam, goes to Shechem to negotiate with the leaders of the northern tribes, and his failure to meet their demands leads to the division of the kingdom (1 Kings 12:1–19).

is centrally located within the territory now claimed by the Israelite tribes, its choice as the place for such an important ritual may also be based on its association with previous events in Israel's national narrative. It is possible to identify a scribal tendency to draw the people back to significant sites for those moments in their history when they have reached a crisis point or are on the point of figuratively turning a corner in their cultural development. This scribal technique is called geographic reiteration.

The Challenges of Settlement in the Hill Country

Whether the taking of Canaan is the result of a conquest, as is depicted in Josh. 1–12, a mass immigration of new peoples combined with a ruralization of the Canaanite peasantry due to the invasion of the Sea Peoples after 1200 BCE, or a rejection of the legal and social constraints of the Canaanite urban centers of the plains, the hill-country villages serve as a new social environment for the settlers. They are faced with new environmental and economic challenges in this marginal region.

Physical Conditions in the Central Hill Country

The physical environment of the central hill country and the level of technology available to the inhabitants placed limits or a productivity threshold on the villages of the twelfth and eleventh centuries BCE.

Geomorphology: The Judean Highlands consist of a low range of hills enclosed within a saddle, bordered by the higher elevations at Hebron in the south and Bethel in the north. The hills have been badly eroded due to deforestation, and thus the best arable land is found in the intervening valleys. A lack of perennial streams requires the digging of wells, use of local springs, and dry farming techniques.

Climate: A Mediterranean climate provides a hot and dry summer and a cold and wet winter. Rainfall amounts vary from more than 1,000 mm (39.37 inches) in the Upper Galilee to less than 300 mm (11.81 inches) in areas south of Beersheba.

Faced with these conditions, ancient farmers engaged in a variety of strategies:

1. In an effort to alter the environment and raise productivity, terraces were constructed on the badly eroded hillsides (see Isa. 5:1–2).

2. While the principal cash crops were wheat, olives, and grapes, it was necessary to engage in a mixed economy as a hedge against drought, insects, and invaders. Herding provided some economic diversity, and interregional trade allowed for the acquisition of products that could not be grown in their own ecosystem, along with social interaction and the sharing of information.

They are also removed from continuous contact with the urban centers of Canaan. The result is a struggle to survive as a viable economic group and as a political entity separate from the urban centers of the plain.

Throughout the biblical period, the village economy of ancient Israel relies on the two basic resources of land and progeny (Gen. 12:1–8), which, according to the covenant, it is committed to develop (1:26–28). Having and controlling their land and progeny distinguishes free households from their slaves.

While these villagers are mostly farmers and herders, the Bible seldom provides details on

Figure 2.5. An ancient stone press used to crush the hard pits of olives in order to abstract the oil. Olive oil was a staple of life in the ancient Mediterranean, used for food, fuel, cosmetics, and medicine. (Baker Photo Archive)

farming or herding practices. Of course, the audience is familiar with life in the villages and understood these jobs so well that no additional details are needed. As a result, farmers are casually portrayed as using the tools and installations necessary for life in the hill country. Plowing, planting, threshing, and winnowing form a part of their everyday life. For instance, the stories of Gideon (Judg. 6:11, 36–40) refer to a threshing floor and winepress at Ophrah, but the writers do not describe them because there is a threshing floor to process grain and a winepress to squeeze their grapes in or near every village. Herdsmen are said to take their flocks to pasture as needed, but there is no detailed discussion of this process (see Gen. 37:12–17 and the allegory of the good shepherd in Ezek. 34:11–24). As a result, any attempt to reconstruct everyday life in these ancient villages is based on a combination of the biblical text and what archaeological excavations and anthropological models can supply.

The range of what each village plants and of the animals they herd is determined in large part by the physical environment of their settlement site. Extreme variability from one area to another meant that the people had to learn to cope with many different kinds of local topography. There is desert to the south and east; highlands to the north and south; slopes and foothills to the west. For instance, the Israelite villages farthest north of Jerusalem live on a land marked by outcroppings of limestone and poor soil. Each village, by necessity, adapts its farming techniques to match the potential of its environmental conditions with existing technology. Among the strategies they employed was the terracing of hillsides. In this way they are able to expand available cultivated space, but terracing also requires massive amounts of labor to construct and maintain. Experimentation undoubtedly takes place, and successful farmers become the models for others until new technology allows for differentiation or expansion into previously unworkable regions.

A standard harvest in the hill country produces ten to fifteen times the grain that is needed to plant it. Positive changes in the quality of the land, the number of farmers available (both men and women would have worked in the fields), and the way in which they work can increase the standard harvest. But there is always a greater risk of negative changes that can destroy the economy of the village and its households. Fields that produce as little as a tenfold to fifteenfold harvest in good years fail in the three years out of ten that bring drought and insect infestations.

To get the most from the labor available in the village, ancient farmers use a variety of techniques. They manage their time, pool their resources, learn to minimize the effort needed to achieve their goals, and have as many children as possible. Farmers stagger sowing by planting a single crop in several stages over a period of time. Although it would be impossible for them to care for a single large crop

The Gezer Almanac

August and September to pick olives,
October to sow barley,
December and January to weed,
February to cut flax,
March to harvest barley,
April to harvest wheat and to pay tithes,
May and June to prune vines,
July to pick the fruit of summer. (OTPar³, 156)

at one time, the same number of farmers can handle the comparable-size crop one section at a time. Planting in stages also provides some insurance against losing an entire crop when the planting and harvesting rains are off cycle. Fallowing a portion of the fields also allows the land to rest and restore its fertility (Exod. 23:10–11; Jer. 4:3).

During the settlement period, farmers plant a variety of cereals along with fruit trees, grape

Figure 2.6. The Gezer Almanac, written in archaic Hebrew script on a pottery shard; possibly a writing exercise for a student and dated to the time of Solomon. The text offers a unique glimpse into the ancient agricultural cycle. (Baker Photo Archive, courtesy of the Istanbul Archaeological Museum)

vines, various vegetables, and nut crops. Such a mixed strategy has two effects. By staggering the sowing of a single crop and varying the kinds of crops they plant, farmers spread out their work over a longer period of time. Trees and vines do not require the farmer's attention during the same season as cereals. Planting more than one crop also restricts the damage done by plant disease. Since the disease or drought that affects one crop does not always affect others, planting a variety of crops prevents the loss of an entire harvest. Even when one particular crop fails, there is still a chance that others will survive.

The Gezer Almanac preserves an example of a typical farm schedule, indicating the kinds of crops being planted, cultivated, and harvested. In about 1000 BCE, a young farmer at Gezer practiced his writing skills on a piece of soft rectangular limestone about four inches long and four inches wide. The text is an almanac that matches each month with a particular chore, and it has the same number of seasonal divisions as the year. Like the agricultural cycle, it arranges the parts of the year in a pattern that rotates the type and level of farm labor. The almanac graphically demonstrates the diversified agricultural picture of the hill country. The use of both wheat, which is a slow-maturing grain, and barley, which matures quickly in poor or salty soil, provided successive harvests and allowed the workforce time to harvest one crop and process it before the next one ripened. Finally, grapes and figs could be harvested at the end of the summer without interfering with major grain harvests. In a region where the labor supply seldom meets labor requirements, the spacing of major farming events is absolutely necessary.

Farmers in the villages in early Israel work long hours and very full weeks. Together they clear land, terrace fields, plant, cultivate, and harvest crops. Living together in four-room, pillared houses makes it easier for farmers to pool their labor. The pillared house is one of the most common dwelling types found in these ancient villages. The houses are designed to meet the same three basic needs: living and working space, space for livestock, and storage space for grain, animal fodder, and products such as wool.

Pillared houses excavated so far reveal a variety of different patterns employed to meet space and environmental demands while adapting themselves to the local topography. However, in general, they consist of three parallel long rooms that are separated by two walls or rows of columns, with an additional broad room running across one end and a second floor providing additional living space. The house is divided lengthwise into three areas by a row of roof-supporting pillars on one side and a solid wall on the other. The row of pillars is nearer to one long wall, creating an area about four and one-half feet wide on the narrow side and about ten feet wide on the other. In some cases, the additional room across the back of the basic rectangle can be entered through a door off the main section of the house or function as an open-air courtyard. Wooden beams six to eight inches in diameter are set into notches in the solid outer wall of the house and extend to the pillars and inside wall. This lower floor, just six feet high, is used to house the family's animals. The roof itself is made up of slats coated with a layer of white clay. Because there are several distinct living spaces, it is possible to dedicate space to particular activities and to maintain purity laws (Lev. 18:19) by isolating menstruating women, who are ritually impure, from the men of the household.

Figure 2.7. The remains of pillared houses at Beer-sheba. (Baker Photo Archive)

Within the living space there is no furniture. People sit cross-legged on the packed clay and stone floor or on a stone ledge along the base of the inside wall of the house. Flat stones are used for stools, and everyone sleeps on the floor on pallets. Several households share a common outdoor courtyard kitchen where bread is baked on a pottery bowl inverted over the coals (Hosea 7:8) or in an oven (Lev. 7:9).

Israelite villagers have little extra clothing and generally wear only a loincloth and a tunic. Everyone also has a cloak that doubles as a blanket. Hence, there is no need for closets in a pillared house. Few villagers regularly bathe or wash their clothes, so there are no rooms set aside for washing or bathing (Gen. 24:63; 37:15).

Most farmers also manage small herds of sheep, goats, and cattle. These grazing animals provide milk, meat, wool, and a reserve food supply in case of a bad harvest or incursions from neighboring peoples (Judg. 6:4). The task of herding is often carried out by children to

prevent the village from losing the services of experienced field hands (1 Sam. 16:11).

Farmers can also bolster their economy by serving as trading partners, especially in metals, which are acquired as imports and shaped into tools. They also create their own pottery, weave linen from flax, and fashion simple tools of wood, flint, and bronze. By combining farming with herding, occasionally raiding caravans (Judg. 11:3), trading, and manufacturing, hill-country villagers distribute their labor more evenly and ensure that they will not face the dry season with no provisions (Joel 1:17).

Another major strategy that ancient farmers use to increase their labor force is to have more children. The major obstacle to this strategy is that the population of the Israelite villages in the hills during the Iron I period (1200–1000 BCE) suffer a high infant mortality rate. For every woman who carries four pregnancies to term, fewer than two children reach the age of five. There is also a danger associated with the attempt to increase the size of the household, since that means there are more mouths to feed. Thus it can be said that increasing the number of workers in and of itself does not necessarily create a higher standard of living.

Farming the hills demands economic and social adaption by these early settlers. It is the process of coping with the uncertainties and heavy labor associated with farming, more than any other challenge, that creates a new people from the villagers who settled in Canaan after 1250 BCE. Both men and women work in the fields in order to meet the demands of peak labor periods. Periods between planting and harvests can be devoted to maintaining facilities, trade, and cottage industries like pottery making and weaving. The lives of these village farmers, while hard, contain both a healthy respect for the environment and an appreciation for its bounty (Judg. 21:19). But even with the concerted efforts of every able-bodied person, no single village can cope in every instance with its local environmental constraints or its labor needs without the help of neighboring villages.

Consequently, otherwise isolated villages build associations in order to share common risks that come with the job of farming in a marginal agricultural region. Their willingness to look beyond the *beth 'ab* (local household) and to place greater reliance on the clan and tribe allow them to forge permanent political networks. Under the necessity to share risks and to defend themselves from raiders and aggressive neighboring cultures, the villagers and their culture of the highlands eventually reach the point where they need stronger leadership. If they intend to expand, compete, and survive, they have to combine their economic and military resources and set aside a portion of their local autonomy. By about 1000 BCE, the tightly knit political relationships into which

the farmers have been drawn have reached the level necessary for the creation of a fledgling state.

STUDY QUESTIONS

1. Why is Joshua portrayed as Moses's successor?
2. Discuss how the story of Rahab fits into the universalism theme (Josh. 2).
3. What is the significance of processing around Jericho seven times (Josh. 6:1–16)? What label would you give to this kind of warfare? How do we compare this account with archaeological evidence from Jericho?
4. Why is Achan's violation of the holy war the reason the Israelites lose the initial battle at Ai (Josh. 7)?
5. Compare Joshua's staging of a covenant-renewal ceremony in Josh. 24 with Moses's ritual in Exod. 24.
6. Evaluate the various theories proposed to explain how Israel came to settle in the land of Canaan. Which theory do you prefer, and why?
7. What strategies did the hill-country villagers employ to diversify their economy and deal with the rigors of their environment?

The Book of Judges

KEY POINTS

- The episodes collected in the book of Judges represent folklore tales from the settlement period.
- While some judges provide a good role model, most are flawed and represent a chaotic period of time.
- The spiral of increasing crisis in the book of Judges provides an argument for the monarchy.

The book of Judges provides both a literary and historical transition between the exodus-conquest sequence of stories and the beginning of the monarchy. This compilation of episodes portrays the difficulties of life as the Israelites began to settle in Canaan. It also provides a strong argument for why the establishment of the monarchy is necessary. Much of this material was probably drawn from oral tradition (especially hero stories), and it tapped the cultural memories of all of the tribes. Some of the episodes are fragmentary, but that also probably reflects the fact that oral tradition is not always as perfectly or completely preserved as what eventually is written down.

Literary Analysis

The distinctive literary characteristic of the book of Judges is that it has an orderly arrangement to describe the rather anarchic events in each episode. The three-part division includes an introductory and explanatory narrative (Judg. 1:1–3:6), a collection of tales about individual judges (Judg. 3:7–16:31), and two extended episodes that do not feature a judge but do contain horrendous stories of a society out of control (Judg. 17–21).

The book of Judges begins with a general introduction, which provides a transition from the rather orderly period of Joshua's leadership to the extremely chaotic conditions that necessitate the raising of judges. What is particularly interesting in these first two chapters is the explanation of why the Israelite tribes are not able to complete their conquest of the Canaanites and other inhabitants of the promised land (see Josh. 13:1–7 for a list of unconquered areas and peoples). One example appears in Judg. 1:19, which states that Yahweh, the Divine Warrior, gives the Israelite tribe of Judah a victory in the hill country, but the Israelites are not able to defeat the people of the plain because those people have iron chariots. This is an unusual admission of failure considering the victories over chariot armies described in Josh. 11:6–9 and Judg. 4:13–16. However, it provides a more realistic appraisal of the Israelites' ability to conquer occupied territory than the idealized narrative in the first twelve chapters of the book of Joshua. It also emphasizes the differences in material culture between the Israelites and the indigenous inhabitants of Canaan in this

The Framework of Judges

The framework used by the biblical editors is quite simple. It contains the following pattern (Judg. 2:11–19):

- The people of Israel sin (defined as turning away from Yahweh and worshiping other gods).
- Yahweh becomes angry and allows the Israelites to be oppressed by their neighbors. This is an excellent example of a theodicy, an explanation for why God allows bad things to happen to the Israelites. It is also not unique to the Israelites. A similar explanation is found in the ninth-century-BCE

Mesha Stele, a stone inscription discovered in 1868 east of the Jordan River (cf. the Israelite version of events in 2 Kings 3:4–27). King Mesha of Moab explains why his people have been oppressed by the Israelites, saying, "Omri, ruler of Israel, invaded Moab year after year because Chemosh, the divine patron of Moab, was angry with his people" (OTPar[3], 168).

- The Israelites repent or at least recognize the source of their present condition, namely, the results of Yahweh's wrath.

- Yahweh responds by "raising up a judge" to deal with the current, local crisis. This usually takes the form of military activity, although it is not always organized warfare.
- A period of peace and order, often in increments of twenty, forty, or eighty years, which coincides with the active period of a particular judge, is almost immediately followed by a return to the sin that had precipitated the original crisis. The cycle then resumes with each successive judge's heralding in an evermore desperate and lawless situation.

post-1200 BCE era referred to by archaeologists and historians as Iron I.

The explanatory material, which is representative of the work of the Deuteronomistic Historian, also contains two statements explaining the remaining villages and cities of some of these enemy peoples in Canaan. Yahweh decides to allow them to survive (i.e., God would not drive them out) in order "to test Israel, whether or not they would take care to walk in the way of the LORD as their ancestors did" (Judg. 2:22). God uses these people "to teach those [Israelites] who had no experience of [war]" in the most effective methods of warfare (Judg. 3:2). Rationalizations or glosses such as these are often placed in parentheses by modern translators to show that they were not part of the original story but represent later commentary on the earlier narrative material. During the period of the judges, it is unlikely that the Israelites would have appreciated the value of having Canaanites as test subjects or military drill instructors, especially while the Israelites were being oppressed by these people. However, the Deuteronomistic Historian viewed these episodes from the perspective of centuries after the events described. Therefore, they are presented in a manner that would illustrate the theological point that the people deserved their punishment and that only Yahweh could relieve them from their oppressors.

The stories in the middle portion of the book are chaotic, and the world described in these stories is clearly anarchic. It seems clear that a very conscious effort has been made by the later biblical editors to tie these episodes into an apparently chronological narrative. Nevertheless, the stories are not really in chronological order, and the only element that they share is the disorder of the times.

The cycle or framework that is used to tie the stories together gives them a sense of unity, but it is artificial.

The final five chapters (Judg. 17–21) are distinct because they do not contain any mention of a judge. The stories are filled with the same sorts of anarchic events as in other portions of the book—rape, murder, civil war, and idolatry—but no judge arises to meet the problems described here. While it is tempting to say that these stories were tacked on to the end of the book simply because of their similarity to other Judges material, it is more likely that they provide a literary transition for the opening of the monarchic period. The theme that "in those days there was no king in Israel; all the people did what was right in their own eyes" (Judg. 21:25) is best exemplified in these final chapters. They provide a crowning argument for the establishment of the monarchy and lay the foundation for the anointing of Saul and David as the first kings of Israel.

Analysis of Distinctive Features

One cannot help but appreciate the ability of the authors and editors of the book of Judges to tell interesting stories. While the stories are often descriptions of events that would shock most modern people, they do have real entertainment value as well as a clear political slant. For example, why does Jephthah sacrifice his daughter (Judg. 11:29–40)? Perhaps more important, why does his daughter take control of the situation and insist that he sacrifice her? What is it about this time period or this culture that could produce such a bizarre set of circumstances, especially when human sacrifice seems to have been implicitly forbidden in the episode with Isaac (Gen. 22:9–13)? The answer appears to be that Jephthah's culture placed a higher value on maintaining a household's honor (keeping an oath) than on the life of the daughter. Furthermore, Jephthah is a desperate general, in need of a victory to retain his position of authority. He is willing to bet his household's future, in the person of his only child, in order to defeat the enemy. He also took the chance that no member of his household would come out to greet him in celebration of a victory (see 1 Sam. 18:6–7). His daughter, recognizing the stakes, sacrifices herself on the altar of her father's ambition in order to retain her family's honor, and in this way she acquires a measure of personal honor in the face of her own death. Of this stuff legends are made.

The modern reader might also ask what value is to be found in the story of the Levite's **concubine** (Judg. 19–20). This story is probably modeled after the story of Lot in Sodom (Gen. 19:1–11). In this version, a woman is severely abused and sacrificed to save her husband from a mob in the Benjaminite village of Gibeah. When the crowd demands that the Levite be given to them, he unceremoniously thrusts his concubine into the arms of a group of ruffians who rape her to death. The aftermath of this tragedy is a civil war between the tribe of Benjamin, in whose territory the outlaw community of Gibeah was located, and the rest of the Israelite tribes. This is the only time when the majority of the tribes fully cooperate in the book of Judges (Judg. 20–21) and the only time that the ark of the covenant is mentioned (20:27–28).

Such violent stories hardly encourage the modern reader or provide a message of hope or inspiration. For that reason, some readers ask why such a story would be preserved. One explanation for its inclusion and one way to interpret the story is to show the value of obedience to God and the problem of disobedience. A second interpretation is to show that God champions the cause of the Israelites, despite their inferior weapons and military might, and delivers them from the Canaanites. Yet a third interpretation is that these stories represent a political strategy designed to mar the reputation of Saul, Israel's first king. Gibeah was his hometown. Tying him, even peripherally, to these horrible events provides an argument for David's later takeover of the government and the elimination of the political faction led by Saul's family. In other words, this story is a disqualification story, like the one in Genesis that justifies Jacob's supplanting his older brother Esau as heir of the covenant (Gen. 26–27).

To understand the Judges material it is necessary to understand the intention of the authors of these stories and the editors who compiled them into an extended narrative. Nations are typically the end product of a long period of factionalism, strife, and disorder—a period that serves as a political crucible for the development of the people into a nation. During the settlement period the Israelites were at best a loose confederation of tribes that occasionally cooperated. Both the Song of Deborah (Judg. 5:12–18) and the feud between Jephthah and the Ephraimites (12:1–6) demonstrate that cooperation was never universal. Rules of law and allegiance to the covenant, elements that bound the people into a single political unit, came later. It might well have been impossible for that union to take place without the chaos of the Judges period as a reminder of the need for order. In this way a case is made, however propagandistic, for law, order, and the establishment of a government that could ensure stability.

A Summary of Judges

The introductory section of the book of Judges, with its explanation of the failure of a total conquest, is followed by the narrative containing the episodes of various judges. Many of the leaders, some of whom are quite heroic, have distinctive physical or social characteristics: Ehud is left-handed; Deborah is the only female judge; Gideon, like Jacob, is a trickster; Jephthah is an outcast; and Samson is a **Nazirite**, technically bound by a religious vow (see Num. 6:1–21). These stories employ a number of motifs, which are signposts for the audience and are designed to heighten human interest. They make the stories easier to follow by using familiar scenes and by providing cues to the audience. In this way the narrative constantly reminds the listeners of what has happened and what will happen again.

For example, the motif of Ehud's left-handedness provides the narrative key to his assassination of the king of the Moabites. Ehud secretly brings a specially designed weapon, a double-edged dagger, into the palace of Eglon (Judg. 3:16–23). Since most people are right-handed, a person's left side would be searched more carefully than the right. Weapons are drawn most effectively across the body, and a left-hander wears a weapon on the right side. By emphasizing a physical characteristic, the storyteller signals to the audience that Ehud will be able to carry out his mission to assassinate Eglon and to become an Israelite hero.

In the only narrative involving a female judge, Deborah predicts that the Israelite general Barak will be given the victory over their enemies, Jabin and Sisera of Hazor, but only through the "hand of a woman" (Judg. 4:9). When Jael, a Kenite woman, kills Sisera, the audience is reminded of Deborah's prediction and can enjoy an ironic twist since it seems at first that Deborah will achieve the victory for Israel (4:17–22). Like other underdog stories, it is the weakest member of society who triumphs because of the intervention of Yahweh. The narrative surprise that produces an unexpected female heroine increases the entertainment value of the story.

Gideon's career is marked by a sequence of crafty tricks: grinding grain in a winepress (Judg. 6:11), repeatedly asking God to demonstrate his power before Gideon will accept his call to be a judge (6:36–40), and using trickery and surprise to win military victories (Judg. 7:9–23). His character is thus part of a long line of trickster figures that includes Abraham, Rebekah, Jacob, and Laban.

Because his mother was a prostitute, Jephthah's brothers force him into a life as a *khabiru*, a stateless person. He becomes the leader of a band of outcasts and acquires a reputation as an effective military commander. When a crisis looms, his tribe and family practically beg him to return and save them from the oppression of the Ammonites (Judg. 11:1–11). His reversal of fortune is a model for the culture of the Israelites under the monarchy, who rose from servitude to sovereignty over neighboring peoples. It also underscores Jephthah's willingness to engage in unorthodox strategies, such as his use of an oath to convince Yahweh to help him obtain a military victory (11:29–33).

One narrative cue found in the story of Samson is his Nazirite status, symbolized by his long hair. However, his violation of all the Nazirite regulations (regarding contact with the dead, cutting the hair, and presumably drinking wine) mark him as a rule-breaker despite his amazing acts of physical prowess. This may indicate that the authors of Judges use the Samson stories for their entertainment value rather than as a model for the Israelites during the Judges period. It quickly becomes clear that Samson's penchant for violating his Nazirite vow and his inability to resist the demands of the foreign women in his life will form the basis for his eventual downfall.

The ironic and comic touches in the narratives of these judges are entertaining, but they also serve as clear warning signals to the audience. Whenever a distinctive physical characteristic (such as long hair) is emphasized, it is a clue that this feature will figure in the resolution of the story.

In addition to the major judges, minor figures are introduced but given only a few lines in the text. Some, like Shamgar, are similar to Samson in style and strength. In a single verse (Judg. 3:31), we are told that he kills six hundred Philistines with an ox goad—a stick used to prod oxen and to break up the clods of dirt turned up by the plow. Others, like Tola and Jair, are not tied to any event or accomplishment other than their tribal affiliation, wealth, and large families (10:1–4). These minor judges seem to serve as literary transitions between the major sections of the narrative. There is too little provided about them to say much more about their value to the book of Judges.

Surprisingly, one character who is not a judge, Abimelech, son of the judge Gideon, receives an entire chapter (Judg. 9). Abimelech may be the perfect example of a ruthless leader in the period of the Judges. He murders sixty-nine of his half-brothers, solicits funds from his mother's clan to hire a mercenary army, and sets himself up as a warlord. Naturally, he comes to a bad end. He is slain by a woman who drops a millstone on his head from atop the wall of a city that Abimelech's army is besieging (9:50–55). Even in death, his name becomes part of popular folklore. In 2 Sam.

11:20–21, Abimelech's demise is cited as the model of the foolish soldier who makes the error of getting too close to the city wall during a battle. In this and in other ways, the Judges material serves as a foundation for later Israelite tradition and self-evaluation.

Cultural Analysis

In approaching the study of the book of Judges, it may be most useful to recall a period in American history when lawlessness and disregard for tradition were rampant. In frontier life during the latter half of the nineteenth century, the man with the most firepower and the ability to trick, cajole, or threaten his way through every situation was heralded as a hero or at least an intriguing rogue. Names like Billy the Kid, Jessie James, and Wild Bill Hickok come to mind, and their excesses and flouting of the law have become as legendary as that of some of the figures described in Judges. They are bigger than life, and the exaggerations recounted about their lives and accomplishments furnish a typology for an era rather than a true chronicle of its history.

The Judges period of Israelite history was a time of new settlements and of the struggle to survive in a difficult social and physical environment. As yet, no evidence has been uncovered that would provide proof of a discernable ethnic difference between the Canaanites and those people who eventually become the Israelites. In fact, many of the Israelite villages were probably made up of Canaanites who had fled their former homes to escape the warfare, civil unrest, famine, and disease that plagued the area of Syria-Palestine between 1200 and 1000 BCE. During this time, when the incursions of the Sea Peoples weakened Egyptian control over the area, new social groups were founded based on a common need to pool their labor to produce crops and establish new settlements in quieter regions of the country.

The culture that did develop in the hill country was initially based on former Canaanite models, but it eventually established a character of its own. These pioneers had to be tough and resourceful to survive in the marginal environment in which they found themselves. The pragmatism of village life directed by elders and idealizing egalitarian virtues like mutual trust and shared responsibility helped to create a distinct people that in time identified themselves as the Israelites.

Life in this village culture depended on the variables of the environment to provide them with the rain in season and to protect them from scorching winds and plagues of locusts. The people worked extremely long hours in their fields. When they made sacrifices, they did so in thanks to Yahweh and in expectation of good fortune and sustained fertility. Their villages consisted of a few dwellings placed in such a way as to provide some protection against raiders. Since the village had to be fairly self-reliant, the potter, tanner, and dye maker all had their shops (probably attached to their houses). These specialists offered simple wares while also working their own farm plots or vineyards.

Village legal proceedings and those occasions when a full assembly of the people was necessary were conducted on the village threshing floor. Threshing floors were the places where grain was processed and distributed, disputes were settled, and the needs of the poor were evaluated and supplied. In this way the village cared for its own and managed its harvest to the benefit and survival of the entire community. Such a shared system worked best on a small scale. Once the monarchy was established, its need for revenues to support the bureaucracy and the military tapped the resources of the villages and drained them with heavy taxes. The establishment of the monarchy would also weaken any sense of **egalitarianism** as a structured, multilevel social system began to replace the simpler village culture.

The material culture of the hill-country settlements survived on a subsistence level. Generally just enough grain was produced to maintain the local population. When a small surplus was produced, it could be used for trade or stored against the inevitable bad years. Population growth could provide a larger work force, but it would also put a strain, at least temporarily, on the food supply. In other words, life was a gamble. For the Israelites to master their new environment and expand beyond the hill country they had to do three things: increase their population, borrow many of the useful aspects of the material culture of the Canaanite cities of the plains, and relinquish local autonomy to warlords, who could help them compete militarily with their neighbors. It was these latter two requirements, however, that were the principal danger. When one culture borrows cultural ideas or practices from another (**syncretism**), the temptation is to become just like that other culture. It tends to allow the distinctive aspects of one's culture to be submerged or lost. The biblical writers continually argue against syncretism, especially with regard to the worship of foreign gods. The stories in the book of Judges suggest that the Israelites were true neither to Yahweh nor to the covenant made at Sinai. Furthermore, as the village elders were forced to merge their authority with larger social groups (clans and tribes) and accept the leadership of warlords, they lost control over their own policies and preferences. Unification will have its price.

Threshing Floors and Gates

Unlike modern cities and towns that have city halls and courthouse buildings, villages and towns in ancient Israel conduct their public business on threshing floors and at city gates. The threshing floor is a flat area near a village or villages where the harvested grain is brought for processing (Job 5:26) by using a threshing sledge (Isa. 41:15), winnowing forks (Jer. 15:7), and sieves (Amos 9:9). After processing, the grain is distributed to its owners, and a portion is set aside for widows and orphans. The economic importance of this installation causes it to be used eventually for legal matters as well. Thus Ruth petitions Boaz to serve as her family's legal representative (**levir**) as he lies on the threshing floor (Ruth 3:6–13). It is a legally significant act for her to approach him there, even though she comes to him in secret and at night.

Walled towns conduct their legal and economic activity in the city-gate area (Deut. 21:18–21; 22:15; 25:7). Some retain the memory of the threshing floor by building the city gate on the site of one of these installations (1 Kings 22:10). Since towns are more dependent on commerce than agriculture, they naturally choose to conduct business in a high-traffic area. Just as merchants today attempt to locate their store in a place where the high volume of traffic will ensure that many people see them, the merchants of ancient Israel set up shop either within the chambers of the gate or immediately on either side of it (see Gen. 19:1). Similarly, trials are held in gateways to ensure public visibility for these legal matters and because of the symbolic value attached to them (Deut. 21:19). Persons who are free to pass back and forth through the city gate are considered citizens (Gen. 34:24), and those entering and leaving the temple are considered ritually **clean**.

Analysis of Point of View

The colonial-era American statesman Benjamin Franklin is said to have remarked during the Continental Congress that "treason is a term invented by the winners to describe the losers." It can also be said that "terrorism is in the eye of the beholder." Many of the characters who are represented as judges are, by modern standards, not models of propriety or good judgment. For example, Ehud murders Eglon, the king of the Moabites, by pretending to have a secret message for the king and arranging to get him alone so that he can stab him (Judg. 3:15–30). If the Moabites had been telling the story, Ehud would have been labeled the worst kind of villain, not a valiant judge who rallied his troops with his courageous action and provided his people with their longest period of peace (eighty years).

Another example of an apparently shocking action is found in Judg. 4:17–22, where Jael plays the trickster in her feigned hospitality for Sisera, the general of the Hazor forces. Ultimately Jael proves herself to be a strong character and a courageous woman. She avoids what may have constituted a planned rape on Sisera's part. After lulling the general to sleep, she drives a tent peg through his temple. Such behavior is certainly not what one expects of a hostess, but that is exactly the point of many of the episodes in Judges. The world of the characters is turned upside down, and no law other than personal self-interest or the household's honor exists. Jael defends her honor and that of her Kenite household through the use of deadly force against a man who may have planned to take over their encampment by force. Although she is not an Israelite, she is proclaimed "blessed" (5:24) for an action that today might put her in the same company with an ax murderer. It is the perspective of the biblical writer that transforms Jael from a monster into a hero.

Even the most famous characters in the book of Judges (Gideon and Samson) engage in activities that may seem unusual for national heroes. Both men perform acts of courage and daring on behalf of their people, but they also display less than noble characteristics. Gideon cheats the Ammonite tribute collectors by secretly grinding his grain in a winepress (Judg. 6:11). He repeatedly requests that Yahweh perform miracles to prove that God intends to provide a military victory over the Midianites (6:36–40). Samson, supposedly a Nazirite from birth, violates every stipulation of the Nazirite's vow (Num. 6:1–12). The storyteller seems to have taken great delight in Samson's sexual excesses and his inflated ego. Most of Samson's exploits center around his dealings with non-Israelite women such as Delilah and are in most cases self-centered. Even his death, while it claims the lives of thousands of the enemy, hinges on his desire for personal revenge for the loss of his eyes (Judg. 16:28).

It may appear that only negative conclusions can be drawn from the Judges narrative; yet, it should be noted that the editors are primarily interested in portraying a world where even God's chosen leaders are far from perfect. They do provide needed aid to the oppressed Israelites—winning a number of battles, staging demonstrations of Yahweh's power as the Divine Warrior, and occasionally setting an example of proper behavior. For example, Gideon musters a huge army of 32,000, but then he is instructed to reduce it through a variety of measures to a ridiculously small 300 men (Judg. 7:2–23). As is the case in the Joshua conquest narrative, this strategy is designed to present the Israelites as underdogs who could not win a battle on their own (6:1–22; 10:8–14; 11:6–15). Only Yahweh can give them the victory, and they and their leader must rely on Yahweh for their deliverance. The Israelite audience, listening to this story, could nod their heads and agree that a small force, led by God's chosen general and using surprise as their ally, could confuse an enemy and win a victory over the Midianites.

Gideon also provides an example as the religious cleanser of his village. Somewhat reluctantly, he pulls down an altar dedicated to the Canaanite god Baal and in its place erects an altar for Yahweh and makes a sacrifice (Judg. 6:25–32). This act then sets the stage for a contest between Yahweh and Baal, reminiscent of the confrontation in Exodus with pharaoh and the contest in 1 Kings 18:20–40 involving Elijah and the 450 prophets of Baal. Gideon's

Figure 2.8. Arad temple courtyard with stone floor and altar. (Baker Photo Archive)

father calls on the outraged villagers to spare Gideon's life and allow Baal, if he is able, to take revenge on the man who has destroyed his altar. If he cannot, then he is no god! The theme of a Canaanite god's inability to defend his altar or take vengeance on the desecrator allows the audience to proclaim that there is no god but Yahweh. This theme is found elsewhere in the Bible (1 Sam. 5), and thus it brings the Judges material into the mainstream of the biblical narrative and its proclamation of Yahweh's power.

Samson's career does contain a few redeeming acts. At one point he goes to the Philistine city of Gaza (Judg. 16:1–3). He boldly walks through the city gate, without any pretense of hiding his intentions, and visits the house of a local prostitute. The men of the city lay a trap for the Israelite hero, but he foils their plans by leaving before dawn. To show them the degree of his prowess (and by extension that of Yahweh), Samson rips the city gates from their sockets and carries them nearly forty miles to a hill near the city of Hebron. They are left there, a monument to the futility of the Philistines to harness Samson's energies. The symbolic value of this action, whether it is intended to be a joke or is a serious attempt to humble the Philistines, is profound. A city's gates represent its power and security. Deprived of these huge protective doors, the city is shorn of its strength and opened to invasion. This is a striking irony considering how Samson loses his strength when he is shorn of his long hair (16:16–19).

Archaeological Analysis

Because this period is not documented except in the biblical account, most of what we can learn about life during the Iron Age in Canaan is based on archaeological remains. Hundreds of small village sites representing the expansion of settlement in the hill country during the Iron Age have been excavated or surveyed during the past twenty-five years. The pattern of these new settlements suggests a migration of the population into this previously underpopulated region during the period between 1200 and 950 BCE. In their examination of these village sites, archaeologists try to identify patterns of culture based on pottery types, architectural styles, and technologies. Often a new people entering an area will bring in a distinctive culture, evidenced by burial styles and possessions such as pottery, jewelry, and weapons.

Although it would be helpful if there were startling differences between Israelite and Canaanite material culture, that does not seem to be the case. Housing styles do change somewhat, but this is due primarily to the environment of the hill country where most new settlements were established. For instance, the so-called four-room house, once considered a marker for the distinctive emergence of Israelite villages in the hill country, has now been shown to be much more widespread and not clearly identifiable with the Israelites. Pottery types remain virtually the same, again with the indication that storage jars were modified for use in a slightly different climatic area or to perform new functions. Innovations such as terracing of hillsides for farming and the plastering of cisterns to prevent seepage of water into the porous limestone seem to be more a matter of the natural developments of life in the hill country than inventions that changed the region or identified a new ethnic group.

What has come out of the ground in the past three decades of archaeological investigation is a fuller understanding of the Philistine presence in Canaan during this period of Iron I.

Sites like Ashdod and Ashkelon reveal well-established urban cultures. They maintained large-scale industry, including the refining of olive oil, and established trade contacts in areas from Egypt to Phoenicia. However, the purported widespread use of iron technology by the Philistines appears to be exaggerated. They possessed the knowledge of refining iron, but bronze continued to be the principal metal used for the fashioning of weapons, farm implements, and industrial tools. The statement in 1 Sam. 13:19 that there was "no smith to be found throughout all the land of Israel" and that the Israelites were forced to rely on the Philistines to sharpen their farm implements suggests a lack of this technology by the Israelites and a likely monopoly on metalworking in general by the Philistines, rather than control of iron technology alone. Intensive specialization of labor would have been less likely to occur in the Israelite villages, where most of their efforts had to be directed to farming and herding. They would most likely have produced their own commonware pottery, tanned their own hides, and woven their own cloth for clothing. Blacksmithing is a dedicated profession, not one that can be practiced part time or learned overnight.

What does seem clear from the tales in Judges is that the Israelites are said to have a much lower level of material culture than their neighbors. Their weapons include farm implements (Shamgar's ox goad [Judg. 3:31]) or what can be picked up (Samson's use of a jawbone to slay Philistines [15:14–17]). They enjoyed celebrations like marriage feasts (14:10) and harvest festivals (21:19). However, they did not always obey the covenant or set aside foreign worship practices (altar to Baal in Gideon's village [6:28–32]; Micah's idols [17:4–5]). Their lack of social cohesion is also found in dialectical differences from one tribe or region to another (pronouncing "Shibboleth" [12:5–6]).

What can be traced in these accounts are the place names mentioned in the biblical text. The Philistine cities of Ashkelon, Ashdod, Ekron, Gaza, and Gath, as well as the Canaanite and Phoenician cities of Megiddo, Acco, Sidon, Beth-Shemesh, Jebus (Jerusalem), and Hazor, have all been located. All these sites furnish evidence that they were inhabited during the Iron Age. It is more difficult, however, to authenticate the social and religious practices of this period. Some Philistine Iron Age I **cultic sites** (e.g., temples and shrines) have been excavated (Tel Miqne-Ekron, Tell Qasile), and cult images have been discovered. Sacrifices from this period are described in documents written in later eras, such as the Iron II period Mesha Stele of the late ninth century BCE. These kinds of data, however, must be examined with caution. Archaeological finds are especially difficult to interpret because they are only mute objects. Drawing conclusions or parallels based on similar but later social customs may be misleading. As is the case with other poorly documented periods of biblical history, reconstructions of the age of the judges must, for now, remain more tentative than concrete.

STUDY QUESTIONS

Assignment: Read the book of Judges with the following questions in mind. Then answer the questions for yourself and be prepared to discuss them.

1. What is a judge? What would be a good job description if you were going to advertise an opening for a judge? Is the position hereditary? Does the judge

administer all the tribes? On this see Judg. 5:12–18; 12:1–6.

2. What is the cycle of history recounted in this book? Look especially at Judg. 2:11–3:4. Try to list the elements in the cycle that are recounted here. Are there any events that are not attributed directly to God or do not fit into the cycle? On this see Judg. 1:19.

3. What indicators exist in the text to demonstrate when this book should be dated? See Judg. 1:21; 17:6; 18:30–31; 19:10.

4. What kind of society is pictured in the book of Judges? Can you think of any parallels to this type of society in the history of your country?

5. Read the story of Ehud (Judg. 3:15–30). What strategies does he employ, and how do you explain the apparent approval of his deception?

6. Read the Deborah narrative (Judg. 4:4–5:31). Why is Jael celebrated as a heroine after her blatant violation of the laws of hospitality?

7. Read the account of Gideon's battle strategy (Judg. 7:9–22). How does this compare with the strategy imposed on the Israelites in Josh. 6:1–21?

8. Read the Samson narrative (Judg. 13–16). Are his excesses simply typical of epic heroes, or do they have a deeper purpose? What is the role of humor in these narratives? What is a Nazirite (Num. 6:1–21)?

9. Read the story of the Levite's concubine (Judg. 19–21). How does this compare with the account of Lot in Sodom in Gen. 19? Why include a story like this in the Bible?

10. While reading Judges, what have you learned about Israel's religion? Are all the people monotheistic? Is there a central shrine for the worship of Yahweh? (a) Read Judg. 6:7–32 and Judg. 8:22–35 in the Gideon narrative. What evidence appears here of faithful Yahweh worship? (b) Read the story of Jephthah (Judg. 11–12). How do his actions conflict with previous law and tradition? (c) Read the story of Micah's idol (Judg. 17–18). How do his actions and those of the Levite conflict with the laws given at Mount Sinai?

11. Note the type of weapons that are used in the book of Judges. What does this tell you about the material culture of the Hebrews? See Judg. 1:19; 3:16, 31; 4:21; 7:16–22; 9:46–55; 15:15; 20:16.

12. Note the named and unnamed women mentioned in the book of Judges. What are their roles? Are these typical or unusual? How much or how little can we generalize about the role of Israelite women at this time from the book of Judges? Explain carefully.

·3·

THE EARLY MONARCHIC PERIOD

The Early Monarchy

The Shift from Judges to Chiefs

KEY POINTS

- Samuel, like Moses, is both a priest and judge. He functions as a transitionary figure.
- The monarchy emerges as a survival strategy for Israel.
- Saul's reign is shaped by the writers as a disqualification story.
- David must take several politically motivated steps to eventually become king.

The career of the last of the judges, Samuel, provides a transition from the anarchic settlement/judges period to the establishment of the monarchy. The tales about this monumental figure contain both the best and the worst of the premonarchic age. Samuel provides single-minded direction of the people as God's representative, and he operates as the first leader to command the loyalties of a large portion of the tribes since Joshua. His efforts to extend his control farther to the south by appointing his sons as judges fail. The old administrative model of the judges period has seen its day, and the people's confidence will eventually be placed in political leaders rather than divinely raised judges.

Like Moses's career, Samuel's story begins with a detailed birth narrative. It has elements of the barren-wife motif found in the ancestral stories: Samuel's mother, Hannah, is childless when she is first introduced. As we know from previous instances of this theme, children born to barren wives are special, and their births are usually announced by an angel or some other agent of God (see Gen. 18:9–14; Judg. 13:2–5). In this case Eli, the priest in charge of the ark of the covenant and its shrine at Shiloh, uses the weight of his office and supports her petition for a child (1 Sam. 1:17).

In contrast to Samuel, Eli and his sons Hophni and Phineas play negative roles in the story. Their inappropriate actions as priests at Shiloh are the first in a series of episodes in 1 Samuel in which the leaders of the people are shown to be corrupt or undeserving of authority. These stories provide one basis for the argument in favor of the establishment of the monarchy in 1 Sam. 8. It is also reminiscent of the disqualification stories in the Jacob narrative that were designed to eliminate Esau as

Map 3.1. Palestine/Israel

the heir to the covenant (see Gen. 25:29–34; 26:34–35; 27:5–46; 33:12–16).

The Samuel narrative includes a number of significant events. One is a dream theophany in which the child Samuel is told that God will remove Eli and his sons as leaders of the people (1 Sam. 3:3–14). The theophany serves as a precursor of Samuel's later career and functions as the basis for Samuel's call as a priest and prophet. The theophany also provides him with the divine authority that he will need later in order to act as a judge and leader of the people.

Another highlight of the Samuel narrative is a sequence of stories describing the deaths

of Eli and his sons, and the capture of the ark by the Philistines. The narrative provides an opportunity for the manifestation of Yahweh's power to take place in a slightly different context. A plague is inflicted on the Philistines, and that leads to the ark's return to the Israelites. Provisions are then made for housing the ark in the absence of an adult member of Aaron's family to officiate before the ark (1 Sam. 4–6).

The ark represents God's presence and was carried into battle in the Joshua narrative of the conquest (Josh. 6:1–7). But the story in 1 Sam. 4:1–11 shows that the ark is only a finely decorated box. Yahweh is not imprisoned within the ark's interior and cannot be convinced to help the Israelites when they are in violation of the covenant and the laws.

A third factor in the Samuel narrative is its description of Samuel's dual role as circuit judge and priestly figure (1 Sam. 7). Samuel, who was not a Levite, replaced the traditional priestly family of Eli as the spiritual leader of the people. He performed sacrifices and served as a prophetic figure, functioning as a Moses-like mediator between the people and God (cf. Num. 11:1–2 and 1 Sam. 7:5–11). Samuel's acquisition of a priestly office may have been typical of the Judges period in which the idea that only Levites could serve as priests was not yet firmly established or enforced.

After assuming his leadership position, Samuel's career as a judge is glossed over quickly, since his primary role in this portion of the narrative is to choose a king for the Israelites. When his sons are proved to be corrupt (1 Sam. 8:3), the days of the judges and their temporary leadership are finished. The elders of the people call out for a king, and there is no turning back despite the antimonarchic arguments made in 1 Sam. 8:11–18 and 1 Sam. 12 (see inset, p. 85).

Arguments for and against Establishing a Monarchy

Arguments for a Monarchy

- Every other nation has a king (1 Sam. 8:5).
- A king provides leadership for national defense (1 Sam. 8:20; 11:1–11 recounts Saul's victory at Jabesh-gilead, showing his ability to command an army).
- A king or his designate function as a diplomatic contact for foreign policy.
- A king is able to develop a national economic policy and marshal the nation's natural resources.
- A king can support the development of the national religion by promoting a location for a central shrine and priestly community.

Arguments against a Monarchy

- Selection of a human king signifies the rejection of Yahweh as the primary protector and ruler (1 Sam. 8:7; 12:12).
- The advantages cited in the arguments for a monarchy are secured at the expense of personal freedoms. A king will impose taxes, institute a military and civil draft, place restraints on travel and trade, and deprive the people of their local religious shrines (1 Sam. 8:11–13).
- A king will abuse his power, including **nepotism** and other corrupt practices (1 Sam. 8:14–18).
- At the heart of each position is the issue of who will protect and feed the nation (see 1 Sam. 12:16–18). To this point, it has been Yahweh's role as Divine Warrior to win battles for the Israelites and to feed them when they call on their God (e.g., manna in the wilderness [Exod. 16:4–8]). Now the people are advocating the replacement of Yahweh with a human king, who will become responsible for their defense (leading the army) and their food (organizing national resources and promoting trade). All that Samuel can do is warn them of the consequences of their decision. Subsequent prophetic figures will then take up this theme, pointing out how Israel's political leaders lead them astray.

At this point, the narrative becomes somewhat complex. Portions of the text are clearly promonarchic while other sections, interwoven with the rest, strongly argue against a king. Having these two opposing positions side by side suggests that a real struggle existed at the time of the establishment of the monarchy and continued throughout its existence. To be sure, some people never reconciled themselves to being ruled by a king. Their position was reinforced during those periods when kings abused their powers or the nation was dominated by outside forces. But because much of the material in the books of Samuel and Kings is based on the court histories of the kings, it is not surprising that the positive information derived from the court histories is retained in the received Samuel–Kings narrative. Perhaps this is not enough to prevent a bad impression of many of the kings, but it is enough to suggest that the monarchy was not as big a disaster for Israel as some of the biblical writers and the prophets would have us believe.

It is possible that the antimonarchic rhetoric dates to the latter part of Israel's history, when the monarchy was about to or had failed. By the time the text was edited, many stories were so well known that they could not be eliminated or drastically changed.

Pro- and Anti-Saul Rhetoric in 1 Samuel

1 Sam. 10:17–22, 27a—Anti-Saul elements

- Tribes come together to choose a king by lot. When the lot falls to Saul, he is "hidden among the baggage" (10:22).
- Although he is acknowledged as king, some people doubt Saul's ability to lead and refuse to give him the gifts and allegiance due to a king (10:27a).

1 Sam. 9:1–10:16 and 10:23–11:15—Pro-Saul elements

- The young, resourceful, and handsome Saul is anointed by Samuel (9:1–10:8).
- On his return home he meets a group of prophets and falls into a prophetic trance himself (10:9–13).
- When news of the Ammonite threat to Jabesh-gilead reaches him, Saul marshals an army and relieves the siege of the city (11:1–11).
- Following his triumph Saul goes to Gilgal, where Samuel and "all the people" proclaim him their king (11:12–15).

Under this scenario, antimonarchic material was interwoven to indicate that from the beginning there were doubts about the establishment of the monarchy.

Saul's Reign as Israel's First King

Samuel is instructed to receive God's chosen candidate and anoint his head with oil (1 Sam. 9:15–10:1). In this way the perception is created that the king is chosen directly by Yahweh. While anointing may have had other significance, in this case it symbolizes the purification of the person designated as king and is a clear tie to the responsibilities the king had to manage and maintain the well-being of the people (olive oil was a major staple of the Israelite economy).

However, Saul's career as king does not begin immediately. He is described as a handsome young man who might have been expected to become a leader someday (1 Sam. 9:2). His openness to God's voice is demonstrated by his ability to be overcome while in the company of dancing ecstatic prophets (1 Sam. 10:10–13). But the idea of a king is still too radical a step for many Israelites to accept at this point. That hesitancy is depicted in the staged event when Saul is chosen by lot as the Israelite king. His shyness or inexperience with public assemblages reflects the antimonarchic position in the narrative. This initial appointment is not conclusive because Saul does not immediately demonstrate his ability to take command, and Samuel appears to sanction the appointment with some reluctance (1 Sam. 10:17–24).

As a result, Saul does not assume the role of king until after a sparkling victory over the Ammonites, described in 1 Sam. 11. This military victory, which lifts the siege of the city of Jabesh-gilead, allows him to claim the loyalty of the people. As a result, he is crowned king at Gilgal, the site where the Israelites crossed the Jordan in Joshua's time. Like politicians of every age, Saul is given credit for recognizing the importance of place for his coronation. Being crowned at Gilgal shortly after winning a military victory creates the impression among the people that Saul is a new Joshua (cf. Josh. 6:27 and the statement, "So the LORD was with Joshua; and his fame was in all the land"). It also takes the ceremony to a more central location, where more of the people and the elders can easily assemble.

Looking at Saul's reign as one that sets a number of precedents, it is easy to recognize why he eventually comes to a bad end. It is difficult to be the first anything, and being the first king is a particularly difficult job. In fact, Saul is more of a war chief than a king. He managed to hold the loyalty of some but not all Israelites. When he called them to war, he did not have a professional army on which to draw. Instead, many of his citizen soldiers were just as likely to find some reason not to come or to leave before the war was over (1 Sam. 13:8). He also had to rely too heavily on nepotism (granting office to members of one's own family), especially in the responsibilities that he granted to his son Jonathan. This policy

---

A Kingdom Lost

And Samuel said,
"Has the LORD as great delight in burnt offerings and sacrifices,
    as in obeying the voice of the LORD?
Surely, to obey is better than sacrifice,
    and to heed than the fat of rams.
For rebellion is no less a sin than divination,
    and stubbornness is like iniquity and idolatry.
Because you have rejected the word of the LORD,
    he has also rejected you from being king."
(1 Sam. 15:22–23)

Obedience Theme: Covenant versus Sacrifice

The key phrase in Samuel's confrontation with Saul is "Surely, to obey is better than sacrifice" (1 Sam. 15:22). The obedience theme implicit in these words reminds the king that the covenant is based on strict attention to God's voice. Sacrifice, while it has its place as part of the people's acknowledgment of Yahweh's gifts, is only secondary and is negated by disobedient behavior. Many of the prophets echo Samuel's words when calling the people and their leaders back to right behavior and fuller commitment to the covenant:

Isa. 1:11–17: "What to me is the multitude of your sacrifices? . . . Learn to do good; seek justice."
Mic. 6:6–8: "With what shall I come before the Lord? . . . What does the Lord require of you but to do justice, and to love kindness, and to walk humbly with your God?"
Hosea 6:6: "For I desire steadfast love and not sacrifice."

ensures that one knows one's employees and advisers, but it also places an additional burden on the leader because of personal relationships and kinship ties.

The most difficult problem Saul faces, other than the continuing military crisis of dealing with the Philistines, is Samuel. At issue is who has the power to do what. Does the king also function as a priest? Are there restrictions that a priestly or prophetic figure can place on the actions of the king (1 Sam. 13:10–14)? Is the king above the law imposed on ordinary citizens (15:10–35)? All these questions and more are brought out in the series of confrontations that take place between Samuel and Saul. In each case the king's role as war chief conflicts with the prophet's role as religious representative and spokesperson for Yahweh. The tension created between Samuel and Saul serves as an introduction to the difficulties that will arise for every king who has to deal with the leaders of the temple community and with the independent representatives of Yahweh (the prophets).

Matters come to a head in what is clearly a disqualification story. Saul fails to obey the prophet Samuel's instructions to wage an all-out war, a *kherem*, against the Amalekites (1 Sam. 15:10–35). As the Deuteronomistic Historian explains it, Saul spares the life of the Amalekite king, Agag, and takes a portion

of the Amalekite herds while destroying all the rest. Yet he greets Samuel with a claim to have fulfilled Samuel's instructions. Samuel sarcastically confronts the king: "What then is this bleating of sheep in my ears, and the lowing of cattle that I hear?" (15:14). Saul's response consists of a blame-casting excuse that the people had spared the animals as a sacrifice to God. Samuel shows no patience with this and predicts God's rejection of Saul's family as future rulers over Israel (15:22–23). Samuel does acknowledge Saul's pleas of repentance, and he agrees at least publicly to support the king before the elders (15:30–31), but the king's violation of the law costs his family the kingdom.

In this series of episodes in 1 Sam. 13–15, the Deuteronomist skillfully disqualifies Saul and prepares the way for David to take over the kingship once Saul is off the scene. The climax is for the new claimant to the throne, David, to be secretly anointed by Samuel (16:1–13). With that accomplished, David's struggle to take power begins.

What follows is what scholars call an **apology**. In this case it is a narrative sympathetic to David that portrays the aging Saul as mentally unstable and incapable of ruling the country. The story of David's rise to power is the story of Saul's demise. It was probably written by members of the royal court of David or Solomon to strengthen their claims to the throne over those of Saul and his family.

David's Steps to Power

The first major episode in David's rise to power is his anointing by Samuel as the future king of Israel (1 Sam. 16:10–13). As it was for Saul (10:1–8), this action symbolically designates David as Yahweh's choice as king. It will be many years, however, before David claims the throne. In this case, however, the theme of the rise of the younger son, which also appears in the ancestral accounts of Isaac, Jacob, and Joseph (Gen. 21–28; 37–50), adds a literary dimension to the story as well as, possibly, a reference to David's lowly status within his family. While it is not possible to prove this, it is possible that the various references to younger sons may be injected into these narratives to bolster David's claim to power. They may also simply be a literary convention of ancient Israelite storytelling that is designed to add tension in the narrative.

David's first public appearance occurs in the Goliath episode (1 Sam. 17). By defeating Israel's enemy David is given an aura of success and provided with hero status. The victory also ties him to the House of Saul through a royal marriage to Saul's daughter Michal. The description of this event resembles the one-on-one combat scenes in Homer's epic poem *Iliad*, which is set in approximately the same time period as the early monarchy. Goliath's huge size and armored body stand in contrast to the young, unarmored David (1 Sam. 17:4–7). Since the Israelites have often been portrayed as the underdog in battles against their enemies (Exod. 17:8–13; Josh. 10:5–14; Judg. 7), David's confrontation with Goliath provides the perfect paradigm for the nation.

The Goliath narrative is problematic because it assumes that Saul does not know David (1 Sam. 17:55–58), although in 1 Sam. 16:18–23 David has already served as Saul's musician and armor-bearer. Furthermore, 2 Sam. 21:19 credits Elhanan with killing Goliath (cf. 1 Chron. 20:5). Another question is whether the royal marriage to Michal is granted in exchange for David's victory over Goliath or is negotiated for a bride price of one hundred Philistine foreskins. In either case it provides David with an official tie to the royal succession through Michal and legitimizes his later claim to the kingship. It is also the initial catalyst for the jealousy theme that dominates David's relationship with Saul for the remainder of the king's life.

Because Saul is jealous of his young rival's popularity and becomes increasingly unbalanced in David's presence, David is forced to flee the royal court. He is aided in his escape by Saul's son Jonathan (1 Sam. 20) and by Michal, who places a *teraphim* (a household idol) in his bed to deceive anyone who might come to see him (19:11–17). The *teraphim* also serves as further evidence that Saul is not maintaining strict obedience to God's demand to have no other gods.

During the next several years, David lives like an outlaw, much like the Robin Hood figure of medieval England (1 Sam. 19–31). During this time he builds a network of support through marriages (Abigail, Ahinoam; 25:39–43), through gifts given to the elders of Judah (30:26), and by gaining the friendship of key individuals. Among his allies is the priest Abiathar, who is the only survivor of Saul's massacre of the priestly community at Nob (22:9–23). By taking the fugitive priest into his company, David is able to draw another contrast between himself and King Saul, who clearly does not respect the sanctity of God's priests. David also obtains the sword of Goliath, a talisman that he can use to remind the people of his military success over the Philistines (21:8–9).

As an outlaw, David is not welcomed or assisted by all the people he approaches. A classic example is the story of Nabal's selfish refusal to provide David's men with supplies even though they have been protecting his shepherds and flocks (1 Sam. 25:2–42). The story stands as a political wisdom tale with the villain caricatured as a "fool" (the meaning of "Nabal" in Hebrew). Foolishness is balanced by the wisdom of Nabal's wife, Abigail. She recognizes the danger to her household and on her own takes David his requested supplies. In her speech to David she addresses him eleven times with the significant title "my lord" (25:24–31), reminding him that God gives him the kingship and will be pleased that he has not "shed blood without cause." She begs that when David does come into his kingdom he will "remember your servant." At each step in her plea Abigail wisely acknowledges David's right to rule and thus gains his promise to grant her petition. When Nabal dies in shock over the news that his household was so close to

extinction, David promptly marries the wise widow, acquiring her fortune and her counsel (25:37–42).

As long as Saul rules as king, David refuses to take any direct action against him. His forbearance highlights the importance of the concept of the Lord's anointed. It also serves as the foundation for the Davidic apology narrative. By showing Saul mercy and respect as the Lord's anointed king, David demonstrates his own worthiness to rule. The audience for these stories will also see him as a sympathetic character in contrast to the sullen Saul.

There are two occasions (1 Sam. 24; 26) when David spares Saul's life because he is the Lord's anointed. The first occurs in a cave near the oasis of En-gedi near the Dead Sea (24:1–7). In this case, David's men urge him to slay the king and thus end the frustrating cycle of hiding and flight that they have suffered. However, David is adamant that no harm should come to the king. He is even remorseful over cutting off a portion of Saul's robe and thus, at least symbolically, depriving the king of a portion of his authority (24:5). This sets a precedent against regicide that would be valuable to David when he in turn becomes king.

During the outlaw period, David spends time as a mercenary leader, working for the Philistine king Achish of Gath. He is given the village of Ziklag as his headquarters and from there stages raids that give him military experience and may have contributed to his knowledge of Philistine tactics and iron technology. To prevent anyone from informing the Philistines of his activities, David orders that no prisoners be taken in his raids against Philistine and Philistine-allied villages. Thus Achish remains pleased with a faithful vassal who supplies him with a large quantity of loot (1 Sam. 27:8–12). Although David is acting as

The Use of a Ritual Pit

- *Odyssey* 11.23–29, 34–42: Here Perimedes and Eurylochus held the victims, while I drew my sharp sword from beside my thigh and dug a pit of a cubit's length this way and that, and around it I poured a libation to all the dead, first with honeyed milk, thereafter with sweet wine, and in the third place with water, and I sprinkled thereon white barley meal. . . . But when with vows and prayers I had made supplication to the tribes of the dead, I took the sheep and cut their throats over the pit, and the dark blood ran forth. Then there gathered from out of Erebus the spirits of those that are dead. (Homer, *The Odyssey*, trans. A. T. Murray, Loeb Classical Library, 2 vols. [Cambridge, MA: Harvard University Press, 1975], 1:387–89)

- Hittite KUB 29.4 reverse side 4.31–36: When at night on the second day (of the ritual) a star leaps, the offerer comes to the temple and bows to the deity. The two daggers which were made along with the (statue of) the new deity they take, and (with them) dig a pit for the deity in front of the table. They offer one sheep to the deity for *enumaššiya* and slaughter it down in the pit. (H. A. Hoffner, *Journal of Biblical Literature* 87 [1967]: 389)

- Gilgamesh Epic 12.83–84: Scarcely had he (Nergal) opened a hole in the earth, when the spirit of Enkidu, like a wind-puff, issued forth from the nether world. (*ANET*, 98)

- 1 Sam 28:7–8: Then Saul said to his servants, "Seek out for me a woman who is a medium [literally, "owner of a pit"], so that I may go to her and inquire of her." His servants said to him, "There is a medium at Endor." So Saul disguised himself and put on other clothes and went there, he and two men with him. They came to the woman by night. And he said, "Consult a spirit for me, and bring up for me the one whom I name to you."

a double agent, his duping of the Philistines (27:5–12) is typical of the trickster figures we have seen in earlier periods of Israelite history (Jacob, Laban, Ehud, Samson).

Saul's reign ends with a disheartening story of an abandoned king who is forced to resort to consulting a medium because God will no longer speak to him. Since Samuel has died, a desperate Saul dresses in a disguise and crosses the northern border of his realm to speak to the witch of Endor. He asks her to conjure up the spirit of Samuel so he can ask him whether God will give them a victory in the next day's battle (1 Sam. 28:8–14). The witch, like all other mediums and magicians, had been expelled from Saul's kingdom. There is an incredible sense of irony in this scene. Saul, who had outlawed those who practiced divination, must now disguise himself and secretly confer with a witch. Consenting to help him, she uses a ritual pit as the symbolic opening to the underworld. The text does not describe her conjuring methods, but similar stories in Hittite and Babylonian texts and in

Homer's *Odyssey* suggest the use of blood or a mixture of bread and honey to attract the spirits of the dead. Samuel's ghostly response does not provide Saul with any comfort. He is told that he and his sons will die in the coming battle and that the kingdom will pass from his family (28:15–19).

When Saul and his sons are killed in battle against the Philistines at Gilboa (1 Sam. 31), a confusing period follows in which the leadership of the people of Israel is divided. David rules for seven years in Judah, with his capital at Hebron. Abner, Saul's general, takes Saul's only surviving son Ishbaal (Ishbosheth) and places him on the throne, where he nominally rules the northern tribes. But Ishbaal must exercise his rule from the Transjordanian city of Mahanaim, since the Philistines now control the area of northern Canaan (2 Sam. 2). These seven years of divided rule are marked by conflict between the forces of David and Ishbaal, but it seems to consist primarily of border skirmishes. No real change is possible until Ishbaal is betrayed and murdered (2 Sam. 4).

Joab: Patriot or Opportunist?

One of the questions raised about Joab, David's general and principal adviser, is whether he is an opportunist or a patriot.

- Joab murders Ishbaal's general Abner to satisfy a blood feud. Abner's murder also eliminates a potential threat to both himself as general of David's army and to David, and it provides David with a scapegoat to shift public opinion in his favor when Joab is shamed (2 Sam. 3:23–39).

- Joab sends his soldier Uriah the Hittite to be killed in the front lines. This is intended to spare David from a charge of adultery, and it puts David in debt to Joab (2 Sam. 11:14–25).

- Joab sends the wise woman of Tekoa to David to convince him to return Absalom to court. This restores royal favor to a strong claimant to the throne and prevents potential unrest if David dies without designating an heir (2 Sam. 14:1–24).

- Joab kills Absalom. This act prevents a recurrence of rebellion but violates a direct order given by David (2 Sam. 18:5–18).

- Joab kills Amasa. This murderous act breaks a stalemate of leadership and allows Joab to put down Sheba's rebellion (2 Sam. 20:4–22).

- Joab backs Adonijah to succeed David. This choice leads Solomon to purge the kingdom of Joab and other leaders when Solomon gains the throne (1 Kings 2:13–46).

The principal figures in this period of unrest are not the kings but their generals, Abner and Joab. Joab is David's general, and Abner serves Ishbaal. Abner and Joab lead the raiding parties, provide advice, and ultimately engineer the unification of the nation under David's rule. Joab is David's first cousin and thus is tied to him by blood as well as service. They make a strong team, although it is sometimes difficult to tell in every episode who the leader of the nation is and who the loyal servant is (see the inset above on Joab's role). The climax of this set of stories occurs when Joab murders Abner. The timing of this murder could not have been worse. Abner had had a falling out with Ishbaal (2 Sam. 3:6–11) and had made overtures to David indicating that he would be willing to give him his support. Joab did not want a rival, and he already had sworn to take revenge on Abner for killing his brother during one of the border clashes. Joab's murder of Abner (in the legally significant gate area [3:27]) precipitates a chain reaction in which Ishbaal is murdered by his own advisers (4:1–3). David, who has been politically embarrassed by these events, is forced temporarily to discharge Joab as his military commander (3:31–39). Ishbaal's death leaves the northern tribes of Israel with no other strong claimant to the throne. The only remaining male representative of Saul's royal family is Mephibosheth, the crippled son of Jonathan (2 Sam. 9). The elders of Israel, therefore, come to David and ask him to assume the leadership of the nation as a whole (5:1–5).

STUDY QUESTIONS

1. Discuss Samuel's role as a transitional figure between the period of the judges and the monarchy.

2. How are Moses and Samuel alike, and why are there so many points of comparison?

3. What is the significance of the capture of the ark of the covenant by the Philistines (1 Sam. 4:1–11; 5)?

4. Does Samuel's response to the people's call for a king reflect the concerns of the people just before the monarchy is established, or is it a reflection of the frustrations of the late monarchy period (1 Sam. 8:1–15)?

5. Why is Saul chosen to be the first king of Israel?

6. What is the significance of the phrase in 1 Sam. 15:22 that it is better to obey than sacrifice?

7. In tracing the steps that lead David to assuming the kingship, which were the most significant?

8. How does David show his wisdom by refusing to kill Saul in the cave at En-gedi (1 Sam. 24)?

9. What does David gain by going to work for the Philistine leader Achish (1 Sam. 27)?

10. What does the story of the witch of Endor suggest about Israelite beliefs in the afterlife and communicating with the dead (1 Sam. 28:10–20)?

11. Is Joab serving David, himself, or the kingship by his actions?

David the King

KEY POINTS

- The narrative of David's reign is shaped by the religious and political agenda of the Deuteronomistic Historian.
- David's reign is marked by the difficulties of newly established states.

Figure 3.1. The Tel Dan Stele, an Aramaic inscription which is the only extrabiblical text to mention the "house of David." (Baker Photo Archive, courtesy of The Skirball Museum, Hebrew Union College, Jerusalem)

- The everlasting covenant with the House of David provides divine right rule.
- Solomon's restructuring of the bureaucracy and construction of the temple help to transform Israel into a nation-state.

It is difficult to make specific historical links to the activities chronicled in the court history of King David (1 Kings 10–20). Numerous difficulties are associated with excavating Iron I levels in Jerusalem (1200–1000 BCE), including the disruption of early levels by later building projects. Excavations over the past thirty years have revealed some structures dated to the tenth century BCE, but it is not possible at this time to conclusively identify them with David or his administration. No extrabiblical texts have been discovered that date to the period of David's reign, although at least one, the Tel Dan Stele, dating to the late ninth century BCE, mentions the House of David. Therefore, most of what we can surmise about this early ruler is based on the account of the Deuteronomistic Historian (1 Sam. 16–2 Kings 2).

Upon David's coronation as king over a united Israel, the narrative explains how he completes a cycle of events that has begun with his anointing by Samuel. To become a true king rather than just a war chief like Saul, David must take a series of steps to create a national identity for the people. The first of these is to establish a capital city for the nation. The criteria for this government center included being in a centralized location, having strong defenses, enjoying political neutrality, and having access to major trade routes.

Since Jerusalem had never been captured by the Israelites during the settlement period (see Josh. 15:63; Judg. 1:21), its political neutrality is intact. A similar example of this type of political decision making is found in the fact that no state in the United States can

David's Significance in Israelite Tradition

Although David has a bit more control over the tribes than Saul had and, at least according to the biblical narrative, more success against the Philistines, he remains primarily a chief rather than a true monarch. The steps he takes to unite the nation, both physically and symbolically, will help his successor, Solomon, transform Israel into a nation-state. Furthermore, the establishment of the everlasting covenant will make hereditary rule possible in Judah after the division of the kingdom. David's true significance for ancient Israel, however, is in the idealized King David, who is God's favorite and the model for all future good kings.

1 Kings 11:38

God's promise to Rehoboam and the kings of Judah: "If you will listen to all that I command you, walk in my ways, and do what is right in my sight by keeping my statutes and my commandments, *as David my servant did*, I will be with you."

1 Kings 15:3–5

Although Abijam "committed all the sins that his father [Rehoboam] did" and his "heart was not true to the Lord,

. . . nevertheless for David's sake the Lord . . . gave him a lamp in Jerusalem, setting up his son after him . . . because David did what was right in the sight of the Lord."

2 Kings 8:18–19

Although Jehoram, son of Jehoshaphat, "walked in the way of the kings of Israel" and "did what was evil in the sight of the Lord, . . . the Lord would not destroy Judah, for the sake of his servant David."

Ps. 89:3–4

"You said, 'I have made a covenant with my chosen one, I have sworn to my servant David: "I will establish your descendants forever, and build your throne for all generations."'"

Isa. 37:35

Faced with an Assyrian siege of Jerusalem, the prophet Isaiah speaks God's words of assurance: "For I will defend this city to save it, for my own sake and for the sake of my servant David."

exercise special privileges by claiming that Washington, D.C., is subject to its sovereign control. Likewise, no tribe of Israel could claim Jerusalem as part of its territory. Since there were no previous Israelite leaders associated with this city, Jerusalem's political neutrality allows the Davidic dynasty to make a fresh start without concern for the entrenched patterns of local politics that would have existed in an Israelite city. Jerusalem's defenses, which have proved invulnerable to this point, also make it a worthy capital city. Its relatively centralized location in the Judean hill country, with easy access to Jericho and the Dead Sea region, and to major sites to the west and north of the city, adds to the conclusion that it is a wise choice.

Once settled in Jerusalem, David needs to expand the city's living space to accommodate a growing population. David therefore initiates a building program to transform the city boundaries (2 Sam. 5:9–12). Whether David's

administration has the resources or the expertise to construct truly monumental structures, such as massive city walls and great palaces, is still in question by archaeologists. Certainly this form of political propaganda would have been desirable, but it is most likely something that has to wait for later kings of the Davidic line. One possible piece of evidence that may be tied to David is based on continuing discussions among scholars regarding the dating of a monumental stepped rampart that may have served as a buttress for a section of Jerusalem's fortifications and administrative district. Based on extensive analysis of pottery forms and styles, an argument can be made that the construction of this architectural feature may be dated to the transition between the Late Bronze Age and the early Iron Age, that is, the time of David. However, his small hilltop fortress city, centered on the Gihon Spring, would not have been impressive by modern standards based on either its size or its structures.

Figure 3.2. This stepped stone structure is located in the ancient city of David in Jerusalem. It appears to be the support for a very large public building currently dated to the tenth or ninth century BCE. (Baker Photo Archive)

As the narrative continues, David orders that the ark of the covenant be brought to his new capital city. The ark serves as the physical symbol of Yahweh's presence. Bringing it to Jerusalem identifies David's capital as the central cultic site for the nation. The text is careful to remind David and future rulers that the ark is Yahweh's symbol and not the property of the monarchy. Along the route one of the men bringing the ark is struck down by God for touching the sacred object (2 Sam. 6:6–11). After a suitable period of repentance and reevaluation, the ark resumes its journey. When it arrives at Jerusalem's gates, David is portrayed in high spirits as he leads the ark in parade into the city (6:12–15). This event marks the pinnacle of David's power and popularity and signals the demise of the last

remnant of Saul's family. When Michal, Saul's daughter, criticizes David for dancing naked before the people, the king relegates her to a life without children (6:20–23). She is never mentioned again, and the book is closed on the House of Saul.

With the ark in place, the next step in strengthening Jerusalem's prestige as the capital city is to build a temple to Yahweh. However, in 2 Sam. 7:5–7, Yahweh's prophet Nathan tells the king that he will not be allowed to build a temple. The reason given by the Deuteronomistic Historian is that God did not desire a house. Such a structure would bring Yahweh's worship into comparison with that of other gods in Canaan. Taking a more practical stance, 1 Kings 5:3 excuses David from building a temple because of the press of military campaigns to protect the nation. The postexilic revisionist version of these events found in 1 Chron. 28:1–19 gives David credit for passing on the structural plans for the temple to Solomon and establishing the priestly bureaucracy to supervise temple worship. However, it also notes that he could not build the temple because he was "a warrior and [has] shed blood" (28:3). If it were possible to consult the people during David's reign, it is possible that they, like modern taxpayers, would have had some negative sentiments about the project. It would cost them higher taxes and labor service to complete the temple's construction. There may also have been some uncertainty about investing so much power in a single cultic site. Whatever the reasons, David relents and leaves the task of temple building to his successor, Solomon.

In place of a temple, David is allowed to construct a dynasty. Nathan provides God's blessing, and the roots of a divine-right hereditary monarchy are born. A new covenant is announced in which Yahweh promises that there will always be a king of the line of David ruling in Jerusalem (2 Sam. 7:7–17). This commitment is known as the everlasting covenant. It functions as a royal insurance policy against assassination and a guarantee of support of the ruling house. Significantly, the text records only two assassinations of a Davidic ruler in Judah's history (Joash, 2 Kings 12:20; Amon, 2 Kings 21:23). During the four hundred years of Judah's existence as a nation, the everlasting covenant successfully maintains the royal ideology granting the Davidic dynasty a divine right to rule.

David's Court History (2 Sam. 10–20)

The account provided by the Deuteronomistic Historian depicts David as both the acknowledged leader of a unified nation and a flawed administrator. He continues to lead military campaigns against neighboring kingdoms early in his reign (2 Sam. 6; 8). But eventually age and the increasing demands of office relegate David to the sidelines. Furthermore, as David becomes identified with the institution of the monarchy, his personal life becomes more restricted. For instance, he no longer leads the army into battle (11:1). If he is killed, his death would throw the nation into turmoil. The idea of hereditary succession is not yet firmly established, and no heir or successor has been identified. Thus David increasingly becomes a full-time administrator. Unfortunately, this does not seem to have been his strongest talent. Much of the narrative about his life as king is filled with the problems he has while trying to manage the activities of the people and his own family. For example, David's justice system is slow and at times even ineffective (15:3). There are periods when David apparently takes little notice of the needs of the people or the actions of his children, and he has to be prodded into action by the ubiquitous Joab (2 Sam. 14).

As a newly installed monarch, David discovers that he will be tested by his allies and enemies. In one case, when David sends emissaries to greet the new king of Ammon and reaffirm previous treaty agreements, Hanun, the son of Nahash, decides to test David's resolve. He orders that the Israelite messengers be disgraced and sent back to David as a symbolic challenge. The Ammonites shame David's envoys by shaving off half their beards and cutting away the lower half of their garments (2 Sam. 10:3–5). This insult to their dignity is a slap in David's face that can be met only with force. David resolves the crisis by sending Joab and the army into Ammon. By defeating them and their Aramean allies, David proves his power and warns other potential opponents (10:6–19).

On the domestic front, David also finds himself using violence to handle a problem. In this case, however, David himself is the culprit, and the point of the story will be to demonstrate that even kings are not above the law. Thus, when David commits adultery and impregnates a woman named Bathsheba (2 Sam. 11:2–5), he fabricates a strategy to cover up his crime. First he tries to have Bathsheba's husband, Uriah the Hittite, spend time with his wife so that everyone will believe that the child is his. But Uriah refuses the comforts of home while his soldiers are in the field. That sparks David to commit yet another crime, arranging for Uriah to be placed in the front ranks where he will be killed (11:14–21). These ruthless acts set the stage for a theme that will dominate relations between kings and prophets throughout the history of the nation. David's adultery is revealed and condemned by the court prophet Nathan, who uses a juridical parable that provides the basis of a motif known as the king's call to justice. It emphasizes that even the king is not above the law and will be called to justice by Yahweh, a justice that will affect his rule and that of his descendants.

Nathan predicts that trouble will be "raised up" against David from within his "own house" and that another man will steal his wives, just as David has stolen Uriah's wife

The King's Call-to-Justice Motif
• The king sins.
• The king is confronted by a prophet about his sin.
• The king repents.
• The punishment that should be imposed on the king is instead imposed on the next generation.

(2 Sam. 12:11). After hearing the prophet's denunciation, David admits to Nathan that he has "sinned against the LORD" (12:13). Nathan replies that the usual punishment for adultery (death) is lifted from David's shoulders, but Bathsheba's child, the physical evidence of David's crime, will die (12:14).

Almost immediately the problems that Nathan has predicted begin as David's sons jockey for position as his successor. The most disruptive of these maneuvers begins with a conflict between David's sons Amnon and Absalom. Each of these potential heirs to the throne seeks to weaken the other's position. The conflict between the two brothers is underscored in the events of 2 Sam. 13 and begins when Amnon rapes Tamar (his half-sister and Absalom's full sister). In response, Absalom arranges the murder of Amnon. He is then forced to spend several years in exile (13:23–39). All the while David does nothing except get angry.

It is not possible to allow matters to drift without resolution. The future of the nation is at stake, and David must be prodded into action. The solution is to find a means of returning Absalom, the most likely heir to the throne, to the royal court. Always sensitive to the potential problems for Israel's future, Joab arranges Absalom's return with the assistance of a **wise woman** (a female elder) from Tekoa (2 Sam. 14:1–24). Once again it is possible to see in this episode that Joab is often David's political reality check. Joab's murder of Abner had opened the way for David to become king, and it is Joab to whom David turns when it becomes necessary to arrange for Uriah's death in battle. Now, since David appears powerless to resolve such a dangerous situation, Joab takes the action necessary to convince David to return Absalom to Jerusalem.

Geographic Reiteration: Hebron

As noted earlier when discussing the city of Shechem, a number of significant sites repeatedly appear in the biblical narrative. Absalom's choice of Hebron as the site of his coronation is another example of scribal use of geographic reiteration (2 Sam. 15:10).

Gen. 13:18: Abram settles near Hebron and builds an altar to mark the entrance of Yahweh worship in the promised land.

Gen. 23: Abraham purchases the cave of Machpelah as a family tomb and gains initial legal title to a piece of the promised land.

2 Sam. 2:1–11: After Saul's death, David rules as king of Judah in Hebron for seven years.

During his period of exile Absalom is convinced that he must take the throne and not wait for it to be given to him. He builds a following among the younger leaders. Again the plan is aided by David's inattention to administrative matters. Absalom is able to exploit his father's failure either to hear legal cases or to appoint judges to hear them (2 Sam. 15:2–6). Having "stolen the hearts" of the people, Absalom stages a successful coup d'état and has himself proclaimed king in Hebron, David's first seat of power (15:6–12). The magnitude of Absalom's popular support forces David to retreat from the capital in disgrace (15:13–37). The final element of Nathan's predictions comes true when Absalom publicly has sexual relations with ten of David's concubines (16:20–22). This act not only displays the young claimant's virility but also indicates that he is now the master of the palace and all within it.

During this crisis, when David is faced with the darkest period of his life, he emerges from the passive role he has played and once again demonstrates himself to be the same decisive leader who outwitted Saul and the Philistines (see inset below for the specific political moves he makes). Perhaps most important, he leaves a double agent, Hushai, in Jerusalem to confuse Absalom's counselors (2 Sam. 15:32–37). This allows him to buy enough time to reorganize his army and ultimately defeat Absalom in battle (2 Sam. 16–19).

The internal struggles contained in the narrative of David's court history are symptomatic of newly formed states that do not yet have an established line of succession. David even has to shame his own tribal elders into publicly welcoming him back as king after Absalom's defeat (2 Sam. 19:9–12). Considerable effort is also necessary to reestablish political ties with potentially dangerous members of his court (Jonathan's son Mephibosheth

David's Strategy to Regain the Kingdom

After being forced by Absalom's army to flee Jerusalem, the narrative records how David takes a series of steps that are designed to make it possible for him to reclaim his throne:

- He leaves ten concubines in the palace to maintain a semblance of his royal presence there (2 Sam. 15:15–16).
- He ascertains the loyalty of his Gittite mercenary troops (2 Sam. 15:18–22).

- He sends the Levite priests and the ark back into Jerusalem, thereby separating his political fortunes from the establishment of Jerusalem as the religious capital of Israel (2 Sam. 15:24–29).
- He sends his adviser Hushai to Absalom as a double agent to disrupt the counsel of other advisers such as Ahithophel, to delay pursuit of David's forces, and to provide information, through the

priests, to David's army (2 Sam. 15:32–37).
- He takes steps to prevent Mephibosheth, Saul's grandson, from taking political advantage of Absalom's rebellion (2 Sam. 16:1–4).
- He does not punish the shaming taunts of Shimei, thus humbling himself and demonstrating his acceptance of Yahweh's judgment (2 Sam. 16:5–13).

[19:24–30]). Perhaps the most important result of these events is the fact that David is never able to satisfy the elders of the northern tribes that his ruling house is their best choice (19:41–43).

The strains caused by Absalom's revolt also spawn another revolt, led this time by a northern tribal leader named Sheba. He voices a cry of secession that will become the rallying call in a later generation: "We have no portion in David, no share in the son of Jesse! Everyone to your tents, O Israel!" (2 Sam. 20:1). Sheba's proclamation of discontent is echoed when the northern tribes become dissatisfied with Solomon's son Rehoboam, and this in turn leads to a permanent division of the nation when they renounce their allegiance to the House of David (1 Kings 12:16).

Once again Joab steps in to quell a storm caused by Sheba's revolt. David has relieved Joab of his command after he disobeyed orders and killed Absalom (2 Sam. 18:5–15). But Amasa, the man who has replaced Joab, is an ineffective commander who delays taking the army into the field to deal with the rebels. Joab swiftly eliminates Amasa, relying on his army to support his callous murder of the hapless general (20:7–13). At the end of the campaign, Joab traps the rebels in the city of Abel Bethmaacah and negotiates there with another wise woman, who speaks for her people and trades Sheba's life for the lives of those of her city (20:14–22). While the nation remains intact

for another generation, the seeds of secession have been sown.

Although David's reign will eventually become idealized as a sort of Camelot, when the nation was ruled by a monarch whom God and "all Israel and Judah loved" (1 Sam. 18:16; 2 Chron. 6:42), the account ends with an embarrassing story of his physical decline. He fails to have intercourse with his last wife, Abishag (1 Kings 1:4), and this signals to his surviving sons and to the audience of this story that it is time to choose his successor. Factions arise favoring two of David's sons, Adonijah and Solomon. These factions split along the lines of the categories "old men" and "new men." One group consists of leaders who have served David throughout his career, and the other is made up of men who come to power only after David has become king in Jerusalem. The conflict is resolved when Bathsheba and Nathan join forces in convincing an apparently senile David to name Solomon as his heir (1 Kings 1). Once this is accomplished, Solomon's succession is assured, and all Adonijah can do is accept the situation. Curiously, David's intellect once again revives long enough to provide Solomon with suggestions on how to purge the administration of its enemies. Joab is executed for past crimes and being too clever to be trusted (1 Kings 2:28–34), and Abiathar, the high priest, is exiled. This latter move is particularly important in the history of the priesthood because from this point onward the priests are led by the descendants of Abiathar's priestly rival, Zadok (2:26–27, 35). Some scholars suggest that this division is also a reflection of the power struggle between a **Mushite priesthood** (those related to Moses) and an **Aaronide priesthood** that traced its authority back to Aaron's position as high priest.

The Contest for Kingship	
Adonijah's Faction	**Solomon's Faction**
Joab	Zadok
Abiathar	Benaiah
	Nathan
	Bathsheba

Solomon's Reign (1 Kings 1–11; 2 Chron. 1–9)

The narrative of Solomon's reign is not as complete or well developed as the narrative of David's reign. In the Deuteronomistic Historian's account in the book of Kings, much more attention is given to Solomon's administrative activities than to his personal life. This could reflect the later editor's interest in the evolution of the monarchy into an institution. During the reigns of Saul and David, the monarchy has functioned more as a personal vehicle of power. Under Solomon's leadership it evolves into a bureaucratic state, with the king functioning more as a chief executive. It is interesting to note that the fifth-century-BCE version of these events found in the book of Chronicles (2 Chron. 1–9) is primarily concerned with Solomon's construction of the temple in Jerusalem. But that can be explained by the dominance of the priestly community in the postexilic era. They had replaced the monarchy as the leaders of the people in Jerusalem, and thus their interest is primarily in the temple, not in politics.

Two themes dominate Solomon's reign.

The Wisdom Theme. This theme is designed to portray the king as the source of wisdom and justice for his people. One of David's principal mistakes has been his failure to appoint judges and to hear cases (2 Sam. 15:1–6). With Solomon's prayer for wisdom (1 Kings 3:9) and the story of the two prostitutes (3:16–28), Solomon's official recorder emphasizes that the new king will have the wisdom to dispense justice fairly from the beginning of his reign.

Perhaps an even better demonstration of Solomon's wisdom can be found in his administrative policies. Recognizing that many of David's problems had been caused by lingering tribal and regional loyalties, the narrative notes that Solomon restructures the national administrative districts. Political boundaries are redrawn in such a way that none of the old tribal territories are left intact (1 Kings 4:7–19). A further demonstration of the desire to unify the nation is found in the policy initiating a program of public works designed to improve the transportation system and basic **infrastructure** (roads, public buildings) within the country. In this way the new administration promotes a national economic policy while making it easier to travel and transport goods. The result is a greater identification with the state.

The Deuteronomistic Historian also lists several fortresses that are constructed or rebuilt along the borders, as well as new defensive systems that are built at major strategic points like Gezer, Hazor, and Megiddo (1 Kings 9:15–19) to ensure internal security. The discovery of six-chambered gates at each of these three cities raises the possibility that their similarity is a reflection of Solomon's building practices. Since other arguments can be made for their uniform shape and construction, such as the diffusion of architectural styles or the use of similarly trained architects on each project, it is best not to make an unequivocal identification of these gates with Solomon or his administrative efforts. Some scholars point to the reign of King Ahab (873–852 BCE) as the most likely period for such monumental construction.

For the Deuteronomistic Historian, the most important of Solomon's policies is the transformation of Israel into a recognizable nation among the nations of the ancient Near East. He is said to have made an alliance with the Phoenician king Hiram of Tyre. They become trading partners, operating a shipping enterprise that sails the Mediterranean and the Red Sea and brings wealth and influence to both countries

Figure 3.3. Remains of the Solomonic gates at Gezer. (Baker Photo Archive)

(1 Kings 10:21–22). Solomon's international reputation is exemplified in the story of the Queen of Sheba's journey to Jerusalem. She is so impressed by the king's wisdom that another trading link is established with the Red Sea spice routes (10:1–13). Among the concrete benefits that come to Solomon as a result of his newfound importance are marriage alliances with neighboring states. Amid a harem of a thousand women is a daughter of an unnamed Egyptian pharaoh (3:1). Such a marriage is an interesting piece of irony given the former status of the Israelites as slaves in Egypt. If these reports, which are not corroborated in any extrabiblical accounts, are correct, then Israel has truly emerged as a nation to be reckoned with.

The Temple Theme. Unlike his father, Solomon is able to construct a temple for Yahweh in Jerusalem (1 Kings 5–7). This temple, possibly located on what is today the Temple Mount in Jerusalem, housed the ark of the covenant

and provided sumptuous surrounding for the ritual practices of Israel's priests. That the ark is almost never mentioned again after Solomon's time suggests that it is not only housed but also submerged in the minds of the people by the temple (e.g., see Jer. 3:16 and 2 Chron. 35:3). The temple serves as the home of the Israelite priesthood, led by Zadok. It will be their responsibility to establish and administer official forms of Israelite religious practice. Solomon's alliance with Hiram proves to be useful in supplying construction materials and the skilled workmen needed to build the temple and design its furnishings.

The temple of Solomon becomes a lasting symbol for the power of the Davidic monarchy. Its site, like Jerusalem, is on politically neutral ground—the threshing floor of Araunah. Based on earliest traditions (2 Sam. 24:18–25), the only previous event tied to this place is the sacrifice that David makes there, marking the end of the plague that God has sent to punish the king for taking a census (however, 2 Chron. 3:1 names Mount Moriah as the site of the temple, tying it to Abraham's [aborted] sacrifice of Isaac in Gen. 22:2). By ignoring or setting aside any previous cultic usage on this site, the Deuteronomistic Historian provides Israel's priestly community with exclusive rights to ownership of the site. David's purchase of the threshing floor (a place associated with dispensing of justice in the village culture) and the building of the temple by King Solomon place royal sanction on the Yahweh cult.

In his dedication speech, Solomon ties the construction of the temple to a fulfillment of God's promise to David (1 Kings 8:15–21). The people are reminded of the covenant between God and the nation; the king employs a phrase that often appears in the text to describe Yahweh, saying that there is "no god like you in heaven above or on earth beneath" (8:23). Such an assertion retains a tinge of henotheism with its acknowledgment of other gods but clearly asserts that none challenge or compare to Yahweh.

Solomon then follows David's example and initiates sacrifices of various kinds (peace offerings, burnt offerings, cereal offerings), followed by a seven-day feast for all the people (1 Kings 8:62–65). This sets a precedent for the king to officiate at sacrifices and initiate worship services. But in the future it will be left to the priests to orchestrate and conduct these religious activities.

Despite the wealth and national spirit created by Solomon, the biblical editors ultimately choose to focus on his failure to obey the covenant with Yahweh. In this way they blame Solomon for the later political division of the kingdom (1 Kings 11:1–13). They point to the **cosmopolitan** (culturally diverse) influence of

---

Yahweh's Attributes as Supreme among the Gods

Deut. 4:39: Moses to the people: "So acknowledge today and take to heart that the Lord is God in heaven above and on the earth beneath; there is no other."

Josh. 2:11: Rahab to the spies: "The Lord your God is indeed God in heaven above and on earth below."

1 Sam. 2:2: Hannah's prayer: "There is no Holy One like the Lord, no one besides you."

2 Sam. 7:22: David's prayer: "There is no one like you, and there is no God besides you."

---

the international builders of the temple, as well as the many foreign wives whom Solomon brings to the capital. Emphasis is placed on the influences of other cultures and the worship of other gods that cause the Israelites to lose sight of the God who has made the kingdom possible. Syncretism, the borrowing of religious and cultural ideas, thus becomes the great sin of the Israelite people and a principal theme in the writing of their history by the Deuteronomistic Historian.

Once again, the motif of calling the king to justice appears in the narrative, and Solomon is confronted with his **apostasy** by Yahweh (1 Kings 11:11–13). He is told that most of the kingdom will be torn away from his descendants, but Yahweh will allow them to retain control over Judah and Jerusalem. Although the everlasting covenant remains intact, the Davidic kingdom is diminished. To complete the process of preparing for the division, the prophet Ahijah announces the divine recognition of a new political figure, a former public-works official named Jeroboam. The stage is set, but the crisis will occur after Solomon's death (11:29–40).

The story of the early monarchic period sets a number of precedents for later rulers. Among these are the establishment of a bureaucratic structure to rule the kingdom, diplomatic relations with other countries, and the fortification of the frontiers. Once the kingdom divides, two paths to leadership will emerge. In the southern kingdom of Judah, the everlasting covenant is employed to ensure the continuation of David's dynasty. In the northern kingdom of Israel, the pattern of succession is often based on the intervention of prophetic figures and the assassination of rulers by rebel leaders.

The establishment of the monarchy marks a centralization of both political and religious leadership. The priesthood quickly becomes linked with the monarchy, and in order to keep their positions of power and privilege, priests often serve the interests of the king rather than God. As has been the case in the stories of the early monarchy (e.g., the prophets Samuel, Nathan, and Gad), in the later monarchic period crises will result in the emergence of prophets who will serve as the loyal opposition to palace and temple.

■ STUDY QUESTIONS ■

1. Why is Jerusalem chosen as David's new capital city (2 Sam. 5:6–13)?
2. What is accomplished by David's bringing the ark to Jerusalem (2 Sam. 6)?
3. What are the implications for future rulers of the "everlasting covenant" (2 Sam. 7:8–17)?
4. Why does Nathan tell David the parable of the ewe lamb (2 Sam. 12:1–15), and what are the implications of the king's call-to-justice motif?
5. Why is David's kingdom threatened by Absalom's usurpation of the throne (2 Sam. 15:1–12)?
6. Why do the editors of the Davidic court narrative sometimes portray the king as

ineffectual and corrupt and sometimes as a decisive figure (see 2 Sam. 15:13–37; 1 Kings 1–2)?
7. What is the significance of Solomon's label as a "wise king"? How is it demonstrated (1 Kings 3; 4:29–34; 9:15–28; 10:23–29)?

The Divided Monarchy

A Kingdom Divides

KEY POINTS

- Poor leadership, divisional differences, and prophetic activity contribute to the division of the kingdom.
- Jeroboam tries to create a firm identity for the new nation of Israel, but the Deuteronomist labels these policies as sin.
- The emergence of superpowers in Egypt and Assyria will drastically affect the minor states in Syria-Palestine after 800 BCE.

Following Solomon's death, his son Rehoboam assumes the throne of Israel. There is no struggle for succession mentioned in the text, giving the impression that hereditary monarchy has become well established by this time. However, Rehoboam inherits a kingdom that has grown discontented with Solomonic rule, and he faces the demands of the elders of the northern tribes, who request that he allow more local autonomy in the various regions of the nation. Rehoboam attempts to intimidate these elders at a meeting held at Shechem and manages only to infuriate them (1 Kings 12:1–15). The elders of the northern tribes denounce Rehoboam and his dynasty: "What share do we have in David? . . . To your tents, O Israel!" (12:16). It is the same rallying cry used during Sheba's revolt in David's time (2 Sam. 20:1). In this case, however, the tribal elders have a divinely appointed leader to step in as their king, and there is no one like Joab

Reasons for the Division of the Kingdom		
Solomon's apostasy, building shrines for the gods of his many foreign wives, making the case for too much foreign influence (1 Kings 11:1–8) Residual discontent from David's reign (cf. 2 Sam. 20:1–2 and 1 Kings 12:16) and the desire for more local autonomy (and probably lower taxes) by the northern tribal leaders	Suppression of the authority of the tribal elders during Solomon's introduction of a complex bureaucratic structure (1 Kings 4:1–28) A prophetic seal of approval for new leaders: Ahijah's appointment of Jeroboam (1 Kings 11:29–39) as king of the northern tribes The political ineptitude of Solomon's successor, Rehoboam, in his	negotiations with the elders (1 Kings 12:6–15) Ability of the elders to take back their political endorsement from Solomon's son Rehoboam and transfer it to a new leader, Jeroboam (1 Kings 12:1–19), when it becomes clear that the central government is too weak to stop them

to step forward and put down the rebellion. As a result, the kingdom divides along a line just south of Bethel.

Within this new political structure, Jeroboam quickly emerges as the king of the northern kingdom of Israel with his capital at Tirzah. His transition to power is supported by the prophet Ahijah (1 Kings 11:26–40) and now is hailed by the northern elders, who acknowledge him as their king. Unable to prevent the national schism, Rehoboam sees his domain reduced to the territory of the southern kingdom of Judah, and he continues to rule from Jerusalem (12:21–24).

Since neither of these new states is particularly large or well defended, both areas are weakened by the division. Their vulnerable position is reflected in the almost-immediate invasion of Judah by the Egyptian pharaoh Shishak. The Egyptian army loots many of Judah's cities, and the pharaoh is said to have taken a ransom from the treasury of the Jerusalem temple (1 Kings 14:25–26). Although the pharaoh's record of the campaign does not mention capturing Jerusalem, it is likely that its ruler had to move quickly to prevent further damage to his tiny kingdom, quite possibly paying tribute or a ransom.

In the north, Jeroboam issues a series of decrees designed to establish an identity for his new kingdom and his emerging dynasty.

These decrees become known as Jeroboam's sin in the biblical narrative. His actions are shrewd political moves, but the biblical editors, through the perspective of the Deuteronomist (a southern-kingdom voice; e.g., 1 Kings 12:19–20), brand them as the worst kind of **heresy**. From this point in the text, all kings are judged based on whether or not they continue to support Jeroboam's policies.

Because of his sin, Jeroboam's House (royal dynasty) is condemned by the prophet Ahijah (1 Kings 14:6–16; another example of a prophet's calling the king to justice). In this case, however, no other specific claimant is designated by the prophet to take the throne. By implication, this omission allows for succession by assassination to become the rule in the

Jeroboam's Sin (1 Kings 12:28–33)
• Jeroboam creates a shrine at the northern and southern boundaries of his kingdom, one at Dan and one at Bethel, to serve as alternatives to Jerusalem. • He places golden calves in each shrine as substitutes for the ark and as symbols of the god "who brought you up out of the land of Egypt" (see Exod. 32:4). • He sanctions the use of **high places** (*bamot*) for worship in the local areas. • He appoints non-Levitical priests to replace the Levites, who are tied politically to the Jerusalem temple. • He changes the religious calendar to reflect better the seasons in the northern kingdom and to prevent his people from traveling to Jerusalem to celebrate major festivals.

northern kingdom. Periodically there will be staged revolts, usually precipitated by military leaders, which result in a change of regime. For example, a military commander named Zimri assassinates King Elah and crowns himself king (16:8–14). However, Zimri holds the throne for only seven days before he is assassinated by yet another military leader, Omri (16:15–20). Subsequently Zimri's name becomes synonymous with the label "traitor" in Israelite tradition, and other usurpers, such as Jehu, who rebel against a ruling king have to face the charge of treason when they attempt to take control of the nation (2 Kings 9:30–33). These political coups disrupt Israel's government and open it to exploitation and conquest by the emerging superpower nations in Egypt and Mesopotamia (i.e., Assyria). It is not surprising, therefore, that the northern kingdom is conquered after only two centuries of existence. Its people are carried off into exile well over a century before similar events take place in the southern kingdom of Judah (720 BCE vs. 587 BCE).

Kings and Prophets in the Divided Kingdom

The division of the Israelite nation could not have come at a worse time. David's kingdom is able to develop in part because the region of Syria-Palestine is not as politically tied to Egypt after the invasion of the Sea Peoples. (Egyptian control in the Beth-sheba Valley and the northern Negev did continue for a generation or two after the Philistine settlement.) From 1100 to 800 BCE, a large number of small states like Israel are formed (e.g., Philistia, Phoenicia, and Syria). They struggle among themselves for control of land and trade routes. The conflicts between Israel and Syria are typical of this period (1 Kings 20:1–35;

22:29–40; 2 Kings 12:17–18; 13:22–25). The diplomatic and military endeavors of these small states are based on their own policies and needs and are not dictated to them by outside forces. Their freedom to act will soon be over.

Local control changes in the period after about 800 BCE. From this point onward, the two small nations of Israel and Judah fall under the **hegemony** of the reemerging superpowers in Egypt and Mesopotamia and become part of the rivalry between these two aggressive empires. Assyria becomes the supreme power in Mesopotamia during the course of the century after 900 BCE. From their capital at Calah (later from a new capital at Nineveh) on the Tigris River, the Assyrian kings first gain control of the rest of Mesopotamia and then expand westward toward the Mediterranean Sea. Assyrian expansion eventually brings Israel and Judah, as well as all of the other small nation-states in Syria-Palestine and Transjordan, into vassal status. As a result, all the economic and political decisions made by the petty kings of these small states are influenced either directly or indirectly by the political chess game played between Egypt and Assyria for the two centuries following 800 BCE.

Our discussion of the period of the divided monarchy will touch on these historical events, but since our primary aim is to present what the biblical writers have to say about the period, we will devote most of our attention to the interaction between Israel's prophets and kings. It is evident in the biblical account that the monarchs have to struggle with internal affairs as well as with the growing demands and threats of the international superpowers. The prophets fundamentally are concerned that Israel and Judah maintain their covenantal obligations to Yahweh. Although they are not unaware of the political events of their time, they often demand that a king take a course of action that makes little political or practical sense (e.g., Isaiah's call for Ahaz to "be quiet" and leave the invaders of Judah to be dealt with by the Divine Warrior; see Isa. 7:3–9).

Once the political fates of Israel and Judah are sealed, the task of the prophets is to help rationalize why these events have been necessary. Their message often centers on a theodicy, an attempt to provide a religious explanation for why things happen the way they do (i.e., why God allows bad things to happen to the people). They try to reassure the people while at the same time letting them know that it is Yahweh, not another god, who has brought about these destructive events. If the people are to continue to worship Yahweh, they have to be convinced that Yahweh has not been defeated when their nation is defeated. It is also essential for them to understand that Yahweh will ultimately restore a righteous remnant. In the end it is the combination of the exilic experience and the message of the prophets that in the postexilic period transform Judaism into a true monotheistic faith and create a people who can survive without an independent nation.

▨▨▨▨▨ STUDY QUESTIONS ▨▨▨▨▨

1. Consider how Ahijah's symbolic act designating Jeroboam as the future king of Israel compares with other scenes in which a new king is chosen (1 Kings 11:29–40). Why is it significant that it is also Ahijah who condemns Jeroboam for his sin?

2. Does the meeting between Rehoboam and the elders in Shechem represent the united kingdom's last chance to remain intact (1 Kings 12:1–19)?

3. What are the elements of "Jeroboam's sin" (1 Kings 12:25–33)? Explain why they serve his political purposes, and then discuss the interpretation placed on them by the Deuteronomistic Historian.

4. Discuss how the encroaching hegemonic ambitions of Egypt and Assyria influence Israel's and Judah's history after 800 BCE.

Characteristics of Prophets

KEY POINTS

- The prophetic figures are called by God to champion obedience to the covenant and warn the people of the consequences of disobedience.
- Prophets are concerned with matters in their own time and place.
- Prophets often confront kings and the establishment and are a catalyst for social justice.
- Prophets are called because God will not destroy the righteous without a warning.

Because so much of Israelite history centers on the interaction between kings and prophets, we present here an extended discussion of the characteristics and social role of the Hebrew prophets. To begin with, it must be understood that these individuals are more than simple religious practitioners. Some of them are members of the priestly community, but when they function as prophets, they stand outside institutions like the priesthood. Their role is to serve as mediators between the people and God. In the process, they will challenge the authority of the establishment and the basic character of Israel's social order. The prophets are called to remind the leaders and the people of their obligation to the covenant with Yahweh and to provide a warning of punishment that accompanies a violation of the covenantal agreement.

The list of the characteristics of true prophets in this chapter is designed to provide a basic overview. Not every prophet will exhibit all of these characteristics. But the student should be familiar with these qualities and should be able to recognize them when they appear in the biblical text or in extrabiblical materials that deal with prophetic activity.

Call Narrative and Its Description

The call narrative describes how a person becomes a prophet. Some call narratives, like that of Moses, are quite elaborate. When a biblical writer includes a more detailed description of a call narrative, the purpose is to enhance the importance of the prophet and the prophet's message.

The call narratives of Isaiah, Jeremiah, and Ezekiel contain elements similar to those that occur during the coronation of monarchs. These major prophets are invested with authority and are placed under heavy obligation to carry out their mission. The literary pattern in these call stories includes a divine encounter or theophany (Isa. 6:1–2), an introductory word or greeting (6:3–5), an objection or demur (6:4–5), a commission (6:9–10), and a sign or talisman (6:11–13). The intention of the stories is to describe how God confers authority on the prophet, not to provide an autobiography.

The call narrative has an important transformational element to it. A person who may have been relatively undistinguished to this point in life is transformed into a dynamic spokesperson for God. An important personage is taken out of one's normal pattern and transformed by the charge to serve as God's representative. In the process, the new prophet is invested with special powers, a message, and a mission.

In addition to the simple calling of a person, the narrative also highlights the majesty of God. Mountains or buildings shake, clouds or fog obscure human vision, earthquakes rumble, and divine beings, including angels, appear in theophanic manifestation (Isa. 6:1–5; Ezek. 1:4–28). The reaction of the human to all this power is fear, hiding one's face, and amazement (Isa. 6:5; Ezek. 1:28).

An identification sequence then takes place, with God providing both a name (although not always "*the* name," i.e., Yahweh) and a reason for appearing at this time and place. Identification is necessary because the Israelites lived their entire existence within a polytheistic milieu. All the other nations had many gods, and it would have been only natural to wonder which god was speaking (note Moses's question to this effect in Exod. 3:13).

The theophany provides the opportunity for the Deity to detail the prophet's mission. Yahweh has identified a problem, and one of the people must be sent to provide a warning

Figure 3.4. Divination was prohibited for Israel but was practiced by other ancient Near Eastern cultures. A question would be posed, an animal sacrificed, and its entrails examined. This clay model of a liver was used to help diviners interpret what the gods were communicating when a liver was inspected. (Baker Photo Archive, courtesy of the British Museum)

(e.g., Amos 7:15). The warning is necessary because, by definition, Yahweh is a righteous and just God. The wicked may be destroyed, but righteous humans must be given a warning that will allow them to rectify the problem and thereby save their own lives.

Faced with the task of becoming a prophet, the person singled out in the theophany generally tries to provide an excuse for why he or she is the wrong person for the job. Perhaps this demur is only a natural human reaction, or perhaps it is part of a formal literary motif as part of the framework for these narratives. For example, Jeremiah claims that he is too young and does not know how to speak in public (Jer. 1:6). When excuses such as this are voiced, they are swept aside by God with assurances of support, dissolved through the provision of special powers, or in the case of Moses, nullified by incontrovertible signs (Exod. 4:1–9).

Among the methods of dealing with the demur is an empowering event. This occurs in the call of Isaiah, who claims that he is not worthy to accept God's call or to speak God's words because he has "**unclean** lips." This means that his mortal lips could never be spiritually clean enough to speak holy words. The solution is for an angel to take a hot coal from the sacrificial brazier near the altar and to cauterize Isaiah's lips (Isa. 6:7). The angel's action is not a physical burning but a spiritual purification that occurs in a vision, not in reality.

Once the excuses have been dealt with, a statement of mission is provided that charges the person who has been called with a sense of what must be done. Sometimes a tone is created, such as in the charge given to Jeremiah, which speaks only of approaching punishment (Jer. 1:11–19). But the primary purpose of the statement of mission is to identify the prophet with the purpose of the call and the urgent sense that the message must be delivered.

Compulsion

A special compulsion is associated with being called as a prophet. A prophet's calling can be denied for a time (e.g., Jonah tries to flee from the Lord [Jonah 1:3–17]). But ultimately the divine call must be answered. Prophetic compulsion includes the irresistible desire or a heightened ability to speak. Many of the call narratives include a reassurance that God will give the prophet the words to be spoken (Exod. 4:12; Jer. 1:7–9). But prophets may be reluctant to speak harsh words or to condemn their own people. In these cases, the prophet experiences a compulsion to speak that cannot be put aside (Jer. 20:9).

At least in the case of Ezekiel, the prophet's speech is shown to be under the complete control of God. Early in his prophetic career he is restrained from speaking any words of comfort or hope (Ezek. 3:25–27). This restriction is then lifted after the fall of Jerusalem to Nebuchadnezzar's army in 587 BCE. Ezekiel is then allowed to speak a more reassuring message that promises an eventual end to the exile and a restoration of the covenant between Yahweh and Israel.

Message

The prophet does not speak his or her own message. It is always spoken in the name of God. Although a prophet may obtain a reputation or become a well-known figure, it is never the case that a prophet says, "Thus says Amos," or "Thus says Isaiah." Many prophetic books begin with a preface or label that functions as a means of noting that this particular prophet has received the "word of the LORD" (Hosea 1:1; Joel 1:1; Amos 1:1). In this way authority is given to the messenger and to the message. However, when that message is presented by the prophet a **messenger formula** is used to make it clear that these are the words of the Deity: "Thus says the LORD (Yahweh)" (see Mic. 2:3; Jer. 5:14). The messenger formula also appears outside the Bible in prophetic texts from the ancient Near East. For instance, the eighteenth-century-BCE Mari letters from northern Mesopotamia contain similar formulaic statements: "Am I not Adad, lord of Aleppo, who raised you in my lap?" and "Thus says Adad" (texts A.2731 and A.1968).

The message is thus the most important aspect of the prophet, not the prophet himself or herself. This may be why prophets seldom mention specific names or dates that could draw the people away from the core of the message. Certainly some prophets, among them Balaam (Num. 22:4–6) and Elijah (1 Kings 18:17), acquire a personal reputation, but this is based on their message and their ability to speak for God.

There are instances in which the message requires that a prophet stand out as an individual. Isaiah parades about in the nude for three years (Isa. 20). Jeremiah marches through the streets of Jerusalem carrying a pot that he later smashes to the ground in a city gate (Jer. 19). Afterward he cries out his frustration from his prison cell and the public stocks (20:7–12). Ezekiel performs acts that are undignified and out of character for a priest (Ezek. 4). But no matter how oddly they may act or how flamboyant they may appear, the issue is ensuring that the people receive the message of God. In every case, these outrageous acts are designed to attract the people's attention to that message and to elicit the question "Why are you

doing that?" or "What is the meaning of your prophetic performance?"

Truth

For a prophet to gain credibility with the people, the message must come true. The Deuteronomic tradition cautions against prophets who call on the people to "follow other gods" (Deut. 13:1–4). It also warns that a true prophet speaks in Yahweh's name alone, and that only a true prophet's words come true (18:18–22). That helps to explain why prophets always begin by saying that they are speaking a message that comes from God. In this way they separate themselves from the words and cannot be condemned for treason, sedition, or doomsaying (Jer. 26:14–15). It is also why some prophets speak an ambiguous message that can be interpreted in more than one way.

The greatest measure of trust and authority, however, comes to the prophet who takes the dangerous path of speaking about the present or the near future. In cases in which the prophet interprets present circumstances as signs of Yahweh's punishment or warns of impending judgment from an angry God, the prophet may arouse the hostility of the people. Under these circumstances, a prophet may face a trial by ordeal or a period of incarceration. The duration of their incarceration may extend until the message is or is not fulfilled (e.g., 1 Kings 22:26–28).

Cognitive dissonance results when both contradictory prophetic messages appear to be true and can be tested only by actual events (see Jer. 28). The tension that results from such an exchange between prophets must have been very difficult for the people, especially since prophetic figures generally appeared during crisis points for the nation. It then became their task to evaluate the truthfulness of each prophet's message. Their decision would in turn determine whether they will obey the prophet's instructions, disobey them, or risk the possibility that the prophet is not a legitimate spokesperson for God.

Vocabulary

Prophets speak in the language of the people being addressed. They want to be understood, and therefore they use familiar images and vocabulary. The result is a large number of pastoral and agricultural illustrations, many of which are difficult for modern readers to understand since most of them have little or no experience of living in small villages or on farms. Prophets also make use of everyday activities, such as a public trial (see Isa. 5:1–7) or the work of a potter (Jer. 18:1–11). Occasionally a prophet may employ formulaic speech, such as the "woe oracle" that originated in funerary ritual (see Hab. 2:6–19). But a prophet's audience is not the same in every case. A prophet's message may be addressed to a large crowd (Jer. 7:1–4) or only to the king and his entourage (Isa. 7:3). Since the biblical prophets operated over a long period of time (ca. 600 years), it must be assumed that their society, their use of vocabulary, and the political situation that they faced changed drastically during this period.

Nevertheless, one way that a prophet identifies himself or herself as a prophet is by using the images or language of a previous prophet. It is not uncommon for one prophet to make statements similar to those of earlier prophets (Jer. 26:16–19 referring to Mic. 3:12). Some portion of a prophet's career (often the call narrative) may have a parallel in the career of a past prophet. The career of Moses frequently plays a paradigmatic role in the lives of later prophets (Deut. 18:15). For example,

Isaiah's call narrative (Isa. 6:1–4) contains a visual image of the ark of the covenant, the earthquake, and the smoke found in Moses's Sinai theophany.

One example of the use of familiar vocabulary or terms by various prophets is the phrase "all flesh." It appears most often in the latter chapters of Isaiah (40:5, 6; 49:26; 66:16, 23, 24; cf. Gen. 6–9), which date to the end of the exile (ca. 539 BCE) and later. But it is also found in the writings of the sixth-century prophets Jeremiah (25:31; 32:27; 45:5) and Ezekiel (20:48; 21:4, 5), as well as in the writings of the postexilic prophets Zechariah (2:13) and Daniel (4:12). This indicates that the phrase "all flesh" becomes a standard part of the prophetic repertoire in the period after 600 BCE.

What most often singles out a prophet from other prophets is the historical context of their message. Elijah speaks to Ahab, not to some future monarch of Israel. Isaiah's prophecy concerning the Syro-Ephraimite war in Isa. 7 is directed to a specific historical event and refers to events in the near future that are directly related to that situation. Haggai's pronouncement on the need to reconstruct the temple in Jerusalem fits only into the immediate postexilic period (ca. 520 BCE).

Enacted Prophecies

Prophets are sometimes called on to be masters of the performing arts. They use not only words but also symbolic acts or pantomimes. Prophets use three kinds of pantomimes: (1) single dramatic gestures (e.g., Jeremiah buries his clothes in the riverbank [Jer. 13:1–11]; Ezekiel shaves his head and beard [Ezek. 5:1–4]), and (2) austere practices or asceticism (e.g., Jeremiah does not marry or attend funerals or celebrations [Jer. 16:1–13]); in this way God provides the interpretation of (3) the silent actions of another (e.g., Jeremiah, like a teacher, draws the attention of his audience to the potter's working at his wheel [Jer. 18:2–4]).

Pantomime emerged from the ancient and universal art of gesturing during social interaction. Anthropologists, sociologists, and dramatists continue to identify a wide variety of pantomimes first celebrated in the cave paintings of the Stone Age and still utilized in the magic practices, rituals, and dances of traditional societies. Technically, pantomime is theater without script. Performers in masks sometimes use words and music to accompany their gestures, but pantomime is primarily a visual art form whose medium is movement. Pantomime grew from a conviction in traditional cultures that only gestures, acrobatics, and dance can appropriately address human realities.

For the Hebrew prophets, pantomime is not solely representational art describing coming events. It also comprises a series of actions designed to bring changes that could alter the course of future events. Pantomime is a catalyst for social change that highlights and sometimes ridicules the faults of the establishment.

Male and Female Prophets

Both men and women function as prophets, and there does not seem to have been any distinction drawn between them as to authority or authenticity (e.g., see Huldah in 2 Kings 22:14–20). This is in harmony with the appearance of both male and female prophets elsewhere in the ancient Near East. Since these persons are chosen by a god to serve as a divine mouthpiece, their individual characteristics, including gender, have no bearing on the message. This is further evidence that prophets are not chosen for their self-importance, status or privilege in society, or personal abilities.

Manner of Prophetic Utterance

Prophetic speech is elicited in a variety of ways and uttered in several different styles, depending on the prophet and the audience. It is sometimes the result of a physical trance state (Ezek. 8:1; 11:1–5). Occasionally prophecy is induced by music or dancing that creates a state of ecstasy (1 Sam. 10:5, 10; 2 Kings 3:15). Most often, however, prophecy is simply spoken or is a report of a vision (e.g., 1 Kings 22:19–22). Occasionally God directs that the message be written down by the prophet (Jer. 36:1–4).

Prophetic words borrow genres from a variety of social institutions. The woe or lament oracle portrays the prophet as a mourner (Ezek. 24:9–10). The parable and the proverb cast the prophet as a teacher (Isa. 5:1–10). The miracle story and the call narrative draw on features found in the stories about monarchs (2 Kings 4:1–7; Jer. 1:14–19). The covenant lawsuit and the oracle imply that the prophet is an emissary or a member of the divine assembly (1 Kings 22:10–17; Hosea 4:1–4). Oracles against nations place the prophet in the role of a war chief (Jer. 48:46).

The miracle stories of Elijah and Elisha are told in villages burdened by the king's tax on their produce and weakened when the monarch drafts their men into his army (1 Sam. 8:11–17; 1 Kings 21:1–29). The miracles that these prophets perform are not so much authorizations of the power of the prophets as they are indictments of the misuse of power by the monarchs. Virtually all the miracles focus on some aspect of feeding and protecting. Miracles demonstrate the effortlessness with which Yahweh can feed and protect the people in contrast to the costly efforts of the monarchs to feed and protect them through treaties with other nations. For example, kings take widows' sons for the army, thus putting them to death, whereas Elijah raises to life the son of the widow of Zarephath (1 Kings 17:17–24). Kings tax widows into starvation, but Elijah gives a widow an endless supply of oil (2 Kings 4:1–7). When a borrowed axhead needed to clear the land is lost, Elisha returns it so that the lender will not foreclose on the borrower's land (2 Kings 6:1–7).

Social Role

In their primary role as the counterbalance to the priestly community and the monarchy, prophets express an **egalitarian ideal** of a society as championing the concept that every person is equal under the law. Sometimes the prophets are mentioned as part of the priestly community (e.g., Isaiah and Ezekiel) or as court prophets (e.g., Nathan). But they always seem to stand apart from these institutions in order to criticize them and to point out where they have broken the covenant with God. Major prophets also attract followings of disciples or create schools of thought that spread their message and preserve it for later generations. It is likely that these disciples and schools ultimately organize the prophecies of their respective founding prophets into written, coherent documents.

Occasionally a prophet, such as Elijah or Elisha, appears to be separate from or peripheral to the mainstream of society. Prophets of this kind are not as isolated as they seem to be. They have a network of support that functions as a sort of underground organization, providing meals, offering a place to stay, and performing other tasks to assist the prophets in carrying out their mission (2 Kings 9:1–10).

In the political realm, the prophets serve as the conscience of the kings. It is their job to remind the monarch that he is not above

the law and can be punished like any other Israelite for an infraction of the covenant code (2 Sam. 12:1–15). Prophets also participate in political acts. For example, Elisha has one of his "sons" (i.e., disciples) anoint the military commander Jehu as king of Israel (2 Kings 9:1–13). Jeremiah counsels King Zedekiah to surrender the besieged city of Jerusalem to the Babylonians in order to spare the people any further pain. He calls on the king and his advisers to recognize that Yahweh is the driving force behind the enemy's efforts (Jer. 21:1–10; 38:17–18).

Prophetic Immunity

Since the prophets are viewed as the messengers of God, they are not to be held liable for the message they speak. Their freedom to speak is based on the principle of **prophetic immunity**, which protects the prophets from the extreme reactions of their audience and the powers that be. However, if for any reason suspicion is raised that the person might not be a true prophet (see the case of Uriah, who flees rather than defend God's message, Jer. 26:20–23), then the message is scrutinized to see whether it does come true (Jer. 28:8–9). Should the message prove false, then the false prophet is subject to execution, either by the people or God (see Jeremiah's trial in Jer. 26:12–19 and the contrasting fate of Hananiah in Jer. 28:16–17). The only case in which a prophet is executed for speaking God's message is in 2 Chron. 24:20–22, when Zechariah is killed by King Joash. But Joash is punished when God allows him to be defeated by the king of Aram (24:23–24).

Just because a prophet is spared from death, however, does not mean that he or she won't face public ridicule and physical punishment at the hands of dissenters. For instance, Amos is publicly denounced by Amaziah, the high priest at Bethel, for speaking without official license in the "king's sanctuary" (Amos 7:12–13). Both Elijah and Jeremiah face public censure (1 Kings 18:17; Jer. 36:21–26). Elijah is forced to flee from Jezebel's wrath following his triumph on Mount Carmel (1 Kings 19:1–3), and Jeremiah is imprisoned (Jer. 38:4–6) and placed in the stocks (Jer. 20:2).

Audience

Prophets are concerned with the present and the near future because their job is to draw the people and the establishment back to the proper covenantal relationship with Yahweh. Repeatedly they express God's desire for obedience and "steadfast love" (*khesed*) rather than rote ritual or pageantry (1 Sam. 15:22; Hosea 6:6; Amos 5:21–24). Sometimes their work is conducted prior to God's punishment (Amos 5:4–6). But many times their words explain why God has punished the people (Ezek. 8). The attempt to explain past or present events as the result of divine punishment is known as a theodicy. Theodicy provides a rationalization for why evil or destruction has happened to God's people.

The major exception to the emphasis on the contemporary context in prophetic speech is **apocalyptic** prophecies. Apocalyptic utterance is concerned with end times (**eschatology**). Apocalyptic prophecy contains elements of earlier traditions and history that are hidden in symbolic language. Zechariah and Daniel are the best examples of apocalyptic prophets in the Bible, but other portions contain apocalyptic literature (Isa. 26–28; Ezek. 1–3; 40–48). In general, this material is dated from the exilic period to the mid-first century BCE. Apocalyptic literature employs many of the ideas and themes of earlier prophets but speaks to a future time

when the problems of the present are solved and God reigns over a restored nation.

Prophetic speech has often been quoted and reinterpreted in later texts. This is done first by other biblical writers (see the reuse of Micah's prophecy against Jerusalem [Mic. 3:12] in Jeremiah's trial [Jer. 26:17–19]). The prophetic materials are later used by the writers of the NT (see Matt. 1:23 for reuse of Isa. 7:14) and Christian theologians as the basis for their pronouncements and doctrines. These later commentaries on the prophetic works have their own intrinsic value in certain academic and religious contexts, but it should not be assumed that the original intent of a particular prophet in the OT/HB is to foretell the events of Jesus's life in the NT or of a specific doctrine that is not integral to Judaism.

Remnant Theme

All the prophets use a remnant theme in their message. The remnant theme emerges from the concept that a righteous God cannot destroy righteous persons without providing them with a chance to survive. The story of Noah and the flood is one good example of this theme. God speaks directly to Noah rather than employing a prophet, but in later Israelite history prophets serve as bearers of a message of retribution by God for the people's failure to obey the covenant. The prophets state that the punishment of the people is certain, but a few (a remnant) may survive the coming destruction and rebuild the nation from the ashes. Ezekiel's vision of the "marking of the innocents" (Ezek. 9) is one of the best examples of this message. In this case, the persons who demonstrate a true repentance and sorrow over the sins of Jerusalem are marked by a divine messenger and spared while the rest of the population is executed and the city is destroyed.

Reinterpretation of Prophecy

It is a common practice among the prophets to reuse or reinterpret major themes or the prophetic message of previous spokespersons for God. One sign of a true prophet is to speak familiar words or to employ themes that the audience knows and considers important to their identity as a people. For example, several of the prophets use themes from biblical tradition, such as universalism or remnant. Several of the prophets, for instance, use the story of the garden of Eden as a foil for lost opportunities or as a hope for an eventual idyllic restoration of the nation.

The process of reiteration and reinterpretation continues as the words of each of the prophets are compiled and recorded. We do not have a great deal of information on the effort to write down the words of the prophets. However, a few references in the biblical text describe how a prophet or one of his support group records a portion of the prophet's message. These include the following:

Isa. 8:1: "Then the LORD said to me, 'Take a large table and write on it in common characters.'"

Isa. 30:8: "Go now, write it before them on a tablet, and inscribe it in a book, so that it may be for the time to come as a witness forever."

Jer. 30:2: "Thus says the LORD, the God of Israel: 'Write in a book all the words that I have spoken to you.'"

Jer. 36:2: "Take a scroll and write on it all the words that I have spoken to you against Israel and Judah and all the nations."

Ezek. 43:11: "When they are ashamed of all that they have done, make known to

> ### Eden in the Prophets
>
> Ezek. 31:8: Ezekiel metaphorically compares Assyria with a "cedar of Lebanon," a type of cosmic tree that stands at the center point of creation. He says it was so beautiful that "the cedars in the garden of God could not rival it." Then, drawing on the lost glory of Eden, he says the mighty "tree" of Assyria has been consigned to the underworld (**Sheol**) as punishment for its wickedness and excessive pride (Ezek. 31:10–18).
>
> Isa. 51:3: The postexilic voice of Isaiah compares the restoration of Zion's "wilderness" (the exile and the destruction of Jerusalem) with a new Eden.
>
> Joel 2:3: Joel contrasts Judah's condition ("like the garden of Eden") prior to its invasion by invading armies to the "desolate wilderness" it has become.

them the plan of the temple . . . and write it down in their sight."

Hab. 2:2: "Then the LORD answered me and said: 'Write the vision; make it plain on tablets, so that a runner may read it.'"

The difficulties entailed in the editing and arranging of the prophetic materials can be seen in what, to Western eyes, is disorganization and a basic lack of chronological sequence in books like Jeremiah and a somewhat jumbled presentation of major themes in Hosea. These problems may be due in part to the tumultuous upheavals of the eighth to sixth centuries BCE that must have contributed to the loss of memory or scrolls containing prophetic speech and action. It may be assumed that the prophets, especially those with long careers (e.g., Isaiah and Jeremiah), spoke on many more occasions than are recorded in the biblical text. As with the historical annals of the kings in the books of Samuel and Kings, there must have been decisions made by editors and redactors on what should be included to make the most impact.

The fact that these prophetic texts did survive and are framed in a coherent corpus

New Testament Use of Old Testament Prophecies

Matt. 1:23: The Gospel of Matthew uses Isa. 7:14 as a proof text for the virgin birth of Jesus.

Matt. 2:5–6: The Gospel of Matthew quotes Mic. 5:2 as a proof text for Jesus being the Messiah.

Matt. 2:18: The Gospel of Matthew quotes Jer. 31:15 as a proof text for the massacre of the innocents by Herod.

by the beginning of the Christian era is evidenced by the use made of these materials by the writers of the NT and later by Christian theologians as the basis for their doctrines. These later commentaries on the words of the Hebrew prophets are not invalid, but it should not be assumed that the original intention of a particular prophet is to foretell the birth of Jesus or the establishment of Christianity. The Hebrew prophets direct their message to an audience in their own time and place. However, their call to return to obedience to the covenant and their reassurance that God would provide relief in times of distress would find a welcome audience in later periods. It would have been only natural for the Gospel writers, Paul, and other early Christian leaders to draw on their own prophetic traditions to bolster their arguments for a fulfillment of these words.

Having outlined and explained these basic characteristics of Israelite prophets, we will now turn to an examination of the message of each of them. The student should seek to identify the characteristics of prophets as they occur in their reading of the assigned texts.

STUDY QUESTIONS

1. What is the principal role of prophets in their society?
2. What must a prophet do to establish that he or she is a true prophet? What happens when cognitive dissonance occurs?

3. What themes are most often cited by the Israelite prophets, and what are the various ways in which they are conveyed?
4. Discuss the various ways the prophets are linked with one another (vocabulary, theme, confrontation with kings and priests).
5. Discuss the implications of the remnant theme. Why must God send a prophet to warn the people?

Elijah and Elisha

The Unnamed Prophet of Judah

KEY POINTS

- Jeroboam's sin serves as a measure of good and evil kings.
- Elijah's confrontation with Ahab and Jezebel highlights the struggle between Yahweh and Baal.
- Elisha's cycle of stories centers on themes of rewarding the faithful and universalism.

In the period immediately after the division of the kingdom, no strong prophetic figure emerges. However, one story particularly demonstrates the tension between prophet and king during this period. The tale involves an unnamed prophet who publicly confronts Jeroboam during a sacrifice at Bethel (1 Kings 13:1–10). Jeroboam is upset that his dedicatory ceremony is being interrupted. He makes a preemptory gesture, stretching out his arm, to signal to his guards to remove the troublemaker. The subsequent withering of the king's arm (13:4b) follows a pattern of events that is common in the Elijah-Elisha cycle where the person who fails to give proper respect to the Lord's representative is slain or wounded (see 2 Kings 1:9–16; 2:23–24; 5:19b–27).

Frightened and publicly shamed, Jeroboam pleads with the prophet to pray to the "LORD your God" to heal his arm. Even though this

Summary of Characteristics of Prophets

- **Call Narrative:** The event when a person is called to serve as a prophet. Some are quite spectacular, including a theophany, a demur by the person called, an empowering event, and a charge for mission. Others simply include the remark that a call has taken place—without any details.

- **Compulsion:** In whatever manner a person is called to be a prophet, the call is unavoidable and, once made, must be obeyed. The person cannot hold back or speak some other message without invoking the wrath of God.

- **Message:** The message of the prophets is from God, and thus the prophets will speak "in the name of Yahweh," not in their own name. Certainly prophets, such as Balaam, do acquire a reputation, but even so they must admit that when they speak as a prophet it is God's word that they are speaking (Num. 23:12).

- **Truth:** When a person speaks in the name of God, does that make him or her a true prophet? The answer is yes, but only if that message comes true. This also applies when two prophets present equally believable, but opposite, messages (cognitive dissonance).

- **Vocabulary:** Prophets are wordsmiths, that is, persons who use words or words plus gestures to get the point across. It is only natural that the prophets speak in the language of the people being addressed and use familiar images and vocabulary.

- **Enacted Prophecies:** The prophets employ easy-to-understand actions, but ones that are out of character for them. The result is that a larger audience is attracted to the performance and requests an explanation. Like all pantomime, enacted prophecies require abstract thinking on the part of the audience.

- **Gender:** The prophetic office is not tied to a specific gender. Both men and women function as prophets, and there does not seem to be any distinction drawn between them as to authority or authenticity.

- **Manner of Prophetic Utterance:** There are various means of receiving and then transmitting prophecies. It is sometimes the result of a physical trance state or occasionally induced by music or dancing (ecstatic prophecy), but most often the prophecy is spoken as a report of a dream experience or what God has told the prophet.

- **Role in Society:** The prophet primarily serves as the loyal opposition to the priestly community and the monarchy. Prophets express an egalitarian ideal of a society in which every person is equal under the law. Sometimes the prophets are mentioned as part of the cult and as court prophets. However, they always seem to be able to stand apart from these institutions to criticize them and to point out where they have broken the covenant with God. Occasionally the prophet is a separate entity,

peripheral to the mainstream of society. These peripheral prophets may have a support network that functions as a sort of underground organization, providing meals, a place to stay, and other aid.

- **Prophetic Immunity:** Even though prophets often tell the people what they do not want to hear, they cannot be killed with impunity when it is certified that the words they are speaking are God's. This does not prevent imprisonment or physical punishment, but at least the messenger is not to be killed for an unpopular or negative message.

- **Audience:** Nearly all of the non-apocalyptic material is directed to the prophets' own time. They are concerned about the present and the near future because their job is to draw the people and the establishment back to the proper covenantal relationship with Yahweh.

- **Remnant Theme:** The remnant theme is based on the concept that a righteous God cannot destroy righteous persons without providing a chance for them to survive. Thus the prophet is sent to warn the nation, but with the expectation that only the righteous will heed that warning, do something about the problem, and therefore be allowed to survive and ultimately rebuild the nation.

is a direct acknowledgment of the prophet's authority, it is a curious response by Jeroboam, who presumably is about to offer incense on the altar to Yahweh. Perhaps in this way the Deuteronomist once again portrays the Israelite king as both an idolater (note the golden calves in 1 Kings 12:28) and a person who is not committed to the obligations placed on members of the covenantal community.

After his arm is healed, Jeroboam is grateful and obligated to reciprocate. He invites the prophet to "come home with me and dine, and I will give you a gift" (1 Kings 13:7). The king's invitation is based on the protocol of hospitality (see Gen. 18:3–5). The protocol, however, allows for the guest to refuse without infringing on the honor of either party, if there is a need to move on or some other abiding reason

Figure 3.5. A small cast-bronze bull found at Samaria dating from the twelfth century BCE. (Dr. James C. Martin. Collection of the Israel Museum, Jerusalem, and courtesy of the Israel Antiquities Authority, exhibited at the Israel Museum, Jerusalem)

that transcends granting the favor of acceptance. In this case, the prophet bases his refusal on a previous command from Yahweh that he "not eat food, or drink water, or return by the way that you came" (1 Kings 13:9). The force with which the prophet refuses Jeroboam's hospitality, however, does seem a bit excessive. He says, "if you give me half your kingdom, I will not go in with you" (1 Kings 13:8). By refusing this offer, the prophet also refuses to grant any legitimacy to the new king or his separatist northern kingdom.

This story is only an isolated incident and not a systematic message of reform. It is not until the mid-ninth century BCE that the prophets Elijah and Elisha emerge to challenge the kings of Israel and the religious establishment in the northern kingdom.

The Elijah Cycle

The cycle of stories that introduce the prophet Elijah is carefully staged by the Deuteronomistic Historian to present Israel in crisis under the poor leadership of King Ahab and his Phoenician wife, Jezebel. In contrast to these villains, Elijah and his successor, Elisha, stand out as bigger-than-life heroes, and the text does everything it can to magnify their actions. For this to be effective, the editors have chosen to portray Ahab as a husband dominated by his wife, weak and vacillating, and unable to stand up for the God of his people. None of what archaeological excavations have revealed about Ahab's activities in rebuilding the fortresses of Israel, or his exploits as the leader of a coalition of kings against the Assyrian invaders in the Battle of Qarqar (853 BCE), are mentioned here. Instead, the Deuteronomistic Historian's agenda is clear. Ahab and Jezebel endanger the people by rejecting Yahweh and by fostering worship of Baal. Elijah is therefore chosen to confront them, just as Moses confronts the pharaoh, to demonstrate whose god is the most powerful of all.

The basis for the confrontation with Elijah begins with the marriage of Ahab and Jezebel. While this marriage represents a logical political alliance between Israel and Phoenicia, the Deuteronomistic Historian presents it as an invasion by the forces of Baal, the main deity in the **pantheon** of the Phoenician religion (cf.

Moses and Elijah Compared

A number of comparisons can be made between the careers of Moses and Elijah. Elijah joins Moses in Israelite tradition as the second great prophetic figure, and in the NT they are paired with Jesus during the transfiguration (Mark 9:2–8).

1. Both Moses (Exod. 3–4:17) and Elijah (1 Kings 19:8–18) receive their call as prophets on Mount Sinai (= Mount Horeb).
2. Both Moses (plague sequence: Exod. 7–12) and Elijah (Mount Carmel contest: 1 Kings 18:17–40) confront monarchs as part of a contest between gods.
3. Both Moses (Exod. 14:21–22) and Elijah (2 Kings 2:8) miraculously open a body of water and cross on dry land.

Solomon's foreign marriages [1 Kings 11:1–8]). Jezebel, whose name becomes synonymous with wickedness and infidelity, is portrayed as a fanatic. She hunts down the prophets and worshipers of Yahweh, killing all she can find (18:4). In the meantime, Ahab does nothing to stop her. This situation is ripe for a hero figure to set things right, just as in the Judges period.

Elijah bursts on the scene and immediately confronts the powers of state and temple. At God's command, he predicts a drought that is to last for three years, and that in turn brings famine throughout the land of Israel (17:1). The significance and the great irony of this prophecy is that Jezebel's god Baal is a god of storms and fertility. Thus the question raised by Elijah in confronting Ahab and the priests of Baal is, "Who really is God?" (18:21).

In yet another ironic touch, Elijah spends the subsequent three-year period east of the Jordan River and then in Phoenicia at Zarephath (1 Kings 17:2–24). While he is there, Elijah demonstrates the power of his God in Jezebel's homeland, another example of the universalism theme. Moreover, the covenant promise to provide land and children is fulfilled in the prophet's performance of life-giving miracles. First Elijah miraculously feeds a starving widow and her son. Then he revives the son after he has apparently died. This stands in stark contrast to the failure of Ahab and Jezebel and Baal to preserve the people of Israel from the drought and the resulting famine. Yahweh is proved to give life while the worship of Baal brings death on the land (cf. the consequences of the tenth plague in Exod. 11:4–7).

Once the three years pass, Elijah is instructed to return to Israel and challenge Ahab to a public competition. In this staged event, Elijah dramatically demonstrates Yahweh's power and Baal's impotence (1 Kings 18:17–40). Not since Moses's confrontation with the pharaoh (a fact emphasized here by the writers) has such a direct, public contest taken place between a political leader and a prophet.

The place chosen for the trial is Mount Carmel, on Israel's northern coast. Mount Carmel overlooks the Mediterranean Sea and could serve as an excellent weather observatory, a quality very useful since the contest is to determine which god will produce rain. At one point this peak had served as a mountaintop shrine, a high place. The question could be asked why the later editor allows Elijah to perform his religious trial in a place forbidden and condemned by the theology espoused by the sixth-century-BCE Deuteronomistic Historian. The likely reasons are that high places are condemned only in the southern kingdom but are accepted as appropriate sacred sites in the north, and the story of Elijah is so well known that the editors cannot change the site of the contest. It should be noted, however, that the altar to Yahweh on Mount Carmel has to be repaired before it can be used, which suggests that it has not been used recently.

The contest is simple. The 450 prophets of Baal and Elijah meet at the top, and each side will construct an altar to their god. They are to call on their god to accept the sacrificial bull and to bring rain and thus end the drought. The suspense, as well as the cosmic nature of the story, is heightened when Elijah lets the opposition go first. Their daylong pleas to Baal receive no answer. Even their "limping" dance and ritual blood letting cannot attract the Phoenician deity's attention (1 Kings 18:26–28). An amused Elijah takes the opportunity to taunt the failed performance and to ridicule their nonresponsive god:

Cry aloud! Surely he is a god; either he is meditating or he has wandered away, or he is on a journey, or perhaps he is asleep and must be awakened. (1 Kings 18:27)

When he steps forward to take his turn, Elijah performs a series of symbolic acts designed to restore the people's confidence in Yahweh as the God of Israel (1 Kings 18:30–40). He gathers the people around him and publicly rebuilds the platform of Yahweh's ruined altar (cf. Gideon's actions in Judg. 6:28–32). He then takes twelve stones representing the twelve tribes of Israel and constructs the altar in Yahweh's name (cf. Joshua's monument of twelve stones in Josh. 4:1–9). Finally, he has a trench dug around the altar and has water poured over the sacrificed bull and wood three times. In this way he fills the trench and saturates the fuel for the sacrifice to symbolize the bounty of rain to come; this process serves as a way to demonstrate that no chance spark has lit his altar (much like a magician who announces to the audience that "I have nothing up my sleeve").

The solemnity of the occasion and Elijah's role are signaled to the audience by two narrative cues. First, the text specifically reports that Elijah presents his prayer to Yahweh "at the time of the offering of the oblation." The Baal priests have worked throughout the day to get an answer from their god, and that means that the time of Elijah's sacrifice is in conformance with the divinely ordained schedule of daily offerings to Yahweh (Exod. 29:38–46). The second cue is the use of the title "prophet" (Hebrew nābî') for Elijah. In point of fact, it is the only time the title is applied to him throughout the cycle of Elijah stories. When Elijah calls on Yahweh to demonstrate that the "God of Abraham, Isaac, and Israel" is the "God in Israel" and that Elijah is his prophetic

servant (1 Kings 18:36), his prayer follows established ritual. Yahweh's divine response is immediate: the sacrifice, the altar, and the water are all consumed by fire from heaven. Such a powerful act elicits two powerful emotions. The first is fear, which evokes a statement of awed submission by the people, "The LORD indeed is God!" (18:39). The second is anger, which leads to a massacre of the prophets of Baal (18:40). All that remains to complete the performance is for the rain to come, which it does after a sevenfold ritual is completed by Elijah and his servant (18:41–46). But Elijah has won only the battle, not the war. Jezebel remains a dangerous enemy to contend with, and when she threatens to kill Elijah, he runs away for fear of his life (19:2).

Elijah's flight highlights one of the curious aspects of his career. He is the consummate outsider. Originally he comes from Gilead, a Transjordanian region, outside the core territory of the kingdom of Israel. He has no permanent ties to any group or person other than a servant. He relies solely on God to feed him or to direct him to persons to care for his needs. In his flight from Mount Carmel, Elijah becomes the ultimate loner in a society that defines itself in terms of familial, economic, and political relationships.

Significantly, Elijah survives his journey to Mount Horeb (= Mount Sinai) only because an angel provides bread and water (1 Kings 19:4–8; cf. the provision of manna and quail to the Israelites in the wilderness in Exod. 16). His journey once again affords an opportunity for the text to link Elijah to Moses and furnishes the setting for the call narrative that is absent in the earlier portion of Elijah's narrative.

Elijah's call narrative on Mount Horeb is staged much like previous encounters with fugitives (cf. Adam and Eve in Gen. 3:8–13 and

Hagar in Gen. 16:7–12). He is addressed with a rhetorical question, "What are you doing here, Elijah?" (1 Kings 19:9). Such a question generally produces an excuse or a justification by the person addressed. Elijah explains that he has been working "zealously" for Yahweh but that he has now taken flight so that there will be at least one voice left to defend God (19:10).

What follows is a mystifying theophany in which the usual signs of power are rejected because they do not contain the essence of God's Spirit. Elijah experiences strong winds, earthquake, and fire; all are also depictions of Baal. But the prophet can perceive the presence of Yahweh only in the silence that follows all these manifestations (1 Kings 19:11–13). This may be because Baal is a storm-god and Yahweh is attempting to create a clear difference between them and show his superiority to Baal. It is also possible that this is an addition by a later editor whose theology has moved beyond simple natural events as signs for God and now wishes to show that Yahweh's presence is both universal and internal.

Whatever the case, God now again asks why Elijah has come to this place. A charge is given to the prophet to perform three acts that will transform Israel religiously and politically (1 Kings 19:15–16). First, he is to anoint Hazael as king of Aram (Syria). Second, he is to anoint Jehu as king over Israel. Third, he is to anoint Elisha as his prophetic successor.

As it turns out, Elijah performs only one of these tasks and leaves the other two for his successor. He designates Elisha as his successor by **casting his mantle** (a length of cloth that serves as a cloak) over Elisha's shoulders. The newly appointed prophet asks and is granted permission to tell his parents good-bye (contrast Jesus's response to the man called to service in Luke 9:61–62). Elisha then disappears from the

Use of Clothing as a Social Symbol

1 Kings 11:29–30: Ahijah removes his own new linen robe and tears it into twelve pieces to signify the division of the kingdom and Jeroboam's claim to rule ten of the twelve tribal districts.

Isa. 20:2: Isaiah graphically displays the danger faced by Judah by stripping off his clothing and walking about naked like a prisoner of war or a slave.

Jer. 13:1–11: Jeremiah removes his "linen belt" (Hebrew *ʾēzôr*) and buries it in the Euphrates riverbank as a signal that Judah's danger will come from that direction. The gesture is an indication that the people, like his piece of clothing, will be exiled in Mesopotamia on God's command.

narrative until 2 Kings 2, where he witnesses Elijah's miraculous departure from the earth.

The Elijah cycle is briefly interrupted at this point by the account of an unnamed prophet who, like Samuel, orders a king (Ahab) to destroy an enemy nation (see 1 Sam. 15). He then condemns the king for failing to complete the devastation of Aram and its king, Ben-hadad (1 Kings 20). The story serves as an apt precursor to 1 Kings 22, which ends with Ahab being killed in battle. However, these two chapters and their unequivocal denunciation of Ahab are superseded theologically by 1 Kings 21, which contains the fullest example of the Deuteronomistic Historian's use of the king's call-to-justice motif.

First Kings 21 contains the story of Naboth's vineyard. It begins with Ahab's desire to own a fine vineyard that adjoins his property. The owner, Naboth, refuses to sell because ownership and inheritance of the land are tied to Yahweh's covenantal promise. Jezebel then demonstrates once again the difference between Phoenician and Israelite royalty by obtaining the land for her husband through deceit and force. In collaboration with the elders of Naboth's hometown, she hires two false witnesses, has Naboth charged with treason and blasphemy, and has him executed, along with his family (2 Kings 9:26). Since the land is left without an heir, Ahab claims it.

At this point, the motif of the king's being called to justice becomes the dominant element in the narrative. As Ahab is stepping off his new property, Elijah confronts him with his sin and condemns Ahab's family to a terrible fate (1 Kings 21:17–24). The king is terrified by Elijah's curse and performs an act of contrition so complete that even Yahweh remarks on it: "Have you seen how Ahab has humbled himself before me?" (21:29). The result is that the punishment is to be deferred to the time of Ahab's successors.

The editors of this material apparently found themselves confronted with two endings to Ahab's story. First Kings 22 tells the story of Ahab's death, concluding with all the chilling aspects of Elijah's curse (e.g., dogs licking up his blood [1 Kings 21:19]). This seems to contradict what has just been resolved in 1 Kings 21, although note the gloss in 1 Kings 21:25–26 that precedes Ahab's repentance and that may have functioned as an alternative ending of that story. One possible solution to this literary incongruity is a decision on the part of the editors to include both stories rather than dispense with a narrative that explains how the wicked Ahab receives his justly deserved end.

The episode in 1 Kings 22 substitutes Micaiah for Elijah as the prophet "who never prophesies anything favorable about" Ahab. Micaiah is forced to withstand ridicule, must contradict the demonstrations staged by the four hundred court prophets of Ahab, and confronts two kings (Ahab and Jehoshaphat) enthroned before the gate of Samaria (22:10–11). In this version of Ahab's doom, Micaiah tells a tale of a "lying spirit" sent by Yahweh to "entice Ahab" to go to his death (22:19–23).

Micaiah's prophecy stands in direct conflic with the word of Ahab's four hundred cour prophets, who have been vehemently predict ing an Israelite victory. Faced with an exampl of cognitive dissonance (two conflicting bu equally plausible statements), Ahab tries to ti the odds in his favor. He orders that Micaia be imprisoned and then disguises himself as common soldier. Unfortunately for him, thi strategy fails. Ahab is mortally wounded, and his blood is lapped up by dogs as it drips from the floor of his chariot (22:29–38).

The cycle of Elijah stories continues with short episode in which Elijah continues to con demn Ahab's family for trusting in every goc except Yahweh (2 Kings 1:3–16). The comi cally dark story of three companies who ar sent to arrest the prophet and who fall victin to Yahweh's divine wrath may have been en tertaining, but it is also disquieting. Still, th transformation of armed men into piles of ash on the hillside must have added to the reputa tion of the prophet and magnifies the belief ir Yahweh's command of the powers of creation

As is only fitting for such a remarkable fig ure, Elijah's chronicle concludes with the story of his being transported to heaven (2 Kings

---

Using Symbols of Power and Significant Space

King Ahab positions himself physically and symbolically in order to control Micaiah's message. He sets the stage for their meeting and tries to overwhelm the prophet with symbols of royal power and by placing the event in a significant location (see italics for these items). When Micaiah arrives, he sees

Two *kings* (Ahab and Jehoshaphat) sitting on their *thrones* and wearing their *robes* of office.

The thrones are placed at the *gate* of Israel's *capital city* (Samaria), on a site that had once been a *threshing floor*.

Four hundred court prophets dancing about and crying out their prophecy that the kings will be victorious in the coming battle.

2:1–14). This narrative includes Elisha's transition as Elijah's successor and Elisha's receipt of Elijah's power. Elisha's new status as Elijah's successor is symbolized by his use of Elijah's mantle to cross the Jordan on dry land (cf. Joshua's crossing of the Jordan after he became the successor of Moses in Josh. 3). Elijah departs as mysteriously as he has arrived. The traditions that surround him have made him unique, especially the fact that he is only one of two persons (Enoch in Gen. 5:24) in the OT/HB who do not suffer death, and he appears along with Moses in the transfiguration (Matt. 17:1–9). In early Judaism, he becomes the precursor of the coming Messiah. Even today, an empty chair and a glass of wine are always left for him at the Jewish Passover celebration.

The Elisha Cycle

Upon his master's spectacular departure, Elisha immediately takes up Elijah's mantle of power. He assumes the prophet's responsibilities as the champion of Yahweh and as the chief critic of Israel's monarchs. The stories about Elisha give more attention to the common people than do those involving Elijah. Much of what is told about Elisha includes episodes in which he helps members of Israelite society or his own support network, the **sons of the prophets** (prophetic apprentices) or their dependents. In that sense there is less real narrative flow in the Elisha cycle than there is in the Elijah material. The way the episodes are woven together makes it seem that Elisha moves from one situation in which he performs a miracle to another (see inset below). The only extended episode in this series is the story of the Shunammite woman (2 Kings 4:8–37). There are parallels with Elijah's reviving the son of the widow of Zarephath (1 Kings 17:17–24). However, the Shunammite story centers more

---

Elisha's Miracles

- Crosses the Jordan River on dry land (2 Kings 2:13–14)*
- Purifies Jericho's water (2 Kings 2:19–22)
- Curses taunting boys at Bethel (2 Kings 2:23–24)
- Multiplies oil in a jar (2 Kings 4:1–7)*
- Revives Shunammite's son (2 Kings 4:18–37)*
- Purifies a pot of stew (2 Kings 4:38–41)
- Feeds one hundred men with just twenty loaves (2 Kings 4:42–44)
- Makes iron axhead float (2 Kings 6:1–7)
- His bones revive a dead man (2 Kings 13:20–21)

*Parallels a miracle of Elijah

---

on elements of the barren-wife motif, rewarding a prophetic supporter, and the woman's persistence in obtaining the prophet's help.

Elisha spends only part of his time directly confronting the kings or priests and is frequently portrayed as helping or encouraging the people of the land. A narrative like this is extremely unusual in what is otherwise a royal annal. Perhaps it functions as a vehicle to show how important the egalitarian ideal is to the Israelite editors. Certainly Elisha's concern for rewarding or protecting the members of his support group (especially in 2 Kings 4; 6:1–7) can be seen as a conscious attempt by the storyteller to demonstrate that the faithful will be cared for by Yahweh and his prophets.

In the cases in which Elisha deals with political matters and political leaders, his role is less confrontational than Elijah's. Instead, Elisha appears to serve as a catalyst for events that Yahweh has previously predicted (see the charges given to Elijah in 1 Kings 19:15–18). Thus, he travels to Syria and reluctantly designates Hazael, a Syrian general, as the new king of that country (2 Kings 8:7–15). Later, Elisha sends one of the "sons of the prophets" to Jehu, an Israelite general, and anoints him as Yahweh's chosen king (9:1–10). The result of both actions is war and murder. The prophet has set in motion the assassination of reigning kings in both countries (8:15). His actions result in a civil war in Israel that ends in a general purge of Ahab's family, highlighted by Jezebel's being thrown from a window as Jehu rides triumphantly into the city of Jezreel (9:30–37). Subsequently, the supporters of Ahab's family and the worshipers of Baal are massacred (9:14–10:27).

Only in the story of the campaign against Moab does Elisha assume the role of a condemning prophet (2 Kings 3). Here he travels with the combined armies of Jehoram, the son of Ahab, and Jehoshaphat of Judah. When their ill-conceived line of march takes them through the wilderness of Edom into dry country that cannot support the army, the prophet is called on to intervene with God and save them (3:12–13). Elisha is reluctant to act, but because the "righteous" king Jehoshaphat is present, he calls for a musician and subsequently enters a trance state. He then predicts life-giving water in the dry wadi bed, which eventually does come as a result of rain upstream, and promises ultimate success for their military expedition (3:13–20).

What is particularly significant about this episode is that it is a direct parallel to the story recounted in the Mesha Stele (see 2 Kings 3:4). King Mesha's inscription is composed from the Moabite viewpoint, and it describes a victory for Moab. Neither the prophet Elisha nor the desperate sacrifice of Mesha's son in the biblical account (3:26–27) are mentioned in Mesha's royal inscription.

One additional theme found in the Elisha cycle of stories is universalism. Both Elijah and Elisha demonstrate that Yahweh is a powerful God with majesty over all nations. In 2 Kings 5, it is left to a Syrian general to make a statement of absolute faith in the total supremacy

Mesha Stele

I am Mesha from Dibon, ruler of Moab. . . . Omri, ruler of Israel, invaded Moab year after year because Chemosh, the divine patron of Moab, was angry with his people. When the son of Omri succeeded him during my reign, he bragged: "I too will invade Moab." However, I defeated the son of Omri and drove Israel out of our land forever. Omri and his son ruled the Madaba plains for forty years, but Chemosh dwells there in my time. (OTPar³, 168)

of Yahweh above all gods. Naaman is a high-ranking military commander afflicted with leprosy. When all other avenues fail to provide a cure, Naaman takes the advice of his wife's Israelite slave girl and seeks an opportunity to consult Elisha. Some difficult diplomatic maneuvering is necessary to gain him safe passage into what is otherwise enemy territory, but

Figure 3.6. This eleventh-century-BCE basalt stele describes the great building projects of King Mesha and celebrates his victories over the Israelite kings, Ahab and Omri. (Baker Photo Archive, courtesy of the Louvre)

eventually he comes to Elisha's dwelling (5:5–9). Ironically, he never sees the prophet face-to-face. Instead, the prophet's servant, Gehazi, relays instructions to the general. The prophet's failure to appear personally violates proper etiquette. It also disappoints a high-status person who has been expecting an impressive prophetic encounter. As a result, the Syrian nearly storms off in anger. But his servants convince him to try the cure suggested by the prophet: to dip himself seven times in the Jordan River. Miraculously, he is cured of his leprosy and rushes back to reward Elisha. In his enthusiasm, Naaman states: "Now I know there is no God in all the earth except in Israel" (5:15).

Elisha refuses any payment, and the general asks him for a future consideration. It seems that as part of his job as adviser to the Syrian king, Naaman is required to participate in an annual religious ritual honoring the Syrian god Rimmon. Naaman assures the prophet that this duty will in no way conflict with his new devotion to Yahweh. He proves this by taking two mule-loads of Israelite soil with him back to Syria (2 Kings 5:17). Naaman's action is based on the belief that gods are localized within the lands in which they are worshiped. By taking Israelite soil back to Syria, Naaman believes he is physically taking the presence of Yahweh back to his country so that he can worship God there.

Elisha dies—unlike his master, Elijah—and his narrative concludes with a story nearly as mysterious as the one in the Elijah cycle. Apparently the site of Elisha's burial is forgotten. When the tomb is reopened for a new internment, the burial party is interrupted by a band of raiders. They abandon the body in their escape. When the corpse falls among Elisha's bones, the dead man revives, jumps from the tomb, and runs after his friends (2 Kings 13:20–21). Just as Elijah's mantle had been left behind and functioned as an object of power, so too do Elisha's bones.

STUDY QUESTIONS

1. Discuss the confrontation between Jeroboam and the unnamed prophet from Judah (1 Kings 13:1–10). Consider how the story contributes both to its own time setting and to the end of the monarchy in Josiah's reign (see 2 Kings 23:15–20).

2. Why is Ahab depicted as a strong king in Assyrian records and as such a weakling in the Bible (1 Kings 16:33; 21:1–4)?

3. Why does Elijah stage the contest with the Baal prophets on Mount Carmel (1 Kings 18:19–40)?

4. What are the most significant aspects of Elijah's theophany on Mount Horeb (1 Kings 19:9–18)? Why has this theophany been called an anti-Baal polemic?

5. How does the story of Naboth's vineyard fit into the king's call-to-justice motif (1 Kings 21)?

6. Why does cognitive dissonance occur in the story of Micaiah (1 Kings 22:5–28)?

7. What is the significance of Elisha's dealings with the "company of prophets" and the Shunammite woman, and why are they rewarded (1 Kings 4)?

8. In what ways are clothing used as objects of power in the Elijah/Elisha cycle of stories and in the story of Micaiah (1 Kings 19:19; 22:10; 2 Kings 2:8)?

9. Compare and contrast the events chronicled in 2 Kings 3 and the Mesha Stele, and discuss the importance of local perspective on these stories.

10. Why is the story of Naaman such a good example of the universalism theme (2 Kings 5)?

11. Why is so much space (fifteen chapters) in the Bible devoted to Elijah and Elisha?

4

The Late Monarchic Period

Political and Historical Overview

KEY POINTS

- Division of the kingdom weakened both Israel and Judah and left them easy prey for emerging superpowers.
- Israel's history is marked by political instability, coups, and Jeroboam's sin. Israel falls to the Assyrians in 721 BCE.
- Judah survives longer than Israel but eventually succumbs to Babylon, and much of its population is exiled.

The divided monarchy contributes to a general lack of stability in Syria-Palestine in the period after 900 BCE. Although Judah benefits from a stable system of hereditary rule, its meager natural resources and population are too limited to allow it to have a significant effect on the region as a whole. As a result, for much of the period from 900 to 750 BCE it is dominated politically by the northern kingdom. In the north, the monarchy is continually disrupted by military coups and assassinations (see 1 Kings 16:15–30; 2 Kings 9:14–27; 15:10), leaving the government and the people without any real sense of stability. This plays into the hands of the reemerging superpower nations

of Egypt and Assyria. While Israel and Judah exhaust themselves in petty wars with Syria (Aram) and the nations of the Transjordanian region (1 Kings 20; 22; 2 Kings 3; 6–7), the superpowers consolidate their power at home and prepare to expand into Syria-Palestine. The last period of relative independence for Israel and Judah comes in the reigns of Israel's king Jeroboam II (786–746 BCE) and Judah's king Uzziah (782–740 BCE), and this is made possible by the conquest of Syria by the Assyrians.

The foreign policies of Israel and Judah also prove to be shortsighted. After 740 BCE, the military might of the Assyrian king Tiglath-Pileser III (Pul, 2 Kings 15:19) transforms the political character of the entire region. The Assyrian war machine first enters the area in 853 BCE. On that occasion, their king Shalmaneser III is defeated at the Battle of Qarqar by a coalition led by kings from Syria-Palestine, including Ahab of Israel. After Shalmaneser III defeats the Syrians in 841 BCE, however, Jehu, king of Israel, is forced to pay tribute to the Assyrians, as recorded in the Black Obelisk Inscription.

Map 4.1. Late Monarchic Period

therefore Israel and Syria combine their forces to drive him from his throne. In desperation, Ahaz allies himself with the Assyrians (against the advice of the prophet Isaiah; Isa. 7:1–9), and this leads to the defeat of the rebels. However, the price Ahaz pays for Assyrian help is full submission to the Assyrian Empire. He even introduces Assyrian worship practices

Black Obelisk of Shalmaneser III

Hazael, king of Damascus, mustered a large army, and fortified Mt. Senir. I fought and defeated him, killing 16,020 of his soldiers. I took 1,121 chariots, 470 horses and his supply train. He ran from the battle to save himself, and I besieged his capital city of Damascus.

Jehu, king of Israel, ransomed his life with silver, with gold bowls, vases, cups and pitchers, with tin, a royal scepter, and spears. (*OTPar*[3], 180–81)

Figure 4.1. The Black Obelisk of Shalmaneser III (ninth century BCE) depicts Jehu's payment of tribute to the Assyrians. (Baker Photo Archive, courtesy of the British Museum)

From that time onward, the Assyrians repeatedly raid Syria-Palestine, devastating large areas and massacring entire city populations. Situated on the major trade routes, Syria, Israel, and the Philistine city-states are soon absorbed into the growing Assyrian Empire as petty vassal states.

These newly established vassal states are always restive under foreign rule. With the encouragement of Egypt they repeatedly revolt. In the midst of these political tensions, in 736 BCE, the kings of Israel and Syria precipitate the Syro-Ephraimite war. Their plan is to reconstitute the coalition of small states in order to drive out the Assyrians. However, King Ahaz of Judah refuses to join their revolt, and into the temple in Jerusalem to show his loyalty (2 Kings 16:1–18). He constructs an Assyrian-type altar, adopts Assyrian sacrificial rituals, and removes cult objects previously used in the worship of Yahweh from the temple in Jerusalem. The explanation given in the text for these actions is simple: "He did this because of the king of Assyria" (16:18b). The Deuteronomistic Historian's conclusion is that Ahaz's **syncretistic** practices (using borrowed cultural and religious ideas) are a sign that he has chosen to follow the practices of the kings of Israel rather than his ancestor David (16:2–4). The editors of the royal annal are not concerned with politics, only with the king's violation of the covenant.

Assyrian patience with Israel finally comes to an end as a result of a revolt by Israel's King Hoshea in 722 BCE. Rather than leave such disruptive forces in place, the Assyrian king Sargon II takes the drastic measure of destroying Israel's capital at Samaria in 721. Subsequently, he orders the deportation of a large portion of the population to some distant part of the Assyrian empire. There is no mention of these exiles returning, and the history of the northern kingdom ends at this point (2 Kings 17:1–6).

The kingdom of Judah generally has more effective leadership and has only a couple of instances in which its rulers are assassinated (2 Kings 11; 14:17–19). Of course, Judah also faces the potential for extinction at the hands of the Assyrians. However, their lesser importance to that empire and stronger leadership on the part of King Hezekiah (727–697 BCE) allows Judah to outlive the Assyrians. The death of the Assyrian emperor Sargon II in 705 BCE gives Hezekiah his chance to free Judah from direct Assyrian control (2 Chron. 32:3–6, 28–29). He briefly ignites a political and religious reform movement that is designed to strengthen Jerusalem's role as the seat of power. Among his preparations for the coming confrontation with Assyria, Hezekiah reinforces Jerusalem's defenses by constructing the Siloam water tunnel (2 Kings 20:20). He also attempts to establish alliances with surrounding states in an effort to create a united front against the Assyrians. The tenuous nature of these alliances, however, can be seen in Hezekiah's refusal to join the Philistine-led Ashdod revolt in 711 BCE. His hesitation to join the revolt may have been influenced by the warning he receives from the prophet Isaiah (see Isa. 20).

Still, Hezekiah's efforts to restore Judah's autonomy could not be overlooked by the Assyrians. As a result, they repeatedly invade Judah and destroy many small cities, including the major fortress city of Lachish. Archaeological investigations have uncovered destruction layers in nearly every city and town site associated with this time period. It is likely that these layers of ash and other debris can be attributed to the Assyrian campaigns. A written record of the events is contained in the propagandistic royal annals of the Assyrian king Sennacherib. He proudly boasts that during the year 701 BCE he captures forty-six cities and enslaves more than 200,000 people (an

---

Josiah's Reform

There are two accounts of Josiah's reform in the biblical text, 2 Chron. 34:1–35:27 and 2 Kings 22:1–23:30. The late-fifth-century Chronicles account describes the reform in three stages (2 Chron. 34:1–8). The sixth-century Deuteronomistic Historian's account in 2 Kings describes the entire reform as having only a single stage. The differences between the two may be traced to the Deuteronomist's closeness in time to Josiah and to the **Chronicler**'s desire to create an ideal, David-like figure out of Josiah. It is also possible that the three-stage account in Chronicles

provided below is the result of the Chronicler's special interest in the Jerusalem temple, the priesthood, and religious reform in the postexilic period.

- Stage 1: In the eighth year of Josiah's reign (632 BCE), when Josiah is sixteen years old, he begins to seek the God of David (2 Chron. 34:3).
- Stage 2: In the twelfth year of Josiah's reign (628 BCE), when Josiah is twenty years old, he purges Judah and Jerusalem of the high places, *Asherim* (cult

objects symbolizing the pagan goddess Asherah), altars of the Baals, and other elements of the worship of foreign gods (2 Chron. 34:3).

- Stage 3: In the eighteenth year of Josiah's reign (622 BCE), when Josiah is twenty-six years old, he completes the purge of pagan worship and orders the renovation of the temple; a biblical-like scroll is found, the covenant is renewed, and the Passover is celebrated (2 Chron. 34:8–35:19).

---

inflated number given the likely size of the population). The biblical account of the siege of Jerusalem credits the miraculous survival of the city to divine intervention (2 Kings 19:32–37; Isa. 37:36–38). But the ransom paid by Hezekiah, also mentioned in Sennacherib's annals, as well as the internal politics of the Assyrian Empire and the appearance of an Egyptian army, may be the primary reasons for lifting the siege. Second Kings 19:37, referring to a second siege, suggests that Sennacherib succumbs to court intrigue and is murdered by his sons upon his return to Nineveh. However, the Assyrian king's death does not come until several years later (680 BCE).

The destruction of the northern kingdom by the Assyrian king Sargon II in 721 BCE, the devastation of Judah's cities by Assyrian invasions, and Hezekiah's death force Judah into a state of quiet vassalage. No prophetic voice is heard during the long reign of King Manasseh (697–642 BCE). Only when civil war and poor leadership cause the Assyrian Empire to begin to crumble in the face of assaults by the opportunistic Babylonians and Medes is Judah once again able to assert a

measure of independence. King Josiah's reign (640–609 BCE) is marked by the inauguration of a religious and political reform movement similar to that of his great-grandfather Hezekiah. Josiah's reform is designed to eliminate the worship of all foreign gods and to expand his kingdom into what had been the northern kingdom of Israel. Like Hezekiah, Josiah makes a concerted attempt to centralize all power and authority in the city of Jerusalem (2 Kings 23:1–14).

According to the account in 2 Kings, Josiah's reform begins in his eighteenth year and is carried out by a group of priests from the city of Anathoth, including Hilkiah, Shaphan, and Ahikam (2 Kings 22:3–13; 2 Chron. 34:20). Their intent and that of the king is to restore the powers of the monarchy and of the Jerusalem priesthood with themselves as its leaders. To do this, they institute a legal code similar to that found in Deut. 12–26, a code that sets Jerusalem apart as the only true place of sacrifice and worship for the people (hence it is sometimes called Josiah's Deuteronomic reform). But all vestiges of Canaanite and Assyrian worship in the land have to be eliminated first. To ensure that this becomes a national effort, the high places and local altars are destroyed, the seasonal religious festivals are localized in the capital, and the service of the Levitical priesthood is restricted to the precincts of the temple in Jerusalem (2 Kings 23:4–20).

Such a radical reform could not be put into effect overnight. Long years of polytheistic religious activity by the people would have made it difficult to enforce the reforms. Even with the backing of the female prophet Huldah (2 Kings 22:14–20), opposition continues to exist within Judah. Presumably there is also resistance in the areas of Samaria where Josiah attempts to extend his influence, such as Bethel (23:15–20). Archaeological evidence from this period points to the reinforcement of Judah's borders by Josiah's government, but evidence of his religious reform is more difficult to find. For instance, the dismantled altars from the sanctuary at Arad that have been cited as proof of Josiah's efforts may date to Hezekiah's time. Few deposits of sacrificial remains at cultic sites derive from this period. But Josiah's reform is enforced for only the thirteen years prior to his death in the battle of Megiddo against Pharaoh Neco II in 609 BCE (23:29–30).

Josiah's death spells the end for most of his reforms and inaugurates a new era of submission to the superpowers. First, Egypt claims much of Syria-Palestine after the defeat of the Assyrians at the battle of Carchemish in 605 BCE. This means a new foreign master and the appointment of a puppet king for Judah. Josiah's son and immediate successor, Jehoahaz, is taken hostage to Egypt, and his brother Eliakim is put on the throne. Eliakim's status as the dutiful servant of the Egyptians is graphically portrayed when the

pharaoh has his name changed to Jehoiakim (2 Kings 23:34; see other name changes in Gen. 17:1–16; 32:22–28).

What follows proves to be the last days of Judah's monarchy. A series of political mistakes and revolts lead the superpowers to crush the troublesome nation. The sequence of events begins with another change of masters. In 604 BCE, the Babylonian king Nebuchadnezzar wrests Syria-Palestine from the Egyptians, and Jehoiakim suddenly finds himself a Babylonian vassal (2 Kings 24:1). Perhaps because of Egyptian promises of aid, Jehohiakim revolts three years later and temporarily resumes his role under the Egyptian hegemony. This arrangement ends in 598 BCE, when Nebuchadnezzar once again invades Judah. He lays siege to Jerusalem and captures the city in 597 BCE. This event marks the first time that Jerusalem has fallen to a siege since David's time.

It is during this period that the prophet Jeremiah emerges and condemns Jehoiakim's policies (Jer. 36:27–31). He also denounces the reliance of the people of Jerusalem on the temple of Yahweh as a guarantee of salvation from any threat (7:1–15; 26:1–6). After Nebuchadnezzar's successful siege of the city, the Babylonian king takes Jehoiachin, the son of Jehoiakim, to Babylon as a hostage along with a group of Judah's leaders and priests (2 Kings 24:10–17). Nebuchadnezzar then installs the last of Josiah's sons, Mattaniah, as his puppet king and changes his name to Zedekiah (2 Kings 24:17).

Again there is a period of relative quiet as Jerusalem licks its wounds. However, in the ninth year of his reign, Zedekiah revolts (probably again under the urging of Egypt; Jer. 37:7). Realizing that this source of continual irritation and rebellion on his borders has to be silenced, Nebuchadnezzar chooses to destroy Jerusalem. While Jeremiah repeatedly urges the people to surrender to the Babylonians (21:1–10; 38:17–18), Zedekiah continues to hold out until the city falls to Nebuchadnezzar's army in 587 BCE. The last reigning king of Judah is forced to watch the execution of his sons, and then his eyes are gouged out (39:6–7). The only remaining member of the royal house, Jehoiachin, continues to live in exile and dies in Babylon without an heir (Jer. 52:31–34).

The fall of Jerusalem and the Babylonian exile spell the end of the Davidic monarchy. When a portion of the exiles returns after 538 BCE, the restored community, now called Yehud by the Persians, is ruled by foreign officials, and its religious activities are monitored by an increasingly powerful priesthood. As we will see in a later section of this textbook, the exile period transforms Israelite religion into an early form of Judaism and creates a sense of Jewish identity that helps the people survive their social dislocation.

STUDY QUESTIONS

1. In what ways are Israel and Judah influenced by the growth of Assyrian hegemony?
2. Why is Manasseh considered the worst king in Judah's history (2 Kings 21:1–18)?
3. Describe the basic elements of Josiah's reform, and then discuss what will be the aftermath of his reform and the centralization of worship in Jerusalem (2 Chron. 34:6–35:27; 2 Kings 22:1–23:30).
4. What is the significance of Nebuchadnezzar's capture of Jerusalem in 597 and his destruction of the city in 587 (2 Kings 24:8–25:21)?

Prophets in the Late Monarchic Period

In the canon of Scripture, the prophetic books of the Bible are not arranged in chronological order. Instead, the major prophets (Isaiah, Jeremiah, and Ezekiel) are followed by books ascribed to ten minor prophets. Such an arrangement can cause difficulties for those who attempt to read the Bible from cover to cover. Therefore we have rearranged them in our discussion to reflect their historical context and chronological sequence. The prophetic books contain a compendium of different literary genres (poetry, narrative, songs, proverbs, oracles, and laments). Their content can be compared with the data found in the books of Kings that have been shaped by the Deuteronomistic Historian's account of Israel's history. However, the message of the prophets is more concerned with the theological underpinning of the people's covenantal obligations to Yahweh. Even though the prophets operate within the social and political context of their time, their primary mission is to bring the people back to God and the covenant and not to support a particular king or political policy.

In working through the prophetic materials, certain cautions are necessary. The prophets, their audience, and subsequent editors are more familiar with terminology, place names, and events than are modern readers. For example, there are several names in the text for the northern kingdom of Israel (see below). The choice of a particular name may be associated with a subtle point being made by the prophet, or it may be poetic license. In any case, it is always good to have a Bible dictionary or some other reference work handy to assist the reader (see our section at the end of this textbook on reference works).

Terms Used for the Northern Kingdom

The Hebrew prophets use several names for the northern kingdom of Israel. As social insiders, the ancient audience would have been aware of this and would have appreciated the meaning tied to the place name used by a prophet.

Israel: This is the official political term for the northern kingdom after the division of the united monarchy and prior to the fall of its capital, Samaria, to the Assyrians in 721 BCE (1 Kings 12:20–2 Kings 17:23). After 721, Israel is once again employed as a collective term for all of the Israelites in the land (Ps. 81:8; Isa. 43:1; Mal. 1:1).

Joseph: The Joseph tribes, identified with his two sons Manasseh and Ephraim, are collectively identified by some prophets with the northern kingdom (Ezek. 37:16; Amos 5:6; Obad. 1:18).

Ephraim: The younger of the two sons of Joseph, his name is equated with the northern kingdom, and this probably is based on the dominance of this tribe over the other northern tribes (Isa. 7:8; Hosea 9:8).

Jacob: The ancestor whose sons become the founders of the twelve tribes of Israel is occasionally equated with the ten tribes that

comprise the northern kingdom, just as the southern kingdom is referred to as Jacob's son Judah. These names are also associated with the geographical and political divisions of the land (Isa. 2:5–6; 10:20; Mic. 2:12). After 721 BCE, the names Jacob and Israel refer to all Israelites (Ps. 14:7; Nah. 2:2; Mal. 3:6).

Samaria: The capital of the northern kingdom, Samaria is occasionally synonymous with the nation itself (Isa. 36:19).

Keep in mind that each prophetic book has been edited into its received form. Therefore, these books should be analyzed as collections of sayings, stories, and prophecies rather than as cogent narratives of events. There are few personal details given about the prophets, and in no case is the full life story of a prophet provided for the reader. These characters step on stage and function as mediators, bringing God's message to the people in times of crisis. They are a reflection of God's intention to spare the righteous remnant while punishing those who do not respect or obey the covenant.

The Book of Amos

KEY POINTS

- Although he is from Judah, Amos is sent to Israel to prophesy.
- Amos condemns the Israelites for their violations of social justice.
- Amos condemns the Israelites for their hollow worship practices.

Chronologically, Amos is the first of the eighth-century prophets. His ministry dates to the period between 800 and 750 BCE. He

is described as a farmer from a small village, Tekoa, in the southern kingdom of Judah. There is no indication that he is a Levite or is trained as a religious professional prior to being called as a prophet. Interestingly, he is instructed to go and prophesy in the northern kingdom of Israel rather than to his own people. The only other individual among the classical prophets who is required to go to another country to carry out his mission is Jonah (Ezekiel is already in Mesopotamia when he is called; Elisha does take a trip to Syria to name Hazael the new king of Syria [2 Kings 8:7–15], but this is not a major part of his mission as a prophet). It is unlikely that Amos has ever traveled more than a few miles from his village, possibly going to Jerusalem but never into Israel. That he must now travel to that neighboring kingdom and specifically to one of its cultic centers makes his work difficult. Although he speaks the same language, his clothing, mannerisms, local dialect, and attitudes cause him to stand out, and as we will see, make him an object of ridicule in some circles.

Amos's status as an outsider sets the tone for his message and attitude. He is an angry

131

Figure 4.2. Jeroboam set up golden calves at Dan and Bethel so the people of Israel would not have to travel to Jerusalem to worship YHWH. This is the cultic site or high place at Dan. (Baker Photo Archive)

prophet, condemning the people of Israel for their social injustices and their unorthodox worship practices. There is little compassion shown in his statements, and he appears relieved to be able to deliver his message and then return home.

When a foreigner comes and speaks in a condemning manner, both the message and the messenger are often dismissed by the audience. Thus Amos wisely begins with a rhetorical strategy that is designed to draw a crowd, not drive the people away (Amos 1:3–2:8). After all, he wants them to hear what he has to say. He cleverly announces the coming of divine judgment on each of Israel's enemy neighbors, using a repetitive opening phrase: "For three transgressions of _____, and for four, I will not revoke the punishment." The blank is filled in geographically, starting in the northeast with Damascus, and then moving south to Gaza (Philistia), north to Tyre (Phoenicia), and east to the Transjordanian kingdoms of Edom, Ammon, and Moab. Even Judah and Jerusalem are condemned. After each recitation it can be

expected that the growing crowd would cheer and urge Amos to continue—at least until he reaches his intended climax, the condemnation of Israel (Amos 2:6–16).

Social Injustice Theme. The list of charges against Israel, starting in Amos 2, centers on violations of the egalitarian ideal that is so often championed by the prophets. Amos

Amos's Use of Geography

Amos uses a geographic oracle to take his audience full circle around Israel's neighbors, touching on each nation, drawing the audience into his message, and then denouncing Israel for its sins.

Amos 1:3–5 condemns Aram (Syria), located northeast of Israel, for its incursions into the Israelite Transjordanian territory in Gilead.

Amos 1:6–8 condemns Gaza, a Philistine city-state on Judah's southwestern border, and uses the city as a collective term for all of Philistia.

Amos 1:9 condemns Tyre, the Phoenician sea port on the Mediterranean coast north of Israel.

Amos 1:11 condemns Edom, the most southern of the Transjordanian kingdoms.

Amos 1:13 condemns Ammon, the Transjordanian kingdom next to Gilead.

Amos 2:1–2 condemns Moab, a Transjordanian kingdom that often rivals Israel's power.

Amos 2:4 condemns Judah for rejecting God's law.

prophesies during the time when Israel is ruled by Jeroboam II (786–746 BCE) and the nation is experiencing a temporary period of peace and prosperity. The capture of Damascus by the Assyrian king Adad-nirari III in 802 BCE eliminates Israel's chief economic and military rival and gives Israelite merchants a period of freedom to trade in previously restricted areas. The change of fortunes for Israel's upper class and well-to-do merchants is not shared with the general populace. It is the blatant lack of concern by these wealthy merchants and landowners that raises Amos's ire and forms the basis for his social-injustice theme.

Amos spends much of his time condemning social injustices such as the bribery of judges (Amos 2:6a), the sale of persons into debt servitude for default on small loans (Amos 2:6b), and the cheating of customers with false balances and contaminated bags of grain (8:5–6). He also levels charges at the greedy merchants who cannot wait for the Sabbath or other religious holidays to end so that they can resume business (Amos 8:5a).

One specific abuse that he highlights is the failure to return the garments of day laborers (Amos 2:8). The wealthy, who employ these men and take their outer robes as a guarantee of a full day's work, are required under the law to return them at night so the men will

> ### An Example of Emendation
> The Hebrew word *harmon* in Amos 4:3 is untranslatable. It does not appear in any other biblical text or any nonbiblical text. The single occurrence of a word in a language is called a **hapax legomenon**. The lack of context or comparison with other related languages makes a *hapax* a real problem for translators. Scholars sometimes deal with this problem by employing an **emendation**, a suggested alternative reading of the text that makes better sense in the context. In this case, the suggestion is to change one similarly shaped Hebrew letter and transform *harmon* into *hadmon,* which means dung heap, the place where the bodies of criminals were left unburied. The text of Amos 4:3 would then read, "You shall be flung out into the dung heap."

have a covering against the cold (Exod. 22:26–27). Here, however, not only are the garments not returned, but the rich sleep on them before the altars of false gods in the hope of obtaining a divine message while they dream.

In like manner, the twelfth-century-BCE Egyptian sage Amenemope includes in his list of admonitions that the wise person is not to "take bribes from the powerful and oppress the poor for their sake" (OTPar³, 300; cf. Ps. 15:5). Amos spares no one in his venomous speeches, even describing the wives of these greedy merchants as sleek "cows of Bashan," who fatten themselves indulgently on other people's grain and then call for more. A just sentence for their Marie Antoinette-like attitude will be imposed when the city of Samaria falls and their impaled bodies are dragged through the breaches in the walls and flung unburied into a dung heap (Amos 4:1–3; see inset).

Hypocrisy Theme. The second major theme in the book of Amos is based on the blatant hypocrisy of the people while engaging in their worship practices. These familiar rituals are described as useless because the Israelites perform them without a true sense of faith in

> ### Social Injustice in Extrabiblical Sources
> The charges made by Amos were unfortunately not uncommon in the business practices of his time. The seventh-century-BCE Yavneh-Yam inscription, found written on a piece of pottery (ostracon), details another case in which a working man fulfills his tasks but the foreman refuses to return his robe. The day laborer is forced to write to the local governor to intervene on his behalf. His plea certifies, "All my fellow workers will testify—all those who work in the heat of the day—... that I am not guilty of any breach of contract" (OTPar³, 355–56).

Hollow Worship Condemned

I hate, I despise your festivals,
   and I take no delight in your solemn assemblies.
Even though you offer me your burnt offerings and
      grain offerings,
   I will not accept them;
and the offerings of well-being of your fatted animals
   I will not look upon.
Take away from me the noise of your songs;
   I will not listen to the melody of your harps.
But let justice roll down like waters,
   and righteousness like an everflowing stream.
         (Amos 5:21–24)

When you come to appear before me,
   who asked this from your hand?
   Trample my courts no more;
bringing offerings is futile;
   incense is an abomination to me.
New moon and Sabbath and calling of convocation—
   I cannot endure solemn assemblies with iniquity.
Your new moons and your appointed festivals
   my soul hates;
they have become a burden to me,
   I am weary of bearing them. (Isa. 1:12–14)

Of what use to me is frankincense that comes from
Sheba,
   or sweet cane from a distant land?
Your burnt offerings are not acceptable,
   nor are your sacrifices pleasing to me. (Jer. 6:20)

Israel and Judah, Bethel is the place to which Amos takes his message. The cultic site has been established as one of two major centers of worship by Jeroboam I when the kingdoms divided. In this way, Amos can condemn the rival temple and make it clear that Bethel is no substitute for Jerusalem. At one point, Amos uses extremely sarcastic speech, "encouraging" the people to come to Bethel, to make their offerings and tithes there, and then to have the amounts published for all to hear about (4:4–5). In the face of such false service, the prophet speaks of Yahweh's rejection of Israel's worship as unacceptable and a raucous "noise" to God's ears (5:21–24).

Naturally such statements cannot be left unchallenged by the king's supporters. Amaziah, the high priest of Bethel, confronts Amos, stating that he has no right to speak in the "king's sanctuary" (Amos 7:10–12). Amos acknowledges that he lacks any establishment credentials, saying, "I am no prophet, nor a prophet's son" (7:14). Instead, he cites the simple call that he has received from Yahweh

Yahweh and often mix them with Canaanite practices (syncretism). Some of these religious practices had been performed for generations. The Israelites and the Canaanites engaged in many of the same sacrificial and festive rituals, and it would not have been uncommon for them to worship the same gods. However, what Amos is particularly concerned about is the rote performance of ritual, chant, and sacrifice with the expectation that the gods can be manipulated into fulfilling human needs and desires. Amos sets a tone here that will be followed in style and vocabulary by Isaiah and Jeremiah when they condemn similar practices as hollow worship (see inset below).

Because of its association with Jeroboam's sin and its proximity to the border between

Geographic Reiteration: Bethel

Bethel is mentioned seventy-one times in the biblical narrative, and this is second only to Jerusalem. Its central location gave Bethel the opportunity to rise to prominence during the emergence of the monarchy. The transference of political power, the installation of the ark of the covenant, and the construction of the temple in Jerusalem eclipse Bethel's importance until Jeroboam makes it one of his two major temple cities.

   Gen. 12:8: Abram builds an altar at Bethel, calls on the Lord's name, stakes out the promised land.

   Gen. 28:19: Jacob renames Luz to be Bethel as a result of his theophanic dream.

   1 Sam. 7:16: Bethel is part of Samuel's judicial circuit along with Gilgal and Mizpah.

   1 Kings 12:29–33: Jeroboam appoints Dan and Bethel as his royal shrines.

   Amos 5:5: Amos urges people to seek God and live, but "do not seek Bethel," for "Bethel shall come to nothing."

to leave his fields and come to Israel to speak his message (7:15). In this way Amos reasserts the position that prophets are free agents, working directly for Yahweh and not requiring any certification other than the truth of their message.

Throughout this prophetic book, Amos prefers to use the pastoral images typical of his country background. For instance, he describes the people as "summer fruit" (8:2)—sweet and full of initial promise but quick to decay and to become worthless. Perhaps reflecting his origins in Judah and his disdain for his northern neighbor, Amos provides little hope for the nation of Israel. There is only a brief, almost offhand use of the remnant theme in Amos 5. Here he tells the people to "seek God and live" so that Yahweh will have an excuse to relent and lessen their punishment (5:4, 6). Though other prophets use similar pleas (Isa. 55:6; Hosea 10:12; Zeph. 2:3), Amos does not elaborate on his admonition. While it seems that this brief glimmer of hope is all he will hold out to them, there is a section in Amos 9:11–15 describing the restoration of the Davidic kingdom. However, it is probably a later addition to the book.

As is typical of the prophetic books, there is no mention of Amos's career after he delivers his message in Bethel. Presumably he returns to his village and his fields. If the experience of serving as a prophet has any further effect on him, the text does not describe it. It is not the individual prophet who matters—only the message.

STUDY QUESTIONS

1. Is Amos's negative and unsympathetic attitude toward his audience simply the result of his being in a foreign land (Amos 1:1; 4:1–5; 5:10–13)?

2. What do you learn about the geography of Israel's neighbors in his repetitious pattern of speech in Amos 1–2?

3. Why does Amaziah react so harshly to Amos's message at Bethel? What qualifications does Amos have to become a prophet (Amos 7:10–15)? What are Amaziah's qualifications?

4. Why does Amos keep referring to those "who trample the head of the poor into the dust of the earth" (Amos 2:7; 5:11; 8:4)?

5. What does it mean to "sleep on garments taken in pledge" (Amos 2:8), and how does this compare with the Yavneh-Yam inscription?

6. What does Amos 5:21–24 mean when it refers to "hollow worship"? Compare this statement with 1 Sam. 15:22–23 and with Isa. 1:13.

The Book of Hosea

KEY POINTS

- Hosea's urgency reflects the growing danger to Israel from Assyria.
- Hosea uses a marriage metaphor to compare his unfaithful wife with Israel's idolatry.
- Hosea's knowledge theme condemns priests and kings for their failure to teach the people about the covenant.

Although he is a contemporary of Amos, the prophet Hosea's message is spoken to his own people in Israel. While harsh in its condemnation of the people's faults, Hosea offers more hope than Amos that reconciliation with Yahweh is still possible. The urgency with which he speaks is reflective of the fact that Hosea speaks at the end of an era. The reign of King Jeroboam II is about to end, and his successors are weaklings who fight among themselves. Assyria, under the emperor Tiglath-Pileser III

Figure 4.3. Tiglath-Pileser III, from Calah (Nimrud), ca. eighth century BCE. (Baker Photo Archive, courtesy of the British Museum)

(745–727 BCE), now emerges as a real international threat and quickly moves to expand its hegemony. Syria-Palestine is a prime target as a buffer between the Assyrian Empire and Egyptian territories. Caught up in the struggle between superpowers, Israel first becomes a client state and then a subservient vassal state. The Israelites are pressured to adopt Assyrian customs and religious practices as a way to prove their loyalty to the dominant culture. Not content to remain a subject people, and after a series of revolts led by the smaller states in Syria-Palestine, Samaria is destroyed and the people of Israel are deported in 720 BCE. It is during this desperate period that Hosea begins to speak. However, he almost ignores the Assyrian threat and instead concentrates on what he perceives as the root causes of Israel's problems: idolatry and the abuse of the land's resources. The lack of concern over the Assyrians may be a reflection of the editing of the material after the destruction of Israel. Or it could be the single-minded approach of a

prophet for whom right behavior toward Yahweh outweighs all else.

Structurally, the book of Hosea is disjointed. Only the first three chapters provide a well-developed theme, and the rest is comprised of a mixture of ideas, admonitions, and evaluations of Israel's problems that reflect this late period of its history. It is likely that what has been pieced together represents only a portion of Hosea's message, but the turbulence of the times is clearly demonstrated in what remains for us to examine.

Idolatry Theme. Hosea first traces his principal theme in a tightly woven, enacted prophecy involving his marriage to a woman named Gomer (Hosea 1–2). The passage, however, raises some important questions. First, is Hosea a Levite? If so, he would not be able to function as a priest since the sin of Jeroboam excludes him from the working priesthood. Such a restriction would have colored his attitude toward the non-Levitical priests who served in Israel's shrines and the kings who supported them. This attitude will be explored in more detail below. Second, is Gomer a prostitute before Hosea marries her? If so, then the tension between his prophetic role and his priestly background would be increased because a Levite is forbidden by law to marry a prostitute (see Lev. 21:14–15). However, if she becomes unfaithful only after they are married, then the metaphorical equation between Gomer and Israel is more appropriate. The resolute faith of Abraham, who had first received the covenant promise from God (Gen. 12:1–4), is transformed in later generations, and God repeatedly laments that Israel is a "stiff-necked people" (Exod. 32:9; 33:5; 34:9) who "turn to other gods" (Hosea 3:1). There is no consensus among scholars on either issue. Certainly it is not necessary for Hosea to have been a Levite for the metaphor to work. However, the social and religious context in which he speaks does suggest that he is an advocate, if not a member, of the Levitical community.

The marriage metaphor ties Gomer's promiscuity to Israel's blatant idolatry. Hosea represents literally and metaphorically the long-suffering husband (God) who laments his wife's (Israel's) actions and finally decides to dissolve the covenant between them. Gomer's chasing after other lovers becomes a metaphor for Israel's worship of the Baals and the Israelites' misuse of the land given to them by Yahweh as part of the covenant (see Ezek. 16:15–58 for another example of this theme).

While this metaphorical understanding is the most common interpretation of this passage, some interpreters have wrongly concluded that Hosea's physical abuse of his wife and his children (Hosea 2:4–5) provides them with the justification for similar action in modern relationships as well. This is a perversion of the meaning of the text. Hosea 1–3 is not a story about the submission of wives to their husbands, nor is it a story giving license to husbands to brutalize their wives for real or imagined transgressions.

The marriage between Hosea and Gomer produces three children, each of whom is given a symbolic name, another form of enacted prophecy.

Jezreel ("God sows"): The first child's name is intended to evoke the memory of the place, the Valley of Jezreel, where Jehu's dynasty defeated Ahab's dynasty and took the throne of Israel (2 Kings 9:15–26). It reminds the reigning king of Jehu's House that he received his power from Yahweh's intervention (9:1–3). It is a threat that God's favor will be withdrawn and the king's authority will be taken away (Hosea 13:11). Furthermore, the Jezreel Valley

---

Hosea's Marriage Metaphor

In the marriage metaphor found in Hosea 1–2, the prophet is instructed to "take for yourself a wife of whoredom and have children of whoredom" (1:2). The metaphor assumes that

Hosea = Yahweh   Gomer = Israel   Unfaithfulness = Idolatry

---

is one of the most fertile areas in Israel. The threats by Yahweh to "take back my grain . . . and my wine in its season" (2:9) suggest both famine and political unrest.

Lo-ruhamah ("Not pitied"): This daughter's name speaks to the level of the current social injustice in which the plight of the poor and the weak is not pitied (see Hosea 4:2; 7:1–3; 10:13; 12:7–8). Yahweh now warns that Israel will receive no pity when the time for its punishment arrives (see 2:4).

Lo-ammi ("Not my people"): This third child, a son, is given a name that signifies a terrible rejection of Israel (see Hosea 13:14–16 for the devastation to come). It negates Israel's pride as God's chosen people. The covenant had assured them that Yahweh would provide them with land and children (the "husband's" gifts of grain, wine, and oil in 2:8–9). Their unfaithfulness in maintaining their allegiance to Yahweh, expressed in ascribing their abundant harvests to Baal, has destroyed this agreement (2:13). As a result, when they finally seek the Lord, "they will not find him" (5:6). The name "Not my people" also suggests that Hosea suspects that the child is not his.

In the face of Gomer's continued unfaithfulness, Hosea punishes her severely, first secluding her and eventually driving her from his home and divorcing her (Hosea 2:3–12). During the effort at reconciliation, Hosea's allusion to the Valley of Achor emphasizes God's willingness to carry out the divine promise of forgiveness and restoration under the most difficult conditions (2:15). Achor refers to the place where Achan and his family are stoned to death for violating the *kherem*. He stole from the loot captured at Jericho and caused the Israelites to lose the battle at Ai (Josh. 7:22–26). Using this as the worst-case scenario, the prophet asserts that Israel's current infidelities, like Gomer's, could be put aside if the wife/nation truly became faithful to her husband/God.

Therefore the prophetic metaphor concludes with an expression of Yahweh's abiding desire to forgive an unfaithful Israel. Hosea agrees to take Gomer back if she agrees to renounce her other lovers forever. Gomer/Israel must acknowledge Hosea/Yahweh solely as her lord. Stepping away from Hosea's personal situation for a moment, this means that Israel must renounce the Baals and return to the covenant obligation that recognizes Yahweh as the only god for the nation (Hosea 2:14–20). When Gomer/Israel makes the decision to return, Hosea/Yahweh assures that a "wife of faithfulness" will enjoy the benefits of "steadfast love and mercy" (2:19–20). The names of Hosea's children are changed to symbolize the reversal of Israel's fortunes as fertility is returned to the land and a new covenantal agreement is put in place (2:21–23).

Additional Expressions of the Idolatry Theme. Although much of the rest of the book of Hosea is not as tightly composed as the first two chapters, the prophet continually returns to the issue of idolatry and its effect on the nation. The nation's rampant idolatry and the syncretistic cultic practices of Israel's shrines and priesthood are chronicled in Hosea's repeated condemnations: "With their silver and gold they made idols for their own destruction" (Hosea 8:4b). They consciously make sacrifices to Yahweh as well as other gods.

This is understandable in the context of the polytheism of their neighbors, who wish to placate and obtain the favor of as many deities as possible. Such offerings will be rejected by Yahweh, however, who demands their exclusive worship: "Though they offer choice sacrifices, though they eat flesh, the LORD does not accept them" (8:13).

To further illustrate his point, Hosea describes the useless practice of consulting "a piece of wood" and using divining rods to determine the will of the gods (4:12). They "sacrifice on the tops of mountains and make offerings upon the hills," a clear reference to the high places that the sin of Jeroboam has perpetuated in the land (4:13). Also referring to Jeroboam's political and religious reforms that endorse idolatrous behavior, Hosea announces that "the calf of Samaria shall be broken in pieces" (8:5–6).

One final recurring expression employed by Hosea to decry Israel's idolatry and foolish attitudes is his use of the metaphor of wind. Although the people seem to be carried away by the wind, literally "wrapped up" in their delight and celebrations associated with their worship of idols by "wings" of the wind, it will transport them to their due punishment (Hosea 4:19; cf. Ps. 35:5; Isa. 57:13). Although they attempt to sow with the assistance of the wind, they will "reap the whirlwind" and not benefit from the expected harvest (Hosea 8:7; cf. Isa. 26:18). Instead of gaining greater prosperity by making treaties with Assyria and Egypt (Hosea 12:1), they will be afflicted by the dry "east wind" that serves God's purpose to oppress them, and shrink their resources, and "strip their treasury" as they attempt to pay their tribute to stronger nations (13:15).

Knowledge Theme. A second element not as fully developed in the book of Hosea is the

---

East Wind as God's Instrument

The east wind, or sirocco, that blows from the desert is a scorching blast that contributes to the difficulties faced by farmers, parches their throats, and dries the skin of all in its path (Isa. 17:13; Jer. 4:11; Ezek. 17:10). As Lord of creation, Yahweh controls both rain and winds (Amos 4:7, 13), and the prophets often use these elemental forces to describe both blessing (Isa. 49:10) and bane for the people.

Isa. 27:8: In a "day of the Lord" prophecy, Isaiah includes the "fierce blast of . . . the east wind" as one of God's weapons.

Jer. 13:24: Using another agricultural image, the prophet describes how the people will be scattered into exile "like chaff driven by the wind from the desert."

Jer. 18:17: Since the people have "forgotten" God in their stubborn idolatry, God will "scatter them before the enemy" as if by "the wind from the east."

The Knowledge Theme in Hosea

My people are destroyed for lack of knowledge;
  because you have rejected knowledge,
  I reject you from being a priest to me.
And since you have forgotten the law of your God,
  I also will forget your children. (Hosea 4:6)

---

theme of knowledge. This is the key to a true understanding of the covenant and of God's relationship with the people. However, once again Jeroboam's sin becomes the source of the problem. As the prophet attempts to reason out the unfathomable decision on the part of the people to "play the whore" (4:14), he casts the blame for Israel's failure to keep the covenant squarely at the doorstep of the monarchy and the priesthood (4:4–6; 5:1). In their greed for power, they "feed on the sin" of the people (4:8), allowing them to forget God's law and rejoicing at their wickedness (7:3). They have made political alliances that have brought ruin on the nation and corrupted the people's worship with false idols (4:12–19).

Some of Hosea's fierce condemnation of the priesthood may be the result of his background as a Levite. In the northern kingdom, he would not have been allowed to function as a priest because Jeroboam I had created his own non-Levitical priesthood when the kingdoms divided (1 Kings 12:31–32). Therefore Hosea is prejudiced against these non-Levitical priests and angry at the monarchy

that installed them. Hosea condemns both of these leadership groups for failing to provide the people with the knowledge they need to obey the covenant. The result is that "there is no faithfulness or loyalty, and no knowledge of God in the land" (Hosea 4:1). As a result, God proclaims a lawsuit against Israel, indicting them for their iniquities and pronouncing judgment on them (cf. Mic. 1:2–7).

Because the people act in ignorance of what is expected of them under the covenant, the Israelites' sacrifices and offerings are unacceptable. They refuse to set aside devotion to other gods despite Yahweh's demand: "For I desire steadfast love and not sacrifice, the knowledge of God rather than burnt offerings" (Hosea 6:6; cf. Samuel in 1 Sam. 15:22). For this reason the people are to be abandoned by God "until they acknowledge their guilt and seek my [God's] face" (Hosea 5:15). The priests who are responsible for this lamentable situation will face a similar fate (4:9).

The term that Hosea uses in parallelism with knowledge in 6:6 is "steadfast love." In Hebrew the word is *khesed*, which is variously translated as "love, abiding love, steadfast love, mercy." *Khesed* is a technical term found most often in the language of treaties and covenants (see inset below).

Hosea 6:6 is also reminiscent of Samuel's condemnation of Saul for failing to keep God's commandments, "to obey is better than sacrifice" (1 Sam. 15:22). The difference, however, is

Khesed as Treaty Language

- *Khesed* is used in the context of a request by Abraham's servant that God adhere to a treaty obligation (Gen. 24:12, 14, 27).
- *Khesed* is used in Yahweh's promise to keep the covenant while giving the people the Ten Commandments (Exod. 20:6).
- *Khesed* is used in a slave's contractual declaration of perpetual servitude (Exod. 21:5).

- *Khesed* is used in a definition of the faithful "who love me and keep my commandments" (Deut. 5:10).
- *Khesed* is used in treaty language following the conquest: "to love the LORD your God, to walk in his way, to keep his commandments" (Josh. 22:5).
- *Khesed* is used in Solomon's citation of God's covenant with

David's "house" (i.e., dynasty; 1 Kings 3:6).
- *Khesed* is used in Yahweh's assurance of compliance: "I act with steadfast love, justice, and righteousness" (Jer. 9:24), for "he is gracious and merciful, slow to anger, and abounding in steadfast love" (Joel 2:13).

that the people lack the knowledge they need to be able to obey. Their kings will be defeated by Assyria, and their idols and temple treasures will be taken away as spoil (Hosea 10:3–8).

Hosea's antimonarchic attitude and his knowledge theme also are contained in a prophecy that alludes to how the people "make kings, but not through me; they set up princes, but without my knowledge" (8:4a). Hosea is speaking to the practice of succession by assassination that has become the standard method in the northern kingdom for ending one ruling dynasty and beginning another. He roundly condemns the practice of foreign alliances and warns that these relationships will bring the destruction of the nation. Hosea predicts that their illegitimate kings, who fail to call on Yahweh (7:7), will be swept away, swallowed up by the very nations that they bargain with as treaty partners (8:8–10; 10:7). The result is that the people and their leaders have failed to keep the covenantal agreement and can no longer expect that Yahweh will be obligated to maintain their safety and prosperity.

Within the context of the political situation facing Israel at the end of the eighth century BCE, Hosea is certain that the conflict between Egypt and Assyria will lead to the ultimate destruction of Israel and its kings. He ridicules

these leaders, referring to them as "silly and without sense" for their courting of both the superpowers (7:11). He assures them that the resources squandered on palaces and walled fortresses will be consumed in the flames of the conquerors (10:14). Instead of listening to God's prophets and seeing them as sentinels placed there to warn the nation, they call the prophet "a fool" and the "man of spirit," a madman (9:7–8). As a result, God will allow the foreign powers to take away Israel's idols and temple treasures as spoil (10:3–8).

Even though Hosea's explicit condemnation of his people and their leaders contains a litany of seemingly unforgivable sins, the prophet cannot leave his own people to be destroyed without warning them of the coming destruction. The primary purpose of prophetic utterance is not just to condemn but also to assure the people that even though they are to be punished as a parent punishes a wayward child (Hosea 11:1–7), Yahweh will redeem them if they return to him (14:4–7). They can be healed and restored, but first they must regain their lost knowledge of Yahweh's power and the covenant. Only in that way will they then understand what they have done and what they must do to return to the proper relationship with their God. If they truly recognize the danger, they will follow the prophet's advice to "hold fast to love and justice, and wait continually for your God" (12:6; cf. Mic. 6:8).

1. How does the growth of Assyrian hegemony threaten Israel's cultural identity and political life?
2. In what ways does Hosea differ from Amos in the tone of his message?
3. How does the sin of Jeroboam relate to Hosea the prophet? See Hosea 8:5 for more on this.
4. Is Hosea's marriage metaphor an effective use of enacted prophecy (Hosea 1–2)?
5. How do the names given to Hosea's three children relate to his prophecy against Israel (Hosea 1:4–9)?
6. Why do the people of Israel stand condemned for their lack of knowledge (Hosea 4:1–6; 5:1; 8:4)?
7. Compare Hosea 6:4–6 and 1 Sam. 15:22, and discuss the desire of God for obedience rather than sacrifice.

The Book of Isaiah (Isa. 1–39)

KEY POINTS

- Isaiah 1–39 contains the eighth-century prophecies related to Judah's struggles with Assyria.
- Isaiah emphasizes the need to stay out of the revolts by petty kingdoms.
- Hezekiah's reforms mark him as a good king, but he also must weather Assyria's wrath.
- Isaiah identifies Assyria as God's instrument of punishment and predicts a restoration led by an ideal Davidic ruler.

At this point in our chronological survey of the prophets, we move to the first of the major prophetic books. Isaiah serves during a time when the northern kingdom of Israel is destroyed by the Assyrians and his own land of Judah is devastated by the Assyrian armies as they repeatedly campaign in the region. It is the task of the prophet to articulate a theodicy explaining the destruction. In this way, the prophet's words will help to explain both why God is justified in punishing the people of Israel and Judah so severely and why the defeated people should still place their trust in Yahweh's promises of restoration and reconciliation. This message will be difficult for both the prophet and his audience to bear, and it will be a test of their courage and endurance both to listen and to respond to what Isaiah has to tell them in the midst of their suffering. Isaiah does engage in direct confrontation and even rather extreme physical displays to get his message across. These methods may reflect either his expectations of being heard by his audience, whether kings or commoners, or the desperate situation faced by the nation at the end of the eighth century BCE.

The book of Isaiah is one of the longest and most structurally complex in the prophetic corpus. Its chapters reflect at least three separate time periods: about 740–697 BCE, 539–535 BCE, and 515–500 BCE. Among scholars, the traditionally accepted breaks corresponding to these three time periods are Isa. 1–39; 40–55; and 56–66. The latter two sections will be dealt with in a subsequent section on the postexilic period. The prophet Isaiah is mentioned by name only sixteen times throughout the book (cf. Jeremiah, who is named more than 125 times in his prophetic book). This interesting statistic suggests a deliberate effort to depersonalize the text, giving the message of Yahweh more prominence than the prophet who delivers it. Although it is possible to trace a fairly coherent narrative in the first section of the book, there are at least two segments (Isa. 24–27, known as the Little Apocalypse; and Isa. 34–35, with its emphasis on a future judgment of nations) that many scholars suspect are later additions and do not reflect the social or historical setting of First Isaiah.

In addressing ourselves to First Isaiah, or the Isaiah of Jerusalem, we notice that his message and activities date to the period of the late eighth and early seventh centuries BCE (ca. 740–687 BCE). He differs significantly from either of his contemporaries, Amos and Hosea, in that he speaks primarily to kings and high-ranking officials and is apparently a member of the religious establishment tied to the temple in Jerusalem. His message reflects a high level of education and a commitment to the Davidic monarchy, the temple, and Jerusalem. Nevertheless, as a prophet it is his task to address individual Davidic kings, the temple community, and the inhabitants of Judah and Jerusalem and condemn them for their failure to keep the covenant with Yahweh.

Call Narrative. Isaiah's call narrative appears in Isa. 6. It contains language that is familiar to many people today because it was used as a source for some of the lines in Handel's great oratorio *Messiah*. The elements of the call help us to date it (the year King Uzziah died [ca. 740 BCE] and determine its site (the inner precincts of the temple in Jerusalem). The mention of **seraphim** (seraphs) or

---

Isaiah's Call Narrative

In the year that King Uzziah died, I saw the LORD sitting on a throne, high and lofty; and the hem of his robe filled the temple. Seraphs were in attendance above him; each had six wings.... And one called to another and said:
"Holy, holy, holy is the LORD of Hosts;
the whole earth is full of his glory."
The pivots on the thresholds shook at the voices of those who called, and the house filled with smoke. And I said: "Woe is me! I am lost; for I am a man of unclean lips, and I live among a people of unclean lips; yet my eyes have seen the King, the LORD of hosts!" (Isa. 6:1–5)

---

angels is based on the imagery of the ark of the covenant, which had crossed wings on the lid representing how angelic beings uphold the throne of God (Exod. 25:17–22).

The manifestations of power in this call narrative include an angelic acclamation of Yahweh's glory, the earthquake, and the smoke that fills the temple. All these manifestations appear in Moses's theophany at Mount Sinai (e.g., Exod. 19:9–23). Also typical is Isaiah's reluctance to take up the prophetic role. As a priest he makes the excuse that his mortal lips are "unclean" (ritually impure) and thus cannot speak the holy words of Yahweh.

Following the pattern established in other call narratives, no excuse is ever accepted by God. In this episode, an angel takes a burning coal from the altar fire and purifies Isaiah's lips with a holy fire. In this way Isaiah is empowered to speak the words that God gives him to speak. Since this is a vision, Isaiah's mouth is not permanently damaged by the coal. Now that Isaiah's self-imposed impediment has been removed, the call is made: "Who will go for me?" Isaiah's only response can be "Here am I; send me" (Isa. 6:8; cf. 1 Sam. 3:4–10).

The commission that Isaiah receives from Yahweh is not easy. He is to speak, but he is told that the people will neither hear nor understand his words. The nation has rejected previous warnings (see Amos 2:12; Hosea 6:5). Now Yahweh's intention is to allow cities to be destroyed and people to be killed. Despite this inevitable punishment, Isaiah is assured that a remnant will survive and will in the future serve as a "holy seed" to restore the nation (Isa. 6:13). This pattern is familiar and establishes Isaiah's message as typical of Israelite prophecy; in its familiarity, it is that much more authoritative to his audience.

One additional aspect of Isaiah's call narrative is the use of the term "holy." Isaiah uses it when he wants to refer to something that is the opposite of human. However, human behavior could become holy, modeling itself after the "Holy One of Israel" whose covenant and laws provide direction for ethical behavior (Isa. 5:16). This term for God is constantly repeated to emphasize the need of the people to "lean on the LORD, the Holy One of Israel" (10:20), so that when they have been purified they will naturally turn their eyes and "look to the Holy One of Israel" (17:7). Isaiah's emphasis on social justice, combined with the obligation to aid rather than oppress the weak, and the requirement to worship only Yahweh, are keys to seeking to be holy. This is not unique to Isaiah. Injunctions against profaning Yahweh's holy name are found throughout the prophets (Jer. 34:16; Amos 2:7; Ezek. 36:22–32).

Oracles of Warning. Two examples of Isaiah's message will be presented here to illustrate his use of condemnation, judgment, and choice. The first is found in Isa. 1:10–23, where the prophet plays on both the familiar tradition of the destruction of Sodom and Gomorrah (Gen. 19:24–26) and the past experience of the people. This passage also has a close parallel with the message in Amos 5:21–24. Both Isa. 1:10–23 and Amos 5:21–24 condemn hollow worship as a form of empty ritual. Yahweh refuses to accept such false service. Instead, the call goes out for a resumption of the covenant stipulations that demand a just society, reflecting God's concern for the nation. Isaiah offers the people of Judah a choice. He states that if they are willing to cleanse themselves of the "innocent blood" that they have shed in oppressing the poor and the weak, then redemption is possible (Isa. 1:16–17). As is made clear in the law (Deut. 19:10–13) and in other

prophetic speech (Jer. 26:15), the shedding of "innocent blood" is one of the greatest of all crimes. Thus Yahweh's willingness to allow them to repent and to step back from such practices makes it possible to enjoy once again the covenantal promise of land and children. However, if they choose to disobey, then the threat of war and destruction will remain, "for the mouth of the LORD has spoken" (Isa. 1:20).

The other example of an oracle of warning is found in Isa. 5:1–7. Here the prophet plays on a familiar agricultural scene, a vineyard planted on a terraced hillside. The use of farming images is common among the prophets (Isa. 28:24–28; Joel 1:11–12; 2:23–24; Amos 8:1). These images reflect the importance of agriculture in their society and demonstrate the effort made by the prophets so that their message is relevant to the people in their own time.

In Isa. 5:1–2, Isaiah describes the farmer's hard work of carving out terraces on a hillside, building a retaining wall, and filling the terrace with fertile soil. Once the land has been prepared, the vines are planted. In the prophetic literature this act serves as a sign of Yahweh's establishment of the covenant with Israel (see Isa. 6:13 and Jer. 31:27–28 for the allegorical reference to "holy seed" or the sowing of a field). Just having the opportunity to develop such a vineyard is described by Jeremiah (35:7) as the sign of sedentary existence as compared with the nomadic life of the landless who do not share in the covenant and who do not have the luxury of waiting years for the vines to mature and to begin to produce fruit.

The wise farmer also takes measures to protect his vines and their fruit from foraging by small animals (Song 2:15) and travelers (Prov. 24:30–31). Therefore, the owner of the vineyard in Isa. 5:2 constructs both a hedge and a stone wall to guard the vineyard from harm.

Figure 4.4. Agricultural watchtower overlooking terraced fields.
(Baker Photo Archive)

He also builds a watchtower to shelter the laborers and to serve as a lookout for marauding bands of animals or humans. The harvesting of the grapes from mature vines takes place in late summer, when new growth has stopped and the bark darkens (Num. 13:20). At this point the grapes are tasted to determine when they are ready to be taken to the winepress. But the grapes in Yahweh's vineyard are sour. What remains is worthless, lacking in any nourishing value, and unfit for its intended use.

The mundane steps of planting, cultivating the vines, guarding its produce, and processing the fruit are also included. But a sour note is struck when the grapes prove to be bitter and therefore worthless (Isa. 5:2).

Yahweh concludes, "What more was there to do for my vineyard that I have not done in it?" (Isa. 5:4a). God's question functions as the initial testimony in a divine lawsuit against the nation and provides the basis for a full indictment of their iniquities. Yahweh's disappointment in the results of such hard labor is evident (5:3–4). Judgment is then pronounced. The sentence is that the vineyard is to be pulled up by its roots and its terraces thrown down. Even the clouds are commanded not to rain on it (5:5–6).

Finally, the meaning of the metaphor in the Song of the Vineyard is revealed (Isa. 5:7). Israel and Judah are identified as the corrupt vines. Their injustices include depriving the poor of their lands by creating huge estates (5:8), drunkenness and self-indulgent living (5:11–12), public deception by the leaders (5:18–21), and bribery (5:23). Their punishment is to be a ruined land, just as the vineyard is to be laid waste. The nation will be left open to the assaults of other people (5:26–30). Furthermore, the "chosen" who "are wise in [their] own eyes" will go into exile because of their lack of knowledge (Isa. 5:13; cf. Hosea 4:1, 2 for the knowledge theme).

Political Message. Many of the major pronouncements of Isaiah are tied to historical events. The final years of the eighth century BCE placed the nations of Israel and Judah

Oracles of Warning

Isa. 1:13–15

Bringing offerings is futile;
    incense is an abomination to me.
New moon and Sabbath and calling of convocation—
    I cannot endure solemn assemblies with iniquity.
Your new moons and your appointed festivals
    my soul hates;
they become a burden to me,
    I am weary of bearing them.
When you stretch out your hands,
    I will hide my eyes from you;
even though you make many prayers,
    I will not listen;
your hands are full of blood.

Amos 5:21–24

I hate, I despise your festivals,
    and I take no delight in your solemn assemblies.
Even though you offer me your burnt offerings and
    grain offerings,
    I will not accept them;
and the offerings of well-being of your fatted animals
    I will not look upon.
Take away from me the noise of your songs;
    I will not listen to the melody of your harps.
But let justice roll down like waters,
    and righteousness like an everflowing stream.

squarely in the way of Assyrian expansion. Isaiah witnesses the destruction of Israel, the northern kingdom, and sees its people taken into exile after 720 BCE. He sees Judah, the southern kingdom, ravaged by Assyrian armies and Jerusalem besieged on two occasions (701 and 688 BCE). These are desperate times, and the message that Isaiah speaks provides little solace to Israel's leaders, despite his repeated use of the phrase "Do not fear" (Isa. 7:4; 10:24; 37:6).

During the 730s, the small vassal states of Syria-Palestine once again are encouraged by the Egyptians to revolt against Assyria. This is and remains a typical ploy of rival superpowers, using the discontent in smaller states in border areas to weaken their opponent and further their own political ambitions. The ultimate goal is to absorb these smaller states into their own empire. Playing into this political ploy, Israel and Syria, along with most of the rest of the Assyrian vassal states in Syria-Palestine, form an alliance. Admittedly, they had been successful in the past when King Ahab had allied himself with other small states in the mid-ninth century to prevent the Assyrians from controlling their region. However, now the Assyrians are much stronger militarily, and their ruthless use of psychological warfare techniques (massacring the population of whole cities and mutilating their prisoners) gives them a decided edge in any conflict (see Hosea 13:16; Amos 1:13).

Because he fears Assyrian reprisal and does not see any advantage in assisting these rebellious states, King Ahaz of Judah refuses to join the alliance. The result is what is known as the Syro-Ephraimite War. Israel and Syria ally themselves against Judah and initiate hostilities. The crisis that Ahaz and his advisers face proves to be even more complex than they have anticipated. On the one hand, as an Assyrian colony, Judah has a legal responsibility to use military force to put down any rebellion against Assyria. On the other hand, as an ally of Israel, Judah has a legal obligation to support Israel's struggle for freedom. Regardless of whether Judah decides to support Assyria or Israel, it faces dire consequences. If Judah does not join the struggle against Assyria, Israel and Syria will invade. If Judah does join in the struggle, Assyria will invade Judah!

Ahaz's advisers, referred to as his "heart," are unable to reach a decision. They shake "as the trees of the forest shake before the wind" (Isa. 7:2). The king takes a recess from their deliberations ostensibly to inspect Jerusalem's defenses. Regardless of Judah's decision, he knows that there will be an invasion and Jerusalem must prepare for a siege. But the strategy of a recess is primarily to offer the deadlocked participants the time to negotiate and to rethink their arguments.

Ahaz's tour takes him outside the city and away from most of his entourage. The crucial scene is set at one of the city's most strategic sites: "at the end of the conduit of the upper pool on the highway to the Fuller's Field" (Isa. 7:3; note the paralleled use of the site for the Rabshakeh's speech in 36:2). This strategic spot is associated with one of the important industries of the city and serves as a crucial link to the city's water supply. It represents the preservation of life for the inhabitants in this time of crisis and is therefore an appropriate place for the prophet to confront the king with a question of life or death.

In this setting, Isaiah also will have the chance to lobby the king and his advisers. The prophet proposes that Judah remain nonaligned in this conflict. His words echo the statement in Hosea 12:1 that indicts Israel for its foreign alliances with both Assyria and Egypt. Both prophets warn that this is a dangerous game. It will result in Isaiah's lifetime in the destruction of the northern kingdom and the exile of its people.

A key assumption in Isaiah's argument to remain nonaligned is the tradition of Jerusalem's inviolability (see Pss. 46:5; 48:8). If Jerusalem's inhabitants are faithful, the city will remain under the protection of the Divine Warrior. In this impregnable position, the city cannot be truly threatened by Syria and Israel's invading forces (Isa. 7:1–9). Furthermore, Judah has only one valid treaty, its covenant with Yahweh. The contractual agreement with Yahweh recognizes Yahweh alone as Judah's true sovereign. It is therefore Yahweh's responsibility as Divine Warrior, not the responsibility of Ahaz, to provide for and to protect the nation. As the climax of his statement to the king, Isaiah announces the verdict of the divine assembly against Israel and Syria. The divine assembly bases its indictment on Syria and Israel's attempts to liberate themselves without asking for divine assistance (7:8–9). Yahweh alone is the liberator of the Israelites, and only Yahweh can set them free. While Assyria is a mighty power, it is no mightier than Egypt, a nation from whom Yahweh has previously delivered Israel.

Having already made other political arrangements, Ahaz refuses to ask for a sign from Yahweh. Isaiah in turn rejects Ahaz's ability to cut off debate and proclaims the sign anyway. He predicts the birth of a child whose name will be Immanuel. On the face of it, this pronouncement is just another example of an **annunciation**, a divine message predicting the birth of a child that is made by a representative of God (cf. Gen. 16:11–12; Judg. 13:3–5). The child's mother, referred to as a "young woman" (Hebrew 'almah, Isa. 7:14), is most likely one of Ahaz's wives who has accompanied the king on his inspection tour. She may have even been

The Heart of Ahaz

The terms "heart of Ahaz" and "the heart of his people" may be more technical than poetic. The context in which these terms are used is political. In a frantic effort to protect Judah against an invasion by Israel and Syria, Ahaz convenes a meeting. The "heart of Ahaz" and "the heart of his people" may identify the two advisory groups that the king summons.

The social structure of ancient Judah provides for a wide range of decision-making and advisory groups. For example, municipal affairs are in the hands of the "bearded" elders, who make up the village assembly (1 Sam. 30:26–31). Monarchs appoint some elders to serve as royal officials and as links between the village culture and the central administration (Jer. 25:19; 38:17; Esther 1:3; 2:18). They could function as military officials (1 Sam. 8:12) or civilian officials (1 Kings 4:2; 20:14; 22:26; 2 Kings 23:8; Jer. 24:8; 26:10; 34:19, 21). Of course, the members of the bureaucracy are especially numerous in the major cities (Jer. 38:24–25; 2 Kings 21:23).

"Heart" is an important anthropological term in the OT/HB. It refers almost exclusively to the human heart (814 times). The word is also used for "the heart of God" (26 times) and "the heart of the sea" (11 times). None of the references have been regularly identified with any advisory or government body. Mesopotamian literature uses "heart" in reference to royal officials, where the phrase "to devote the heart entirely" identifies the monarch's eunuchs, closest advisers, and vassals. In Isa. 7:2 "the heart of Ahaz" could easily refer not just to his own human heart but also to the officials totally dedicated to him.

Thus "heart" becomes an easy metaphor for advisers who function in much the same way for a government as the "heart" does for an individual. A "fat" heart is out of touch with the real needs of the country (Isa. 6:10; 11:8; 13:10; 16:12; 18:12). A heart of "stone" is unapproachable (Ezek. 11:19; 36:26) or unswerving (Job 41:16). A "trembling" heart is indecisive (Deut. 28:65; 1 Sam. 28:5). Yahweh's statement in Hosea 11:9, "My heart turns over within me," parallels the report in Isa. 7:2, "The heart of the king and the heart of the people trembled." Perhaps knowing the difficulties of reaching consensus in a group, Solomon prays for a "hearing heart" (1 Kings 3:9–12), hoping for a cooperative council.

obviously pregnant at the time and thus have served as an easily observable object of the prophet's words.

More important than the identity of the mother, however, is that Isaiah's prophecy is time-specific. Isaiah demonstrates how important his message is, and how dire the consequences that accompany it are, by taking the unusual step of setting a time limit on his prediction. Thus, by the time the child is old enough to know the difference between right and wrong (between 5 and 13 years), Israel and Syria will have been destroyed and Judah's people will be impoverished (Isa. 7:13–25; left to eat only curds and wild honey). The child's name, Immanuel, means "God is with us." Ordinarily that would be considered to be an appropriate name for a child, but in this instance it is a sign that the power behind the coming destructive forces, embodied in Assyria, is Yahweh. They should therefore fear the coming of the Lord more than the approach of the Assyrians. Isaiah matches this prediction with a second annunciation, this time predicting the birth and naming of his own son, who will see the destruction of Samaria and Syria before he can say the words "my father" and "my mother" (8:1–4).

Unwilling to take Isaiah's advice that he maintain quiet patience and trust in the Divine Warrior, Ahaz chooses to request aid from Assyria. The Assyrians in turn use the opportunity to intervene before the rebellious states have sufficient time to organize their resistance. Any hopes of freedom from Assyrian rule are dashed, and the states are placed under even more restrictive treaty obligations. Judah also is forced to pay for Assyria's help. Their local autonomy is weakened, and an even heavier tribute payment is imposed on the tiny state. Isaiah's prediction of destruction and impoverishment thus comes true within the time frame he had set.

The End of the Northern Kingdom. The Syro-Ephraimite War (730s BCE) is symptomatic of the discontent within the Assyrian Empire. When more revolts occur, the Assyrian emperor Shalmaneser V and his successor Sargon II decide to make an example of some of the rebels. Israel, once again a leader among the small states, is targeted and in 722 BCE is invaded. Shortly thereafter Israel's capital city of Samaria is captured, and the nation of Israel effectively ceases to exist. Though many escape to Judah, the majority of the survivors are deported in 720 BCE by the victorious Assyrians, and the legend of the "ten lost tribes of Israel" is born (2 Kings 18:9–12). Israel's population is culturally absorbed, and they lose their identity as a distinct people. The Assyrian rebuilding

Figure 4.5. Sargon and high official. The Assyrian king Sargon II captured Samaria ca. 721 BCE. (Marie-Lan Nguyen/ Wikimedia Commons, courtesy of the Louvre)

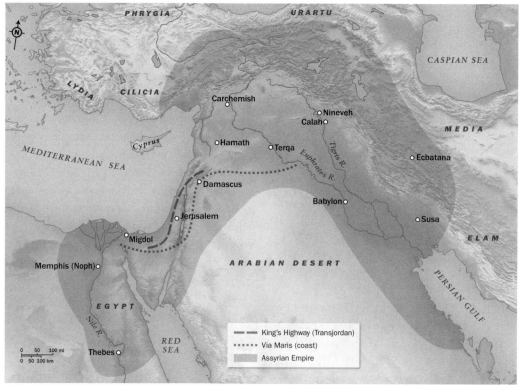

Map 4.2. Assyrian Empire

of Samaria contributes to the eradication of Israelite culture. Sargon II repopulates the area with peoples from other parts of his empire, including Arab tribes (2 Kings 17:24).

The traumatic effect of Israel's destruction on Judah is reflected in the prophets, who point to the northern kingdom's fate and warn Judah and Jerusalem of a similar ending (Isa. 28:1–4, 14–22; Jer. 7:13–15). Some people, including the editors of 2 Kings, take Israel's demise as vindication of the Davidic monarchy and its covenant with Yahweh. Israel, which has broken away and has perpetuated the sin of Jeroboam, has finally been punished (2 Kings 17:2–18, 21–23). But with the Assyrians remaining a threat to Judah's existence, these self-righteous views seem shortsighted. It is

likely that most of the people of Judah felt shock, fear, and apprehension about the future, perhaps fueled by the lurid tales of Assyrian atrocities carried south by the refugees from Israel's cities.

It is into this atmosphere that Hezekiah succeeds his father, Ahaz, as ruler of Judah. While his perspective on the political situation is similar to his father's, he is portrayed as a king who is more open to the message of Isaiah. The much more sympathetic assessment formula in the book of Kings that describes Hezekiah's reign indicates that "he did what was right in the sight of the LORD" (2 Kings 18:3). It is helpful that Hezekiah's actions are part of a noncombative political strategy that defies Assyrian efforts to impose set boundaries, their religion, and their culture upon Judah. Since they do not represent open revolt or military action, they are less likely to be suppressed immediately.

Among Hezekiah's accomplishments is a religious reform. He attempts to purify the temple in Jerusalem of foreign influences (2 Kings 18:4–6). He orders the removal of all the images of other gods, including the Nehushtan, the bronze serpent that Moses had made (Num. 21:9). He also adds a portion of the Philistines' territory to his holdings and strengthens royal control over critical supplies of grain and oil (see inset above on *lmlk* jar handle seals). In addition to his religious reforms and his tightening of administrative procedures, Hezekiah makes preparations for the inevitable confrontation with the Assyrians. He orders the construction of a water tunnel that is intended to connect the pool of

Figure 4.6. Stamped *lmlk* jar handle from Lachish, eighth or seventh century BCE. (Baker Photo Archive, courtesy of the British Museum)

Siloam to the city and provide a secure water supply during a siege (2 Kings 20:20).

Hezekiah is able to survive these initial moves of defiance because the Assyrians are distracted by more active rebellions elsewhere within the empire. For example, in 711 BCE the Philistine city-state of Ashdod organizes a revolt at the instigation of the Egyptians. Hezekiah is invited to join the alliance, but he chooses to remain passive and officially loyal to the Assyrians. Isaiah may have influenced this decision by performing an unusual **enacted prophecy**. He parades around the city naked for three years to demonstrate the fate of those who rebel against the Assyrians (Isa. 20:3; cf. Mic. 1:8). His actions graphically portray the condition of war prisoners and undoubtedly had an effect on the decision not to support Ashdod and Egypt (Isa. 20). At the same time, the prophet makes it clear who is the real power in these events, naming the Assyrians as "the rod [of Yahweh's] anger" (10:5). His characterization of Assyria as the instrument of God's punishment also swings the pendulum of responsibility and of power away from Assyria's gods and toward an all-powerful Yahweh.

Ultimately, Hezekiah's attempt to gain a greater measure of independence brings his small kingdom to the attention of the Assyrian overlords. In 701 BCE, the emperor Sennacherib invades Judah and ravages the countryside. Archaeological excavations at Tell ed-Duweir (Lachish) have revealed the siege ramp employed by the Assyrian army during their siege of that important border city. Sennacherib's own chronicle, despite its boasting style, closely resembles the account found in 2 Kings 18:13–15 (see inset). The destruction of many of Judah's cities (2 Kings 18:14) forces Hezekiah into a situation in which his only way to save the kingdom is to pay a huge ransom (cf. an earlier ransom to end a siege by Hazael of Syria [2 Kings 12:17–18]). This payment saves the city of Jerusalem from destruction at that point. However, that is little solace to the villagers outside its walls (cf. below on the condemnation of Jerusalem by the prophet Micah).

Additional details of the siege are also provided in an interesting diplomatic exchange found in Isa. 36–37. These chapters contain two detailed taunting speeches delivered by an Assyrian diplomat with the title "the Rabshakeh" (chief cupbearer). Under a truce, he stands outside the walls of Jerusalem, at the spot where Isaiah had once confronted King Ahaz (7:3): at "the conduit of the upper pool on the highway to the Fuller's Field" (36:2). Here he negotiates with Hezekiah's officials, who are standing on the city wall. The people, who have retreated inside the walls for safety, may be presumed to be straining to hear the negotiations despite the protests of Hezekiah's advisers. The shrewd Rabshakeh makes sure they can understand his message since he speaks in their own Hebrew language (36:11–12).

An analysis of his formal discourse shows that he is a skillful orator. He first chides them, describing Judah's alliance with Egypt in sarcastic terms as a worthless exercise that ties them to a "broken reed." He then makes a sanctimonious judgment of their situation, pointing out in disparaging tones that King Hezekiah's decree to have all altars torn down in the shrines and villages outside Jerusalem has angered Yahweh. Next, in a comic and ingratiating manner, he ridicules Judah's lack of soldiers, saying that even if the Assyrian king supplied the necessary horses, Hezekiah could not provide the riders. Then, returning to the results of Hezekiah's efforts to centralize worship in Jerusalem, he tells them that the Assyrian army is besieging Jerusalem at the behest of Yahweh: "Is it without the LORD that I have come up against this land to destroy it? The LORD said to me, go up against this land, and destroy it" (Isa. 36:10). The obvious goal of the Rabshakeh's speech is to weaken resistance and bring about Hezekiah's surrender. This use of a theodicy by a foreign diplomat is a powerful, but not unusual, tactic. Isaiah himself describes Assyria as Yahweh's tool designed to punish the nation (10:5–11). Similar claims of divine sanction for the actions of a non-Israelite ruler can be seen elsewhere, both in the Bible (Jer. 21:4–10) and in other ancient Near Eastern documents (see the inset on the Cyrus Cylinder, p. 195).

Isaiah's version of a second siege (Isa. 37) is difficult to separate from the first one (Isa. 36; 2 Kings 18:13–16 does contain additional information that seems to separate the two events). But the episode in Isa. 37 more directly involves Yahweh's assurances that the city of Jerusalem shall be saved: "For I will defend this city to save it, for my own sake, and for the sake of my servant David." What is found here is another example of an apology narrative (a literary style used to defend a character). The text promotes Hezekiah as a "faithful [Davidic] ruler." Hezekiah prays for Yahweh's assistance, and the response is an angel who brings a plague that kills 185,000 Assyrians overnight (Isa. 37:36; cf. Exod. 12:29–30).

Mention is also made of political problems that face Sennacherib in Nineveh and the assassination of the emperor after his return (Isa. 37:37–38). Plague in overcrowded army camps is certainly well known in the ancient world, and the evidence is clear from Assyrian sources that Sennacherib is assassinated, but there is no reason to connect that event with Isaiah's prophecy. Isaiah's explanation for the survival of Jerusalem, however, perpetuates the idea of the inviolability of the city and the temple (37:35). One hundred years later, Jeremiah will be almost killed by a mob for prophesying the destruction of the city and the temple (Jer. 7:12–15; 26:4–6) because of this myth of inviolability. The idea that Yahweh is somehow required to spare the city of Jerusalem is disproved in due course when the Babylonian king Nebuchadnezzar besieges and destroys both the city and the temple in 587 BCE. Simply put, Yahweh will not defend a city that violates the covenant (Isa. 28:14–15).

Remnant Theme. While Isaiah describes the punishment of the people on several occasions, he matches nearly every prediction of destruction with a promise of restoration by a faithful remnant of the people (see Isa. 10:20–23; 37:30–32). Coupled with these hopeful statements are the prophet's assurances that on the day when God restores the fortunes of the nation, a representative of the ruling House of David will lead the remnant. The phrase beginning "For a child has been born for us" (Isa. 9:6–7), which the Gospel writers in the NT interpret as authentication for Jesus's tie to the House of David and to the role of Messiah (Matt. 1:16; Luke 2:11) represents Isaiah's promise of hope to a nation under siege and in danger of destruction. The words also demonstrate once again the emphasis that the prophet places on national leaders who will establish justice and rule as righteous kings. Thus in Isa. 11:1–2, Isaiah's reference to "a shoot from the stump of Jesse" (David's father) is a promise that the nation will not be left to wither away. Their leaders will spring forth once again from the ruins of the nation. This future Davidic ruler will have Yahweh's wise counsel and will be the proper model for a people who must have the knowledge and fear of Yahweh to survive (see Ps. 111:10; Prov. 1:7).

On that day of restoration, God will extend a hand to bring back "the remnant that is left of his people" (Isa. 11:11), and they will once again "lean on the LORD" to give them strength (10:20). When God returns the blessings of the covenant to the land, "the surviving remnant of the house of Judah shall again take root downward, and bear fruit upward; for from Jerusalem a remnant shall go out, and from Mount Zion a band of survivors. The zeal of the LORD of hosts will do this" (Isa. 37:31–32).

Additional attention will be given to the other two sections of Isaiah later in this textbook. Isaiah of Jerusalem apparently ends his activities at the conclusion of Hezekiah's reign in 697 BCE (see Isa. 38–39). It is apparent from an examination of the similarities of language and theme that appear in Isa. 40–66 that Isaiah's message is passed on to a school of his disciples (see the group mentioned in 8:16 who receive his testimony and teachings). They keep his message, vocabulary, and style alive and give it new life after the exile in speaking to the needs of those who returned to Jerusalem to rebuild their lives and the temple.

▰▰▰▰▰ STUDY QUESTIONS ▰▰▰▰▰

1. In what ways do the visual images in Isaiah's call narrative (Isa. 6) compare with those in Moses's theophanic experience (Exod. 3–4)?
2. What can be learned about ancient agriculture in Isaiah's Song of the Vineyard (Isa. 5:1–8)?
3. With the Syro-Ephraimite War as the background for Isa. 7, why does Ahaz ignore Isaiah's Immanuel prophecy?
4. How does Isaiah's reference to Assyria as "the rod of God's anger" (Isa. 10:5) relate to the universalism theme?
5. Why is Isaiah's remnant theme in Isa. 11:1–9 so committed to the restoration of the nation through a "shoot from the stump of Jesse"?
6. Why does Hezekiah take the chance to cleanse the temple and engage in administrative reforms that violate his treaty with Assyria?
7. How effective is the theodicy employed by the Rabshakeh to convince Hezekiah to surrender (Isa. 36)?
8. What is the significance of the Siloam Inscription and Sennacherib's Assyrian Annals in reconstructing the story of the siege of Jerusalem (2 Kings 20:20)?

The Book of Micah

▰▰▰▰▰ KEY POINTS ▰▰▰▰▰

- Micah speaks from a rural perspective during the Assyrian invasion of Judah.
- Micah condemns Samaria and Jerusalem as the root of the nations' problems.
- Micah emphasizes social justice and a simpler form of covenant theology.

The prophet Micah, an exact contemporary of Isaiah of Jerusalem, has a distinctively different perspective on the events during the last three decades of the eighth century and the beginning of the seventh century BCE (the reigns of Jotham, Ahaz, and Hezekiah; Mic. 1:1). Coming from Moresheth, a small village in southwestern Judah, Micah represents the feelings and concerns of the rural farmers and villagers who are forced to bear the brunt of Assyrian pillaging. While the people of Jerusalem are under siege by Sennacherib's army, the rest of Judah's population is subject to rape, violent death, and enslavement as the Assyrian troops strip the countryside of all food and livestock. As a result, Micah is highly critical of Jerusalem, the monarchy, and the temple community. Micah's message is divided into four main themes: a covenant lawsuit against the nation (Mic. 1); the condemning of hollow worship (6:1–8); a concern over social injustice (Mic. 1:2–2:11; 3:1–12; 6:9–16; 7:17); and a depiction of future restoration, including a royal messiah figure (4:1–5) and a shepherd image for God (2:12–13; 7:8–20).

Covenant Lawsuit against the Nation. Following the typical messenger formula that identifies the prophet as one who speaks in the name of Yahweh (Mic. 1:1), Micah frames his denunciation of Jerusalem, Samaria, and their leaders in the form of a divine lawsuit. Isaiah also uses a lawsuit form in his Song of the Vineyard (5:1–7), but Micah, like Amos, is a product of village culture, and it is therefore not surprising that he points more specifically to the urban centers as the cause of the people's despair and destruction. Now

Charges Filed against Israel and Judah

All this is for the transgression of Jacob
and for the sins of the house of Israel.
What is the transgression of Jacob?
Is it not Samaria?
And what is the high place of Judah?
Is it not Jerusalem? (Mic. 1:5)

weary and sick of the waves of relentless destruction, Micah identifies the true enemies of the people, in a sharply critical oracle, as the Israelite capital of Samaria and Judah's capital at Jerusalem.

The idolatry fostered in Samaria's and Jerusalem's cultic centers and the foreign alliances that they have forged have incurred both God's wrath and the heavy hand of the conqueror (Mic. 1:15). Just as the invaders have trampled the countryside, so now they will devastate and depopulate the capital cities, which will become "a heap in the open country, a place for planting vineyards" (1:6). This harsh message is quoted again in Jer. 26:18 as a part of Jeremiah's trial, demonstrating the transmission of prophetic speech over a period of a century.

When Samaria falls after a prolonged siege to the Assyrians in 721 BCE, Micah notes that its once-mighty walls "pour down . . . into the valley" (1:6). The path of destruction created by the Assyrians may be reflected in the list of cities, from Gath to Maroth to "the gate of Jerusalem" found in 1:10–15. As the helpless peasant farmers in neighboring villages attempt to defend their homes, they too are slaughtered or deported. In the wake of such general destruction, the prophet calls on the people to repent and mourn their fate. Like Isaiah (20:2), the mourners are to strip themselves naked and walk barefoot into exile to the sound of scavenging jackals (Mic. 1:8). Their shaved heads will indicate that they are

no longer "pampered children" but prisoners of war (Mic. 1:16; cf. Ezek. 5:1–4).

Hollow Worship Condemned. In keeping with his central theme of condemning those in positions of authority, the prophet also takes aim at the hollow rituals orchestrated by the priesthood and performed by the people. He makes it clear that they cannot expect that by presenting their sacrifices on the altar, they have in some way obligated God to protect them. Micah's *rib*, or "contention," over hollow worship begins with Yahweh calling on all of creation to witness the testimony that will be presented (6:1–2). This is an unusual feature since most lawsuit oracles are addressed to the "people of Judah" (Isa. 5:3–4) or the "people of Israel" (Hosea 4:1). Here, however, in a series of questions and answers in Mic. 6:3–8, the prophet makes his case by presenting the traditional litany of saving events that has previously characterized God's care for the people of the covenant (Mic. 6:3–5; see Ps. 78). They have been "brought up" from Egypt; "redeemed from slavery"; guided by Moses, Aaron, and Miriam; blessed by foreign prophets like Balaam (Num. 22:5–6); and forced to recognize divine anger and retribution when they fell into idolatry and disobedience at Shittim (Num. 25:1).

Some scholars suggest that the next set of questions (Mic. 6:6–7) is a whining, almost sarcastic response by the people, who believe that God is burdening them by making extravagant demands on their resources. Instead, the mounting tone of indignation over the query "With what shall I come before the LORD," which ends with proposing impossibly large offerings like "ten thousands of rivers of oil" and the "firstborn" child (6:7), more likely represent Micah's harsh criticism of Israelite cultic practices (cf. a similar sarcastic tone in

Amos 4:4–5). Like Amos's contention in Amos 5:21–24, rejecting their "solemn assemblies, . . . burnt offerings," and the noise of their songs, Micah drives a stake into a belief system based on quantity rather than the quality of faith.

To finalize his point and to provide a much simpler expression of devotion to Yahweh, Micah lays out, in much the same way that Samuel does (1 Sam. 15:22), that obedience is more important than sacrifice. They must "do justice . . . love kindness, and . . . walk humbly with your God" (Mic. 6:8). His statement is very similar to that in Hosea 12:6, which calls on the people to "hold fast to love and justice, and wait continually for your God," and is echoed in a later generation by Jeremiah (7:21–23), who indicates that God does not require burnt offerings. Instead, the people are to "walk only in the way that I command you, so that all will be well with you" (see Exod. 15:26). In each case, it is the peace that comes with the knowledge of God (Hosea 6:6), which then is reflected in an adherence to and a true understanding of *khesed*, "everlasting love."

Better to Obey Than Sacrifice

With what shall I come before the LORD,
and bow myself before God on high?
Shall I come before him with burnt offerings,
with calves a year old?
Will the LORD be pleased with thousands of rams,
with ten thousands of rivers of oil?
Shall I give my firstborn for my transgression,
the fruit of my body for the sin of my soul?"
He has told you, O mortal, what is good;
and what does the LORD require of you
but to do justice, and to love kindness,
and to walk humbly with your God? (Mic. 6:6–8)

For I desire steadfast love and not sacrifice,
the knowledge of God rather than burnt offerings.
(Hosea 6:6)

Has the LORD as great delight in burnt offerings and sacrifices,
as in obeying the voice of the LORD?
Surely, to obey is better than sacrifice. (1 Sam. 15:22)

Concern over Social Injustice. The failure of Israel's leaders to provide justice, as is their responsibility, is a common charge of the prophets (see Amos 2:6–8; 5:10–12; Hosea 4:6–10). There is a real sense of the world turned upside down in Micah's remarks, which are similar to those found in Egyptian literature during the First Intermediate Period (2258–2050 BCE), when the social and economic structures of that country were crumbling. In the Egyptian story of the Farmer and the Courts, an eloquent peasant pleads for justice when a corrupt official's greed has cost the man his donkey. So too Amos and Micah, both prophets from the rural area of Judah, champion the weak and proclaim that God will have no mercy on avaricious judges, who devour the people like cannibals (Mic. 3:1–4). The prophets assure their audience that when judgment comes upon their oppressors, "they will cry to the LORD, but he will not answer them" (Mic. 3:4).

Framing his prophecy in the form of a covenant lawsuit, Micah details God's indictment of the people before a court whose witnesses are the physical structures of creation (mountains and foundations of the earth). In the midst of the turmoil caused by the succession of political crises in the late eighth century, Micah points to large landowners and wealthy individuals who seek to prey on small farmers, seizing their land for debt, squeezing them of their holdings, and depriving them of their covenantal inheritance (2:1–2). Isaiah makes a similar charge against those who "join house to house, who add field to field" (Isa. 5:8). Micah taunts these ravenous, landed gentry, defying them to close their eyes and ears to his words when God directs the Assyrians to dispossess them and deprive them of their ability to pass on their lands to their heirs (2:4–6).

A World without Justice

Those who distribute the grain put more in their own ration. Those authorized to give full measures short their people. Lawmakers approve of robbery. Who is left to punish the wrongdoer? The Inspector pushes aside the infirm. The respectable condone what is crooked. One is publicly criminal, the other tolerates injustice. Do not learn from such as these. (Farmer and the Courts, *OTPar*³, 234)

They hate the one who reproves in the gate,
  and they abhor the one who speaks the truth.
  (Amos 5:10)

Hear this, you rulers of the house of Jacob
  and chiefs of the house of Israel,
who abhor justice
  and pervert equity,
who build Zion with blood
  and Jerusalem with wrong!
Its rulers give judgment for a bribe,
  its priests teach for a price,
  its prophets give oracles for money;
yet they lean upon the LORD and say,
  "Surely the LORD is with us!" (Mic. 3:9–11)

The conclusion to the indictment comes in a typical form of prophetic speech, including a retelling of God's saving acts (Mic. 6:3–5; see also Jer. 2:6; Amos 2:10). The prophet frames a solution to what he perceives as the nation's ills. The people must return to the Sinai covenant and its simple injunctions. Like Samuel and Hosea, he places ritual and ceremony second to obedience to the law. God will not tolerate those who, for their own gain, adulterate what is designed to serve the people's needs (Mic. 6:10–15).

Restoration. Although there is some concern that the passages in Micah dealing with restoration of the nation and the monarchy have been inserted by later editors, it is not out of character for a prophet in the seventh century BCE to use these themes. One of Micah's most important statements concerns the rise of a new Davidic ruler from Bethlehem (Mic. 5:2; see the NT interpretation in Matt. 2:6). Having the future leader come from this insignificant village serves two purposes. First, it takes the monarchy back to its roots, since this is also David's birthplace. Second, it removes the taint of career politician or insider from the position of king. The new king will be obedient to Yahweh's voice, "feeding the flock" (cf. Ezek. 34:23–24) and providing the people with security and peace by eliminating the Assyrian threat (Mic. 5:4–5).

The restoration also includes a cleansing of the nation, that is, a removal of idols and other signs of foreign worship (Mic. 5:12–14; see Isa. 17:8 and Jer. 17:2 for other examples of this type of worship practice). When Yahweh has removed the evildoers from the land and justice is restored, then the shame that was upon the nation will be removed. In what is termed a prophetic litany because it contains alternating voices and a combination of themes, Mic. 7:8–20 announces that in the time to come the nations of Assyria and Egypt will become desolate and will "stand in fear" of Yahweh. Like many prophets, Micah becomes a voice of both condemnation in the present and of hope for a better future when God will once again shepherd the people (7:14).

STUDY QUESTIONS

1. Why is Micah's perspective different from that of his prophetic contemporary Isaiah?
2. On what basis does Micah condemn the cities of Jerusalem and Samaria (Mic. 1:2–16)?
3. Why would a prophet who condemns Jerusalem predict an ideal Davidic king, coming from Bethlehem, as the restorer of the nation (Mic. 5:1–2)?
4. Compare Micah's emphasis on covenant obedience with the statement in 1 Sam. 15:22.

5. Why do the prophets find sarcasm such an effective rhetorical method (1 Sam. 15:13–19; Amos 4:4–5; Mic. 6:6–7)?

6. Is Micah's simpler view of covenantal obedience naive or a real alternative to temple worship (Mic. 6:8)?

Prophetic Voices of the Late Seventh Century BCE

KEY POINTS

- The prophets in the late seventh century BCE anticipate the fall of the Assyrian Empire and the approaching conquest of Judah by the Neo-Babylonians.
- Nahum, Zephaniah, Obadiah, and Habakkuk voice prophetic themes like the "day of the LORD" typically found in other prophets.
- The message of these minor prophets primarily addresses specific events just prior to Josiah's reform in the early sixth century.

It may seem like a curiosity that there are no prophetic voices associated with the mid-seventh century BCE. The very brief chronicle of events that describe this period in 2 Kings 21:2–9 indicates that Judah is completely under the political and cultural control of Assyria during Manasseh's long reign (697–642 BCE). With no immediate sign of change, there may not have been a crisis to spark prophetic speech. What little is known of the period is recorded in 2 Kings 21:1–18, which is a litany of the king's crimes and religious apostasies (esp. 21:2–9). Manasseh is only a child at the time that he is crowned king. His advisers would have been careful to see that their tiny nation made no move that would once again bring the wrath of Assyria down on them. In contrast to the Deuteronomist's harsh appraisal, the postexilic Chronicler's account portrays Manasseh as a repentant sovereign and reformer (2 Chron. 33:1–9) who

could not be blamed for Jerusalem's fall to the Babylonians (as 2 Kings 21:10–15 does). The Chronicler may be responding to the length of Manasseh's reign (fifty-five years). It is possible that the Chronicler chose to discount the Deuteronomist's negative appraisal in order to demonstrate to the postexilic community that even the worst individual can be redeemed.

Several decades pass between the pronouncements of Isaiah and Micah at the end of the eighth century and the restoration of prophetic activity during the reign of Josiah (640–609 BCE). Perhaps they have all gone into hiding as they did in Ahab's reign (1 Kings 18:4), or it may be that the harsh words of Isaiah and Micah have served to keep a flame of belief alive even during this period. As we will see, the four short books written by Nahum, Zephaniah, Habakkuk, and Obadiah provide a transition reflecting the demise of the Assyrian Empire and the, at times, hopeful and rather confused era of the late seventh century BCE. They also complement and augment the prophetic message found in the works of Jeremiah and Ezekiel.

The Book of Nahum

Nothing is known about the author of the book of Nahum, and he is not referred to as a prophet, although his message is identified as an oracle (Nah. 1:1). His short book cannot be dated with certainty, although its mention of the Assyrian sack of the Egyptian capital of Thebes in 663 BCE (3:8–10) provides a chronological time frame for the destruction of Assyria's capital at Nineveh in 612 BCE. In addition, the general optimism of the text suggests a date prior to the end of Josiah's reign (609 BCE). Perhaps because of the many atrocities committed by the Assyrian armies as they ravaged both Israel and Judah, it is not so unusual to find a work so single-mindedly devoted to cheering the defeat of an enemy city. However, since no nation or tyrant remains in power forever, the prophet Nahum, whose name means "comfort," can be allowed his brief moment of glory. He is probably joined by many others in that era who celebrated the imminent destruction of Nineveh to a combined army of Chaldeans/Babylonians and Medes. It is clearly the view of the prophet that the hated Assyrians at last are about to receive the justice they so richly deserve.

Nahum begins with a theophanic hymn (1:2–8) that depicts, in a partial alphabetic **acrostic** poem, a God who is both "jealous and avenging" (1:2) as well as "slow to anger" (1:3). The assurance is that God will not allow the oppressors to go unpunished. God's "vengeance" is a further example of the contest theme found in Exod. 6–12 and 1 Kings 18. No other god will be allowed to supplant or conquer Yahweh. The appearance of Yahweh as commander of the winds is reminiscent of the theophanies found in Habakkuk (esp. 3:10) and Job (38:1), and is representative of the powers of the high gods of Israel's neighbors. The hymn's typical imagery of the storm-God, who is wrapped in thunderclouds and commands the sea and the rivers (Nah. 1:3–4), allows clear comparisons with the Canaanite/Ugaritic storm-god Baal. This suggests both literary borrowing of these motifs as well as their conversion by the Israelite poet in order to portray Yahweh's complete power over all creation (see similar imagery in Pss. 18:15–16; 104:6–7).

These theophanic manifestations—including Yahweh's triumphant march, his thundering voice, and the convulsions of the mountains at his stride (Nah. 1:4–6)—tie God's presence to the threats made by the prophet against Assyria and its king. In the midst of divine manifestations of towering rage, God is still portrayed as open and caring to those who trust in him (Nah. 1:7–8; cf. Isa. 8:8). Yahweh's dual character provides a sense of comfort that wrongs will be addressed and the faithful will be restored.

The use of a theodicy to indicate that Yahweh is the force behind the newly emerging Neo-Babylonian (Chaldean) leader Nabopolassar's army is typical of Israelite prophecy. When Nah. 2 opens, the herald or courier of God appears to predict Nineveh's fall in graphic detail. The mass confusion of a city being sacked, its strength ebbing like the scattered waters of a shattered fountain (2:8), would be welcomed by Israelites who believed that a just God never leaves the guilty unpunished. The gory description of shields dripping

Figure 4.7. The land of Judah was also devastated by the Assyrians. This scene from a Nimrud palace wall relief shows the attack on the city of Lachish by Assyrian slingers and archers. (Baker Photo Archive, courtesy of the British Museum)

with blood and war chariots careening through the streets (2:3–4) must have been satisfying to the people of Judah, who have suffered great devastation at the hands of Assyrian armies.

It must have been heartening to the people of Jerusalem to hear the prophet's voice proclaiming Yahweh's threat against Nineveh: "I am against you" (Nah. 3:5).

In the face of such a divine threat, Nahum taunts the Assyrians, asking, "Are you better than Thebes?" (3:8). The Egyptian city of Thebes, also dedicated to a god (Amon), had been captured and destroyed by the Assyrian emperor Ashurbanipal in 663 BCE. Lots had been cast (3:10) to distribute its nobility as slaves to the conquerors (a practice also found in Homer's *Iliad* and in Joel 3:3), and its rich palaces had been plundered. Now Nahum asserts that it is Nineveh's turn. Although the city is admonished to prepare for a siege (3:14), the people of Nineveh are told that their efforts will not save them because their "troops are women in your midst" and "the gates of your land are wide open to your foes" (3:13). Then, using a phrase common in the Assyrian Annals identifying the kings as the shepherds of the people, Nahum tells them that their "shepherds are asleep" (3:18) and their enemies now "clap their hands" over the anticipation of their demise. This common gesture of derision also appears in Lam. 2:15, where Jerusalem is the destroyed city. In this case, Jerusalem is scorned by those who witness its ruined state, and they signal their disdain by clapping, hissing, and wagging their heads (cf. Ezek. 6:11).

The nation of Judah is able to revel in Nineveh's destruction for only a few years. As the seventh century comes to an end, they are quickly swept up in the empire-building aims of Egypt and Babylonia. King Josiah, whose religious reforms and political ambitions have temporarily rejuvenated the nation, is killed by the Egyptians at Megiddo in 609 BCE, and the nation falls under the strict hegemony of new rulers who are just as demanding as the Assyrians.

The Book of Zephaniah

As the Assyrian Empire came to an end and Judah emerged from Manasseh's puppet rule, new prophetic voices began to be heard condemning the failure to eliminate Baal worship and encouraging the people and leaders of Judah to restore Yahweh as their supreme deity. Among them is Zephaniah, whose name may be an assertion that "Yahweh is Zaphon," a claim that Yahweh is the sole source of power even over the Baal stronghold/sacred mountain of Baal. Dating to the period of Josiah's reign (640–609 BCE), the book of Zephaniah contains oracles against idolatry and confirms God's judgment of Judah's sins and those of its neighbors. One image he, like several other prophets, repeatedly employs is the image of the "day of the LORD [Yahweh]" (1:8–18; 2:2). This image is associated with God's judgment of Judah and all other nations (1:14–15). For instance, in Isa. 13:9–11 and 17:7–9, the day of the Lord will coincide with the nations' being confronted by the reality of true power, when God will put an end to their pride, their arrogance, and their useless altars. In Zephaniah, the people are warned to show proper respect in the face of the coming manifestation of divine justice when "princes" and those who have become wealthy by promoting foreign influences will be punished (1:12). God will rain down bloody ruin and destruction in a display of such wrath that it can be compared with the blaring of battle trumpets and the clashing of arms associated with human battles, leaving the survivors to walk about in a daze like the blind (1:14–18).

Following the messenger formula in Zeph. 1:1, the book can be divided into three segments: 1:2–2:3 contains a pronouncement of judgment on Jerusalem and Judah; 2:4–15 is a collection of oracles against foreign nations; and 3:1–20 includes a promise of ultimate transformation of Judah and salvation for its people.

The most pervasive image used is the day of the Lord (Zeph. 1:8, 14, 18; 2:2) and the judgment of God on the people (1:14–15). The day of Yahweh is usually considered to be a day of expected hope and restoration. However, in this instance and often in other prophetic writings, it is tied to a stern recital of the bitter fate that can be expected for those who have violated the covenant (cf. Amos 5:18–20). This momentous day is a "day of ruin and devastation" (Zeph. 1:15) for Jerusalem, not just for Judah's oppressors (see Isa. 13:6–22). Zephaniah's fierce condemnation of Judah's syncretized religious practices (1:2–6; 3:3–4) is an indication that these prophecies were uttered prior to the institution of the Deuteronomic reform (pre-621 BCE). That position is supported by the fact that Josiah is never mentioned by name. However, Zephaniah's concentration on syncretism could also be one of the arguments used to support the cleansing of Judah's religion during the midst of Josiah's reform movement.

The prophet's vision is one of annihilation for the whole of creation:

> I will utterly sweep away everything
> from the face of the earth, says the
> Lord.
> I will sweep away humans and animals;
> I will sweep away the birds of the air
> and the fish of the sea.
> I will make the wicked stumble.
> I will cut off humanity
> from the face of the earth, says the
> Lord. (Zeph. 1:2–3)

Such massive destruction recalls Noah's flood story (Gen. 6–9). It may have also been influenced by the vision of devastation described in Isaiah's call narrative: "Until cities lie waste without inhabitant, and houses without people, and the land is utterly desolate" (6:11). Even with its all-inclusive devastation, Zephaniah states that God is not satisfied with condemning whole lands and cities. Specific groups are targeted for God's judgment. All who have bowed to gods other than Yahweh and turned their back on the Lord (1:4–6) are condemned. The expression "cut off" (*hakrît*) in Zeph. 1:4 refers to the extinction of households that are denied children (see 2 Sam. 14:7 for the devastating effect of a house without an heir). Like other prophets who predict calamity for the nation, Zephaniah still voices a feeble hope for the righteous remnant that chooses to "seek the Lord" (Zeph. 2:3).

One particularly poignant image in Zephaniah is that of Yahweh searching Jerusalem with a lamp for "those who say in their hearts, 'The Lord will not do good, nor will he do harm'" (Zeph. 1:12). These complacent people have convinced themselves that God takes no

> ### The Remnant Theme
>
> Seek good and not evil,
>   that you may live;
> and so the LORD, the God of hosts, will be with
>   you,
>   just as you have said.
> Hate evil and love good,
>   and establish justice in the gate;
> it may be that the LORD, the God of hosts,
>   will be gracious to the remnant of Joseph.
>   (Amos 5:14–15)
>
> Seek the LORD, all you humble of the land,
>   who do his commands;
> seek righteousness, seek humility;
>   perhaps you may be hidden
>   on the day of the LORD's wrath. (Zeph. 2:3)

direct role in the affairs of history, for good or evil. They must therefore be shaken out of their drunken stupor by the plundering of their houses and the stripping of their storehouses (1:13). This single-minded determination to cleanse the city of evil is also found in Ezekiel's vision of the marking of the innocents prior to Jerusalem's destruction (Ezek. 9). Jeremiah reverses Zephaniah's image, with Yahweh instead searching for "the one person who acts justly and seeks truth" (Jer. 5:1). In the face of God's anger, Zephaniah offers little hint of mercy and leaves only a simple path for survival of a remnant (cf. Amos 5:14–15).

Only when God has completed the coming judgment on the nation is there a hope for restoration. At that point, once the "proudly exultant ones" have been purged from their midst, a "people humble and lowly" will reemerge to "seek refuge in the name of the LORD" (Zeph. 3:11–12). Such a lack of compromise is typical of a zealous reformer who recognizes the harm that syncretism has caused and the value in establishing a clear cultural and religious identity for Judah.

Zephaniah balances his horrific statements of Judah's doom by providing an assurance that Judah's foes will also suffer God's judgment. He speaks a number of oracles against the nations, including Philistia, Moab, Ammon, Ethiopia, and Assyria, and they are even more graphic in their descriptions of Yahweh's wrath:

> Moab shall become like Sodom
>   and the Ammonites like Gomorrah,
> a land possessed by nettles and salt pits,
>   and a waste forever. . . .
> The LORD will be terrible against them;
>   he will shrivel all the gods of the
>   earth. . . .
> And he will stretch out his hand against
>   the north,
>   and destroy Assyria;
> and he will make Nineveh a desolation,
>   a dry waste like the desert. (Zeph.
>   2:9, 11, 13)

The ultimate human boast of the Assyrians, "I am, and there is no one else" (2:15a), will not be left unchallenged but will be the basis for total desolation and loathing: the abandoned city of Nineveh will be the home to wild animals, and "everyone who passes by it hisses and shakes the fist" (2:15b).

After his condemnation of the foreign nations, Zephaniah turns his attention once again to Judah's shortcomings. He does this in the form of a woe oracle directed at Jerusalem in Zeph. 3. His charges may be based on the failure of the people to continue the Deuteronomic reform after the death of Josiah in 609 BCE, or may be the result of their rejection of the prophet (cf. Jeremiah's personal laments in Jer. 20:7–18). Zephaniah 3 also contains another promise for the righteous remnant. He declares that for this select group there will be a transformation of their words into "pure speech" (3:9), perhaps in the same manner as Isaiah's lips are purified (Isa. 6:5–7). The nation also will have been purified of the "proudly exultant ones," leaving the humble and lowly, who "will pasture and lie down" as Yahweh's flock (Zeph. 3:12–13). In this new era, the people will trust in Yahweh rather than in human leaders, and the result will be the peace and security that had been denied them during the time when rampant political ambitions had held sway.

The final segment of the book (Zeph. 3:14–20) contains a proclamation of salvation for the people and the restoration of Jerusalem. It does tie fairly well into the theme in the previous segment in Zeph. 3. There is a promise that the prophets will no longer need to pronounce woe oracles against the people (3:18). However, there are also elements of postexilic literature in this passage that compare quite well with the words of comfort found in Isa. 40:1–2 and Isa. 54:1. Therefore, this portion of Zeph. 3 is probably a later addition to the prophetic text.

The Book of Habakkuk

The book of Habakkuk consists of three distinct sections, suggesting that these materials may have been edited and put into final form by the prophet or his followers in the decade or so after Josiah's death in 609 BCE. The oracles found in Hab. 1 can probably be dated to the reign of Jehoiakim and, more specifically, to before 605 BCE, when the Chaldean armies of Nebuchadnezzar defeated the Egyptian-Assyrian coalition at the battle of Carchemish. Habakkuk reflects the prophet's familiarity with the Chaldean presence in Judah in the period after 605 BCE and possibly as late as 598 BCE. By 597 BCE, the Neo-Babylonians capture Jerusalem and take king Jehoiachin as a hostage (2 Kings 24:10–14), ending the effective period of Habakkuk's

> ## Postexilic Words of Comfort
>
> Sing aloud, O daughter Zion;
>   shout, O Israel!
> Rejoice and exult with all your heart,
>   O daughter Jerusalem!
> The LORD has taken away the judgments against you,
>   he has turned away your enemies. (Zeph. 3:14–15)
>
> Comfort, O comfort my people,
>   says your God.
>
> Speak tenderly to Jerusalem,
>   and cry to her
>   that she has served her term,
>   that her penalty is paid,
> that she has received from the LORD's hand
> double for all her sins. (Isa. 40:1–2)
>
> Sing, O barren one who did not bear;
>   burst into song and shout,
>   you who have not been in labor!
> For the children of the desolate woman will be more
>   than the children of her that is married, says the
>   LORD. (Isa. 54:1)

message. The first segment of this short book (Hab. 1:2–2:5) contains a theodicy in the form of a litany of the world's ills and the seeming victory of evil. Faced with the oppression of first Egyptian and then Babylonian rule and the misrule of their own king, Jehoiakim, Habakkuk raises the question of "how long" the people must wait for God to intervene (Hab. 1:2; cf. the complaint in Job 21:7–30). This unjust situation, as he describes it, is similar to that found in the Egyptian tale of the Eloquent Peasant, who defines a world without justice as one in which "judges take sides in a dispute" and "magistrates are corrupt," while merchants are free to give "short measure" when distributing grain (*OTPar³*, 234–35).

The intent here is to pose this question: if Yahweh is involved in the world situation at that tumultuous time, then has Yahweh committed an unjust act against the people in unleashing the Babylonians? "The wicked surround the righteous—therefore judgment comes forth perverted" (Hab. 1:4b). God responds (1:5–11) by saying that the Babylonians have been chosen to punish Judah as well as the other nations (cf. Isaiah's similar reference to the Assyrian threat in 10:5).

Habakkuk then voices a second complaint (1:12–17), asking why God uses the wicked Babylonians as the instrument of judgment against Judah. A brief transition is then provided (2:1), stationing the prophet as a sentry awaiting God's response to this complaint. God then orders the prophet to write down the elements of a vision (cf. Isa. 8:1–4), which contains divine judgment on proud, arrogant Babylon (Hab. 2:2–5).

At this point, five statements of reassurance and of judgment or woes are declared against the people and/or nations that temporarily prosper through illegal and violent means (Hab. 2:6–20). The woe oracle is a commonly employed genre of prophetic speech, introduced by the particle *hoy*, an **onomatopoeic** word designed to express deep emotions like anger, grief, and fear. The pattern of the woe oracle includes a threat that accompanies the charge, which is then spelled out, often in gruesome detail, in the accompanying verses. Examples of the form are found in Isaiah's "Woe to those who . . ." statements (3:9; 5:8) and in Jeremiah's beseeching cry, "Woe to you, O Jerusalem!" (13:27). Each of these cries of woe is followed by the threat of punishment to come.

In his use of the woe oracle, Habakkuk first points to the looting of the invading Babylonians: "Alas for you who heap up what is not your own! How long will you load yourselves with goods taken in pledge?" (2:6). The object here is to warn them that their oppressed creditors shall "suddenly rise," and "you will be booty for them" (2:7). In a similar manner,

Isaiah condemns the wealthy landowners who have driven the small farmers off their land in order to "join house to house." He assures them that their beautiful houses will soon be lying desolate "without inhabitant" (5:8–9; cf. Hab. 2:9–10).

Habakkuk completes his list of woe pronouncements with a condemnation of idolatry and the charlatan practices of priests who call on wood and stone images to "Wake up!" or to "Rouse yourself!" (2:19). The intention of the prophet may be to cry out against the Babylonian ritual of "opening the mouth" that is designed to transform a manufactured object into the physical embodiment of the god. But he also joins many other prophets who ridicule the very idea that an idol can be considered a god or can be relied on for help (see Isa. 40:18–19; Hosea 4:12; 13:2).

Also embedded in this section is a taunt song that decries plundering the nations (Hab. 2:6b–8), unjust gain (2:9–11), bloodshed (2:12–14), and debauchery and rape (2:15–17). It concludes with a condemnation of idolatry (2:18–19). The reassurance of God's reigning presence in his holy temple silences all possible dissent or unbelief (2:20).

> Shall not everyone taunt such people
> and, with mocking riddles say about
> them,
> "Alas for you who heap up what
> is not your own!
> How long will you load yourselves
> with goods
> taken in pledge?" (Hab. 2:6)

Another interesting aspect of the book is its use of elements found in psalms of lament (Pss. 22; 137) and in Wisdom literature. These literary elements place value on the person who can hope for the eventual triumph of Yahweh and the people of Judah over their enemies: "If it seems to tarry, wait for it; it will surely come, it will not delay" (Hab. 2:3b). Taking such a patient view over the rash demand for action is found in many wisdom pieces from the ancient Near East. The emphasis placed by the prophet on "living by faith" (2:4) will have a great effect on Martin Luther and the leaders of the Protestant Reformation.

The third section of Habakkuk (Hab. 3) is a psalm, structured much like those in the book of Psalms. It contains a **superscription** including the technical term *shigionoth*, which may refer to a lament or perhaps the meter of the psalm (cf. Ps. 7). This is the only place outside the Psalms in which the word *Selah* appears as a segment divider between portions of text (on this, see the section on Psalms, beginning on p. 250). The poem contains the marching forth of a transcendent Creator using the elements of nature to manifest divine power and to save the people: "In fury you trod the earth, in anger you trampled nations.... You trampled the sea with your horses, churning the mighty waters" (Hab. 3:12, 15).

Throughout, the psalm employs natural phenomena to emphasize Yahweh's transcendent power as the Divine Warrior. It is possible that the prophet is intentionally drawing on figurative images common in Ugaritic and Canaanite epic poetry. Habakkuk describes God's divine rage displayed against the sea (cf. Baal's epic battle against the sea god Yamm in *OTPar³*, 269–70), the slaughter of enemy soldiers (Hab. 3:13–14; cf. the goddess Anat's "wading knee-deep in warriors' blood" in *OTPar³*, 265).

A tension is expressed in the song at this point as the prophet anticipates the day when God will fulfill his petition. This expectation in turn suggests a basic liturgical character to

---

Wisdom's Affirmation of Patience

- The plans of the diligent lead surely to abundance, but everyone who is hasty comes only to want. (Prov. 21:5)
- Thorns and snares are in the way of the perverse; the cautious will keep far from them. (Prov. 22:5)
- If one strains to seek perfection, in a moment he has marred it. Keep firm your heart, steady your heart. (Instruction of Amenemope, *COS* 1:47, XX.1–3.120)
- Blessed is the man who thinks before he speaks. (Teachings of Ankhsheshonq(y), *OTPar³*, 312)
- Look at the proud! Their spirit is not right in them, but the righteous live by their faith. (Hab. 2:4)
- I wait quietly for the day of calamity to come upon the people who attack us. (Hab. 3:16)

---

the composition and the use of this poem in a priestly procession or dramatic ritual. However, it may also provide an opportunity for an audience familiar with Israelite hymnic tradition to join in the chorus, singing of their hope for eventual liberation. In the face of the devastation suffered by the people at the hands of the Babylonians, the faith of the author comes through in a final victory hymn (Hab. 3:17–19), "rejoicing in the LORD" and knowing that God will be their "savior" (cf. Ps. 13:5–6).

The Book of Obadiah

This brief prophetic book consists of a single chapter (just 21 verses) and dates to the period after the final Babylonian invasion and conquest of Judah (post-587 BCE). Nothing is known of its author, whose name means "servant" and may be a title rather than a personal name. Throughout this short book, the poet draws on familiar prophetic themes and languages. Thus the "day of Yahweh" (Obad. 8, 11, 15) is also found in Amos 5:18–22 and Isa. 2:12–22. By contrasting pride and humiliation in reference to the overthrow of Edom (Obad. 4–6), the prophet echoes similar statements in Isa. 2:5–17 and in Ezekiel's oracle against Tyre (Ezek. 28:2–10).

Figure 4.8. Eighth-century-BCE relief of a procession of Hittite musicians. Music played a role in the religious, political, and social life of ancient peoples. (Kim Walton, courtesy of the Istanbul Archaeological Museum)

The prime targets of Obadiah's oracles are Edom and other nations that exploited Judah's weakness by raiding and pillaging defenseless cities and towns. Edom's occupation of southern Judah and the hatred of the Herods (Idumeans/Edomites who rule under Roman authority some five hundred years later) generates an animosity toward Edom that continues into the rabbinic period (70–500 CE), when Edom is equated with Rome in rabbinic denunciations of foreign oppressors. The theme fits into a collection of anti-Edomite literature from this period (see Joel 3:19; Jer. 49:7–22; Ezek. 25:12–16) and may even relate back to the struggle between Jacob (Judah) and Esau (Edom) in Gen. 27:41–45.

There are occasional references to Edom as an ally of Israel in the biblical narrative (2 Kings 3:9). However, its relationship with Judah (from the reign of Jehoram [853–841 BCE] until Jerusalem's fall [587 BCE]) is filled with violence and harsh dealings. A sign of the enmity between these two nations is found in Amos's geographically based oracle against the nations surrounding Israel. In the section on Edom (1:11–15), the prophet refers to brandishing swords, perpetual anger, and a lack of pity that would lead God to rain down fire on Edom's major cities, Teman and Borzah. These traditions may be based on incidents throughout the period of the monarchy (1 Sam. 14:47; 2 Sam. 8:12–14; 14:7) as well as events in Amos's own time, when King Uzziah captures and rebuilds the Edomite port of Elath on the Gulf of Aqaba (2 Kings 14:22; 2 Chron. 26:2).

The principle on which Obadiah justifies his call for revenge and destruction of Judah's enemies is based on the law of reciprocity. All nations, not just Judah, must observe the maxim that a people who are not at war should not do violence to their neighbors or gloat over their misery (Obad. 12). The principle applies especially to the case for those who are already in distress because of natural or human-related catastrophe. Thus Obadiah confidently states, "As you have done, so shall it be done to you" (Obad. 15). His statement provides a corollary to the legal principle of lex talionis found elsewhere in biblical law (Exod. 21:23–25; Lev.

> ### Legal Principle of *Lex Talionis*
>
> As you have done, it shall be done to you;
>   your deeds shall return on your own head.
>   (Obad. 15)
>
> Anyone who maims another shall suffer the same injury in return. (Lev. 24:19)
>
> If the father of one household breaks a bone of another, then his bone is to be broken. (CH 197 in OTPar³, 112)
>
> If a man without grounds accuses another man of a matter of which he has no knowledge, and that man does not prove it, he shall bear the penalty of the matter for which he made the accusation. (from the Lipit Ishtar Code; quote in M. Roth, *Law Collections from Mesopotamia and Asia Minor*, SBL Writings from the Ancient World Series 6 [Scholars Press, 1995], 29)

24:19–20) and in the law codes of the ancient Near East (see inset above).

In its reflection on the dislocation of the people of Jerusalem, who have been taken into captivity by the Babylonians and told that their God has forgotten them, the postexilic author of Ps. 137 creates a pattern that is also found in Obadiah. Instead of giving in to depression, the psalmist provides assurance that God will never allow the people's vision of Jerusalem to dim or their desire to return to their land to diminish. With this assurance, the poet then calls on God for recompense against their enemies. A similar pattern to this complaint-assurance-petition structure is found in the oracle against Edom in Obadiah. However, it comes in a slightly different order: petition-assurance-complaint-assurance.

Rhetoric such as this (cf. the similar language in Jer. 49:7–22) expresses the range of emotions over betrayal and destruction and the hope for a day when Yahweh will bring judgment on their enemies. In that sense the lament form is a means of purging the sufferer of bitterness through the assurance that evil cannot prevail.

Obadiah's Lament Pattern

Petition: "A messenger has been sent among the nations:
'Rise up! Let us rise against it for battle.'"
(Obad. 1)
Assurance: "On that day, says the LORD,
I will destroy the wise out of Edom,
and understanding out of Mount Esau."
(Obad. 8)
Complaint: "On the day you stood aside, . . .
you should not have gloated over your brother. . . .
You should not have boasted on the day of distress." (Obad. 11–12)
Assurance: "As you have done, it shall be done to you;
your deeds shall return on your own head."
(Obad. 15)

Obadiah's oracle of restoration contains the familiar image of Yahweh triumphant on Mount Zion (cf. Isa. 30:19–26; 31:4–9; Zeph. 3:14–20). The day of the Lord will bring justice to the plunderers and the occupation of Edomite, Phoenician, and Philistine territories by the people of Judah (Obad. 19–20). Such a remarkable political reversal of fortunes is matched by the restoration of Yahweh's name as Lord of all nations: "Those who have been saved shall go up to Mount Zion to rule Mount Esau; and the kingdom shall be the LORD's" (Obad. 21; cf. Ps. 22:28).

STUDY QUESTIONS

1. According to the tradition found in the Deuteronomistic account of the monarchy, what makes Manasseh the worst king in Judah's history (2 Kings 21:1–18)?
2. How do the prophets make use of the "day of the LORD" theme?
3. How helpful is Habakkuk's use of the woe oracle to the people of Judah? What purpose is served by detailing such gruesome threats against the nations by the Divine Warrior?
4. Why is Edom targeted so often by the prophets as an archenemy of Judah?

The Book of Jeremiah

KEY POINTS

- Jeremiah's message unfolds in the midst of tumultuous political events.
- Jeremiah's message focuses on exploding the myth of the inviolability of Jerusalem.
- Jeremiah reassures the exiles that they can continue to worship Yahweh outside of Judah.
- Jeremiah's "redeemed field" points to eventual return from exile and a restoration of the covenant community.

There are a wide variety of literary genres in the book of Jeremiah: poetry and prose, personal dialogues, prophetic speech, biography and autobiography, wisdom material, and sermonic pronouncements. All this material is set within the context of very turbulent times (626–587 BCE). As is often the case with the prophetic books, Jeremiah is not organized in chronological order, and therefore careful attention is necessary to determine precisely where an oracle or sermon fits into the events of his day. Throughout the book the prophet is an active participant in the events that signal Judah's declining political fortunes and the eventual destruction of Jerusalem by Nebuchadnezzar and the Neo-Babylonians. Although his prophetic role begins during the reign of Josiah (640–609 BCE), Jeremiah's first public appearance does not occur until the time of King Jehoiakim (ca. 604 BCE).

The fact that Jeremiah's public role does not occur prior to Josiah's death suggests that he was initially a supporter of the king's reform measures. It does seem curious that it is the otherwise unknown female prophet Huldah rather than Jeremiah who is consulted to authenticate the "scroll of the law" for Josiah (2 Kings 22:13–20). However, Jeremiah's extreme youth (Jer. 1:6) and his association with Anathoth, the site of a community of exiled priests of the line of Abiathar (1 Kings 2:26–27), may have worked against him. In addition, Huldah's husband is said to be a ranking member of the temple priesthood, and she may well have been an established court prophet. In any case, the death of Josiah at Megiddo in 609 BCE spells the end for his expansionist plans

Time Line of Events during Jeremiah's Prophetic Period

640–609	Josiah reigns as Judah's king.		600–598	Jehoiakim revolts; Nebuchadnezzar besieges and captures Jerusalem, takes a segment of the upper-class population as hostages back to Babylonia, including King Jehoiachin, and places Zedekiah on Judah's throne as his new puppet ruler (2 Kings 24:1–17).
627	The Assyrian emperor Ashurbanipal dies, and his empire begins to fall apart.			
622	Josiah begins his reform movement, centralizing authority in Jerusalem and taking initial steps to reclaim territory in the former northern kingdom (2 Kings 22:3–23:27).			
			598–588	Jeremiah engages in a series of enacted prophecies (Jer. 16–19) and writes at least one letter to the exiles in Babylonia (Jer. 29).
609	Josiah is killed in battle of Megiddo by Egyptian pharaoh Neco II (2 Kings 23:29).			
609–605	Jehoiakim serves as puppet king of Judah under Egyptian auspices.		588–587	Zedekiah revolts; Nebuchadnezzar besieges and captures Jerusalem and destroys the city and the temple. A much larger segment of the population is taken into exile in Babylonia (2 Kings 24:18–25:21). Jeremiah warns the people and King Zedekiah to "submit to the yoke of Babylon" as God's instrument of punishment (Jer. 27:11–12) and redeems a field as a promise of eventual return to the land (Jer. 32).
605	Battle of Megiddo signals Assyria's final defeat and emergence of Neo-Babylonian king Nebuchadnezzar as the new power in the Near East.			
ca. 605	Jeremiah delivers his temple sermon (Jer. 7; 26).			
ca. 604	Jeremiah sends Baruch to read a prophetic scroll in the temple (Jer. 36).			
ca. 604	Nebuchadnezzar claims control of Syria-Palestine, and Jehoiakim now becomes a puppet king for the Neo-Babylonians.		586	Gedaliah is appointed governor of Judah but is assassinated. Jeremiah is taken to Egypt by fleeing exiles (2 Kings 25:22–26; Jer. 41–43).

and for most of his reforms and sparks the beginning of a new era of submission by Judah to the superpowers.

Jeremiah's prophetic message unfolds within a poignant portrayal of the final years of Judah's monarchy. It reflects the prophet's efforts to warn and preserve a remnant of the people as they face the certainty of exile. The book itself appears to be a combined effort of the prophet Jeremiah, Baruch (Jeremiah's scribe and friend), and an unknown editor or editors. The portions that are written in the first person are powerful demonstrations of the emotions of anger, frustration, and great personal loss for the prophet. In many ways Jeremiah's distress is a mirror of Judah's disintegration as a nation. While the third-person accounts are more dispassionate, they allow the reader to step away from the anguish, analyze why it has come on the people of Judah, and understand the theodicy of a righteous God who punishes the nation but expects eventually to restore them as the people of the covenant.

Jeremiah's hometown may be a clue to understanding the focus of his message and in particular his fierce hatred of the monarchy and the temple. It is possible that Jeremiah is a descendant of the Levitical group that is exiled to Anathoth in Solomon's time as punishment for Abiathar's support of Solomon's brother Adonijah (1 Kings 2:26–27). With the appointment of Zadok as high priest, Abiathar's priestly group is forever frozen out of that prestigious office. Thus Jeremiah's words condemning the "unrighteousness" of the current rulers of the House of David (Jer. 22:13–17) and prophets and priests, who "deal falsely" with the people (8:10) and have "no knowledge" (14:18), may play into the desire of the Anathoth priesthood for revenge. Furthermore, his condemnation of lavish offerings of incense suggest a tie to previous prophets who decried elaborate cultic ceremonies while the leaders of the temple ignore God's warnings to reform their worship practices (Jer. 6:16–21; cf. Amos 5:21–24).

Jeremiah's Call Narrative

The actual date of Jeremiah's call as a prophet is still debated, but it is generally considered to be in the thirteenth year of Josiah's reign (627 BCE), the same year that the last great emperor of Assyria, Ashurbanipal, dies. The prophet's statement that he is "only a boy" (Jer. 1:7) suggests that he is a young adult, certainly younger than twenty-one, at this time. The question of dating his call also depends on his age when he confronts the people before the Jerusalem temple (Jer. 7; 26). His confidence level is quite high in that narrative, and the temple sermon is known to have occurred in the early reign of Jehoiakim (ca. 605 BCE). It therefore seems likely that Jeremiah receives his call sometime during the reign of Josiah (640–609 BCE), experiences Josiah's Deuteronomic reform (622–609 BCE), and then becomes an accomplished spokesman and prophet during the turbulent years following Josiah's death. Thus the bulk of Jeremiah's active work occurs during the time when Judah is subjugated first by Egypt (609–605 BCE) and then by Babylon (604–587 BCE).

As is the case with other prophets, Jeremiah's call narrative describes a change of status, accomplished through a ceremonial transformation of his person. It is similar to an initiation ritual into a fraternal order, installation as a priest, or coronation as a king. Each involves a programmed set of actions designed to apply a new label to the person and provide him or her with the symbols of membership peculiar to this new status. These symbols are designed to transform the individual in the eyes of the public. The new label can then be used to further the initiate's agenda or increase his or her authority.

The commissioning or ordination ritual of the prophet Jeremiah (Jer. 1:4–18) contains some familiar stages (see Moses in Exod. 3:2–4:23 and Gideon in Judg. 6:11–24). There is a theophanic appearance; a statement by the Deity of intention and relationship; an objection by the candidate and a negative label applied by the candidate to himself; a transforming action; an injunction and a legal empowerment; and a sign given by the Deity to reassure and strengthen the chosen one.

Yahweh appears to Jeremiah (no particular location is cited) and announces that a divinely ordained plan has existed for him as a prophet even "before I formed you in the womb" (Jer. 1:5; also found in Isa. 49:1). The concept of a designation "from the womb" is well known in ancient Near Eastern literature, although it is usually reserved for kings (see inset below).

Jeremiah pleads that he is powerless to fulfill the task that Yahweh has set before him because he is "only a boy" (Jer. 1:6). He is reassured by Yahweh that this is no impediment and is empowered to speak when God's hand touches his lips (Jer. 1:9; paralleling events in

---

Called from the Womb

A king am I; from the womb I have become a hero. (*Hymn of Shulgi,* Ur III king [c. 2050 BCE; *ANET,* 585])

Amun says: It was in the belly of your mother that I said concerning you that you were to be ruler of Egypt; it was as seed and while you were in the egg, that I knew you, that (I knew) you were to be Lord. (*Stele of Pianchi* [25th Dynasty of Egypt, 751–730 BCE]; M. Gilula, "An Egyptian Parallel to Jeremia I 4–5," *Vetus Testamentum* 17 [1967]: 114)

Deut. 18:18 for Moses, in Judg. 6:15 for Gideon, and in Isa. 6:6–7 for Isaiah).

At this point, a legal formula similar to the one used at royal coronations is employed (Pss. 2:7–9; 89:19–37). Jeremiah is told that when he speaks in his divinely chosen role as a prophet, he will wield the power usually reserved for kings or gods and is elevated above kings in authority (Jer. 18:7; 31:28). A similar formula is used by the divine assembly in the *Enuma Elish* creation story when they inaugurate the reign of the Babylonian god Marduk (see inset, p. 169). His commissioning ceremony transforms Jeremiah. Not only does he obtain the title of prophet, but also he now has the legitimate authority to speak and act in the name of God. In that sense, he obtains a measure of the power of the God for whom he performs his prophetic duties. Such a close parallel suggests either a familiarity with the Babylonian story by the biblical writer or a standardization of enthronement language in the Near East.

The final step in the transformation process is the giving of a sign by Yahweh or the divine messenger. The sign is designed to provide a sense of the prophet's mission as well as to serve as a reassurance that the prophet will receive divine assistance. In Jeremiah's case, this involves a pair of visions and their interpretations that indicate the source from which God's judgment will arise and a reassurance of divine protection (Jer. 1:11–16; visions of an almond branch and a boiling pot). Yahweh also gives Jeremiah a final charge and imposes the additional symbolic labels of "a fortified city, an iron pillar, and a bronze wall" to denote his invincibility (Jer. 1:18).

Jeremiah's Temple Sermon

The first major event in Jeremiah's prophetic career is his temple sermon. It is delivered at

The Power to Command

Henceforth your command cannot be changed, to raise high, to bring low, this shall be your power. Your command shall be truth, your word shall not be misleading. (*Enuma Elish* 4.7–9; *COS* 1:111, 397)

See, today I appoint you over nations and over kingdoms,
    to pluck up and to pull down,
    to destroy and to overthrow,
    to build and to plant. (Jer. 1:10)

the beginning of Jehoiakim's reign (Jer. 26:1) and reflects Yahweh's concern over Egypt's growing influences over Judah. There is also an acknowledgment of the emerging threat posed by the Neo-Babylonians (ca. 605 BCE). Jeremiah is aware of the political realities of the time, but like other prophets, he focuses on covenant and proper worship practices. Accounts of his sermon and the reaction it receives are found in Jer. 7 and Jer. 26. Jeremiah 7 is written in the first person and provides a detailed account of the sermon's themes as spoken by the prophet. Jeremiah 26 is written in the third person, possibly by Baruch, who is a professional scribe. It provides only an abbreviated version of the sermon while concentrating on the public reaction to Jeremiah's indictment of Jerusalem's people and the myth of the city's inviolability.

Location is always an important ingredient in giving speeches. Visibility and spatial symbolism are combined when God directs Jeremiah to stage his confrontation with the powers of Jerusalem at the entrance to the temple. This place serves as the physical conduit between secular and sacred space. It marks the boundary between contact with the world and contact with Yahweh. By standing here and blocking free movement back and forth, Jeremiah is assured of drawing a crowd. He comes to the temple on a major feast day (possibly the Feast of Booths, implying a date in either September or October). Because of this he can expect not only the people of Jerusalem but also persons and officials from all over the kingdom to hear his message.

The sermon focuses on two crucial themes. First he tells them that the presence of the temple dedicated to Yahweh does not ensure that Jerusalem will never be destroyed. The myth of inviolability has been growing since the time of Hezekiah, when the Assyrians failed to capture Jerusalem (2 Kings 19:20–37). It is reinforced by the reforms instituted by Josiah, which centralize sacrificial and festival practices in Jerusalem, the place God has chosen "as a dwelling for his name" (Deut. 14:23; 16:2; 26:2). Jeremiah's second major point is that obedience to the covenant and the stipulations of the Ten Commandments is necessary to prevent Yahweh's destruction of Judah and Jerusalem (cf. Josh. 1:7). Jeremiah uses a framework for his message based on repetition of the phrase "Amend your ways and your doings" (7:3, 5). He also mocks the popular chant "the temple of the LORD" (7:4). That phrase or chant is apparently both a ritual utterance used when entering the temple and a slogan reassuring the people of Yahweh's protection. It holds no significance for a people who only mouth the words while continuing to violate the covenant.

Jeremiah draws on the people's memory of the priestly community led by Eli at Shiloh (see 1 Sam. 1:3). The prophet uses that former shrine to Yahweh (about 20 miles north of Jerusalem) as his example of destruction. Although Shiloh has once served as the seat of Yahweh worship (1 Sam. 1–4), it has been destroyed by the Philistines because of the unfaithfulness of Eli's sons (1 Sam. 2:12–17). No amount of staged ritual behavior or sacrifice

Covenantal Obligations

Jer. 7:22–23

For in the day that I brought your ancestors out of the land of Egypt, I did not speak to them or command them concerning burnt offerings and sacrifices. But this command I gave them, "Obey my voice, and I will be your God, and you shall be my people; and walk only in the way that I command you, so that it may be well with you."

Mic. 6:6–8

With what shall I come before the Lord,
   and bow myself before God on high?
Shall I come before him with burnt offerings,
   with calves a year old?
Will the Lord be pleased with thousands of rams,
   with ten thousands of rivers of oil?
Shall I give my firstborn for my transgression,
   the fruit of my body for the sin of my soul?"
He has told you, O mortal, what is good;
   and what does the Lord require of you
but to do justice, and to love kindness,
   and to walk humbly with your God?

Geographic Reiteration: Shiloh

Jeremiah's reference to the destroyed sanctuary at Shiloh draws on a number of Israelite traditions at that site. Once again geographic reiteration seems to play a part in strengthening the point made by a biblical writer or, as in this case, a prophet.

Josh. 18:1	Joshua assembles the people at Shiloh following the conquest to redistribute the land among the Israelite tribes. The tent of meeting and the ark are present to signify God's presence during the distribution (see also Josh. 21:1–2).
Josh. 22:10–12	Representatives of Israelite tribes assemble at Shiloh to discuss the construction of an altar east of the Jordan River by the tribes in Gilead.
Judg. 18:31	Reference is made to a competing shrine at Dan that exists as long as "the house of God was at Shiloh."
1 Kings 2:26–27	Solomon banishes Abiathar and his priestly group to Anathoth, "fulfilling the word of the Lord that he had spoken concerning the house of Eli in Shiloh" (see 1 Sam. 2:31–35).
Ps. 78:60	The psalmist recounts the covenant history and states that God "abandoned his dwelling at Shiloh."

could save Eli's sons or the place of worship at Shiloh (1 Sam. 3:11–14) because without due respect for Yahweh's covenant, sacrificial ritual was merely hollow worship. Jerusalem is therefore not free from the threat of destruction if similar conditions reign there.

Like Micah in the previous century, Jeremiah decries mindless ritual behavior that does not contain the fervent desire to obey Yahweh's covenant (Jer. 7:23; cf. Mic. 6:6–8). Once again we see the familiar theme that sacrifice without the love (*khesed*) of Yahweh and the covenant has no worth. We have already seen this theme in Samuel's confrontation with Saul (1 Sam. 15:22) and in the words of Hosea, "For I desire steadfast love [*khesed*] and not sacrifice, the knowledge of God rather than burnt offerings" (6:6).

Thus the people of Jerusalem could not expect the temple to save them, despite previous occasions in which the city had been spared (Isa. 37). They could not freely violate every law and then blithely call on Yahweh's name, expecting forgiveness (see inset for this wisdom theme of both right and improper behavior in Jeremiah and Ezekiel). Yahweh is not blind to their actions (Jer. 7:11b) and will abandon them, just as the people of the northern kingdom have been left to their fate (7:15). Faced with a similar future, the crowd reacts angrily.

Jeremiah's attack on the foundations of Judah's belief system and on the icon that they had come to consider their safety net cannot go unanswered. Baruch's version of the scene describes an immediate outcry against Jeremiah. A trial is organized on the spot, with the religious establishment (priests and prophets) serving as his accusers and prosecutors, the king's advisers serving as judges, and "all the people" (a collective phrase meaning the

Two Kinds of Behavior: A Wisdom Theme

Right Behavior

Do not oppress the alien, the orphan, and the widow, or shed innocent blood in this place, and . . . do not go after other gods to your own hurt. (Jer. 7:6)

If he does not eat upon the mountains or lift up his eyes to the idols of the house of Israel, does not defile his neighbor's wife or approach a woman during her menstrual period, does not oppress anyone, but restores to the debtor his pledge, commits no robbery, gives his bread to the hungry and covers the naked with a garment, does not take advance or accrued interest, withholds his hand from iniquity, executes true justice between contending parties, follows my statutes, and is careful to observe my ordinances, acting faithfully—such a one is righteous. (Ezek. 18:6–9a)

Improper Behavior

Will you steal, murder, commit adultery, swear falsely, make offerings to Baal, and go after other gods that you have not known? (Jer. 7:9)

[He] eats upon the mountains, defiles his neighbor's wife, oppresses the poor and needy, commits robbery, does not restore the pledge, lifts up his eyes to the idols, commits abomination, takes advance or accrued interest. (Ezek. 18:11b–13a)

citizens present at the time) serving as a jury (Jer. 26:7–11).

Once the charges of blasphemy and false prophecy are levied against Jeremiah, he stands up to speak in his own defense. Jeremiah freely admits that he has "prophesied against this house [the temple] and this city" (26:12–13). But he insists that his message is Yahweh's words, not his own. If the people of Judah choose to kill him, they will be shedding "innocent blood," which is one of the worst crimes an Israelite can commit (Exod. 23:7; Deut. 19:10–11).

The final verdict of the officials and the people is to release Jeremiah, based on the principle of prophetic immunity: a prophet must not be killed for speaking Yahweh's words (Jer. 26:16). Their decision is augmented by the "elders of the land" (regional officials probably in Jerusalem for the feast day), who cite the case of the prophet Micah. They remember that Micah also spoke out against the city of Jerusalem in Hezekiah's day (715–687 BCE) and was not punished (Mic. 3:12). The elders also express the hope that as in Hezekiah's day the Lord will "change his mind about the disaster" (Jer. 26:19). Clearly no one in the crowd has listened to Jeremiah's warning or the conditions that he has set forth for God to relent. It is not enough to spare the prophet. They need to listen to his words and take action on them.

Although Jeremiah is somewhat vindicated by the court's decision, it is less than clear that he has made his point. However, he is quickly removed from the scene by one of the king's officials, Ahikam the son of Shaphan, in order to prevent any possible harm to Jeremiah. A real threat of reprisal must have still existed. Precedent for attacking false prophets is found in Jehoiakim's order that Uriah be executed for prophesying the same fate for Jerusalem that Jeremiah had predicted (Jer. 26:20–23).

Baruch's Mission to the Temple. Apparently Jeremiah's temple sermon creates enough of an uproar that the prophet is forced into hiding. During the fourth year of Jehoiakim's reign (ca. 604 BCE) Jeremiah uses Baruch to deliver another scathing denunciation of Jerusalem and its leaders (Jer. 36). Having been barred from entrance into the temple precincts, Jeremiah dictates his message to Baruch (36:4). In the process, he elevates, at least in this instance, the importance of the scribal class and the written word and diminishes that of the prophet and the oral presentation. Baruch carries the scroll containing Jeremiah's words to the temple on a "fast day" when a large audience will be present, including the leaders from the temple and the palace (36:5–8). In this way he begins to forge a link between the space in which the scroll is created, read, destroyed, and then re-created.

It may be surmised that the words of the prophet indict Jehoiakim for choosing to be faithful to one foreign monarch (Neco II of Egypt) and then to another (Nebuchadnezzar of Babylon) while leading the people away from the covenant. Baruch first reads the prophet's message "in the hearing of all the people" inside the temple, "in the chamber of Gemariah . . . , which was in the upper court, at the entry of the New Gate" (Jer. 36:10). Micaiah, the grandson of Shaphan, is the first royal official to hear Baruch's performance in this more public chamber (36:11), and he discusses it with other royal officials, who become alarmed (36:16). They order Baruch to retell parts of the story for them in a place set aside for a select group of the king's personal advisers, within "the secretary's chamber" (36:11–15). They will then decide whether to "report all these words to the king" (36:12–18). These officials are apprehensive, and they ask Baruch, "Tell us now, how did you write all these words? Was it at his dictation?" (36:17). Baruch's answer certifies that both the scroll and Jeremiah's role as a prophet are authentic. After due deliberation, the officials report the substance of their concerns to the king and send Baruch back to Jeremiah (36:20). Jehoiakim has a second adviser, Jehudi, read the scroll before the king and his officials "in his winter apartment," an area of the palace restricted to a very select group (36:21–22). Each location in which the scroll is read represents spaces with defined spheres of influence. There is also a clear sense that as the scroll travels from place to place, it

is read in locations with increasingly stricter rules of accessibility and closer proximity to increasingly powerful individuals.

Once the message has progressed in stages into the presence of the king, a public performance occurs. Jehoiakim plays to an audience that likely includes not only his own advisers but also curious Babylonian officials. He haughtily denies Jeremiah's indictment without speaking a single word. Instead, using a nearby charcoal brazier, Jehoiakim burns the scroll piece by piece as it is read. In this way he disputes its contents as the word of the Lord (Jer. 36:22–23). Although Jehoiakim's gesture may have been convincing to foreign members of his court, it is scandalous to the people of Judah who remain loyal to their covenant with Yahweh. Even though the king does not want to provide the Babylonians with any evidence of his disloyalty to Nebuchadnezzar, his political gesture denies his official role as a protector of the covenant.

Publicly Judah will remain faithful to its covenant with Nebuchadnezzar and abrogate its treaty with Yahweh. For his crime, Jeremiah sentences Jehoiakim to a shameful death (Jer. 36:32). Privately, however, the political overtures of Egypt, Jeremiah's indictment, and the stories of Baruch and Jehudi may have contributed to Jehoiakim's declaration of Judah's independence from Babylon. Thus, by 600 BCE, Judah is once again an ally of the Egyptians. Jehoiakim's revolt causes the Babylonians to lay siege to Jerusalem, and he meets his end at this point as the monarch of an embattled minor state.

Enacted Prophecies. In an age when animated storytelling is a developed art, Jeremiah makes effective use of physical acts, symbolic gestures, and street theater in presenting his prophecies to the people of Jerusalem. For instance, Jer. 16–19 contains several enacted prophecies that allow him to demonstrate his theatrical skills while playing on recognizable aspects of Judah's social customs and traditions. Each prophetic performance portrays a sense of urgency on the part of the prophet as well as a graphic enactment of the events to come. An **emic**, or insider's understanding of the prophet's actions and symbolic gestures, allows the enacted prophecy to convey a message without a long explanation to its original audience. Such prophecies may be intended to shock the audience or to present to them the common sense of the situation. Unfortunately, our **etic**, or outsider's viewpoint on these prophecies, makes it somewhat more difficult to understand their full significance.

In Jer. 16, the prophet's personal life and his normal emotional reactions are severely restricted. He is forbidden to marry and raise a family (16:2–4). His enforced celibacy symbolizes the fast-approaching doom of the city and its people. Celebrations at this time would be inappropriate, and it would be cruel to bring children into a world in which they could expect to experience disease, destruction, and pain.

Jeremiah is further prohibited in Jer. 16:5–9 from participating in acts of mourning, even for his parents. Such a restriction has previously been placed only on the high priest, who must not on any account come in contact with the dead or display the signs of ritual mourning (Lev. 21:10–11). Jeremiah is told that he may not gash himself or shave his head, nor can he attend funeral rites in which the dead are memorialized and the mourners comforted. These actions for an individual's death could only serve as a mockery of the approaching death of the whole nation. There will be so many dead that their bodies will lie like piles

---

Emic and Etic Perspectives

Emic: The insider viewpoint is represented by what the original audience or community knows about its own social setting. Thus, in their storytelling and literature, they share a common vocabulary and a set of geographic references, social distinctions, and gestures that are intrinsically meaningful to native speakers. The members of this culture are therefore the sole judges of the validity and meaning of any emic description, just as native speakers of a language are the sole judges of the accuracy of the full range of meaning for the words they speak and write.

Etic: The outsider viewpoint is that of observers of a society other than their own. It is therefore the external researcher's interpretation of customs or beliefs. While an emic perspective may be postulated by observers, they cannot claim the full range of understanding that is implicit for members of the insider group.

---

of cordwood in the streets, unburied and unmourned by the few survivors, and food for wild animals (cf. Amos 8:3; Nah. 3:3).

Using his theme from the temple sermon, "amend your ways and your doings" (18:11), Jeremiah provides another metaphorical warning in Jer. 18. Here the prophet is instructed to go to the potters' district of the city and to watch a craftsman work with the clay. What he witnesses is a common occurrence. When the potter grows dissatisfied with his newly formed creation, he stops his wheel and crushes the clay back into a shapeless ball. At that point, the potter begins once again to rework the clay (18:3–4). The explanation that Jeremiah receives of this scene is that the clay symbolizes the nation of Judah, and Yahweh is the conscientious potter. Like the initial pot formed on the wheel, the nation has not taken proper shape, according to the desires of its maker. As a result, Yahweh is free to remold the clay and begin again, using the essence of the potential pot to shape a new vessel (18:7–10).

Jeremiah has provided an excellent example of the remnant theme. The prophet warns the people that punishment is inevitable if they

Figure 4.9. Statuette from an Egyptian tomb showing a potter at work. (Baker Photo Archive, courtesy of the Oriental Institute Museum, Chicago)

do not "turn now, all of you from your evil way" (18:11). The destruction of the nation is not God's plan. Just as the clay is saved to be used in the forming of a new pot, so too a remnant of the people will be spared in order to restore the nation.

A third example of Jeremiah's use of enacted prophecies is found in his **execration ritual** (Jer. 19). The prophet engages in a public prophetic performance to get his message across to the people. The climax, when he smashes a pot in the city gate, functions in the same way as the detailed lists found on Egyptian incantation bowls that denounce their enemies. His performance also provides a remarkable opportunity for the prophet to challenge the temple establishment and make the point that Yahweh has condemned the temple and the city of Jerusalem. He purchases a pottery vessel and then marches in an informal procession to the Potsherd Gate, picking up witnesses and supporters along the way.

When he reaches his destination, he lists a bill of particulars of the people's sins: idolatry, the shedding of innocent blood, and the sacrifice of children. Jeremiah then describes the utter devastation of the city and its population: "Everyone who passes by it will be horrified and will hiss because of all its disasters" (Jer. 19:8; cf. Zeph. 2:15).

Then, to enact the curse, he smashes the pot within the city gate and makes the statement that Yahweh will "break this people and this city, as one breaks a potter's vessel, so that it can never be mended" (Jer. 19:11). The curse is horrible enough, but to smash the pot in a gate, a place associated with law and judgment, makes his action a living reality for the people who witness it. Jeremiah cannot have chosen a more profound way to make his point to his contemporary audience that the city of Jerusalem is doomed.

A challenge like this cannot be left unanswered. Pashur, one of the chief officials of the temple, arrests Jeremiah and places him in the stocks (Jer. 20:2). The object is to silence Jeremiah by humiliating him. The comic posture of someone in the stocks is an easy thing to ridicule. Pashur and the rest of the religious establishment expect that Jeremiah's credibility and that of his prophecies will be damaged along with his pride. By sentencing him to such

Egyptian Execration Text

The Middle Kingdom (mid-12th Dynasty, 1991–1786 BCE) execration texts do not contain specific curses, but instead they list all those persons who will be destroyed along with the pottery figurines or vessel on which the inscription is written.

Their strong men, their messengers, their confederates, their allies, who will plot, who will fight, who will say that they will fight, who will say that they will rebel, in this entire land. (*COS* 1:32, 51)

Why Do the Wicked Prosper?

Why does the way of the guilty prosper?
Why do all who are treacherous thrive?
You plant them, and they take root;
they grow and bring forth fruit;
you are near in their mouths
yet far from their hearts. (Jer. 12:1b–2)

a disgraceful fate, there is a very real possibility that the hated doomsayer may even die while he is restrained in this ignominious posture.

Jeremiah's reaction shows both his anger and his personal despair. He calls on Yahweh to take revenge on his enemies (Jer. 20:12), as he has done when his neighbors in Anathoth plotted against him (11:18–12:6). He then draws on a traditional ancient Near Eastern wisdom theme employed in times of personal and national crisis. Jeremiah questions why the wicked are allowed to prosper and to mislead the people (cf. Hab. 1:2–4). Jeremiah also questions himself, cursing his own birth and the task that has brought him to this inglorious fate (Jer. 20:14). But the prophet also acknowledges that even if he wishes to keep silent, and thereby stop his persecutors, he cannot. He feels an inner compulsion to speak that cannot be denied:

> If I say, "I will not mention him,
>   or speak in his name,"
> then within me there is something like a
>   burning fire
>   shut up in my bones;
> I am weary with holding it in,
>   and I cannot. (Jer. 20:9)

Cognitive Dissonance and Opposition to Jeremiah's Message. In the uneasy period between Jerusalem's initial fall to the Neo-Babylonians in 597 BCE and its final destruction in 587, Jeremiah and the people, both in Judah and in the exile, have to cope with conflicting prophetic voices. Even while Jeremiah continues to warn of the ultimate destruction of Jerusalem, other prophets and officials speak of a quick end to the exile. These voices of false hope speak of a return of their exiled king Jehoiachin, the people who have been taken to Mesopotamia, and the sacred objects that were stolen from the temple. They also call for divine retribution against the Babylonians (Jer. 28:3–4), as Nahum did against Assyria (1:3–6) and Obadiah did against Edom (12–15). The overly optimistic and vengeful message of these prophets is much more pleasing to the people than Jeremiah's words of approaching doom. As a result, Jeremiah faces both overt hostility and open opposition from the people of Jerusalem.

The most dangerous of these prophetic opponents is Hananiah, an apparently well-known prophet from Gibeon. Confronting Jeremiah in the temple in the presence of the priests, Hananiah predicts that within two years the exiles will return and Babylon's power will be broken (Jer. 28:1–4). A message so diametrically opposed to Jeremiah's position demands a response from Jeremiah, though he does not have an immediate message from God. Jeremiah first affirms the hope that

The Babylonian Theodicy

Those who seek not after a god can go the road of favor,
Those who pray to a goddess have grown poor and destitute.
Indeed, in my youth I tried to find out the will of (my) god,
With prayer and supplication I besought my goddess.
I bore a yoke of profitless servitude: (My) god decreed (for me)
Poverty instead of wealth.
A cripple rises above me, a fool is ahead of me,
Rogues are in the ascendant, I am demoted. (COS 1:154, VII.493)

this message will come true, but then he makes the point that peace is not typical of prophetic speech: "The prophets who preceded you and me from ancient times prophesied war, famine, and pestilence against many countries and great kingdoms" (28:8).

In this way Jeremiah explains the role of the prophet as he might explain it to a child. The job of the prophet is to alert the people and their leaders to deviations from the covenant. They are to warn the people of Yahweh's righteous anger. It is their duty to present the proper course of action that will bring the people back into compliance with their obligations to their God. Peace in times of crisis, however, is not part of the usual prophetic message because it implies two things: there will be a satisfactory end to current troubles without a change of heart by the people, and the people can without qualification call on Yahweh to intervene and end their present troubles. Jeremiah concludes with a reminder of the adage that the true prophet is the one whose words come true (see Deut. 18:21–22):

As for the prophet who prophesies peace, when the word of that prophet comes true, then it will be known that the Lord has truly sent the prophet. (Jer. 28:9)

Faced with a classic example of cognitive dissonance (a situation in which two conflicting statements are both credible), Hananiah performs a physical act to gain the advantage. He breaks the wooden yoke off of Jeremiah's neck (Jer. 28:10). Jeremiah had been wearing this as a symbolic prop to remind the people that they must submit to the "yoke of Babylon" and thus to Yahweh's will (27:2–8). By breaking the yoke, Hananiah symbolically negates Jeremiah's message and reaffirms his message

that Yahweh intends to "break the yoke of King Nebuchadnezzar" within two years (28:11).

Temporarily defeated, Jeremiah leaves the field to Hananiah. When he later receives a new revelation from Yahweh, he returns to confront Hananiah with a new symbol of submission—an iron yoke. The wooden yoke may have been broken, but Yahweh has forged an even stronger restraint to hold his people in submission to Babylon (Jer. 28:12–14). Jeremiah also announces that Yahweh will discredit the false message and bring an end to the dissonance. The prophet predicts the death of this false messenger. The text then reports that Hananiah dies that same year (28:16–17). What is especially interesting is that both prophets give testable prophecies, and only Jeremiah's comes true.

Apparently there are also voices of dissension among the exiles (Jer. 29:8–9). Jeremiah attempts to deal with these purveyors of false hope by writing a letter to the exilic community (29:4–7). First he discounts any idea that the exile will be over soon. They must understand that it is Yahweh's plan to provide for a seventy-year period during which the people are to seek the Lord "with all their hearts" before they can be returned to their land (29:10–14; cf. the Israelites' forty-year period of purification in the wilderness [Num. 14:26–35]).

Jeremiah's Letter to the Exiles

Thus says the Lord of Hosts, the God of Israel, to all the exiles whom I have sent into exile from Jerusalem to Babylon: Build houses and live in them; plant gardens and eat what they produce. Take wives and have sons and daughters; take wives for your sons, and give your daughters in marriage, that they may bear sons and daughters; multiply there, and do not decrease. But seek the welfare of the city where I have sent you into exile, and pray to the Lord on its behalf, for in its welfare you will find your welfare. (Jer. 29:4–7)

Jeremiah also removes the limits on worship that have been placed on the people by the reforms of Hezekiah and Josiah. They no longer have to be in Judah or Jerusalem to worship. The people may worship Yahweh in exile—even without the temple priesthood to direct them. They are assured that God will hear their prayers in the exile. Yahweh is not just a local God. Jeremiah's message sets the stage for the development of **diasporic Judaism** in the next two centuries. His letter is also the first sign of what will take place after the exile, divergence between the Judaism of the exile and the Judaism of the return (see The Jewish Identity Movement, pp. 200–202).

Jerusalem's Final Days

In 589 BCE, after nearly ten years of relative peace, Zedekiah once again is prodded by Egypt to revolt against the Neo-Babylonians. In order to make an example of Judah, Nebuchadnezzar now resolves to eliminate the troublesome kingdom, and in 588 he again besieges Jerusalem. In the midst of the siege, King Zedekiah sends messengers to Jeremiah to see if Yahweh will once again intervene to save the city (Jer. 21:1–2). The prophet offers them no consolation. He warns that Yahweh, the Divine Warrior, will fight on the Babylonian side against the city. Its defenders will be slaughtered without mercy (21:4–7).

Jeremiah states that there is only one way to save their lives: surrender to Babylon. "Those who stay in this city shall die, . . . but those who go out and surrender to the Chaldeans . . . shall have their lives as a prize of war" (Jer. 21:9). Even though Jeremiah is applying a current situation to the Deuteronomistic injunction to "choose life" (Deut. 30:11–20), he is touching on a sore spot for Judah's leaders. But, of course, his message is intended to shock the king and his advisers. Once again, however, their reaction is to close their minds to the prophet's warning. They proclaim Jeremiah's word to be blatant treason and a real danger to the people's morale in the midst of the Babylonian threat. It is no wonder that they imprison Jeremiah in a dry cistern to prevent him from demoralizing the city's defenders (Jer. 38:4–6).

Just before the end, Zedekiah releases Jeremiah and in a private interview asks him again for some ray of hope. Jeremiah elicits an oath from the king that Zedekiah will not kill him for speaking disturbing words. Then he repeats his warning that surrender to the Babylonians is the only chance for survival (Jer. 38:16–23). The king places Jeremiah under house arrest, and there he remains until the fall of the city (38:28).

In the final days before Jerusalem's walls are breached, Jeremiah engages in one last symbolic act. He receives a message that one of his relatives has died and uses his kinship right to redeem the man's fields as a final enacted prophecy (Jer. 32:6–8). Real estate at this point is worthless because the people are about to be captured and taken into exile. In spite of this, Jeremiah goes on with the normal business process of weighing out the money and signing and sealing a deed before witnesses (32:9–10).

Jeremiah's redemption of the field once again demonstrates the symbolic importance attached to land transactions. In Gen. 23, Abraham establishes his stake in the promised land by purchasing the cave of Machpelah. He has a document drawn up and witnessed to prove that his descendants have title to that land and in this way obtains legal rights to a portion of the covenant promise. Now Jeremiah too preserves for future generations a title to the land. He gives the copies of the documents to Baruch in front of witnesses and charges him to "put them in an earthenware jar, in order that they may last for a long time" (Jer. 32:11–14). His action assures the people that when Yahweh's plan is fulfilled, they will be returned from exile. Jeremiah's deed is therefore more than a means of keeping a plot of ground in his clan's inheritance. Like Abraham's burial cave, it serves as a deed to the entire promised land and will serve as the returned exiles' legal claim to its ownership.

Just before the fall of the city, Jeremiah delivers a series of oracles of restoration and return. In Jer. 31, he describes a future end to the exile and a reversal of the current destruction (31:27–28). He also addresses the issue of individual responsibility and the casting of blame for the exile in much the same terms as Ezek. 18 (Jer. 31:29–30). The exiles must recognize that they are not paying for the sins of their ancestors but for their own. He also envisions a new covenant that God writes on the heart of each member of the community.

I will put my law within them, and I will write it on their hearts; and I will be their God, and they will be my people. No longer shall they teach one another, or say to each other, "Know the LORD," for they shall all know me, from the least to the greatest. (Jer. 31:33b–34; cf. Ezek. 11:19)

Then, in a series of "oracles against the nations" (Jer. 46–51), the exiles are prepared for the inevitable fall of the city. They are also reassured that the Babylonians and their allies will not always benefit from their conquest and looting of other nations. Eventually God will demand an accounting for "all the wrong that they have done in Zion" (51:24). When this happens, God will turn against them,

transforming their country into a wasteland and calling on foreign armies to campaign against them (50:11–16; 51:25–29).

When the city of Jerusalem does fall to the Babylonian forces, the entire city, including Solomon's temple, is destroyed. The monarchy and the royal court are dissolved. Zedekiah is forced to watch the execution of his sons and then is blinded before being taken into exile (2 Kings 25:7). The monarchy of Judah effectively ends at this point, although Jehoiachin lives on as a king in exile (25:27–30). Jeremiah, who has spoken so often of surrender to the people, is well treated by the Babylonians, who probably see him as the voice of reason (Jer. 29:11–14). However, after the Babylonians appoint a non-Davidic official, Gedaliah, as Judah's governor, a dissident group of Judeans assassinate him after he serves only a short time in office (2 Kings 25:22–26). Jeremiah continues to plead with the remnant who are not taken into exile to remain in the land and rebuild as best they can (Jer. 42). However, Gedaliah's assassins flee to Ammon (41:10), and a portion of the people flee to Egypt, taking Jeremiah with them. This is the last we know of Jeremiah. His career has spanned the period from the glorious expectations of Josiah's nationalist movement to the dregs of despair as Judah and Jerusalem meet their fate at the hands of Nebuchadnezzar.

STUDY QUESTIONS

1. What is it about Jeremiah and Isaiah that make their call narratives different (Isa. 6; Jer. 1:4–19)?
2. Why does Jeremiah work so hard to explode the myth of Jerusalem's inviolability in his temple sermon (Jer. 7; 26)?
3. What is the significance of the repeated readings of Jeremiah's scroll in the temple,

the office of royal officials, and in the king's audience chamber (Jer. 36:5–26)?

4. How does Jeremiah's lifestyle become the basis of an enacted prophecy in Jer. 16:1–13?

5. How does Jeremiah's visit to the potters' district display and explain the remnant theme (Jer. 18:1–11)?

6. What is an execration ritual, and how do we know that Jeremiah's action is effective (Jer. 19–20:6)?

7. What is the basis for the argument between Hananiah and Jeremiah (Jer. 27–28)?

What is the test of a true prophet (cf. Deut. 18:20–22)?

8. Why does Jeremiah write a letter to the exiles (Jer. 29:1–23), and what are the implications of what he tells them?

9. Why does Jeremiah agree to redeem the field of his relative in Anathoth during the siege of Jerusalem (Jer. 32:1–25)?

10. Why is Jeremiah treated with respect and restraint by the Babylonians (Chaldeans) after the fall of Jerusalem in 587 (Jer. 39:11–18)?

$\cdot5\cdot$

THE EXILE
AND THE PERSIAN PERIOD

Exilic Prophecy

The Book of Ezekiel

KEY POINTS

- Ezekiel describes the same events as does Jeremiah but from the vantage point of the exile.
- Ezekiel's prophetic compulsion shifts from judgment to restoration after Jerusalem falls in 587 BCE.
- Ezekiel uses street theater to perform his message.
- Ezekiel's visions provide the theodicy for Jerusalem's fall and the people's eventual return to the covenant.

The Deuteronomistic History comes to a close with the destruction of Jerusalem in 2 Kings. Thereafter, what we can learn of the history of the nation is found in the prophetic literature and writings from the exilic and postexilic periods.

The book of Ezekiel can be divided into three distinct sections: Ezek. 1–24 contains the prophet's oracles of judgment against Judah; Ezek. 25–32 consists of oracles against foreign nations (Ammon, Edom, Tyre, Egypt); and Ezek. 33–48 provides oracles of hope and restoration for the people of Israel. Unlike much

of the book of Isaiah, which has been heavily edited and supplemented in later periods, scholars consider the majority of the book of Ezekiel as dating to the period of the exile and to represent a fairly unified and consistent set of prophetic themes.

Social context and the historical background of the last days of Judah are the keys to understanding the message of the prophet Ezekiel. Carried off with the first group of exiles in 597 BCE (including Jehoiachin, the royal family, and many of the chief priests and influential people), Ezekiel the priest has a dual perspective. He has a definite tie to Jerusalem and its temple priesthood, but he also is a member of the exilic community and must deal with their anxieties and concerns. Like many other prophets, Ezekiel's message is divided into two parts: judgment and restoration.

In what might be considered a throwback to earlier prophetic style, Ezekiel repeatedly describes how he is filled with the Spirit of God, carefully instructed about what to do, or placed into a trance that presages a vision (see

Ezek. 2:2; 3:12; 8:3). None of the other writing prophets whose names are attached to a book use this language, which is associated with the miracle-working prophets Elijah and Elisha (1 Kings 18:46; 2 Kings 3:15). It may be that Ezekiel is seeking to authenticate his message by describing how much power God exercises over his actions and speech.

The force that God imposes on Ezekiel is demonstrated by the prophet's dual message. Initially he is unable to speak anything but words of judgment, doom, and destruction. His restriction lasts until the final fall and destruction of Jerusalem. Such control over the message is called selective compulsion (see Ezek. 3:25–27). Any other ideas the prophet may have are immediately suppressed by God. After the destruction of Judah's capital, Ezekiel is released from his enforced silence and can begin to assure the exiles of the merciful intentions of Yahweh. Once the people have been purged by their exilic experience, they will be returned to their homeland and restored as God's covenantal nation (36:24–25).

The principal theme in the book of Ezekiel is the presence of Yahweh. When God's presence and **glory** depart from the temple in Ezek. 10, it is clear that the nation is doomed. In like manner, Yahweh's return to the throne in the temple in Jerusalem in Ezek. 40–48 is the crowning vision of restoration.

Call Narrative. Although Ezekiel's call narrative is similar to those of Moses, Isaiah, and Jeremiah, it has its own distinctive characteristics. Perhaps the most important difference is its sense of mystery. There is also a muted anthropomorphic character to his theophany. Whenever the prophet speaks of God's appearance, he uses a qualifying phrase ("something like") so that he does not have to describe Yahweh in exact human terms (Ezek. 1:26–28). The

result is a sense of majesty similar to Isaiah's "temple filled with smoke" (Isa. 6:4). The clear distinction that Ezekiel's vision draws between the human and the divine is emphasized by the phrase used by Yahweh when addressing the prophet. Yahweh refers to Ezekiel as a "son of man," that is, a "mortal."

The sense of Yahweh's glory as a separate, roving aspect of the Deity also is evident in this scene. Instead of being a fixed entity, like the seated figure in Isa. 6:1, God is placed "above the likeness of a throne" (Ezek. 1:26), a being of ever-changing motion ("wherever the spirit would go"; 1:12) in Ezekiel's vision. The universality implied by such an indescribable appearance may have also been intended to separate Yahweh from the somewhat human-like characteristics applied to the gods of Mesopotamia. Such a frenetic image would make it more difficult to determine the extent of Yahweh's glory or the degree of power that is behind its continuous movement (see especially 1:12–28). All the prophet can do in response is fall on his face in awe and fear of the divine manifestation (1:28b).

As is the case in other call narratives, Ezekiel is confronted with a vision of God and called to serve as a spokesperson. His task is not easy, but unlike Isaiah and Jeremiah, Ezekiel does not voice his reluctance. Instead, while expressing a sense of fear and respect for the divine manifestation, he makes no excuses for why he cannot serve. Instead, he obediently consumes the scroll presented to him (Ezek. 2:9–3:3). This gesture is similar to the purification of Isaiah's lips and the touching of Jeremiah's mouth. It empowers him to speak God's word. A period of seven days of muteness delays Ezekiel in taking up his task. For this amount of time he sits "stunned" among the exiles (3:15). His temporary paralysis suggests the magnitude of Ezekiel's message as well as his reluctance to take on the prophetic mantle. It is also the period of time set aside for the ordination of priests (Exod. 29:35) and their ritual purification (Lev. 13:5–7), and therefore may represent the process of transformation that Ezekiel is to undergo in order to carry out his mission.

Ezekiel is also presented with an image of his prophetic responsibility. The prophet is portrayed as a "guard" or "sentry," whose task is to cry out an alarm when an enemy approaches (Ezek. 3:17–21). Failure to do this will result in the condemnation of the sentry for failing to warn the people. Just as in Isaiah's declaration (7:17–25), the imminent danger faced by the people is the anger of Yahweh. Once again God intends to use a foreign power to punish Judah (see Isa. 10:5–6). Ezekiel differs from other prophets, who offer a hope that God will relent if the people repent and return to their covenant obligations (see Hosea 6:1–3; Amos 5:4–6). The hope of being spared ultimate destruction does not appear in Ezekiel, and that seems consistent with someone already in exile whose expectations are that he will soon be joined by a new group of exiles.

As noted earlier (see Mesha Stele inset, p. 122), the belief that a god is in control of historical events is not limited to Israel. This belief provides two important keys to the purpose of Israelite prophecy. The role of the prophet is to call the people back into compliance with the covenant and to warn them of Yahweh's judgment and punishment when they do not respond as they should. The failure of the people to respond to the prophet's message can then be used as the basis for the theodicy explaining why Yahweh has allowed Israel to be oppressed and defeated by foreign nations. It also serves as the basis for the belief in the essential righteousness of a God who is willing to provide a warning even though this warning may be heard only by a core group of righteous persons within the nation. But it has always been for the benefit of the righteous, who respond to divine warnings that Yahweh has chosen to act (see Gen. 6:9–22). Without this set of beliefs in place, there would be no reason for the Israelites to continue to worship a God who apparently has failed to protect them.

Enacted Prophecies. During the period prior to the final fall and destruction of Jerusalem, Ezekiel uses a series of enacted prophecies to present his message. He performs symbolic and outrageous acts that draw attention to his person and his message and make an indelible impression on his audience. In Ezek. 4, the prophet employs a simple strategy to portray Jerusalem's fate. He is instructed to take a clay brick (an item used in the construction of all the buildings in Mesopotamia) and to inscribe an outline of the city of Jerusalem on it. Then this linen-clad priest dispenses with his personal dignity and plays like a small boy with his toy soldiers, besieging the brick/city and showing how it will be destroyed. For a grown man, especially a priest, to do this must have raised questions and heightened apprehensions of the impending doom of Jerusalem.

A second action taken by Ezekiel involves lying on his side for an extended period: 390 days on his right side and 40 days on his left side. He explains that this painful regimen symbolizes the number of years that the people of the northern and southern kingdoms respectively will remain in exile (Ezek. 4:4–6). The number 40 is particularly significant here because it is the number of years the people were condemned to wander in the wilderness following the exodus (Num. 14:33; Ps. 95:10). In the same way, the current exile is to serve as a new period of winnowing and transformation.

The reuse of the wilderness motif follows the pattern in which aspects of Israel's history and tradition are retold in order to speak to events in a later period (cf. Nehemiah's idealized image of the wilderness period in Neh. 9:15–21).

During the time that Ezekiel undergoes his difficult ordeal, he is required to prepare sparse meals. Such a starvation diet demonstrates the hardship faced by the exiles and by those who are besieged in Jerusalem (Ezek. 4:9–13). At first God commands him to cook these meals on an "unclean" fire (made with human dung), but at this point Ezekiel finally protests. As a priest, he has dedicated his life to maintaining a "clean" (ritually pure) existence. Eating an **impurity** would not only make him gag but also would be more than he can bear. He therefore asks God's indulgence so that he will not have to contaminate himself. God relents, allowing him to use conventional fuel (animal dung) to cook his meal (4:14–15).

Ezekiel's next piece of street theater occurs in Ezek. 5. The prophet is told to shave his head and beard. Shaving the head or beard is normally an act of persons in mourning or something done to humiliate prisoners (cf. 2 Sam. 10:4; Job 1:20; Jer. 48:37). Ezekiel then divides his hair into three piles and chops up one pile with a sword, scatters another into the wind, and throws the third pile into the fire. Only a few hairs, a remnant, are left, bound up in the edges of the prophet's robes (Ezek. 5:3). Ezekiel's visually oriented performance would be most impressive in the open air, where the wind could play its part and the fire and sword could be used effectively.

Yet another pantomime predicting the exile of the people occurs in Ezek. 12:1–16. Here the prophet is instructed to take up "an exile's bag" and carry it about with him in public

both day and night. He is even told to dig a hole through the wall of his house and carry the bag with him like someone who is forced to exit the breached walls of Jerusalem with only what can be carried. This performance is hauntingly similar to the images on the walls of Sennacherib's palace in Nineveh that depict the prisoners from Lachish (701 BCE) as they trudge from their destroyed city with nothing but a few clutched possessions (*OTPar*[3], 190).

In the final stage of this enacted prophecy, Ezekiel is forbidden to even look on the land. He is instructed to cover his eyes as if he is blind and in effect to renounce his citizenship

Figure 5.1. Relief from the walls of Sennacherib's palace in Nineveh depicts the prisoners from Lachish (701 BCE) trudging from their destroyed city with nothing but a few clutched possessions. (Baker Photo Archive, courtesy of the British Museum)

in that place. Each of these symbolic actions is a sign to King Zedekiah of the inevitable fate of both the city of Jerusalem and of himself. His people will be taken into exile, "dispersed among the nations" (Ezek. 12:15), while a select few will survive "the sword, . . . famine and pestilence" to tell the tale of "their abominations among the nations" (Ezek. 12:16; cf. similar language in Jer. 21:9–10). An additional example of Ezekiel's use of graphic performances and gestures is found in Ezek. 6:11, where he claps his hands and stamps his feet at the people being condemned by his oracle. In 21:11, on God's command, the prophet groans continually. Each of these apparently unjustified behaviors, coupled with his later failure to perform the usual mourning rituals on the death of his wife (24:17–19), requires his audience to question him. That in turn provides the opportunity to tie his actions to his prophetic message.

Explanations of Judgment. Condemnations and predictions of doom have to be justified for the prophetic theodicy to be understood and accepted. Ezekiel's visions provide more than adequate explanation for Yahweh's anger. The most devastating image of disobedience appears in the multifaceted vision of the abominations in the temple in Ezek. 8. The structure of this vision confirms Ezekiel's priestly background and demonstrates that he is a man who is both intimately familiar with the temple and highly concerned with issues of **ritual purity** and proper worship practices. In his vision, he is instructed to take an inspection tour of the temple precincts. The tour provides vivid evidence that the temple has been corrupted from one end to the other by the worship of foreign gods.

His vision begins when Ezekiel is cast into a trance while sitting with the exiled elders of

Judah. These authority figures are included to serve as his witnesses and to authenticate his experience. In what might be described as an out-of-body experience, he is unceremoniously grabbed by the hair and carried back to Jerusalem. On arrival, he finds himself in front of the temple, but he is unable to enter by the gate. His way is blocked by an abhorrent "image of jealousy" (probably an idol; cf. "jealous God" in Exod. 20:4–5). Ezekiel is instructed to go to a sidewall, where he finds a hole, and is told to tunnel his way into the building. The prophet emerges into a chamber whose walls are covered with the pictures of other gods and their symbols. Even more abhorrent is the presence of the seventy elders, who are burning incense and worshiping other gods (Ezek. 8:10–12). The elders have previously appeared in positive contexts and represented the people's acceptance of the covenant (Exod. 24:9–10). Their presence and actions in this scene represent how the entire nation's idolatry has reached such a level of audacity that it is openly practiced within Yahweh's temple.

As Ezekiel continues his tour of the temple compound, he finds one example after another of blatant idolatry. He witnesses a scene in the outer court in which a group of women are "weeping for Tammuz" (Ezek. 8:14). Tammuz is the Babylonian god of new growth and fertility who dies each year during the dry season. He will be released by the gods of the underworld only in response to the tears of his worshipers. The worship of Tammuz represents a rejection of Yahweh as the sole provider of land, including its produce, and children (i.e., fertility).

Next Ezekiel moves to the inner court, between the porch and the altar. There he sees twenty-five men prostrating themselves as they worship the sun. Their ritual performance requires them to bow down with their backs to the altar and to the holy of holies (Ezek. 8:16), a sign of gross disrespect for Yahweh. Throughout his tour of what should have been God's temple, Ezekiel finds nothing associated with and no person engaged in worshiping the God of Judah.

The vision of the abominations in the temple provides a firm legal foundation for Yahweh's decision to abandon the temple in Jerusalem (Ezek. 10). Central to this vision is the appearance of Yahweh's glory, once again depicted in motion, but this time the movement signals the departure from the sacred precincts. The glory that has filled the temple (cf. Isa. 6:1) does so one last time (Ezek. 10:4) and then is carried away amid clouds and fire in a chariot drawn by cherubim (10:6–19). Just as Jeremiah warns the people that their failure to "amend their way" will prevent God from being able to "dwell with you in this place" (7:3–4), now Ezekiel describes the result of that failure—the abandonment of the temple by its God.

Ezekiel provides one other powerful explanation for Yahweh's decision to abandon the temple and the nation. His oracle in Ezek. 16 contains a parenting image similar to those associated with the exodus (Exod. 3:7–10; Deut. 1:30–31; cf. Hosea 11:1–7). Ezekiel portrays Jerusalem as an abandoned female child. Unwanted, the infant has been left to die (Ezek. 16:6a). This image is especially poignant because exposure of female infants was fairly common in times of famine or among impoverished families. It is Yahweh who takes pity on the infant Jerusalem and serves as her surrogate parent (16:6b–7). All of her needs are met, and when she grows up God marries her, providing her with rich robes and jewelry (16:8–14). But just like a new bride who is not satisfied and seeks other lovers, Jerusalem becomes unfaithful to Yahweh and seeks the favor of other gods (16:15; cf. Hosea's wife in Hosea 2:1–13).

All that had been given to her, including her children, are dedicated to other gods as sacrifices (Ezek. 16:17–22). She constructs "high places" (cf. Hosea 4:13) and makes alliances with Egypt instead of trusting Yahweh (Ezek. 16:24–26; Isa. 30:1–7). She is a peculiar harlot who pays her lovers instead of receiving payment from them (Ezek. 16:33–34). For these crimes, Jerusalem will be given into the hands of her enemies. Her "older sister," Samaria, the capital of the northern kingdom, and other disobedient "sisters" (like Sodom) also sinned and were destroyed (16:46–50). Now the "younger sister," whose sins make her older siblings appear righteous, must face the same judge.

Despite this condemnation, God still is willing to "remember my covenant with you in the days of your youth" and will establish an "everlasting covenant" so that the people will at last and truly "know that I am the LORD" (Ezek. 16:60–62). The generosity expressed by divine forgiveness is intended to shame Judah so profoundly that she will "never open her mouth again" to betray the covenant (16:63). Typical of prophetic speech elsewhere, the divine judge condemns but also promises to forgive (16:60–62; see Hosea 2:14–23).

Amid the inevitable destruction is an opportunity for a righteous remnant of the people of Judah to survive. In his vision in Ezek. 9, the prophet sees seven men, six executioners and a scribe. The divine servants are instructed to pass throughout the city of Jerusalem. Wherever they find someone mourning the sins of the people, that person is to have the Hebrew letter *taw* (an X shape) inscribed on the forehead as a mark of righteousness. Then, during a second circuit of the city, the executioners are commanded to slay everyone who does not have this mark of innocence. In this way the righteous are set aside for survival (cf. the effect of the blood placed on the doorpost in Exod. 12:7 and Rahab's crimson cord in Josh. 2:18). These marked innocents form the core of the future. They will rebuild the temple and the city of Jerusalem. Ezekiel's warning comes horribly true when Jerusalem falls. The unity between his word and the actions of the Neo-Babylonians marks an end of one period and the beginning of a new one.

Oracles against the Nations. Ezekiel's enacted prophecies and statements of judgment are separated from his message of restoration and hope (Ezek. 33–48) by the "oracles against the nations," found in Ezek. 25–32. The separation may have been an intentional editorial decision, intended to serve as a transition or buffer between the two parts of Ezekiel's message before and after the destruction of Jerusalem. The oracles may also function as signs of the promised restoration since they indicate the punishment that God will exact on Judah's oppressors. In these oracles, Egypt, as well as several of Judah's neighbors (Ammon, Moab, Edom, Philistia, and Tyre in Phoenicia), are condemned. The oracles against the nations are not in a genre unique to Ezekiel. They also appear in Amos (1:2–2:3), Isaiah (13–23), and Jeremiah (46–51).

Structurally, the oracles are arranged geographically (cf. a similar rhetorical device in Amos 1:3–2:5). Ezekiel begins his cycle of condemnation by first looking east toward Ammon. He figuratively moves in a clockwise manner, addressing Moab, Edom, Philistia, Tyre, and Sidon in turn. The oracle against and lamentation for Egypt is treated separately by the editors, perhaps because there is such a contrast in political influence between the petty

---

Oracles against the Nations

See, the Lord is riding on a swift cloud
    and comes to Egypt;
the idols of Egypt will tremble at his presence,
    and the heart of the Egyptians will melt within
      them. (Isa. 19:1)

Woe to you, O Moab!
    The people of Chemosh have perished,
for your sons have been taken captive,
    and your daughters into captivity.
Yet I will restore the fortunes of Moab in the latter
    days, says the Lord. (Jer. 48:46–47)

Because with unending hostilities the Philistines acted in vengeance, and with malice of heart took revenge in destruction; therefore thus says the Lord God, I will stretch out my hand against the Philistines . . . and destroy the rest of the seacoast. I will execute great vengeance on them with wrathful punishments. *Then they shall know that I am the Lord,* when I lay my vengeance on them. (Ezek. 25:15–17)

Thus says the Lord:
For three transgressions of Tyre,
    and for four, I will not revoke the punishment;
because they delivered entire communities over to
    Edom,
    and did not remember the covenant of kinship.
So I will send a fire on the wall of Tyre,
    fire that shall devour its strongholds. (Amos
    1:9–10)

---

states of Syria-Palestine and Egypt. Dating the oracles is uncertain, although they all assume a knowledge of the fall of Jerusalem in 587 BCE.

Visions of Restoration. Prior to the fall of Jerusalem, Ezekiel makes it clear that the misfortune and destruction that have afflicted the people of Jerusalem are caused by their own sins. He also emphasizes that the current punishment will not extend into later generations if they prove to be faithful to Yahweh. To make his point, Ezekiel provides two related statements in Ezek. 14 and Ezek. 18. In the first case he lists three righteous wise men of the past: Noah, Daniel, and Job. All three are non-Israelites, yet they all survive trials because they are righteous. Noah, chronicled in the primordial era, survives the flood. Daniel (not Ezekiel's contemporary) may be the wise king in the ancient Ugaritic epic of Aqhat who judges his people fairly and is rewarded with a son and heir. Job of Uz (Edom) survives a legendary test of afflictions only to rise from the dustheap to regain God's favor. Always before (Gen. 18:17–21; Jer. 5:1), tradition had held that the presence of righteous persons could help spare a city from destruction. Now, however, Ezekiel assures the people that even if these three exemplary characters were all assembled at that moment they could save only themselves. In this new scheme, no one may through their own righteousness set aside the punishment due to a land that has acted "faithlessly" (Ezek. 14:13).

Ezekiel further develops his new principle of taking responsibility for one's own actions in Ezek. 18, where he quotes an old proverb, "The parents have eaten the sour grapes, and the children's teeth are set on edge" (18:2). This proverb expresses the legal principle of corporate identity, under which children are viewed as participants in the sins of the parent. Thus Achan, who stole from the goods placed under the *kherem* ban at Jericho (Josh. 7:16–27), is condemned. However, based on the legal principle of corporate responsibility, his entire family also is condemned to be stoned to death in order to purify the nation of Achan's sin.

In the new world of the exile, however, Ezekiel assures the people that they will not have to pay for the sins of their parents. Only "the person who sins . . . shall die" (18:3). Keep in mind, however, that Ezekiel is not making an argument for individual responsibility as we understand it in modern Western culture. His message applies to the entire exilic community and is an exhortation for them to recognize the exile as a period of purification and rededication. Individualism is a Western concept. It is a concept that is unfathomable for the communally oriented people of the ancient Near East. The issue of individual responsibility and the casting of blame for the exile are also addressed by Jeremiah (31:29–30) in much the same terms as Ezek. 18. In both of these prophetic books, the exiles are told that they must recognize they are not paying for the sins of their ancestors but for their own. Jeremiah and Ezekiel make this claim in response to those exiles who refused to repent or change and instead excuse themselves by blaming their parents and ancestors for their punishment in the exile.

Once the city of Jerusalem falls to Nebuchadnezzar's army, God no longer compels Ezekiel to speak only words of judgment. His new task is to explain what is ahead for the exiles in relation to their God. They must recognize that the exile is a direct result of their iniquity and Yahweh's decision to leave them unprotected. It is analogous to the time spent in Egypt, when they lived "among the nations." They will be tested and purged in the exile, as they were in the wilderness period. The people who measure up to the stipulations of the covenant will be allowed to return to the land of Israel (Ezek. 20:33–38). Furthermore, the name of God will be restored among the

Cause and Effect of the Exile

And the nations shall know that the house of Israel went into captivity for their iniquity, because they dealt treacherously with me. So I hid my face from them and gave them into the hand of their adversaries, and they all fell by the sword. (Ezek. 39:23)

Now I will restore the fortunes of Jacob, and have mercy on the whole house of Israel; and I will be jealous for my holy name. They shall forget their shame, and all the treachery they have practiced against me, when they live securely in their land with no one to make them afraid, when I have brought them back from the peoples and gathered them from their enemies' lands, and through them have displayed my holiness in the sight of many nations. (Ezek. 39:25–27) nations when they recognize Yahweh's power to return the exiles after the period of "instruction" is complete (Ezek. 39:25–29). Whatever tarnish may have been attached to Yahweh's apparent failure to protect the people in 587 BCE will thereby be removed (cf. the oracles against Tyre and Egypt in Ezek. 28–29 and against Gog in 39:1–16).

A new world is envisioned by the prophet. In that new day, old injustices, poor leadership by kings and priests, and even the desire to violate the law and covenant will be inconceivable (cf. Jer. 31:33b–34). The prophet's use of the good shepherd image in Ezek. 34 plays on a familiar theme of contrasted leadership also found in Jer. 23:1–6, which condemns the "shepherds . . . who have scattered my flock" and indicates that their right to rule the people has ended.

Ezekiel (34:11–23) picks up this judgment oracle and describes how Yahweh, the owner of the flock, will take it away from the false shepherds (kings and priests) who serve only themselves and neglect the sheep. Yahweh is the perfect shepherd who takes them to good pasture during the day, brings them to a safe haven at night, cares for the sick, and seeks out the strays (cf. Ps. 23). Once order has been reestablished, a new shepherd from the line of David will be appointed, one who will follow Yahweh's example and properly care for the sheep (cf. Jeremiah's language: God "will gather the remnant of my flock" and "raise up for David a righteous Branch" to rule over them with wisdom and justice [23:3–5]).

What makes this new world possible is the exilic experience. It puts a truer understanding

Figure 5.2. Modern shepherd with his sheep. Shepherding imagery is often used in the prophets where YHWH is the perfect shepherd. (Baker Photo Archive)

of Yahweh's power and wisdom into the people's minds. As the prophet says, Yahweh will place a "new heart" and a "new spirit" of obedience within them (Ezek. 36:26–32). These new sources of obedience will make the experience of the exile worthwhile. The example of a God who allows the nation to be taken away and who then brings them home again will demonstrate to all nations the power of Yahweh (36:22–24; 39:27–28; cf. Isa. 40:5–26). God promises that the barren and depopulated land of Israel will blossom because the people will "soon come home," and all its fields and pastures will be restored to fertility (Ezek. 36:8–12).

Ezekiel tells his audience that the exile is only one phase in their covenantal history, not the end of all things. In his vision of the "valley of dry bones" (Ezek. 37:1–14), the prophet plays off the language of the creation story in Gen. 1–2. In the vision, the Spirit of the Lord takes Ezekiel to a battlefield and asks him whether the dry bones of the long-dead warriors can rise and live again. Realizing that this is a question that only Yahweh can answer (as in the sequence of questions in Job 38–39), Ezekiel says, "O Lord GOD, you know" (37:3).

Having once again established the vast range of difference between mortals and God, the prophet is commanded to speak the word of God to the bones. It is the creative power of this word, as in the first creation story (Gen. 1:1–2:4a), that causes the bodies to rearticulate and take on flesh again. A second action is needed to animate the bodies. The breath of God is called on to fill them. Because "breath" and "spirit" are the same word in Hebrew (*ruah*), the reference to the "breath" is another allusion to the creation story. The first sign of order and life within the primordial earth's watery void is the Spirit of God passing over

Spirit of the Lord in the Prophets

One of the most commonly used images in the prophetic literature for God's power is the "spirit of the LORD." It sometimes refers to the spirit of God as the motivating power behind prophetic speech, sometimes as a means of travel or rescue, and occasionally as a term synonymous with the person of God.

Isa. 11:2	"The spirit of the LORD shall rest on him, the spirit of wisdom."
Ezek. 37:1	"He brought me out by the spirit of the LORD and set me in . . . a valley."
Zech. 4:6	"Not by might, nor by power, but by my spirit, says the LORD."

the waters (Gen. 1:2). Ezekiel's description of the "breath" also recalls the second story of creation, in which Yahweh "breathed . . . the breath of life" into the body of the first human (Gen. 2:7).

Ezekiel's vision describes the reanimation of these dead bodies. It is not the basis for a belief in a general resurrection of the dead in Judaism. Resurrection as a theological concept does not enter Jewish thought until the Hellenistic period (fourth to second centuries BCE) and appears in the OT/HB only in Dan. 12:1–2, which dates to the time of Persian and Greek influence on Judaism (second century BCE). The vision relates to their covenant relationship and how the people's disobedience had killed that pact with Yahweh. Now, when God takes the initiative, a new creation is made possible. The divine word and the Deity's breath revive a dead nation.

The crowning vision of restoration in the book of Ezekiel is found in Ezek. 40–48. Here the prophet, in great detail, describes the reconstruction of the Jerusalem temple. In this vision, the temple's grand scale and monumental construction are designed to approximate the power and majesty of Yahweh's restorative act. Within this narrative the key point is the reestablishment of the throne of Yahweh when God's presence returns to the temple (43:7–12). God's presence is equated with the receipt of God's blessings. Full restoration of the land and the people is not possible without this divine return. When it occurs, the covenantal promise of land and progeny will once again be in full effect (47:1–12).

The reality does not match the vision. When a new temple is built after the exile in 515 BCE, inaugurating the Second Temple period, it is only a fraction of the size of Solomon's temple and is not as beautifully decorated. It is not even constructed immediately after the return of the exiles (Hag. 1). The discrepancy between the vision and the reality is the basis for concerns in the postexilic priestly history (1 and 2 Chronicles) and for the fifth-century-BCE reforms of Ezra and Nehemiah in the Persian period. The people had to wait until the time of Herod the Great (30 BCE) for a truly magnificent temple to appear once again in Jerusalem. However, Herod's edifice reflects the political connections that he has with the Romans and his own desire to demonstrate his power through the construction of monumental structures, not the fulfillment of Ezekiel's vision.

STUDY QUESTIONS

1. Why does Ezekiel's call narrative avoid the direct description of God (Ezek. 1–2)?
2. Why is Ezekiel prevented from speaking words of comfort and hope to the people prior to the fall of Jerusalem?
3. How effective are Ezekiel's attempts at street theater to graphically portray his prophetic message (Ezek. 4–5)?
4. Which of Ezekiel's theodicies (tour of the temple or the abandoned child) do you find most compelling (see Ezek. 8; 16)?

5. Discuss how the marking of the innocents in Ezek. 9 parallels the story of the tenth plague (Exod. 12), and consider if it would have had a major impact on Ezekiel's audience.
6. Why is God's departure from the temple in Ezek. 10 central to Ezekiel's message? Draw on Ezekiel's vision of restoration in Ezek. 40–48 to shape your answer.
7. Consider why there is a shift in Ezekiel's interpretation of the law of corporate responsibility. Look at Ezek. 14 and Ezek. 18 and discuss how his use of righteous individuals and a proverb make a case for this shift. Why is Ezekiel not talking about individualism in the modern Western sense?
8. Consider whether Ezekiel's vision of the valley of dry bones in 37:1–14 is effective in representing covenant obligation and God's desire for a restored nation.

The Book of Lamentations

KEY POINTS

- The fall of Jerusalem in 587 BCE provides the theme for these five poems of lament.
- Comparisons can be drawn between Lamentations and other ancient Near Eastern laments.

With Jerusalem in ruins and the exiles taken away to Mesopotamia, this is the appropriate place to introduce the book of Lamentations. It is a short book that consists of five poems dealing with the destruction of Jerusalem in 587 BCE. Lamentations has been placed among the Writings in the Hebrew canon. Its placement right after Jeremiah in the Christian canon is supported by its appearance at that point in some Septuagint manuscripts and subsequently in the Vulgate. In later periods, Lamentations will be used as part of the Jewish liturgy commemorating the fall of the city of

Ancient Israelite Grief Rituals		

• Weeping, wailing, or lamenting
    Amos 5:16–17
    Jer. 9:18
• Tearing clothes
    2 Sam. 1:11
    2 Sam. 13:31
    Job 1:20
• Wearing sackcloth (coarse material)
    Gen. 37:34
    2 Sam. 3:31
	• Cutting hair or shaving head
	    Jer. 7:29
	    Mic. 1:16
	• Putting hands on or over head
	    2 Sam. 13:19
	    Jer. 2:37
	• Putting dust or ashes on one's head
	  and rolling on the ground
	    Ezek. 27:30
	    Mic. 1:10
		• Fasting
		    2 Sam. 1:12
		
		Other Examples of Mourning
		• Wives mourning in separate groups
		    Zech. 12:12–14
		• Professional mourners, usually
		  women, being hired
		    Eccles. 12:5
		    Amos 5:16

Jerusalem on the ninth of Av and the celebration of the fast of Tisha b'Ab, which usually falls in August.

Lamentations is most likely composed in the period immediately after 587, when the pain of loss is still fresh. Since there is no mention of the rebuilding of the temple, it is probably put together prior to the end of the exile in 539 BCE. Authorship is unknown, and the traditional view (see 2 Chron. 35:25; Jer. 9:1) that Jeremiah composed these emotional laments is unlikely because of a dissimilarity of style and vocabulary (cf. Lam. 4:17 with Jer. 2:18; 37:5–10). Lamentations depicts in graphic detail extremely gruesome images of destruction and depravity. The voices of the surviving community are heard in its five poems as they respond to Jerusalem's fall: blame, lament, accusation, and consolation.

There are other short examples of the lament form in biblical narratives (e.g., David's lament over Saul's death, in 2 Sam. 1:17–27). Laments are also a common genre in the Psalms, where they may represent either collective or individual sorrow (Pss. 12; 22; 44; 69; 137). In the book of Lamentations, the lament form is written specifically to commemorate the fall and destruction of the city of Jerusalem and the deportation of its people.

There are close parallels between Lamentations and a Sumerian work known as the Lamentation over the Destruction of Sumer and Ur (see p. 193) that dates to the period between 2000 and 1500 BCE. Both works depict a city that is destroyed by enemies and is seemingly abandoned by its patron deity. In addition to the physical tragedy and loss of life, there is a crisis of the spirit. Although there is no way to prove direct literary borrowing between the Mesopotamian examples and biblical lament, we repeat that ancient Israel benefited from the full range of ancient Near Eastern literature, its genres, and its motifs. What it chose to imitate or adapt, however, always takes on a distinctly Israelite character.

In form the book consists of a series of alphabetic acrostics in the first four chapters. The acrostic structure requires that each line or stanza begin with a consecutive letter of the Hebrew alphabet. The fifth chapter provides a variation on this structural device. It contains the same number of verses as there are letters in the Hebrew alphabet. Such a programmed piece of poetic literature, using a 3:2 meter, suggests close adherence to a set style of writing designed for public recitation on days commemorating the fall of Jerusalem. It also serves as a mnemonic aid and symbolically expresses the notion of the end of an era. Completeness has been achieved for this era (symbolized in the inclusiveness implied in using all the letters of the alphabet, as A to Z in English). The central theme throughout is the agony caused by the abandonment of the city by Yahweh (cf. Ezek. 10):

> The LORD determined to lay in ruins
>   the wall of the daughter Zion;
> he stretched the line;
>   he did not withhold his hand from
>   destroying;
> he caused rampart and wall to lament;
>   they languish together.
> Her gates have sunk into the ground;
>   he has ruined and broken her bars;
> her king and princes are among the
>   nations;
>   guidance is no more,
> and her prophets obtain
>   no vision from the LORD. (Lam.
>   2:8–9)

Even in the face of such massive destruction, there also exists an expressed hope that God will eventually return to rule a humbled nation once again:

> Let us test and examine our ways,
>   and return to the LORD.
> Let us lift up our hearts as well as our
>   hands
>   to God in heaven. (Lam. 3:40–41)

The book depicts typical Israelite grief rituals (see inset). The physical destruction of the city and its people is recounted, and a catharsis is achieved through these expressions of grief (e.g., Lam. 5:1–18). In the process the people show repentance as they attempt to demonstrate to Yahweh that they deserve another chance under the covenant (2:10; 3:48–57). Like the Babylonian lament that concludes with the

---

Lamentations and the Lament for Ur

> Even the jackals offer the breast
>   and nurse their young,
> but my people has become cruel,
>   like the ostriches in the wilderness.
> The tongue of the infant sticks
>   to the roof of its mouth for thirst;
> the children beg for food,
>   but no one gives them anything.
> Those who feasted on delicacies
>   perish in the streets;
> those who were brought up in purple
>   cling to ash heaps.
> For the chastisement of my people has been greater
>   than the punishment of Sodom,
> which was overthrown in a moment,
>   though no hand was laid on it. (Lam. 4:3–6)

On that day, the storm was removed from the Land, and that city was in ruins! Its people like potsherds littered its sides. . . . In its high gates where they were wont to promenade, corpses were piled; in its boulevards, where feasts were celebrated, heads lay in heaps. (Lamentation over the Destruction of Sumer and Ur, COS 1:166, 210–14.536)

---

fervent prayer "Enough! . . . May Anu rebuild Ur" (OTPar³, 254), the author of Lamentations exhorts Yahweh to be the people's enemy no longer (2:5). He pleads, "Restore us to yourself, O LORD" (5:21). In that way, the people will be able "to praise you once again in your temple" (OTPar³, 255).

Lamentations, like the prophetic books, does contain a message of hope in the midst of suffering. As might be expected of such an artful piece of literature, the author(s) has placed the divine promise of hope in the center of the book (3:21–24). A rhetorical device called a chiasm places the most important message of all not at the end but in the middle of the text, that is, at its heart.

STUDY QUESTIONS

1. How do laments and other forms of mourning serve as a catharsis for the people of Judah after the destruction of Jerusalem?

193

2. How do the authors of Lamentations reshape ancient Near Eastern laments to fit their needs after the fall of Jerusalem?

3. Given its poetic nature, how could Lamentations be used most effectively in the liturgy of the Israelite community?

Isaiah of the Exile (Isa. 40–55)

KEY POINTS

- Second Isaiah represents an exilic prophetic voice that builds on the themes of Isaiah of Jerusalem.
- Comparisons between the Decree of Cyrus and Isa. 45 indicate literary borrowing and an opportunity to celebrate Yahweh's role in ending the exile.
- The Servant Songs function as a theodicy of the exilic experience.

Second Isaiah and His Historical Context. As the period of exile comes to an end, a prophet or perhaps representatives of a prophetic school use the name of the great eighth-to-seventh-century prophet Isaiah to strengthen their message to the people in Mesopotamia. It seems likely that Isaiah of Jerusalem becomes such a dominant figure in Israelite prophetic tradition that a school of disciples is formed to perpetuate his ideas and his admonitions to Israel and Judah. The descendants of some of these original disciples are included among the exiles, and they produce the material for the latter half of the book of Isaiah (Isa. 40–66). Thus, a Second Isaiah (Isa. 40–55) as well as a Third Isaiah (Isa. 56–66) have been identified by many scholars. Each of these sections of the book of Isaiah will be treated here (see p. 207 for Third Isaiah).

This second voice of Isaiah begins to speak starting in Isa. 40, which dates to the end of the exile in 539 BCE. The section begins with a call to speak words of "comfort" to God's people, a message that clearly is not in the repertoire of the first Isaiah, who has to shock the people of his time with God's harsh judgment in the face of Assyrian aggression and Israelite unfaithfulness. Second Isaiah speaks of a later time, when the capture of Babylon by the Persian king Cyrus will make it possible for the exiles to be released from their captivity. They will be given the opportunity, if they wish, to return to their own land. It is therefore the task of this second voice of Isaiah to accomplish two things: to provide a theodicy for the exile, explaining to the people why it has been necessary and what it has accomplished; and to convince the people to begin thinking about their return to Judah and Jerusalem.

The most spectacular aspect of their change in fortunes, according to Second Isaiah, is that it will be accomplished by a God whose people have been vanquished and exiled. That is a piece of news that is deserving of being shouted from Mount Zion to "all the cities of Judah" (Isa. 40:9). Previously this would have been taken as proof that the God of Israel was a failure, no longer worthy of the people's worship. Undoubtedly this opinion has led many within the exilic community to become assimilated into Babylonian society and to transfer their allegiance and worship to the gods of Mesopotamia. By freeing them from their second period of captivity (the prophet compares the exile with the Egyptian experience), Yahweh now proves to the Israelites and to "all flesh" that there is no God but Yahweh (Isa. 49:26). This "new thing," once again making "a way in the wilderness" for a defeated people, is something that has never been accomplished by any other god. It distinguishes Yahweh as truly supreme and will become the basis for the formation of the monotheistic belief of the Jews with the proclamation, "I am the LORD, and there is no other" (45:5; see also Isa. 42:9; 43:19).

Second Isaiah states without reservation that the physical instrument of liberation for the exiles will be the Persian king Cyrus. This foreign monarch begins his career in 550 BCE by consolidating control over Persia and Media in the region east of the Tigris River. During the next ten years, he systematically conquers and pacifies the northern and western portions of the Chaldean Empire, leaving only Babylon and its immediate area for last. By 539, Cyrus is prepared to take on the final bastion of Babylonian power. He is aided in this endeavor by the dissatisfaction of the priests of Marduk in Babylon. Nabonidus, Nebuchadnezzar's successor, has de-emphasized Marduk's worship in the capital city, refuses to participate in the New Year festival staged by the Marduk priests, and elevates his own patron deity, the moon god Sin, to a position of supremacy. These policies significantly reduce the importance of the Marduk priests and cost them a fortune in uncollected offerings and other revenue. In addition, Nabonidus spends a great deal of his time and efforts in the areas

southwest of Babylon, especially around what is now the Saudi Arabian city of Teima (Tema), protecting that important trade route. His long absences provide ample cause for complaint and unrest within the capital, a condition that is not controlled effectively by Belshazzar, the son and coregent of Nabonidus.

Although what we know of Cyrus's campaign is based on his self-aggrandizing account, it is not surprising to find that as the Persian army approaches Babylon, discontented leaders and captive peoples such as the Israelites welcome Cyrus. Second Isaiah hails Cyrus as a savior in Isa. 45. He even takes the extraordinary step of applying the title "anointed one" (Hebrew *meshiakh*, which is the source of the English word "messiah") to the Persian king. No other non-Israelite is ever given this title, but as Yahweh's tool of liberation, Cyrus is truly a savior in the eyes of Second Isaiah and the people.

Second Isaiah's statements about Cyrus are closely paralleled in a document prepared by Cyrus's administration, justifying the capture

Cyrus Cylinder and Isaiah 45

Marduk, the ruler of the divine assembly, heard the people of Babylon when they cried out, and became angry. Therefore, he and the other members of the divine assembly left the sanctuaries which had been built for them in Babylon [cf. Ezek. 10:18–9]. Marduk . . . searched all the lands for a righteous ruler to lead the *akitu* New Year procession in Babylon. He chose Cyrus, the ruler of Anshan. Marduk called his name and made him ruler of all the earth. . . . Because Marduk . . . was pleased with Cyrus' good deeds and upright heart, he ordered him to march against Babylon. They walked together like friends, while the vast army of soldiers accompanying Cyrus marched into

Babylon without fear of attack. Marduk allowed Cyrus to enter Babylon without a battle [Isa. 45:1–2] . . . and delivered Nabonidus, the king who would not revere Marduk, into the hands of Cyrus. (The Decree of Cyrus, *OTPar³*, 208)

Thus says the LORD to his anointed, to Cyrus,
whose right hand I have grasped
to subdue nations before him
and strip kings of their robes,
to open doors before him—
and the gates shall not be closed:
I will go before you
and level the mountains,

I will break in pieces the doors of bronze
and cut through the bars of iron,
I will give you the treasures of darkness
and riches hidden in secret places,
so that you may know that it is I, the LORD,
the God of Israel, who call you by your name.
For the sake of my servant Jacob,
and Israel my chosen,
I call you by your name,
I surname you, though you do not know me. (Isa. 45:1–4)

of Babylon and the removal of Nabonidus. Cyrus's victory decree is a piece of political propaganda and must be read very carefully. It refers to Nabonidus's crimes against the god Marduk and Marduk's eventual decision to seek out a champion to liberate his people. As a result, Cyrus's army is allowed to travel unmolested through the countryside. When the army reaches Babylon, the priests of Marduk open the city's gates. Cyrus is able to take the Chaldean capital with only a minimum of fighting (see Isa. 43:14).

Cyrus uses the image of a discontented god, Marduk, and the dissatisfaction of the Babylonian priesthood to gain the support of the people. Employing propaganda as a military tactic is not unusual in the ancient Near East. Since the statues of gods are often held as hostages along with their conquered people, Cyrus voices his intention to release the captive gods, as well as to restore their destroyed temples (see Isa. 44:28b). Like many other ancient and modern politicians, Cyrus understood the political value to be gained in the use (manipulation) of religious objects and beliefs. Thus his decree includes the command that these divine prisoners be freed along with their worshipers.

It may be that Second Isaiah's exuberant message is written after Cyrus captures

Figure 5.3. Cyrus Cylinder (ca. 535 BCE). This political propaganda justified the Persian king Cyrus's conquering of Babylon. (Baker Photo Archive, courtesy of the British Museum)

Babylon and issues his victory decree. The prophet's familiarity with the details of the decree suggests at least an adaptation of its text. His use of the term "anointed" and his recital of Cyrus's easy victory would have been pleasing to the Persians. But Second Isaiah's insistence that Yahweh has chosen Cyrus, even though the king does not know Yahweh, stands in contrast to the Persian's statement that Marduk has sought out a ruler who would keep Marduk's religious festivals and honor him as the chief god of Babylon. It also raises some question about whether the Persian ruler would have ever heard this flattering statement read. More likely, it is the exilic community that is being addressed, and Cyrus is simply God's tool amid these momentous historical events (cf. Isa. 10:5).

Second Isaiah insists that Yahweh alone is responsible for Cyrus's victory. No other god has helped Yahweh, the creator of the earth and humankind (Isa. 45:12). That is because Yahweh is the only true divine being: "there is no god besides him" (45:14). The idols that Cyrus so magnanimously liberated are simply objects. It is the God of Israel who has taken these steps to save the people (45:16–17).

Servant Songs (Isa. 42:1–4; 49:1–6; 50:4–9; 52:13–53:12). The other major contribution in the second voice of Isaiah is the composition of four Servant Songs, which provide a theodicy of the exile. If the people are to resume their allegiance to Yahweh and return to their devastated homeland, they must recognize some value in the dislocation and pain caused by the exile. Thus it is not surprising that the prophet closely parallels the exile with the exodus. Just as the people are to be purified in the wilderness prior to the conquest of the land (see Deut. 1:34–45), so the exiles are purified in the cauldron of Mesopotamia. Now that "she

[Jerusalem] has served her term" (Isa. 40:2), the way to freedom is open for their return to Zion.

What is not taken into account here is the historical fact that some of the people of Judah were taken into exile, some were killed in the destruction of Jerusalem, and some remained behind in Judah. What sense can God or the prophet make of this division of the nation? Why do any of the people have to suffer at all? The answer comes in a classic theodicy. The exile is necessary because the people violated their covenant with Yahweh. The pain and suffering associated with their period of exile is a demonstration of Yahweh's justice. For "was it not the LORD, against whom we have sinned," and therefore the Lord who "poured upon him [the nation] the heat of his anger" (Isa. 42:24–25)?

The suffering of Israel, God's servant (Isa. 49:3), is intended to expiate Israel's sin. Now that their period of suffering is about to end, the prophet assures the people that the gods of the other nations are merely idols made of wood and metal (see his satire of idols in 44:9–20). They have no power to oppress or control the exiles once Yahweh has determined that the time is right for the return. Second Isaiah proclaims woe oracles against any who would question or oppose Yahweh, the creator of heaven and earth (Isa. 45:9–19; cf. Zeph. 3:1–5; Hab. 2:6–7). Indeed, Yahweh's purpose cannot be thwarted by any nation or king (Isa. 46:10–13).

With the end of the exile comes a new purpose for the servant. God uses this opportunity to make known the fact that the "former things" no longer have any hold on the exiles. God is about to perform a "new thing" (Isa. 42:9) so that the nation will "sing to the LORD a new song" of praise to the ends of the earth (Isa. 42:10). Suffering for the sins of the nation

(53:3–6) is now at an end, and the servant, despite his "marred appearance," will triumph and astonish kings and nations by returning to the promised land (52:14–15). The prophet assures the people that as Yahweh's servant their faith will be vindicated, and they shall not be put to shame for their belief in their God (50:7–11).

In the midst of their rejoicing over the triumph of Yahweh, the servant is given a new mission. It is not enough that Yahweh's power is demonstrated by the return of the people from exile. They must now become "a light to the nations," to serve as witnesses to the Lord's majesty (Isa. 43:10) and to spread the news of Yahweh's power that requires the obeisance of kings and rulers (49:6–7). While this may be an indication of universalism and a further strengthening of the emerging concept of monotheism, Judaism did not become a proselytizing religion. Conversion has never been one of its principal tenets. It is unlikely that the prophet is encouraging his audience to engage in a mission to the surrounding nations. More likely, he is seeking to demonstrate Yahweh's power, not a divine command to convert the people of the world to Judaism.

The identification of the servant has been a problem for scholars. In some passages, Israel (Isa. 49:3) or Jacob (44:1; 48:20), that is, the nation, is clearly identified as the servant. In other cases, the servant appears to be an individual (52:13–53:12) or perhaps the prophet (49:1–5). The indeterminate nature of this person or group known as the servant allows for multiple interpretations of these passages.

Predictive Prophecy. One of the most difficult issues in dealing with Second Isaiah and the other prophets is whether their prophecies are intended to predict future events, including events in the NT. For some of the writers of the NT and many other Christians, the servant song in Isa. 52:13–53:12 is seen as a description of Jesus's suffering and his role as redemptive Savior. However, like many prophecies, this one is imprecise. While similarities can be observed, neither an actual naming of names nor indications of dating occurs in 52:13–53:12.

Another proof that is often cited as an example of predictive prophecy is the passage in Hosea 11:1, "Out of Egypt I called my son." A careful study of the context here shows that the writer is retelling the story of early Israel and its apostasy (cf. a similar retelling in Ps. 78). Yet it is cited by the Gospel writer in Matt. 2:14–15 as a fulfillment of the prophecy of Jesus's birth and sojourn in Egypt when his family is forced to flee from Herod's murderous intentions. Such use of OT/HB prophetic speech by the NT writers must be recognized as an argument made to insiders, just as rabbinical arguments were designed to appeal to Jewish insiders. It is designed to reinforce the faith of the early Jewish-Christian community and follows the pattern of discourse common to that time, in which ancient texts are cited to demonstrate the validity of a group's interpretation of current events. The people of ancient Israel and in the period of formative Judaism believed that past events could foreshadow future events and that interpretations could focus on key terms and phrases, even if taken out of context. Thus Hosea can speak of Israel's origins in the exodus, while at the same time later interpreters can legitimately use the prophet's words to bolster their claims about Jesus.

These insider, or emic, arguments are satisfactory proof for members of the insider group. But it is too much to expect that outsiders would find them convincing. Outsiders, or etic, observers tend to interpret the words of

Hosea and Isaiah in context and not see them as the basis for their own belief. Just as Cyrus shapes historical events in his victory decree to suit his view of what happened, so too the NT writers use the body of prophetic materials from the OT/HB to make a case for their newly established religion. The object is to reinforce the prophetic ties to events in Jesus's life and ministry (see the quotation of Zech. 9:9 as part of the story of Jesus's triumphant entry into Jerusalem as recorded in Matt. 21:5). Neither interpretation is invalid, but both must be seen for what they are. If outsiders try to understand the positions of insiders, they should be able to develop an appreciation of other positions while continuing to hold to their own conclusions. Ultimately mutual respect is the basis for peace and harmony in a pluralistic society (one made up of many diverse groups).

Response to the Call to Return. Despite Second Isaiah's rallying cry to return to Zion, the question that sticks in the minds of most of the exiles is, "Why should we leave all that we have created in Babylonia to go back to Judah?" Throughout the roughly sixty years of the exile, they have obeyed Jeremiah's injunction (Jer. 29:4–6) and started businesses, purchased land, and established their families. The *golah*, or exilic community, has been given opportunities by both the Babylonian and the Persian administrations that allow them to become a part of the economy of their new region (e.g., farmers, herders, fishermen). As a result, many of the exiles have assimilated into the dominant culture and lost their own cultural identity. For those who continue to maintain a clear sense of their Israelite heritage, the choice of whether to return still remains difficult. If they return to their homeland, they can expect to have to start over in a land with large areas that have lain unattended for generations. It would have taken persons of real idealism and conviction to decide to go back. As a result the majority choose not to leave. In a series of waves over a period of nearly a hundred years, perhaps 15 percent of the exiled community returns to Judah.

Then who are the people who make the difficult decision to return to Jerusalem to rebuild the nation?

1. One group consists of political appointees of the Persian government whose job it is to rebuild the area and transform it into a tax-paying province.

2. A second group has a vested interest in the temple and the status associated with the cult community. Priests and their families expect to play a major role in the revitalized nation, especially since there will be no restoration of the monarchy.

3. A third group likely to make the trek are speculators and opportunists, who see this as a type of land rush in which they can claim large tracts of land and make a fortune. Among these will be younger sons who cannot inherit their families' property in Mesopotamia and therefore see this as their chance for economic independence.

4. Finally, there are those who see the return as their religious duty to Yahweh and the covenant. Like Second Isaiah, they envision a glorious procession proclaiming the glory of God from the heights of Zion.

The Cyrus Cylinder Decree

I returned the statues of the divine patrons of Ashur, Susa, Agade, Eshnunna, Zamban, Meturnu, Der, and Gutium to their own sanctuaries. When I found the sanctuaries across the Tigris in ruins, I rebuilt them. I also repatriated the people of these lands and rebuilt their houses. (*OTPar*[3], 209)

What these people will discover when they arrive will shock them. Nebuchadnezzar's systematic destruction of the city of Jerusalem has left it in ruins. It is overgrown after about sixty years of neglect. In addition, recent archaeological surveys have demonstrated that the land of Judah is not totally depopulated after the Babylonian conquest in 587 BCE. It would have been in the economic interests of both the Babylonians and the Persians to keep this region productive enough to pay its taxes, feed its people, and serve as a reliable buffer zone on the border with Egyptian territory. The remaining inhabitants would be hard-pressed to continue to cultivate all the fields, and therefore many areas must have been allowed to lie fallow. A lack of sufficient labor force would have also meant that in some areas the carefully constructed terraced hillsides had crumbled and eroded. In addition, the Samaritans, who now inhabit the former northern kingdom of Israel, claim political control over the entire area of what had been Israel and Judah. They are not pleased to see these returnees with their claims to the land and to political independence from the Samaritan governor's rule (see the conflicts described in Neh. 4:1–9; 6:1–14).

All these factors will result in the returning exiles' turning their primary attention to the immediate needs of the community: building housing, the backbreaking task of restoring and planting the fields and terraces, and the management of water resources. These tasks not only occupy their time but also exhaust the funds that the Persian government has provided to rebuild the temple. During the first twenty years after the return, the exiles complete only the foundation of the temple before turning to more pressing matters.

1. What evidence do you find in the text that Second Isaiah is not the same prophetic voice as the eighth-century Isaiah of Jerusalem?
2. Why is Cyrus honored with the title of "messiah" (Isa. 44:28–45:1)?
3. In what ways do the accounts of Babylon's fall in the Cyrus Decree and Isa. 44:24–45:7 compare and contrast?
4. Are the four Servant Songs in Isa. 42–53 an effective theodicy for the exile?
5. Discuss the reasons why some exiles choose to return to Jerusalem and some choose to remain in the diasporic community.

The Jewish Identity Movement

■■■■■■KEY POINTS■■■■■■
- The exilic experience sparks an identity movement to combat cultural assimilation.
- Facets of the identity movement include developing a canon of Scripture, circumcision, Sabbath worship, endogamy, and ritual purity.

The exilic experience provides the impetus for the formation of Judaism as a distinct religion separate from its Israelite and Canaanite roots. It becomes a religion that is able to maintain its tenets and values amid cultural diversity and the pressures of assimilation. Judaism's commitment to maintain a distinct identity may be the result of the combined shock associated with the destruction of Jerusalem, the demolition of Solomon's temple, and the demise of the monarchy as an institution. Added to that is the prolonged period of roughly sixty years that the people of Judah spent in exile.

An intensification of devotion to Israelite institutions seems peculiar because such disasters must have driven many Israelites to abandon their "failed" god and to seek the gods and the culture that now dominates their lives. But for those who choose to listen to Jeremiah and Ezekiel and agree with the premise of the theodicy that Yahweh is triumphant rather than defeated by the Babylonians, closer ties to their religion make perfect sense. To think otherwise would be to discount their entire cultural heritage. Perhaps the grief, the hope, and the anger expressed in Ps. 137 (see inset on songs of lament, p. 201) are clues to what is forming in their minds.

It is fair to say that the exile provides the catalyst for the basic elements of what are included in the Jewish Identity Movement. These elements include the following:

1. The formal process that will lead to a canon of *Scripture* begins during the exile. Previous documents, including royal annals, primordial stories, ancestral narratives, and legal documents are compiled, edited, and arranged. It seems likely that a formal attempt is made at this point to give these compiled written and oral materials a definite slant to sustain the understanding that Yahweh is the sole, transcendent, creator God; Israel is the chosen people; special legal obligations have been placed on them; and ultimately they will regain their special status and their country.

2. *Hebrew* is now used as a liturgical language. There is a comparable example of this practice in Mesopotamia, where Sumerian continues to be used in cultic contexts for thousands of years after it ceased to be a spoken language. For many centuries, Latin was used this way in the Roman Catholic Church.

3. An emphasis is placed on *Sabbath* worship. The increased importance attached to the celebration of the Sabbath is a direct result of the destruction of the Jerusalem temple and the sorrow generated by that destruction.

Songs of Lament

By the rivers of Babylon—
    there we sat down and there we wept
    when we remembered Zion.
On the willows there
    we hung up our harps.
For there our captors
    asked us for songs,
and our tormentors asked for mirth, saying,
    "Sing us one of the songs of Zion!"
How could we sing the LORD's song
    in a foreign land?
If I forget you, O Jerusalem,
    let my right hand wither!
Let my tongue cling to the roof of my mouth,
    if I do not remember you,
    if I do not set Jerusalem
    above my highest joy.
Remember, O LORD, against the Edomites
    the day of Jerusalem's fall,

how they said, "Tear it down! Tear it down!
    Down to its foundations!"
O daughter Babylon, you devastator!
    Happy shall they be who pay you back
    what you have done to us!
    Happy shall they be who take your little ones
and dash them against the rock! (Ps. 137)

Judah has gone into exile with suffering
    and hard servitude;
she lives now among the nations,
    and finds no resting place;
her pursuers have all overtaken her
    in the midst of her distress.
The roads to Zion mourn,
    for no one comes to the festivals;
all her gates are desolate,
    her priests groan;
her young girls grieve,
    and her lot is bitter. (Lam. 1:3–4)

Lacking a working priesthood in the exile, private family celebrations of the Sabbath accomplish several things. They commemorate Yahweh's creative act. Yahweh is affirmed as the sole creative force as part of a weekly ritual that reinforces the argument for monotheism. The simplicity and repetition of the Sabbath celebration serves as a teaching device helpful in explaining theology to children. When the temple is rebuilt in Jerusalem, the priests once again seek to justify their existence by laying additional requirements on the worshipers. In the face of this attempt to increase the power of the priesthood, Third Isaiah (see Isaiah of the Return, p. 207) opposes the cultic community with the claim that all that is necessary to be a faithful Jew is to engage in Sabbath worship (Isa. 58:13–14). After the destruction of Herod's temple in 70 CE, Sabbath worship becomes the center of rabbinic Judaism.

4. There is a renewed emphasis on *circumcision* as a necessary ritual act of initiation for Jewish males. While a precedent for circumcision is found in Gen. 17:11–14, the origin of circumcision is unknown. The emphasis it receives in the royal annals, where the Philistines are labeled as the "uncircumcised," may suggest a possible date, but it may be a practice borrowed from the Egyptians during the monarchic period or even earlier.

5. There is an intensification of interest in ritual purity. Ritual purity takes several forms, including ritual bathing and strict dietary laws (Lev. 11:1–47; Deut. 14:3–21). It is unknown when these laws were first instituted, although

Elements of the Jewish Identity Movement

- The Hebrew canon of Scriptures begins its formal development.
- Hebrew is used as a liturgical language for cultic practices and sacred texts.
- Sabbath worship by families is emphasized.
- Circumcision is practiced to distinguish the people from other communities.
- A Holiness Code is formulated and enforced to maintain ritual purity through personal hygiene and diet.
- Strict adherence to **endogamy**, marrying only within one's own group, is enforced.

there is evidence of the practice of ritual purity in Hittite texts (1600–1200 BCE). Endorsement of purity laws in the Daniel stories (Dan. 1:5–19), which date to the Hellenistic period (332–63 BCE), suggests a formal acceptance by the Jews at least by the time of the postexilic period.

6. There is an insistence on endogamy. Marriage within a group makes sense if the group is trying to protect its culture from outside influence. The mother is always the child's first teacher. If the mother comes from a non-Jewish household, she is likely to present mixed signals that could draw the child away from Judaism. The only other time in which the biblical tradition emphasizes endogamy is in the ancestral narratives (Gen. 24; 26:34–35; 28:1–9). As is the case in the postexilic period, the ancestral narratives enforce endogamy as a strategy for cultural survival. Otherwise endogamy makes little economic or political sense. It does not seem to be an issue during the monarchic period. Interestingly, it has to be enforced on the descendants of the returned exiles by the more stringent diasporic Jews Ezra and Nehemiah (Ezra 9:1–4; 10:6–17; Neh. 13:23–31).

The exile does not produce a single, monolithic Judaism; in fact, several branches exist. These include the normative, which requires strict adherence to the dictates of the law, and the wisdom group, which advocates a life of moderation and rational thought. There are also the more extreme apocalyptic movement, which advocates an eschatological vision of battles and last judgment, and the universalism movement, which takes its cue from Isaiah's image of "light to the nations" and sees the sharing of the law and Yahweh as the true mission of the Jews. It is this latter group that is most likely responsible for the stories of Ruth and Jonah, with their clearly universalistic motifs.

What seems curious is that the writings of all these groups have found their way into the canon. Each has been allowed to voice its vision of Judaism even though normative Judaism ultimately becomes dominant.

Persian Rule

> ### KEY POINTS
>
> - Without a restoration of the monarchy, the Jerusalem priesthood increases its influence on matters of religion.
> - A clear separation takes place between the Samaritans and the Jewish community after the return from exile.

A number of factors contribute to the significant changes that transform Jewish culture during the Persian period. First, the exiles who return to Jerusalem and the Persian province of Yehud enjoy a period of nearly two hundred years of relative peace under Persian rule. They are allowed to rebuild their destroyed cities and reestablish economic stability within their province. Agricultural lands are reopened for cultivation, and widespread business activity resumes after being practically dormant during the Babylonian exile.

Second, there is a greater emphasis on urbanization in the Persian period. Jerusalem, once its walls are rebuilt (Neh. 2–4) and the temple is functioning, becomes a major center of religious and social activity (Ezra 6:13–15). The temple provides a focal point for life, and Jerusalem becomes a model of urbanism for the other cities and towns of Judah. The strength of Persian authority throughout the empire assures a continuous stream of foreign businessmen into Yehud and the creation of a more cosmopolitan culture. A greater acceptance of the outside world during this period will make

Figure 5.4. The remains of Nehemiah's wall at the top of the stepped stone structure in the city of David, Jerusalem. (Kim Walton)

the transition to Hellenistic domination in the late fourth century BCE easier for many Jews.

The third major factor influencing the formation of Jewish culture during the Persian period is the elimination of the civil office of the king of Judah. As a direct result of this policy, the position of the high priest in Jerusalem is enhanced. He becomes the titular religious and civic head of the Jewish community, bowing only to the authority of the Persian king and his governor. The high priest's position is confirmed by the Persian government (Ezra 7:11–26) and further solidified by his control of the sacrificial cult in Jerusalem.

According to tradition, the office is to be held by a member of the Zadokite priestly family (Ezra 7:1–6). The connection that this family has to temple worship during the pre-exilic period provides legitimacy for the position of high priest (see 1 Kings 1:38–40; 2:35; 4:2). It also reassures the people that, at least in matters of religion, nothing has changed. The power wielded by the office of high priest leads to a gradual process of increasing secularization of the high priesthood. In the period of Hasmonean rule (165–63 BCE), when the Jews are able to free themselves from the Seleucid Hellenistic rulers, the office of high priest and the privilege of choosing who will hold that post are transformed into coveted political prizes.

A fourth important development during the Persian period is the initiation of the canonization process. Canonization is related to the growth in importance of the priestly community. Among the concerns of the priesthood is that the oral as well as written traditions of the people of Israel need to be compiled. After the traumatic experience of the exile, the priests want to ensure that sacrifice and other cultic acts are performed regularly and correctly. They hope to gain God's continued goodwill by a strict conformity to the law, and they want to formalize and strengthen their own influence over the people. These goals require that the law be written down and canonized into an authoritative document, the Torah, that can be consulted to prevent future mistakes or misunderstandings of what is expected of the people.

Once this process has begun, almost continuous interpretation and evaluation of the entire body of traditional writings take place until the final form of the Hebrew canon of Scriptures is certified in the early centuries of the Common Era. The compilation and editing process, which took several centuries to complete, also sparks increased study of the text and the development of a group known as scribes or rabbis (teachers). They become authorities on the law and its interpretation and are consulted on these matters by the religious community.

A final development that can be ascribed to the Persian period is the separation that takes place between the Jews of Judah and the Samaritans. Historically, this break has its roots in the political conflicts and religious differences between the Persian provinces of Yehud (Judah) and Samaria. It is also tied to the prejudice that the returned exiles have for the "people of the land" (Ezra 4:4) who did not experience the exile and are therefore not considered to be a part of the newly reformed covenant community. A sign of this growing separation is found in the decision by the returning exiles to exclude the Samaritans from participation in rebuilding the Jerusalem temple (Ezra 4:1–3). Later Nehemiah also stands up to Samaritan pressure and their governor, Sanballat, when they argue against the rebuilding of Jerusalem's walls. Nehemiah literally throws the Samaritan representatives out of the temple precincts (Neh. 13:4–9). With the Jews denying them participation in the cult in Jerusalem and calling them unfit because of their mixed cultural heritage, it is no wonder that the Samaritans reject Jerusalem as the true temple site and place of God's presence. Instead, they declare Mount Gerizim near Shechem as their place of worship. In 325 BCE the Samaritans take advantage of Alexander the Great's political goodwill to construct an alternative temple there and thereby formally separate themselves from the Jerusalem cult (Josephus, *Jewish Antiquities* 11.346–347).

STUDY QUESTIONS

1. What evidence is there that the exile helps to produce a single, monolithic Judaism?
2. Discuss the various elements of the Jewish Identity Movement and how they reflect either earlier traditions or a new understanding of the covenant and God.
3. Discuss the ways in which Judaism begins to become a distinct religious movement during the Persian period.

Postexilic Prophecy

The Books of Haggai and Zechariah (Zech. 1–8)

KEY POINTS

- Lack of funds, opposition from neighboring political groups, and immediate concerns bring the construction of the Jerusalem temple to a halt.
- Haggai and Zechariah both urge the returned exiles to rebuild the temple to complete the process of restoring the covenant.
- The temple is rebuilt, but only after Persian permission and funds are made available.

The postexilic community that established itself in Jerusalem and its environs are citizens of the emerging Persian province of Yehud. The period immediately after the arrival of the returned exiles is busy, filled with the rebuilding of houses and the return of long-neglected fields to productivity. The funds that are provided by the Persian king Cyrus to rebuild the Jerusalem temple cover only the laying of a foundation, and for years no further construction takes place. In light of this stalemate, two prophetic voices are heard that call the people and their leaders' attention back to the priority of rebuilding the temple of Yahweh. Nothing about the background or personal lives of these prophets is provided in their books. It is their message alone that is emphasized.

During a three-month period of the second year of the reign of the Persian king Darius (518 BCE), the prophets Haggai and Zechariah (Zech. 1–8 only) begin to provoke the people to rebuild the temple in Jerusalem. Haggai uses a negative approach, pointing to crop failures and other natural disasters as evidence of Yahweh's displeasure at the people's delinquency in completing this task (Hag. 1:9–11). In doing this, he follows a pattern set by previous prophets, who also proclaimed that famine, war, and natural disaster are signs of God's wrath (cf. Hosea 2:8–9 and Amos 4:6–11). For example, Jer. 14:1–11 contains a lament in which the people call on God for help in the midst of a drought and the suffering that it has caused them. However, the answer that they receive, like that in Haggai, is that because they have continually "wandered" into idolatry and disobedience, "I do not hear their cry" (14:10–11). Haggai structures his message to the people by beginning each argument with the phrase "consider how you have fared" (1:5, 7), a wake-up call to reassess their priorities.

His repeated harangues are designed to get the leaders and the people to recommit to building the Lord's temple. To spark them to action, he uses a phrase that is suggestive of the perceived social identity of the community of returned exiles in Yehud and Jerusalem. He refers to them as "the remnant of the people" (Hag. 1:14; 2:2). The words echo the terminology employed in Ezra's prayer (Ezra 9:8–15), in which he also refers to them as "a remnant." This designation also separates the returned exiles from the "people of the land," those who had not gone into the exile (2 Kings 25:12; Ezra 4:4), and from other peoples who had settled in the land during the period of exile. It singles out those who may take part in the building of the temple from the "adversaries

of Judah and Benjamin," who are rebuffed by Zerubbabel and Jeshua in Ezra 4:1–3.

In his parallel effort to convince the leaders and the people to restore the Jerusalem temple, Zechariah describes a series of eight night visions, each with a distinctive pattern: vision, question, and response. These interrelated visions present the prophet's concept of the universe as Yahweh's personal domain within which all the nations are given the opportunity to rule the earth. One major feature of the visions is the appearance of an angelic guide who interprets the various symbolic images shown to the prophet. Reliance on an angelic interpreter is characteristic of apocalyptic literature. This feature is designed to move the prophet to the background and place God's power and message in a more complicated and mysterious light (see Dan. 7–12; Zech. 9–14).

Zechariah employs a hopeful tone, in which Yahweh promises a return to prosperity and a restoration of comfort for Zion when the temple is rebuilt (1:16–17; 8:1–3). Full restoration of the nation's fortunes and of the covenantal relationship with Yahweh are assured when God once again dwells in the midst of the chosen people in the "holy land" (2:12 [2:16 in Hebrew]). Note in particular here that this is the only reference in the Hebrew canon in which Judah is referred to as the "holy land."

Despite their initial reception, both postexilic prophets continue to pressure the leaders in Jerusalem to move forward with the construction of the temple. Haggai calls on Zerubbabel, the Persian-appointed governor and possibly a grandson of the last king, Jehoiachin, to take on the mantle of Davidic kingship. The prophet uses the title "the signet ring" for Zerubbabel, indicating the legitimacy of the governor's Davidic origins and his right to exercise the power of the office. That would include using the signet ring to stamp and certify official documents in the same manner as previous Davidic rulers (Hag. 2:23). Haggai encourages him to trust in Yahweh's support to aid the people in their work.

Haggai's prompting is probably unrealistic, given the political situation of the times and that Zerubbabel is an appointed governor rather than a true heir to the House of David. Were Zerubbabel to "take courage" and trust in the "abiding spirit of God" (cf. Hag. 2:4–5), and act without explicit instructions from the Persian government, he would have been quickly replaced. Haggai is employing prophetic speech in much the same manner as Isaiah when he confronts King Ahaz in Isa. 7. The real message, in both cases, is to trust that God will provide what the people need. In Haggai's case, that includes "the treasure of all nations" to "fill the house with splendor" (Hag. 2:7).

Perhaps because Haggai's efforts bear no fruit, Zechariah, the bulk of whose prophecies are in the form of his seven visions (1:7–6:15), directs his lobbying efforts toward the high priest, Joshua. In his fourth vision, Zechariah describes Joshua "standing before the angel

of the Lord, and the *satan* standing at his right hand to accuse him" (Zech. 3:1, emphasis added). Here the term "satan" (Hebrew for "adversary") refers to an angelic being in Yahweh's heavenly court. Like the satan character in the book of Job (Job 1:6–12; 2:1–7), this angel's function is to bring human sins to God's attention. In this case, the accuser points out that Joshua's priestly robes are filthy. Here again clothing is used as a social or status symbol (see Gen. 37:3; 1 Sam. 24:4–5). Joshua's soiled robes are representative of the sins of the people and the priesthood. Yahweh orders that Joshua be given a new, clean set of clothes and a fresh turban (Zech. 3:3–5). A divine directive ordering new garments for the high priest plays on the exilic theme voiced in Second Isaiah (Isa. 51:9–11), in which the restoration of the exiles is based on Yahweh's decision, not human actions (cf. Ezek. 36:22–32). The injunction is repeated that obedience to the covenant is necessary to ensure God's continued blessings. Obedience also ensures Joshua's place as high priest and the continued role of the priestly community in administering the temple and the courts (Zech. 3:6–7).

At this point Zechariah draws on the traditions associated with the House of David and the concept of a messianic figure who will restore the temple and the nation under Yahweh's guidance (3:8). This figure can be compared with the ideal Davidic ruler, who is called "the branch of the Lord" in Isa. 4:2 and Isa. 11:1. When this ruler appears, he will usher in an era of restoration and justice that will also include the return of Yahweh to Zion (Zech. 8:2–3) and an ingathering of people from all nations "to seek the Lord of hosts" (8:21).

Zerubbabel, fearing possible political repercussions from the Persian government, does not accept the royal messianic titles assigned by Haggai and Zechariah. Perhaps that is why Zechariah changes his target and directs his use of "the Branch" in 6:9–15 to Joshua.

Despite the urging of these prophets, Zerubbabel does not resume the construction of the temple in Jerusalem until additional funds and a political confirmation are received from Darius's court. Opposition from the "people of the land" (persons who had not been taken into exile) and from the Samaritan leaders further complicate the political situation (Ezra 4:1–6; 5:1–17). Once these impediments are resolved through bureaucratic and diplomatic means, Darius gives the order and construction begins in earnest. The temple is completed in 515 BCE (Ezra 6), but it is in no way as grand as the one envisioned in Ezek. 40–48. Still, it provides a setting for the resumption of priestly offices and of the ritual sacrifice of animals. It also provides a religious focal point for the returned community in Judah as well as a beginning date for the Second Temple period, which extends until Herod's Jerusalem temple is destroyed by the Romans in 70 CE. Zerubbabel's political success in obtaining these funds from the Persian government may be an indication that he and Jerusalem are being favored over the politically suspect rulers of Samaria, Ammon, and Philistia.

■■■■■ STUDY QUESTIONS ■■■■■

1. Discuss why Haggai and Zechariah are so adamant that the temple be rebuilt in Jerusalem. Why are the Samaritans so opposed to it?
2. Why do Haggai and Zechariah draw a line between the returned exiles and those persons, including the Samaritans, who have not experienced the exile?
3. Discuss the value of using royal images to urge Zerubbabel to rebuild the temple in light of the political realities of that time period.
4. Compare Zechariah's use of "the satan" with that angelic figure in Job.

Isaiah of the Return (Isa. 56–66)

The anonymous prophetic voice of Isa. 56–66 dates to the period after the rebuilding of Jerusalem's temple in 515 BCE. Its link to earlier prophets is made by asserting that "the spirit of the LORD God is upon me, because the LORD has anointed me . . . to bring good news to the oppressed, . . . to proclaim liberty to the captives, . . . to proclaim the year of the LORD's favor, . . . to comfort all who mourn" (Isa. 61:1–2). Connections with Second Isaiah are found in the vocabulary and themes of Third Isaiah. Thus both prophetic voices set aside "former things" (43:18; 65:16–17) and look to the eventual fulfillment of "new things" that are to come with God's help (42:9; 65:17; 66:22). The return of the exiles that had been prophesied in Isa. 40:1–11 is envisioned in Third Isaiah in terms of a restored Zion, whose light shines so brightly that nations and kings shall be drawn to it (60:1–3). Furthermore, Second Isaiah's servant image (43:5–13) is transformed in Third Isaiah into the righteous remnant that has returned to the land (60:21–22).

However, the "new age" that Second Isaiah portrayed in his vision has been delayed by social and cultic abuses. Third Isaiah speaks of these problems by using terms like "blind sentinels," shepherds without understanding, and leaders filled with wine (Isa. 56:9–12). These complaints are echoed in the charges of hollow worship found in earlier prophetic messages (Amos 4:4–5; Jer. 6:20; Isa. 1:12–15). In the face of a resumption of the problems tied to God's judgment of the preexilic community, the prophet lays out a guide to deal with the situation that centers on what God truly expects for the people (Isa. 58:1–14; cf. Mic. 6:4–6). He uses fasting as one example of religious ritual that has no real value because it is performed "to serve your own interest" (Isa. 58:3–6). What is required is "to loose the bonds of injustice, . . . to let the oppressed go free, . . . to share your bread with the hungry, and bring the homeless poor into your house" (58:7–8). This is another example of the often-voiced statement (see Mic. 6:6–8; James 1:27) that God's interest in ritual is based on proper motivation.

KEY POINTS

- Third Isaiah (Isa. 56–66) speaks to the period after 515 BCE.
- Third Isaiah voices concerns over restrictions on temple worship and hollow worship practices.

The restoration of the temple in Jerusalem becomes a source of pride for the people of the province of Yehud. The temple and its community quickly establish itself as one means of defining Jewish religious identity. However, the restoration of the priesthood authority brings with it the enforcement of strict rules on the use of the temple and its facilities. Among the restrictions are detailed criteria to determine who is a Jew (thus the importance of genealogies as in Ezra 8:1–14). These criteria are primarily based on kinship (Ezra 2:59–63), but they may also include considerations of gender and physical infirmity (see Deut. 23:1–2), given that Third Isaiah gives the reassurance that the "eunuchs who keep my Sabbaths" shall have a place "in my house" (Isa. 56:4).

The formulation of these regulations reflects the purpose and design of temples in general. Temple architecture is intended to create defined areas of sacred activity. Concentric zones, from the outer courts to the holy of holies at the center of the temple, have increasingly restrictive rules for entrance. For example, all unblemished and ritually pure male members of the community can enter the outer courts of the temple to worship. However, only priests can move into the inner courts where sacrificial ritual takes place. Finally, only the high priest can enter the holy of holies and that only on one day each year (Exod. 28:40–43; Lev. 16:2–5). By diminishing the number of worshipers (all of them male) who can enter its gates and then to further restrict the number who could proceed within its boundaries to only a select few increases both its sacred character as well as the power of the priests. Such rigid guidelines can also be traced in the Second Temple period to competing challenges between the returning exiles and the "people of the land," who are the descendants of the people of Judah and Israel who never were deported (Ezra 4:1–5; 6:6–12).

Turning his attention to the restrictive measures applied to temple worship, Third Isaiah challenges the restrictions that have been

Figure 5.5. Only the high priest could enter the holy of holies. (Baker Photo Archive)

placed on eunuchs and proselytes (converts) keeping them from entering and making sacrifices in the temple. Other than obedience to the covenant, the sole criterion established by Isaiah is the celebration of the Sabbath (Isa. 56:2–8). During the exile, Sabbath became a centerpiece of the Jewish Identity Movement because it does not require a temple or an active priesthood. Although the restrictions on work associated with the Sabbath are intended to honor God as the Creator and to set the exiles aside from their neighbors, once the community is reestablished in Jerusalem, this practice is not being kept with the solemnity it requires (see the reforms that Nehemiah enforces on Jerusalem to keep the Sabbath in Neh. 10:31; 13:15–21). Thus, Third Isaiah's focus on Sabbath observance may be a call to return to proper respect for this commandment (Exod. 20:8–11). It also is tied to his call for the people to maintain justice and refrain "from doing any evil" within their community (Isa. 56:1–2). By proclaiming that no person, not even foreigners and eunuchs, should be excluded from entrance into the temple if they "keep the sabbath . . . and hold fast my covenant" (Isa. 56:3–6), the prophet is also upholding the rights these powerless persons have to justice. Furthermore, at the heart of this extension of rights to all Sabbath keepers is the prophet's concern over the growing separation that has been created within the Jerusalem community in labeling "those of Israelite descent" as superior to "all foreigners" and "the peoples of the lands" (Neh. 9:2; 10:28). Third Isaiah's more inclusive vision of those who will be gathered to God's holy mountain, to "my house of prayer" (56:7), reminds us again that prophetic voices are often minority viewpoints and do not always have a profound effect on those in control of events or institutions.

> **Emphasis on Sabbath Worship**
>
> All who keep the Sabbath, and do not profane it, and hold fast my covenant—
> these I will bring to my holy mountain,
> and make them joyful in my house of prayer;
> their burnt offerings and their sacrifices
> will be accepted on my altar;
> for my house shall be called a house of prayer
> for all peoples. (Isa. 56:6b–7)

The period after the return from exile is one of readjustment and an effort to return to a measure of normalcy. The prophets call for the restoration of the temple as a way to refocus the attention of the people on the former modes of living in Jerusalem and the covenant that they had made with Yahweh. But constructing a new temple does not eliminate the abuses of power and excesses of exclusivism that are a part of any institution and its leaders. Third Isaiah's prophetic voice is raised to remind the nation of the basic simplicity of its covenant agreement.

The Book of Zechariah (Zech. 9–14)

KEY POINTS

- The final chapters of Zechariah provide a shepherd metaphor and an apocalyptic vision.
- A final gathering of nations to Jerusalem will acknowledge Yahweh's rule.

The final chapters of the book of Zechariah contain two segments: Zech. 9–11, which most likely dates to the late Persian period and includes oracles against the nations and an autobiographical narrative using a shepherd metaphor; and Zech. 12–14, which comes from the Hellenistic period and consists of descriptions, some apocalyptic in style, of conflicts between nations and a triumphant Yahweh. As a whole, this final portion of Zechariah continues the theme of the establishment of a messianic era, which is first described in Zech. 6–8.

The focus of the final chapters in the book of Zechariah are two oracles that contain many familiar prophetic elements: indictment of foreign nations (9:1–8), the use of the image of "on that day" (12:4, 6, 8), and condemnation of false prophets (13:3–6). They also contain elements of apocalyptic literature, similar to that found in Dan. 7–12, including the vision of the final victory of Yahweh over the earth (Zech. 14:9).

For the use of the image "on that day" or the "day of the LORD," we can compare Jer. 30:8; Hosea 1:5; Obad. 1:8; and Zeph. 1:7–18. Examples in the latter chapters of Zechariah include the following:

> On that day the LORD their God will save them for they are the flock of his people. (Zech. 9:16)

> On that day the LORD shall shield the inhabitants of Jerusalem so that the feeblest among them on that day shall be like David, and the house of David shall be like God, like the angel of the LORD, at their head. (Zech. 12:8)

The first oracle (Zech. 9–11), written in poetry, is concerned with a call for the exiled people to return to Jerusalem (9:12; 10:6, 10–12). The vision contains a militant image, as the people are transformed into Yahweh's bow against the Greeks (Zech. 9:13–14; contrast Hosea 1:5). This reference most likely alludes to the repeated Greek mercenary and allied presence in Syria-Palestine during the fifth century BCE (see Ezekiel's sixth-century reference to the Greeks in 27:13). In Zechariah's time, Greeks were political allies of Egypt and trade rivals of the Persians. Zechariah would therefore see them as an enemy people, to be condemned by Yahweh. The prophecy then concludes with a description of a "wicked shepherd" who oppresses the people and may represent the officials ruling in Judah after the exile or possibly a foreign ruler.

The militant tone continues in the vision of the prophet-shepherd, sheep dealers, and the breaking of the staffs named "Favor" and "Unity" (Zech. 11:7). The first key to this vision is found in 11:6–10, with its abdication of control over human actions, allowing world leaders the opportunity to exploit the people and engage in savage slaughter. These actions are sanctioned, symbolically, by the breaking of the first staff, annulling the covenant with the nations (Zech. 11:10; cf. Jer. 12:7). There is then an interlude involving the payment of thirty shekels of silver as wages to the prophet-shepherd, a pittance so unacceptable that God calls on him to throw it back into the temple treasury (Zech. 11:12–13). This act, plus the breaking of the second staff (11:14), is symbolic of the dissolving of any recognized political link between the kingdoms of Israel and Judah and sets the stage for God's command that a "worthless shepherd" be raised up, who will act in a manner completely foreign to that of the true shepherd (cf. the good shepherd in Ezek. 34:11–16). The false shepherd will not care for the flock or seek out the "wandering, or heal the maimed, or nourish the healthy" (Zech. 11:16). Instead, the task of this shepherd is to devour rather than to guide, to literally strip the flesh from their bodies, even "tearing off their hoofs" (11:16). At this point the prophet cries out against such an abomination in a woe oracle, cursing the "worthless shepherd" with the sword, a withered arm (see 1 Kings 13:4), and blindness (Zech. 11:17). His cry in turn provides a transition to the second oracle, which is more eschatological in tone and envisions a world at peace at last.

Zechariah's Vision of Peace

On that day there shall not be either cold or frost. And there shall be continuous day (it is known to the Lord), not day and not night, for at evening time there shall be light.

On that day living waters shall flow out from Jerusalem, half of them to the eastern sea and half of them to the western sea; it shall continue in summer as in winter.

And the Lord will become king over all the earth; on that day the Lord will be one and his name one. (Zech. 14:6–9)

The second oracle (Zech. 12–14) is written in prose style and includes a series of statements that begin with the phrase "on that day." This provides a greater sense of future action by God rather than the more immediate acts intended to aid the returning exiles, found in the first oracle. In these chapters there is a mixture of military action and lamentation over the losses incurred in the fighting (12:7–11).

Of particular interest here is the restructuring of the cosmos after a long and devastating struggle in which Jerusalem, as well as the nations, suffer greatly (cf. Dan. 10). In the final scene, peace will at last come to Jerusalem, and the survivors of the war are required to come there to worship Yahweh at the Feast of Booths, celebrating Yahweh's rule and the restoration of the covenant (Zech. 14:16–19).

The Book of Malachi

KEY POINTS

- Dating to the early Second Temple period, Malachi addresses the abuses of the priesthood.
- Malachi's six oracles call for a return to the covenant while maintaining sacrificial offerings and proper behavior.

The book of Malachi stands as the final volume in both the Hebrew and Christian canons. Authorship is uncertain, since Malachi is not a personal name but means "my messenger," a reference perhaps to the promised messenger of God mentioned in Mal. 3. Malachi probably dates to the period between 500 and 450 BCE; it reflects the activities of the priestly community immediately after the reconstruction of the temple and just prior to the coming of Ezra to Jerusalem. Even though the Jerusalem temple is rebuilt in 515 BCE, the hopes that are raised by the prophets Haggai and Zechariah about a restored and prosperous community in Yehud have not been fulfilled. In addition, tensions are created by the priesthood, with its desires to increase its power and maintain complete control over ritual and sacrifice.

The book of Malachi addresses some of these concerns in six oracles, the last five of which deal with the failures of Judah and the priests to obey the covenant. The first oracle, a condemnation of Edom (1:2–5), is out of character with the rest. But this may indicate that the author has adopted the traditional theme of enmity between Edom and the Jews found elsewhere in the OT/HB (cf. Ps. 137:7; Obad. 6–14, 18–21).

In Malachi's second oracle (Mal. 1:6–2:9), the accusations made against the priests are similar to those found in Hosea 4:4, 6 and Jer. 6:13–14. The writer begins with a proverb categorizing the duties of a son to his parent (cf. Exod. 20:12; Prov. 29:3). The proverb evokes poignant emotions related to unfaithful and forgetful children. It also draws on themes in ancient Near Eastern wisdom literature:

A son honors his father, and servants their master. (Mal. 1:6a)

When Israel was a child, I loved him,
    and out of Egypt I called my son.
The more I called them,
    the more they went from me. (Hosea 11:1–2)

The faithful have disappeared from the
    land, . . .
for the son treats the father with
    contempt;
    the daughter rises up against her
    mother. (Mic. 7:2, 6)

Those who do not honor their parents' name
are cursed for their evil by Shamash, the divine judge. (Teachings of Ahiqar, *OTPar*³,
308)

Honor your father and mother and you
will prosper. (Teachings of Ankhsheshonq,
*OTPar*³, 310)

The emphasis on parental concern and
filial obedience continues in Malachi's third
oracle (2:10–12). The complaint here is that the
people are profaning the temple by introducing
aspects of foreign worship, including that of
the "daughter of a foreign god," possibly Asherah (see 1 Kings 15:9–13; 18:19 for Asherah
worship). That veneration of the Canaanite
goddess Asherah is still common in the Persian
period testifies to the conservative nature of
religious practices in that area and the people's
unwillingness to change. In addition, Yehud's
mixed population, made up of both returned
exiles and "people of the land," practically
ensures that "Yahweh alone" adherents live
side by side with practitioners of the old Canaanite religion. The prophet denounces the
worshipers of false deities, calling them unfaithful persons who must be "cut off from the
tents of Jacob," a metaphor for the community
of the faithful (see Jer. 30:18; Zech. 12:7). Such
a harsh measure is necessary in order to maintain the purity of temple practice and ritual.
This emphasis on purification and abhorrence
of any contamination of Yahweh worship ties
Malachi to the themes of the preexilic prophets

Elijah (1 Kings 18:20–40) and Hosea (2:13–17),
who also call for Israel to abandon its mixed
allegiances.

Malachi returns to his criticism of the
priesthood in Mal. 3. He has already denounced the priests for improper attention
to their sacrificial duties: "You bring what
has been taken by violence or is lame or sick,
and this you bring as your offering!" (1:13).
Even though the law is explicit that sacrificial
animals are to be healthy and without blem-
ish (Lev. 22:17–25; Deut. 15:21), the priests'
greed makes them think they can cheat God.
They are cursed for "robbing God" of the required tithes and offerings (Mal. 3:8–9). Only
those who do bring their tithes into the temple
storehouse, not skimping even in harsh times,
can be assured that Yahweh will reward their
faithfulness by giving them abundant harvests
and protecting their crops from locust plagues
and other natural calamities (3:10–12).

Weary of such unfaithful servants, Yahweh
resolves to send a messenger who will "prepare
the way" for the Lord's coming to the temple
and for the reestablishment of the covenant
(Mal. 3:1). An appendix to the book identifies the messenger as the prophet Elijah (Mal.
4:5–6 [3:23–24 in Hebrew]). This mysterious
figure, who does not die like other mortals
(2 Kings 2:11–12), is an appropriate harbinger
of change. The NT writers, seeing the coming
of a new age, apply Malachi's prophecy to
John the Baptist, as in Luke 1:17.

Another theme developed in Malachi is a
condemnation of divorce (Mal. 2:14–16). If
this theme refers to human marriages, then it
contrasts with the demands of Ezra and Nehemiah that mixed marriages between Jews and
non-Jews be dissolved (Ezra 9:1–10:5; Neh.
13:23–30). Malachi asserts, "Have we not all
one father? Has not one God created us all?"

Charges against the Priesthood

For the lips of a priest should guard knowledge, and people should seek instruction from his mouth, for he is the messenger of the LORD of hosts. But you have turned aside from the way; you have caused many to stumble by your instruction; you have corrupted the covenant of Levi, says the LORD of hosts. (Mal. 2:7–8)

> With you is my contention, O priest.
> My people are destroyed for lack of knowledge;
>   because you have rejected knowledge,
> I reject you from being a priest to me.
> And since you have forgotten the law of your God,
>   I also will forget your children. (Hosea 4:4, 6)

> From prophet to priest,
>   everyone deals falsely.
> They have treated the wound of my people carelessly,
>   saying, "Peace, peace,"
>   when there is no peace. (Jer. 6:13–14)

(2:10). This apparent example of universalism may be part of the minority voice within Judaism that argues for the extension of the covenant to all nations (see Isa. 63:16; 64:8). The prophet's argument against divorce may also be an effort to convert spouses to Judaism so that they do not remain "the daughter of a foreign god" (Mal. 2:11) and so that their families will produce "godly offspring" (2:15).

However, it is also possible that this passage is a metaphorical reference to the marriage between Israel and Yahweh under the covenant. If that is the case, then Israel is the husband who by law (Deut. 24:1–4) may divorce his wife, and the "wife of his [Israel's] youth" is Yahweh. But in a reversal of the situation described in Hosea 1–2, it is the idolatry of the husband/Israel that is covered up by rejecting the wife's/God's charges of infidelity/idolatry. The marriage garment should symbolize the conjugal agreement (see Ezek. 16:8), but here it disguises the husband's crimes (cf. the web of lawsuits that form an iniquitous garment in Isa. 59:4–6) instead of providing the legal

protections due to a wife under the covenant. In this way what should have been a festal covering, symbolizing the couple's union with its garlands and jewels (see Isa. 61:10), has become a physical indictment of broken pledges. Therefore divorce is a sham, allowing Judah/the husband to claim the status of a victim while continuing to worship other gods. Such a strategy cannot be allowed, and therefore the divorce between Israel and Yahweh is denied and all are called on to "act faithfully" under the covenant. The conclusion of the book is a reference to a horrific day of judgment when those "who revered the LORD" will be recorded in a "book of remembrance" (cf. Dan. 12:1) and will be spared when God separates out the righteous from the wicked (Mal. 3:16–4:3 [3:16–21 in Hebrew]). The image of a divine oven consuming the wicked is followed by two appendices: the first commands the reader to obey the law as given to Moses, and the second identifies Elijah as the messenger whose coming will presage the "day of the LORD." These verses serve as a **colophon** to the entire set of prophetic books (see Hosea 14:9 for another example of a wisdom colophon).

The Book of Joel

KEY POINTS

- The book of Joel describes how a locust swarm serves as God's means of punishing an unfaithful nation.
- The day of the Lord then becomes a time of renewal and restoration in Joel's apocalyptic vision.

The lack of any mention of identifiable historical events in the text prevents an accurate dating of the book of Joel. The book's placement in the canon among the preexilic prophets reflects a traditional understanding of its historical setting, but most scholars today place its origins in the Persian era. For instance,

Return to Eden-like Conditions in the Restored Nation

Joel's prediction of a revival of Judah's fortunes follows the pattern set in earlier prophets of the restoration of the land's fertility to an almost Eden-like perfection. The transformation will take place when the people are once again obedient to the requirements of the covenant. On that day and with God's help, all their needs will be met, and the land and people will reach their full potential.

Amos 9:13: In the early eighth century, Amos predicts a time when the land's fertility is so great that its fields

and vineyards outproduce the efforts of the workers to cultivate them, and "the mountains shall drip sweet wine, and all the hills shall flow with it."

Hosea 2:21–22: In the late eighth century, Hosea envisions the "day of the Lord" as an idyllic time when the earth responds to the "answer" provided by the creative word of God. The result is an abundance of grain, wine, and oil for the people of the covenant.

Joel 2:18: Joel echoes Hosea's words, stating that God has become

jealous for the land and now will have pity on the people by sending "grain, wine, and oil" to satisfy their needs and to prevent other nations from mocking them.

Joel 3:18: Joel echoes Amos's message, describing how creation rejoices: "the mountains shall drip sweet wine, the hills shall flow with milk, and all the stream beds of Judah shall flow with water."

the author's intimate knowledge of the Jerusalem temple and its priesthood (see Joel 2:17) suggests a date after 500 BCE. Furthermore, the mention of Jews being sold as slaves to the Greeks (3:6 [4:6 in Hebrew]) requires a date closer to 400 BCE, when, under cosmopolitan Persian rule, more frequent contacts are made with Greek merchants.

Written by an otherwise unknown author, the book of Joel reflects the uncertain existence of the Jewish community in Yehud. Their world is so fragile that a plague of locusts can create a famine and the specter of starvation. They can also be victimized by their neighbors and sold into slavery. Into this reality of want and misery, Joel injects a ray of hope for a day of the Lord that does not involve the punishment of the nation, but rather a newly revived creation and vengeance on the enemies of God's people.

The principal theme in this short prophetic book is the day of the Lord. The day of the Lord is first symbolized in a locust plague (cf. Nah. 3:15) that strips the land like an invading army (Joel 2:1–11; cf. Amos 5:18–20). In the midst of the devastation, the prophet reiterates the familiar theme that it is better to repent than to perform rituals: "Rend your

hearts and not your clothing" (Joel 2:13a; cf. 1 Sam. 15:22; Hosea 6:6). He also reminds the people that if they are not true penitents, God will not hear their pleas (cf. Isa. 59:2; Mal. 2:2). Their return to God must be characterized by full submission, "with all your heart, with fasting, with weeping, and with mourning" (Joel 2:12).

Then Joel provides God's promise to respond to the pleas of the priests to spare the people (2:17). The devastation will end, and the land will be restored as plenty replaces want and the presence of God is made manifest in the people's words and hearts (2:18–32). A distinctive literary pattern, a plea followed by a reassurance of hope and restoration, identifies this portion of Joel as a cultic liturgy (cf. Ps. 22). Thus the plea to "spare your people, O Lord" (Joel 2:17) is immediately followed by a series of clauses outlining what God will do to redeem them. In the repeated instruction "Do not fear" is an assurance of the divine promise to the land, its creatures and vegetation, and its people (Joel 2:21–27).

Joel also contains apocalyptic language and visions. Among them is a passage (Joel 2:28–32 [3:1–5 in Hebrew]) that is quoted in the NT book of Acts (2:17–21) as an example of the

> **Apocalyptic Vision**
>
> Then afterward
>   I will pour out my spirit on all flesh;
> your sons and your daughters shall prophesy,
>   your old men shall dream dreams,
>   and your young men shall see visions.
> Even on the male and female slaves,
>   in those days, I will pour out my spirit.
> I will show portents in the heavens and on the earth, blood and fire and columns of smoke. The sun shall be turned to darkness, and the moon to blood, before the great and terrible day of the LORD comes. (Joel 2:28–31 [3:1–4 in Hebrew])

last days and final judgment. However, the Judaism in Joel's time has not incorporated the idea of resurrection of the dead or a specific afterlife following judgment. This postexilic prophet refers to a day when the world will be transformed and judgment will be rendered on Judah's enemies (Joel 3:1–8 [4:1–8 in Hebrew]). The emphasis that Joel places on the use of war as a means for righting injustice and gaining revenge is also found in Esther 9 and Nah. 2. Such a blatant justification of war sounds cruel, but it speaks to the pain and suffering of an oppressed people who wish to strike out in their anger against Edom, Phoenicia, and the Philistines (cf. Ps. 137:8–9). Like other minor prophets (minor with reference to the length of the book), Joel includes only a few familiar images, not fully developed sets of teachings like the ones that appear in Isaiah or Jeremiah. He draws on both his own experience of his world and on the views of the growing apocalyptic movement, which are more completely developed in Daniel, the Qumran texts, and the writings of the NT.

STUDY QUESTIONS

1. Discuss the implications of Third Isaiah's emphasis on the importance of Sabbath worship.

2. Discuss the concern over tithing in the book of Malachi (3:8). Why is the prophet so critical of the priesthood?

3. Discuss the positive apocalyptic images of the day of the Lord in Joel 2:18–27 and in Zech. 12:4–9 and compare them with the negative use of that image in Amos 5:18–20.

4. What does Joel's admonition "Rend your hearts and not your clothing" say about mourning practices and previous prophetic injunctions about proper obedience to the covenant?

The Book of Jonah

KEY POINTS

- The story of Jonah promotes Yahweh's universal role and concern for all of creation.
- Jonah's reluctance to prophesy to Nineveh is based on national hatred of the Assyrians.
- Jonah is forced to speak and learns that God's mercy is extended to all people who obey the divine command to repent.

The book of Jonah is set in the period of Assyrian control over much of the ancient Near East (850–605 BCE). However, the author does not provide the name of Nineveh's ruler (cf. Jer. 1:1–3; Hosea 1:1). The story's principal character, Jonah, son of Amittai, is mentioned elsewhere as a prophet in the time of Jeroboam II of Israel (2 Kings 14:25), but no direct tie can be made in the text of this prophetic book to that earlier king or the political conditions of that time. Most scholars therefore consider that the book of Jonah is composed during the postexilic period (after 500 BCE). Their judgment is based on the strong emphasis on the universalism theme and the inability to trace the events in this book to any established historical sources.

Figure 5.6. Assyrian encampment. The Assyrians were well organized, well equipped, and usually conquered their enemies easily. (Baker Photo Archive, courtesy of the British Museum)

Purpose of the Book. The purpose of the book of Jonah is to provide a showcase for the principle that Yahweh has the power to control the fate of all peoples, even the sworn enemies of Israel. In that sense, it champions a position that is not acceptable to those who view Yahweh as the exclusive "property" of a single nation or people. One important literary device employed by the author in this tale of a reluctant prophet is comic irony. For example, when called to serve as a prophet, Jonah acts as though he can "flee from the presence of the LORD" by sailing away to the "ends of the earth" (Jonah 1:3a). Such a radical response to his mission hardly fits the awed and humble acceptance found in other call narratives (cf. Isa. 6:8 and Ezek. 1:28). Even more ironic is the pious reaction of the king and people of Nineveh to Jonah's warning, not only adopting the outward signs of mourning (e.g., sackcloth) but also displaying true remorse and causing God to "change his mind" about the city's destruction (Jonah 3:6–10; cf. 1 Kings 21:27–29). Jonah may have thought he was protecting his own people by refusing to save the Assyrians from destruction at the hands of Yahweh.

It is understandable that he would not have wanted to aid the enemy who has destroyed the northern kingdom of Israel and devastated the towns and villages of Judah. Like many of his audience, he may have preferred to join in the seventh-century prophet Nahum's invitation to "Celebrate!" (Nah. 1:15) for the Assyrians are no more!

Jonah's task, however, is to go to Nineveh, the Assyrian capital, and "cry out against it" (Jonah 1:2). Knowing that Yahweh intends to give the Assyrians an opportunity for repentance (cf. the angels' mission to Sodom in Gen. 19:13), the prophet flees in the opposite direction. He boards a ship from the port of Joppa that is sailing to Tarshish in Spain (Jonah 1:3). What he discovers is that there is no place to hide from Yahweh.

Universalism Theme. Throughout much of the narrative, Jonah appears to be stubbornly avoiding or actively resisting God. His actions stand in stark contrast to the keen awareness of Yahweh's power by all the non-Israelites he deals with in the story. For example, during the voyage a storm tosses his ship about amid the mounting waves. The sailors fervently pray to every god they revere for deliverance, but Jonah sleeps through the storm, seemingly oblivious to the danger (Jonah 1:4–6). These men, all non-Israelites, are very aware of God's

Assyrian Atrocities

I tore out the tongues of those whose slanderous mouths had uttered blasphemies against my god Ashur and had plotted against me, his god-fearing prince. . . . The others, I smashed alive with the very same statues of protective deities with which they had smashed my own grandfather Sennacherib—now (finally) as a (belated) burial sacrifice for his soul. I fed their corpses, cut into small pieces, to dogs, pigs, *zibu* birds, vultures, the birds of the sky and (also) to the fish of the ocean. (*ANET*, 288; the annals of Ashurbanipal [668–627 BCE]) anger, and acknowledge tacitly God's power over nature. When they ask Jonah to call on his god, he merely advises them that they should throw him overboard in order to appease Yahweh. There is no emotion from Jonah! The sailors are reluctant, but eventually they carry out this strange request (1:6–16).

Jonah's three-day sojourn in "the belly of the fish" provides him with a place of solitude and the time to mull over his actions (Jonah 1:17). Finally, convinced that his call to prophetic activity cannot be denied, he prays for his release (2:2–9). The fish and the storm function in the story as evidence of God's control over the natural world (1:17; 2:10; see Job 41:1; Ps. 104:26). Later in the story, a bush that provides Jonah with shade serves the same literary function, although Jonah will have to be reminded of this fact (Jonah 4:6–11). Having at last accepted his mission, however reluctantly, Jonah approaches the Assyrian capital city.

The resolution of the drama comes when Jonah enters Nineveh and reluctantly begins to proclaim his message: "Forty days more, and Nineveh shall be overthrown!" (3:4b). Even while carrying out this critical task, he once again shows his stubborn and rebellious nature. He walks a full day into the city before saying anything, perhaps hoping to find some corner where no one will hear him speak it (3:4a). The ironic thing about this tactic is that the people of this "great city," so large that it takes a person three days to walk from one end to the other, immediately believe Yahweh's prophet: "They proclaimed a fast, and everyone, great and small, put on sackcloth" (3:5). In a comic twist, at least to some, the order is even extended to clothe their animals in mourning garments (3:8)! In this way all of Nineveh repents, both humans and animals.

> **The Decree of the King of Nineveh**
>
> No human being or animal, no herd or flock, shall taste anything. They shall not feed, nor shall they drink water. Human beings and animals shall be covered with sackcloth, and they shall cry mightily to God. All shall turn from their evil ways and from the violence that is in their hands. (Jonah 3:7–8)

Unlike Sodom, which has showed that all its citizens are evil (Gen. 19:4–17), Nineveh's entire population, including the king, demonstrate their contrition and willingness to repent. Their change is based on the hope that Yahweh may relent and spare the city (cf. Joel 2:12–14). There is a close parallel between their voiced hope (Jonah 3:9)—"Who knows? God may relent and change his mind; he may turn from his fierce anger, so that we do not perish," and the explanation given at the end of Jeremiah's trial for his acquittal and release: "Did he [Hezekiah] not fear the Lord and entreat the favor of the Lord, and did not the Lord change his mind about the disaster that he had pronounced against them?" (Jer. 26:19b). Obviously these people recognize the possibility of changing God's mind, and they are willing to go to extremes in making the attempt.

Ironically, Jonah's reaction to his phenomenal success as a prophet is sullen anger (Jonah 4:1). The prophet is so beside himself over Nineveh's survival that he asks for God to take his life (4:3). This plea is not an unheard-of request. Elijah, after fleeing into the wilderness from Jezebel's wrath, asks God for the comfort of death, saying, "It is enough, . . . O Lord, take away my life" (1 Kings 19:4). And, perhaps justifiably, after struggling with the suffering that is inflicted on him, Job issues a similar desire for "death rather than this body" (Job 7:15–16). Neither example, however, is based on the frustration brought on by too much success. Jonah is so excessive in his self-centered demand that he is a laughable curmudgeon.

In fact, Jonah's anger allows the author to once again inject the universalism theme into the story. What we learn is that the same sense of justice that is extended to the Israelites causes God to be concerned about the most bloodthirsty people in the ancient world. Jonah, realizing that Yahweh is a just God, is beside himself because God acts justly and relents. Thus the key to the prophet's stubborn nature is found in Jonah 4:2. In this verse, Jonah reveals the reason why he refused his initial call to be a prophet. He is willing to proclaim Yahweh's loving and forgiving nature, but Jonah cannot forgive the Assyrians and thus does not want God to do so either.

> O LORD! Is not this what I said while I was still in my own country? That is why I fled to Tarshish at the beginning; for I knew that you are a gracious God and merciful, slow to anger, and abounding in steadfast love, and ready to relent from punishing. (Jonah 4:2)

The final expression of the universalism theme occurs when Jonah constructs a booth outside of the city and God causes a bush to sprout and give the prophet shade from the heat of the day (Jonah 4:5–6). Then God creates a catalyst for further conversation with Jonah by stripping him of his pleasant vantage point. God sends a worm to destroy the bush and a hot wind to parch Jonah's throat (Jonah 4:7–8). As he did when Nineveh is spared, Jonah responds angrily at the unfairness of life. He pitifully moans: "It is better for me to die than to live."

Jonah's self-centered philosophy is then condemned by God, who teaches him that he must be concerned for all creation. The prophet's anger is not based on the death of the plant but on the fact that he is deprived of its comfort-giving shade. His concern over this petty matter is then analyzed in a typical wisdom statement (cf. the questioning of Job in Job 38–41):

> You are concerned about the bush, for which you did not labor and which you did not grow; it came into being in a night and perished in a night. And should I not be concerned about Nineveh, that great city, in which there are more than a hundred and twenty thousand persons who do not know their right hand from their left, and also many animals? (Jonah 4:10–11)

The book ends with a question and leaves the reader to ponder Jonah's rigid nationalism and lack of basic human compassion.

Connection with Postexilic Period. Those who decide to remain loyal to Yahweh during the exile and in the subsequent postexilic period generally identify their God with themselves and their own country. Some, like Isaiah of the exile (Isa. 40–55), attempt to broaden the scope of Judaism and portray God as universal. This is a pleasant task when it allows the prophetic writers to show Yahweh as crushing their oppressors and demonstrating through their return from exile that the God of Israel is supreme over all other nations and gods (Zech. 14:13–15; Mal. 1:4–5).

What is not so pleasant is when Yahweh helps their enemies to repent and be delivered from justified destruction. This message would have been difficult to accept in the period of Assyrian control of the Near East. At that point, the people's hopes were kept alive by prophecies of the impending annihilation of Nineveh and its rulers (Nah. 2–3; Zeph. 2:13). The book of Jonah, however, comes from the postexilic period, when some voices within the Jewish community argue that if Yahweh is truly the only God (Isa. 49:7; 60:8–14), then all peoples, even the seemingly unredeemable Assyrians, deserve a chance to accept a message of repentance.

1. Why is Jonah reluctant to prophesy to the people of Nineveh (cf. Jonah 1:1–3; 4:2)?
2. Why do the sailors ask Jonah to call on his god during the storm (Jonah 1:4–16)?
3. Suggest several purposes behind the writing of the book of Jonah.
4. How is God depicted in the book of Jonah?
5. How often is the big fish mentioned in the book of Jonah? Does it have major significance or minor significance?

Postexilic Narrative

The Books of Chronicles

▨▨▨▨▨▨▨▨ KEY POINTS ▨▨▨▨▨▨▨▨

- The fifth-century BCE Chronicler provides a revised version of Israel's history.
- Careful attention is given to emphasizing the positive character of David and Solomon.
- The temple and the priesthood are a major focus of the Chronicler.

The Hebrew canon comes to an end with the books of Chronicles. In modern translations it is divided into two books, 1 and 2 Chronicles, but originally it was composed as a single volume. The work of the Chronicler (a modern designation for the editor or editors of 1–2 Chronicles) begins with an extensive genealogy, starting with Adam, detailing the descendants of the Israelite tribes, and concluding with the list of Levitical families that return from the exile (1 Chron. 1:1–9:34). At

that point the narrative shifts to a description of David's reign (1 Chron. 11–22, 28–29). Sandwiched between David's exploits are a number of chapters (1 Chron. 23–27) that describe the temple community and its functions. Second Chronicles contains a long recitation of Solomon's reign (1:1–9:31) followed by a recital of the history of the kings of Judah down to the destruction of Jerusalem (10:1–36:21). The final words recorded in Chronicles contain the decree of Cyrus that provides the exiles with the opportunity to return to Palestine (36:22–23; cf. Ezra 1:1–4). The Persian king's decree gives the exiles a promise of a brighter future and the hope for a restoration of the relationship with God. Chronicles is a revisionist history, written in the period after the reconstruction of the Jerusalem temple by the returned exiles (after 500 BCE). Its purpose, in addition to retelling the story of Israel's history from Adam to the time of the exile, is to establish a link between the ideal worship community of David's reign and the community of returned exiles who are living in Yehud during the Persian period. Such a selective and focused history is designed to help the scribes who compiled Chronicles to legitimize their restored community and its priesthood. The Chronicler attempts to create the impression that their own community is a continuation of that created by David and Solomon. They do this in order to encourage the people to hold fast to their cultural and political identity.

The sources used by the Chronicler include large portions of the Deuteronomistic History (1 Sam. 31–2 Kings 25). A number of other lost sources are also cited, such as "the records of the seer Samuel, . . . the records of the prophet Nathan, and . . . the records of the seer Gad" (1 Chron. 29:29). Since none of these

The Chronicler's Revision of the Narratives of David and Solomon

- The Chronicler juggles the chronological sequence of events, interposing episodes from David's outlaw period (1 Chron. 11:10–12:40) between the story of his being anointed king of Israel and his capture of Jebus/Jerusalem (11:1–9). There is a reversal of the narrative order of two events: the story of the transport of the ark of the covenant to Jerusalem (2 Sam. 6:2–11; 1 Chron. 13) and the episode in which David obtains materials and workmen from Hiram of Tyre to construct his palace (2 Sam. 5:11–25; 1 Chron. 14:1–17).

- The Chronicler edits out some of the less flattering aspects of the story of David that are presented in Samuel–Kings. David's unclothed dance before the ark as it is brought into Jerusalem and his confrontation with Michal (2 Sam. 6:14–23) are omitted in the parallel story in 1 Chron. 16. The episodes involving David's adultery with Bathsheba, Absalom's rebellion, and David's flight are also omitted (2 Sam. 11–16).

- The Chronicler changes the title for David's sons from "priests" to "chief officials" (2 Sam. 8:18; 1 Chron. 18:17) in order to maintain the ideology that only descendants of Levi and Aaron can serve as priests.

- Second Samuel 9, with its story of David's care for Jonathan's son Mephibosheth, is omitted by the Chronicler. First Chronicles 10:6 asserts that all of Saul's family is dead.

- The political purge at the beginning of Solomon's reign is omitted, and his first official act is to visit and sacrifice at the high place at Gibeon, where the tent of meeting is erected (2 Chron. 1:2–6).

- The story of the two prostitutes who come to Solomon for a decision (1 Kings 3:16–28) is omitted.

- Hiram of Tyre's name is changed to Huram, and Chronicles adds a letter from the Phoenician king that does not appear in 1 Kings 5. The letter expands on the statement, "the Lord God of Israel, who made heaven and earth" (2 Chron. 2:11–16).

- The Chronicler exercises editorial prerogative by omitting verses 27–37 from the description of the temple equipment in 1 Kings 7:23–51 (2 Chron. 4:1–22).

- The story of bringing the ark into the temple (based on 1 Kings 8:1–11) has an additional section on the priests and Levitical singers that reflects their increased importance in the Second Temple period (2 Chron. 5:11b–13a).

- Solomon's offering of incense (1 Kings 9:25) is qualified in 2 Chron. 8:12, where it explicitly notes that his altar is built "in front of the vestibule," thus reserving sacrificial service within the temple for priests alone.

documents currently exists, it is impossible to determine how extensively they were used or even whether they are real or fictitious. It has been suggested that Chronicles was originally part of a larger work that included the books of Ezra and Nehemiah, but this proposal is not accepted by all scholars and requires further linguistic and historical analysis before a final determination can be made.

What is unique about this revisionist version of Israel's history is its selective use of material. For example, the period from Adam to the death of Saul is told through the recitation of genealogies. The choice of what data to provide here ensures that the reader will be drawn along by the editor(s) to view Israel's history as a human stream that flows from the beginning of time to the reign of David. It then culminates with the designation of Jerusalem as the religious and political capital of the newly established monarchy.

In addition, where the Chronicler deems it appropriate, the Deuteronomistic narrative of Samuel–Kings is rearranged or heavily edited. Usually the goal of these modifications is to put greater emphasis on cultic rather than political motives and to cleanse from the text the scandalous behavior of David and his court. Therefore the reader is confronted with more detail on the furnishings of the temple than on David's or Solomon's administrative activities.

Only in 1 Chron. 21:1–4 is there an indication of the complexities of making the right decisions as king. David is "incited" by one of his advisers, who is not identified by name, but instead by the Hebrew word *satan*, "adversary." Like the member of the divine assembly depicted in Zech. 3:1–2 and Job 1:6–12, this anonymous human character becomes the catalyst for action in the story. It is his counsel rather than Joab's advice that prevails, and David orders a census of the nation. The parallel story in 2 Sam. 24:1 describes God as the one who "incites" David to this unwise action. The Chronicler chooses, however, to avoid having Yahweh involved in David's policy making and instead places the blame for something that will "displease" God (1 Chron. 21:7) at the feet of a foolish adviser.

David's role as the originator of Israel's cultic practice and the organizer of the priestly groups who serve in various capacities is also described at great length. For example, David commands the chiefs of the Levites to appoint long lists of persons who will serve as singers and musicians (1 Chron. 15:16–24). As part of his final instructions to Solomon, David organizes the body of officials who will administer and serve in the temple (23:2–32). Chronicles also shows at least a cursory interest in the administration of the government and provides lists of officials. However, these records in Chronicles contain some differences from those in Samuel. In Chronicles, information about David's officials serves primarily to magnify the importance of David's position rather than to describe a realistic account of the size of his court (e.g., 1 Chron. 27:1–15 gives the inflated figure of 288,000 for the number of David's royal guards).

When the narrative moves to Solomon's reign, again it is evident that the emphasis is on cultic matters. Of particular importance is the construction of the temple in Jerusalem. The Chronicles version tends to condense and revise the material that is found in 1 Kings 6–7. Throughout the process, Solomon is portrayed as faithfully carrying out the work that his more important father, David, would have done if he had been permitted to do so by circumstances and by God's command (see 2 Chron. 6:7–9, 14–17; 7:17–18).

As with the chronicle of David's reign, the Chronicler's account of Solomon's reign focuses on his wealth, the temple, and his wise policies. There is nothing here that is unfavorable to his administration (2 Chron. 9:22–31). In contrast to the description of Solomon's many wives and the shrines built to their gods in Jerusalem (1 Kings 11:1–8), the Chronicler has Solomon build a house for his Egyptian wife so that she will not contaminate the palace precincts where the ark had once resided (2 Chron. 8:11). With the transition to the reign of Rehoboam and the division of the kingdom, it becomes clear that the Chronicler's loyalties are with the Davidic kings, and this attitude colors every event. Even Manasseh, who is considered to be the worst of Judah's kings (2 Kings 21:1–16), is rehabilitated in the Chronicles account when he repents and restores the altar of the Lord (2 Chron. 33:10–17).

The chapters narrating the history of Judah after the division of the kingdom (2 Chron. 10–36) describe the misdeeds of kings and the basis on which Yahweh became angry with the nation (see 2 Chron. 20:33, 35–37). But the Chronicler, like the Deuteronomistic Historian (2 Kings 8:18–19), makes a point of declaring that the actions of evil individuals cannot negate the covenant that Yahweh has made with David.

> Yet the LORD would not destroy the house of David because of the covenant that he had made with David, and since he had promised to give a lamp to him and to his descendants forever. (2 Chron. 21:7)

This assertion could then be used as the basis for the claim of a restored people after the exile.

The Chronicler often adds a short comment to the narrative to ensure that the reader understands the reason why certain acts are considered wicked. For example, in 2 Chron. 21:8–10, the text describes the Edomite revolt in the time of King Jehoram. The Chronicles story is based on the same account found in 2 Kings 8:20–22. But the Chronicler adds an explanation for the revolt (2 Chron. 21:11): "[Jehoram] made high places in the hill country of Judah, and led the inhabitants of Jerusalem into unfaithfulness, and made Judah go astray" (cf. 2 Chron. 21:16–19). The rewriting of 2 Kings 16 to magnify the portrayal of Ahaz's sins is typical of the Chronicler's commentary style of presentation and basic theological agenda (2 Chron. 28).

The kings who are righteous are singled out for special attention by the Chronicler and generally given longer treatment than in 1–2 Kings. Jehoshaphat, Hezekiah, and Josiah all are pictured as reformers and faithful kings who ordered the people to return to proper worship. The Chronicler also takes the opportunity to note kings who are at first just rulers and then are convinced by evil advisers to turn from God and right behavior (Joash in 2 Chron. 24:1–22) and others who are restored to favor when their evil ways end (e.g., Manasseh in 2 Chron. 33:10–17). The heightened role of the Levites in these reforms is also typical of the Chronicler's desire to enhance the authority of the priesthood (see 2 Chron. 29:12–19; 31:2–19).

Another example of the way that the material from the Kings' account has been revised to reflect the fifth-century attitudes of the Chronicler is the account of the siege of Jerusalem by the Assyrian king Sennacherib (2 Chron. 32:1–23). Even though the speech of the Rabshakeh is paraphrased and condensed, it contains most of the same taunts employed by the Assyrian official in the 2 Kings account (cf. 2 Kings 18:17–35; 19:1–37). But it fails to reflect the Assyrian's aggressive rhetorical style and omits the Rabshakeh's theodicy that claims Yahweh has sent the Assyrians in response to Hezekiah's unfaithfulness (2 Kings 18:22). In addition, the monotheistic theology of the Chronicler's time is injected into 2 Chron. 32:19 with the editorial comment, "They spoke of the God of Jerusalem as if he were like the gods of the peoples of the earth, which are the work of human hands" (cf. Isa. 40:18–20; 42:21–24).

Josiah in particular is singled out as the true successor to King David. Again, however, the Chronicler's narrative of his reign is rearranged. Here the Deuteronomic reform movement occurs prior to the discovery of the tablets of the law in the temple (2 Chron. 34:3–7; contrast 2 Kings 22–23). The Passover celebration is described in much greater detail in the Chronicler's version to give it the prominence that the priestly community associated with this major religious festival (cf. 2 Kings 23:21–23 with 2 Chron. 35:1–19). Even Josiah's death at Megiddo is given a more theological foundation with the inclusion of a speech, not found in 2 Kings, in which the Egyptian pharaoh Neco II commands Josiah to stand aside while the pharaoh obeys Yahweh's command to go to war (2 Chron. 35:21).

The confusing years of Josiah's successors are given little attention, and the fall of Jerusalem to the Babylonians is condensed into only a few verses. At the end of the Chronicles' account, the decree of Cyrus is highlighted to demonstrate that Jerusalem's fall is not the end for the nation. Interestingly, Solomon's dedication prayer also includes similar sentiments of hope for the exiles (much of it verbatim to 1 Kings 8:46–53):

> The LORD, the God of heaven, has given me all the kingdoms of the earth, and he has charged me to build him a house at Jerusalem, which is in Judah. Whoever is among you of all his people, may the LORD his God be with him! Let him go up. (2 Chron. 36:23)

> [If your people] repent with all their heart and soul in the land of their captivity . . . and pray toward their land, which you gave to their ancestors, the city that you have chosen, and the house that I have built for your name, then hear from heaven . . . their prayer and their pleas . . . and forgive your people who have sinned against you. (2 Chron. 6:38–39)

This sets the stage for the postexilic community's restoration of the Jerusalem temple and its priestly orders. In the present arrangement of the Jewish canon of the HB, this statement completes the canon on a positive note.

STUDY QUESTIONS

1. Discuss the idea of a revisionist history. What makes the Chronicler's account so different from the royal annals found in Samuel–Kings?
2. Why are David and Solomon portrayed in a different manner and given so much attention in the Chronicler's account?
3. Why are kings Jehoshaphat, Hezekiah, and Josiah given such a positive depiction by the Chronicler?
4. What is significant about the ending of the Chronicler's history? Why might later editors choose to place it at the end of the canon?

The Books of Ezra and Nehemiah

KEY POINTS

- Ezra and Nehemiah bring the stricter interpretation of Jewish identity from the Diaspora back to Jerusalem.
- Both Ezra and Nehemiah operate with the backing of the Persian government to pacify Yehud and prevent conflict with Samaria.
- Ezra's covenant-renewal ceremony marks the final phase in the traditional history of Israel.

One of the things that becomes clear in the books of Ezra and Nehemiah is that there has been a cultural separation between the Jewish communities that remain in the Diaspora and the newly reconstituted one in Yehud. Distance contributes to these differences, but high on the list is the restoration of the temple and the priestly community in Jerusalem. There is nothing comparable in the Diaspora. There the community relies on the elements of the Jewish Identity Movement, including rituals associated with the Sabbath, which do not require priestly intervention or interpretation. In Jerusalem the reconstituted priesthood is quick to establish its authority and exercise control over the religious activities of the people. Yet the pragmatic nature of this same priesthood allows intermarriage with families that are not part of the returned exilic community, access to markets and commercial activity even on the Sabbath, and some political accommodation that brings them into close contact with their neighbors.

The restoration of the community in Yehud also brings about some frictions with the Samaritans and their allies that have the potential to lead to conflict and Persian intervention. When concerns over civil unrest and leadership problems in the province of Yehud do reach the ears of the Persian administration, steps will be taken to prevent it from getting out of hand.

During the period after 450 BCE, two Jews from the diasporic community are dispatched to Jerusalem to help administer its affairs and seek solutions.

The books of Ezra and Nehemiah contain the story of the return of the exiles to Jerusalem and the measures taken to preserve the Jewish Identity Movement in Yehud. Ezra and Nehemiah could have worked side by side, but if that were the case, it seems likely there would have been many more direct contacts and references to each other in the text. In any case, the issues they deal with in Jerusalem are similar. The real difference between them is that Ezra consistently appears as a priestly figure. His activities are almost exclusively concerned with the temple and with religious conformity. In contrast, Nehemiah is clearly a political figure who is interested in the efficient administration of this Persian province and in what he considers to be necessary religious and civil reforms. The orders he issues are designed to bring the people back into his vision of the covenant while at the same time pacifying the area so that he can assure the Persian government that no direct intervention is necessary.

Since there is no record in the biblical narrative of major events other than the rebuilding of the temple in the province of Yehud and Jerusalem during the reigns of Cyrus's successors, it is possible to surmise that the Persian government ignores the region for nearly sixty-five years. There is no mention of any of the affairs in Judah between 515 BCE and the reign of the Persian emperor Artaxerxes I (465–424 BCE). It is possible that this break in the record is due to the Persians' preoccupation with wars against the Greeks. These conflicts drain their resources during the period from 490 to 449 BCE. It is only after the Peace of Callias (449 BCE) that the Persians once again turn their attention to the minor complaints of their outlying provinces.

Nehemiah's Administration. The story of the Jewish community in Yehud resumes with a controversy over the reconstruction of the walls of Jerusalem. There is a series of counter-charges submitted in formal petitions by both Samaritans and Jews. As is so often the case in dealing with a large bureaucracy, many of these letters are not sent directly to the king. Instead, petty officials and persons who have the king's ear are consulted to see if they will intercede in the case. Nehemiah, the cupbearer of Artaxerxes I, was one of these officials (Neh. 2:1). The title "cupbearer" is probably ceremonial, but Nehemiah is a trusted member of the Persian court.

What is particularly interesting is that Nehemiah is also a Jew, which suggests that at least for some positions the Persians appointed persons based on merit, not just on ethnic origin. Sympathizing with his fellow Jews, Nehemiah obtains a commission as governor of Yehud and begins a career that will include two separate terms of office. His narrative is written as an apologetic memoir. It includes an impassioned defense of his policies (Neh. 5:14–19), as well as a list of charges against his enemies, who have plotted to harm him and foil his efforts (6:1–14).

Upon arrival in Jerusalem, Nehemiah shows good judgment by making a surprise inspection of the wall system (Neh. 2:11–16). This tactic allows him to see it with his own eyes and assess the difficulty of rebuilding the walls, the probable costs, and the dangers involved. The next day he entertains the arguments for and against the project and makes the decision to push ahead with construction. But why is the reconstruction of the walls of Jerusalem such an important matter to the people of Yehud?

Figure 5.7. Assyrian relief showing King Ashurnasirpal with his cupbearer and other attendants, ninth century BCE. Nehemiah was the cupbearer to Artaxerxes I. (Baker Photo Archive, courtesy of the British Museum)

It is unrealistic to think that they expected to use these rebuilt walls to declare their independence or to protect themselves from Persian armies. The real answer lies in the symbolic value of the walls. Jerusalem's defense system has lain in ruins since the time of Nebuchadnezzar. Now, as Yehud attempts to restore itself as a Persian province separate from Samaria, its capital city must be restored for appearances' sake if for no other reason.

A cosmetic restoration of Jerusalem's physical appearance will mean greater recognition for Yehud. That fact causes Sanballat, the Samaritan governor, to oppose rebuilding the walls. He has ambitions to oversee all of what once was the kingdom of Israel. An independent Yehud will be a threat to his plans. As a result, when Nehemiah agrees to begin the construction, Sanballat and his allies, Tobiah of Ammon and Geshem the Arab, threaten to complain in very strong terms to the Persian government and even to physically attack the workers (Neh. 2:19; 4:1–3, 7–8, 11).

Despite these threats, Nehemiah keeps the workforce on the job with an armed escort and completes the project in fifty-two days (Neh. 6:15). Such a short period of time raises questions about how much work really had to be done or how extensive the wall system was. Nehemiah probably rebuilt only the walls around the citadel and Temple Mount, the most important political structures in the city. Even this limited construction project answers the need for a symbolic wall and quiets the opponents. Once the initial phase is complete, additional construction can be done on the rest of the city as time and finances allow.

Once his position is firmly established, Nehemiah initiates a series of social reforms, some of which make him extremely unpopular. It seems clear that his intent is to put the province on a sound administrative and financial

Nehemiah's Reforms

- Prohibition of charging interest on loans (Neh. 5:7–13)
- Institution of a lottery requiring 10 percent of the people to live in Jerusalem (Neh. 11:1–2)
- Appointment of temple treasurers to monitor the gathering of the tithes (Neh. 12:44–47)
- Return of Levites and singers to temple service and the institution of practices designed to ensure their upkeep (Neh. 13:10–11)
- Closing gates and prohibiting commerce on the Sabbath (Neh. 13:15–22)
- Dissolution of mixed marriages to enforce the practice of endogamy (Neh. 13:23–27)

footing and ensure that Persian administrative policy related to small provinces like Yehud is upheld. He appoints temple treasurers to collect and to distribute the produce of the land to the people and the Levites in the temple community (Neh. 12:44–47). He deals with the corrupt practices of the priestly hierarchy by expelling Tobiah, a relative of the priest Eliashib, from his rooms in the temple complex. This precious space is then restored to its original function as storage for the sacred vessels and commodities given as tithes (13:4–9). These and similar actions are components of a plan to solidify Yehud's position as a Persian province separate from Samaria.

Locking the gates on the Sabbath (Neh. 13:15–22) and prohibiting mixed marriages (13:23–27) serve a dual purpose. First, these actions reflect the exclusivism that forms an integral part of the Jewish Identity Movement in the Diaspora. Nehemiah feels that the people should maintain themselves as a separate nation. To do that, they need to adhere to recognizable and unique social institutions such as the Sabbath regulations and a refusal to marry individuals outside of the group (endogamy). Nehemiah's control over commerce, inheritance through marriage, and charging interest on loans (5:7–13) strengthens his administration and centralizes his authority within the province. His actions reflect established Persian policy. Such a vast empire means that the bureaucracy needs to establish ways to easily recognize the many ethnic groups within their domain. Any variation from the government's understanding of what constitutes a particular ethnic group could endanger their political privileges and their recognition as citizens of a province. Mixed marriages are therefore a signal to Nehemiah that the Jerusalem community is in danger of losing its ethnic focus.

Nehemiah serves two terms as governor of Judah. His strong-handed treatment of the people probably did not win him many friends, but in his memoir he seems satisfied with his accomplishments. He concludes his chronicle with an administrator's epitaph: "Remember me, O God, for good" (Neh. 13:36).

Ezra the Priest. The initial portion of the book of Ezra is a continuation of the history found in the books of Chronicles. This is one of the reasons that has led scholars to conclude that Ezra is Nehemiah's predecessor. But the chronology of events in the careers of Ezra and Nehemiah is still unclear, and it is not possible to determine with certainty whether they are contemporaries or whether one comes before the other. Both mention Artaxerxes as king, but there were two kings by that name: Artaxerxes I (465–425 BCE) and Artaxerxes II (404–359 BCE). There is also a mention of a restored temple and "a wall in Judea and Jerusalem" (Ezra 9:9) that may indicate Nehemiah's wall, or it could be a metaphor for the law. For now the question of chronology and even the historicity of Ezra and Nehemiah must be left unanswered.

The first six chapters of the book of Ezra contain a recital of the return from exile, the problems associated with rebuilding the temple (including mention of the prophets Haggai and Zechariah in Ezra 5:1), and the opposition the community faces from the Samaritans. When Ezra himself enters the story, we are told that he has been appointed by the Persian king to journey to Jerusalem. His credentials list him as a "scribe skilled in the law" but not as a priest (Ezra 7:6). After gathering a group of Levites and others who wish to join them, Ezra's company travels without an armed escort to fulfill an unspecified mission in Yehud (8:21–36).

A Decree of Artaxerxes

I, King Artaxerxes, decree to all the treasurers in the province Beyond the River: Whatever the priest Ezra, the scribe of the law of the God of heaven, requires of you, let it be done with all diligence, up to one hundred talents of silver, one hundred cors of wheat, one hundred baths of wine, one hundred baths of oil, and unlimited salt. Whatever is commanded by the God of heaven, let it be done with zeal for the house of the God of heaven, or wrath will come upon the realm of the king and his heirs. We also notify you that it shall not be lawful to impose tribute, custom, or toll on any of the priests, the Levites, the singers, the doorkeepers, the temple servants, or other servants of this house of God.

And you, Ezra, according to the God-given wisdom you possess, appoint magistrates and judges who may judge all the people in the province Beyond the River who know the laws of your God; and you shall teach those who do not know them. All who will not obey the law of your God and the law of the king, let judgment be strictly executed on them, whether for death or for banishment or for confiscation of their goods or for imprisonment. (Ezra 7:21–26)

Even though we do not know as much about Ezra's background or his mission as we might like, he seems to function in a much different capacity than Nehemiah. He is given a letter written in Aramaic from the Persian king empowering him to serve as chief administrator of the province of Yehud (Ezra 7:12–20; see a slightly different version in Josephus, *Jewish Antiquities* 11.121–130). But this decree may have been intended to ensure the cooperation of the temple community when Ezra arrives rather than give him real administrative authority over the province. Its chief attributes are tax-exempt status for all members of the temple community; a grant of authority to appoint magistrates and judges who administer the "law of the God of heaven"; a grant of authority to educate the people in this law; and an empowerment clause that gives Ezra executive powers of life, death, and confiscation. Ezra's powers are probably granted to keep order and are delegated to administrators as part of any royal decree (see reference to the letter given to Nehemiah in Neh. 2:7–9).

Ezra's purpose for returning to Jerusalem is not explained in any detail in his narrative. It simply states that he is to "make inquiries about Judah and Jerusalem according to the law of your God" (Ezra 7:14). Gold and silver are also to be transported to purchase sacrificial grain and animals for dedication in the temple (7:15–20).

It appears that this new attempt to entice people to return to Jerusalem is not initially successful. Ezra has to make a special effort to recruit Levites (Ezra 8:15–20), and he is unwilling to ask for a group of soldiers to accompany them, despite the treasures they are transporting (8:22). Clearly he envisioned this as a procession much like the one that Moses led out of Egypt or the one that journeyed into Canaan in Joshua's time. Such an image would be appropriate for a people that considers the exile a second wilderness period.

As the book of Ezra describes it, the principal matter facing Ezra upon his arrival is the issue of mixed marriages (Ezra 9:1–2). To us that may seem like a small thing, considering all the administrative matters that might have been brought to his attention. However, by focusing on this one issue, the writer can bring the crisis to a climax and present Ezra as the stern enforcer of the law of Moses. After assembling the heads of households and forcing them to stand in a driving rain while he chastises them (10:9), a committee is formed to investigate individual cases and to demand that the culprits divorce their inappropriate spouses (10:14–16).

It is now necessary to switch from the narrative in the book of Ezra to the one found in Neh. 8–9 in order to complete the story. In these chapters, Ezra stages a covenant-renewal ceremony (cf. earlier examples in Exod. 24; Josh. 24; and 2 Kings 23:1–3). He assembles the people, reads them the law, and then asks them to pledge obedience to it (Neh. 8:1–12). Once they have made this affirmation, a period of celebration and sacrifice is observed during the Feast of Booths (8:13–18).

One curious aspect of this scene is the appearance of men in the crowd who "helped the people to understand the law" (Neh. 8:7–8). This service is probably necessary because the law is written in Hebrew, and by this time Aramaic has become the common language of the people. The help provided by these persons who are so well-versed in the law also creates a precedent in a later period for rabbis to explain the law. In later periods, the community rabbi becomes the heart of interpretative Judaism.

The final step in Ezra's attempt to rejuvenate what he conceives to be the proper worship of Yahweh and right behavior by the people is the recitation of the covenant history (Neh. 9:6–37). Such a recital is probably a part of every covenant-renewal ceremony in the period after the establishment of the monarchy. Psalm 78, for example, is designed to be recited during a ceremony just like this one. After Ezra reads the law, the leaders and the people pledge not to intermarry or to violate the Sabbath (Neh. 10:28–31). These two principles appear to be the basis of diasporic Judaism and are imposed on the Jerusalem community by Ezra and Nehemiah.

The End of an Era. The tradition is that prophecy comes to an end with Ezra. Thereafter the canon is supposed to be closed, and no further revelation is expected or needed. The law has been given to the people, and it is now their task, in the centuries ahead, to obey it. The reality is that a great deal of additional material is written after 400 BCE, including Jonah, Ruth, Esther, Daniel, and the Apocryphal/Deuterocanonical books. The postexilic period gives Judaism the impetus to begin to institutionalize itself, but its greatest test, Hellenism, is yet to come.

STUDY QUESTIONS

1. Why are there cultural and religious differences between the Jewish communities in the Diaspora and in Yehud?
2. Why do the people in Jerusalem wish to rebuild the city walls? Why do the Samaritans and their allies oppose the rebuilding of Jerusalem's temple and walls (Neh. 2:10, 19; 4:1–5; 6:1–14)?
3. What is the purpose of Nehemiah's social reforms in Neh. 11; 12:27–13? Is he enforcing elements of the Jewish Identity Movement or just being a good Persian administrator?
4. Are powers granted to Ezra in Artaxerxes' decree in Ezra 7:21–28 designed to enable his work as an administrator, or do they indicate that he has Persian backing?
5. Compare the covenant-renewal ceremony in Neh. 8:1–13 with those in Exod. 24; Josh. 24; and 2 Kings 23. What is distinctive about each time period that makes such a ceremony necessary?

The Book of Ruth

KEY POINTS

• The book of Ruth is set in the period of the judges but is composed in the postexilic period.

- The central themes of Ruth are the establishment of personal identity, a wisdom theme, and levirate obligation.
- The ancestral tie between Ruth, Boaz, and David is an argument against endogamy.

The book of Ruth is one of two books in the HB in which a woman is the principal character. (One additional example in the Deuterocanonical works, Judith, is discussed in ch. 6 below.) Ruth is a tightly written composite tale that contains a relatively authentic look at the social world of a small village in ancient Israel. Although this short story is set in the period of the judges, its theme, vocabulary, and use of legal structures from the Deuteronomic Code (especially Deut. 25:5–10) suggest a date of composition in the postexilic period. The opening phrase, "in the days when the judges ruled," may indicate a once-upon-a-time quality that adds to the sense of antiquity for this material and allows the storyteller to focus on matters of the social order without tying them more specifically to actual historical events.

In the Hebrew canon, Ruth follows Proverbs and precedes the Song of Songs (Canticles). Its placement in the Christian canon immediately after Judges is based on similarity of story type as well as an attempt to connect the period of the judges with the story of the rise of David in the books of Samuel. It may be useful, however, to compare the story in Ruth with the stories in Judges to demonstrate that a tale set in this period does not have to contain lawlessness or violence.

The book of Ruth contains three major elements: the theme of **levirate obligation**; a segment of the Davidic genealogy; and an assimilation ritual, allowing foreigners to reestablish their identity and become a part of the Israelite community. These elements are all interrelated within the story, indicating a careful editing of the original tale. The primary agenda of the author(s) is to argue against the increasing emphasis on endogamy that is being forced on the Jerusalem community during the time of Ezra and Nehemiah (Ezra 9–10; Neh. 13:23–27). In this way the book forms the basis for a more universal understanding of the covenant and of Yahweh's concern for all the peoples of the earth (cf. Isa. 56:1–8).

Initial Premises. The story begins with an Israelite family from Bethlehem that migrates to Moab in order to escape a famine in their own area (Ruth 1:1). Similar migrations for the same ecological reason are described in the ancestral narratives (Gen. 12:10; 26:1). While they live in Moab, the family's sons marry Moabite women. A turning point comes for them when something, possibly a plague, strikes down all of the men in the family. Naomi, the mother, decides to return to Bethlehem to spend the remainder of her life with her own people (Ruth 1:3–7). Realizing that it would be difficult for her sons' widows to find a life for themselves in Israel, Naomi offers them the opportunity to return to their families in Moab without further obligation to her. Orpah chooses to return, but Ruth pledges to remain with her mother-in-law and adopt Israelite ways:

> Where you go, I will go;
> where you lodge, I will lodge;
> your people shall be my people,
> and your God my God.
> Where you die, I will die—
> there will I be buried.
> May the Lord do thus and so to me,
> and more as well,
> if even death parts me from you! (Ruth 1:16–17)

Ruth's statement is a classic example of an **assimilation ritual**, a ceremony that requires a person to renounce his or her former condition or status. In what is clearly treaty language, including a curse on those who break the oath, Ruth transforms herself from a Moabite into an Israelite. Ruth's action is apparently motivated by her deep commitment to Naomi, her desire to support her mother-in-law, and her resolution to continue the family line. Ruth's decision to accompany Naomi will require more than words and a verbal commitment. Her vow, similar in form to that taken by a slave who chooses to remain in his master's household after his six years of debt servitude are completed (Exod. 21:2–6; Deut. 15:16–17), will also require right behavior and recognition by the people of Bethlehem before her new identity is established.

Legal Obligations. Fortunately for the two widows, they arrive in Bethlehem at the beginning of the barley harvest. Israelite law (Deut. 24:19–21) allows them to glean in the fields and to survive without male support (Ruth 1:22–2:3). Naomi has the right to do so as a poor widow, and Ruth, the Moabitess, can exercise this right as a resident alien.

Ruth's diligence, obedience, willingness to work hard, and concern for Naomi are continually emphasized in the narrative (Ruth 2:6–7, 11–12, 17–18, 22–23; 3:5, 10). In this way she exemplifies one of the central tenets of the wisdom theme (right behavior), and a sympathetic case is made for a foreigner, who might otherwise be distrusted or treated badly (2:22). The first sign of her social transformation takes

---

Gleaning Rights

When you reap the harvest of your land, you shall not reap to the very edges of your field, or gather the gleanings of your harvest. You shall not strip your vineyard bare, or gather the fallen grapes of your vineyard; you shall leave them for the poor and the alien: I am the LORD your God. (Lev. 19:9–10)

The New Kingdom Egyptian (1250–1000 BCE) Instruction of Amenemope contains an injunction not to "arrest widows gleaning your fields." (*OTPar³*, 302)

---

place when Boaz's foreman states that she "has been on her feet from early this morning until now, without resting even for a moment" (2:7). Boaz confirms that her diligence has become well known in the village: "All that you have done for your mother-in-law since the death of your husband has been fully told me" (2:11).

Perhaps recognizing the opportunity presented by Ruth's hard work, Naomi then devises a strategy to meet the needs of both herself and Ruth and to provide an heir for her deceased husband's property in Bethlehem. Since she no longer has either a husband or sons, the law of levirate obligation comes into play. According to this law, the nearest male kin is required to impregnate and take legal responsibility for the widow. In this way the extended family takes the initiative to provide an heir for the dead man and to provide for the needs of the widow until her son is old enough to take legal responsibility (see Gen. 38:7–11). Naomi, because she is beyond childbearing age, sends Ruth to Boaz to ask him to serve as their levir, guardian (Ruth 3:1–5).

Ruth's plea is made on the village threshing floor, where the harvesters, including Boaz, sleep overnight in order to protect their grain. The threshing floor in the village culture is the equivalent of the gate in walled towns and cities. It serves as a place for business transactions

---

The Conversion Ritual for a Slave

But if the slave declares, "I love my master, my wife, and my children; I will not go out a free person," then his master shall bring him before God. He shall be brought to the door or the doorpost; and his master shall pierce his ear with an awl; and he shall serve him for life. (Exod. 21:5–6)

and for legal decisions (see Judg. 6:36–40; 2 Sam. 24:18–25). The main function of the threshing floor is to provide a place in which seed can be separated from the stalks of harvested grain. All the farmers transport their harvest to this flat and open space where the prevailing west winds help in separating the wheat from the chaff (Hosea 13:3). During the harvest and the subsequent distribution of grain, the threshing floor commands the attention of the entire community. The seed will be distributed here to the field owners and to the protected classes (widows, orphans, and strangers), who also can claim a portion of the harvest under a societal/covenantal obligation to protect the destitute and the weak (see Deut. 14:29; 26:12–13). Presumably any disputes that might arise over distribution or some other related matter would also be handled on the spot.

Based on the same legal tradition, Ruth's meeting with Boaz at the threshing floor in Ruth 3:10–14 concerns both the redemption of her father-in-law's fields and the establishment of an intimate contact with the person she will eventually marry. Her request, "Spread your cloak over your servant, for you are next of kin" (3:9), is a legal formula obligating Boaz to take action (cf. Ezek. 16:8). His response is in the form of a blessing that recognizes Ruth's legitimate claim, and he congratulates her for serving her mother-in-law and not just her own desires (Ruth 3:10–11). Once again Ruth's right

The Use of a Threshing Floor for Legal and Judicial Purposes

• In the Laws of Eshnunna 19, a man who has made a farm loan "shall make (the debtor) pay on the threshing floor" (*ANET*, 162).
• In the Ugaritic epic of Aqhat, King Danil is portrayed as "sitting before the gate, under a mighty tree on the threshing floor, judging the case of the widow" (*ANET*, 153).

behavior is acknowledged, and that is a narrative indicator that her needs will be met.

Legal Resolution. Boaz reveals that he is not Naomi's closest kin. He can be their advocate before the elders, but it is up to another man to decide whether he will carry out the levirate obligation (Ruth 3:12–13). Boaz's gift of six measures of barley may therefore serve as either a bride price, if the levir refuses his duty, or as a kinsmen's gift to Naomi, the poor widow (3:15–18).

In the formal courtroom scene that follows, Boaz adheres to a strict legal protocol by going to the gate and asking the next of kin to join him in determining what should be done with Ruth and Naomi (Ruth 4:1). Ten elders (a legal quorum) are asked to sit in judgment, and Boaz puts the first of two questions to the levir: Since you are the nearest male kin and thus have the first right of refusal to purchase Naomi's field, do you wish to buy it (Ruth 4:3–4; cf. Jer. 32:6–15)? He is happy to say yes to this. Then Boaz asks the second question: When you purchase the field, are you willing also to take Ruth, "to maintain the dead man's name on his inheritance"? The levir refuses to do this since it would mean he could not pass the field to his own heirs (Ruth 4:5–6).

At that point the narrative breaks off and a legal gloss (addition) is inserted that refers to the custom of removing the sandal of the levir who refuses his duty. This gloss assumes that the audience is familiar with a practice based on the law in Deut. 25:7–10. However, the characters do not follow that law exactly. The gloss demonstrates that the date for this version of the story of Ruth is most likely after the compiling of the Deuteronomic law code (after 600 BCE).

Boaz then claims possession of the property of Naomi's husband and asserts his right to

231

take Ruth as his wife in front of the elders who are witnesses. Through her hard work, perseverance, and exemplary behavior, Ruth is officially acknowledged as a member of the Bethlehem community.

> Today you are witnesses that I have acquired from the hand of Naomi all that belonged to Elimelech and all that belonged to Chilion and Mahlon. I have also acquired Ruth the Moabite, the wife of Mahlon, to be my wife, to maintain the dead man's name on his inheritance, in order that the name of the dead may not be cut off from his kindred and from the gate of his native place; today you are witnesses. (Ruth 4:9–10)

Concluding Issues. The response of the elders is to echo Boaz's claim and bless the marriage. The blessing, like the subsequent genealogy of Boaz's family, is political. In Ruth 4:12, the witnesses refer to Perez, the son of Judah and Tamar (Gen. 38:29), and then the genealogy of Perez is found in Ruth 4:18–22. Boaz is listed as a descendant of Perez and as the ancestor, with Ruth, of King David. In this way these two stories of levirate obligation (Gen. 38 and Ruth) are tied together, and the line of David is allied with the concepts of concern for the law and the freedom to marry outside the Israelite tribes. The presence of a foreigner in the lineage of David, the king of Israel's golden age, is a particularly effective argument against any insistence on endogamy in the postexilic period (cf. Ezra 9–10).

Finally, the song of blessing sung by the women to Naomi (Ruth 4:14–15) celebrates Yahweh's role as the covenantal provider of land and children. Like so many barren women before her, Naomi can now rejoice in children. When she places the child on her breast and gives him a name, Naomi claims Obed as her

son, born in a surrogate fashion through Ruth. The child is now the legal heir of Naomi's husband, Elimelech (4:16–17). The legal complication that motivates the story is resolved at the same time that the author makes the final point in his argument for legitimizing mixed marriages and the rights of converts to Judaism (see Isa. 56:3–8).

STUDY QUESTIONS

1. Discuss how the establishment of personal identity and the wisdom theme are linked in the story of Ruth.
2. How is Ruth's diligent gleaning tied to a wisdom theme (Deut. 24:21; Ruth 2:2–13)?
3. Why does Ruth go to meet Boaz at the threshing floor (Ruth 3:1–13)?
4. Compare the administration of levirate obligation in Ruth with that found in Gen. 38 and Deut. 25:5–10. Why does the levir refuse to redeem Naomi's land and impregnate Ruth (Ruth 4:3–6; cf. Gen. 38:8–10)? Can you suggest why he remains nameless in the story?
5. Discuss the implications of Ruth's Moabite origins and her status as an ancestress of David in light of Ezra and Nehemiah's insistence on endogamy.

The Book of Esther

KEY POINTS

- The book of Esther provides an entertaining tale centered on the dilemma of whether to save oneself or others.
- The characters in the story are easily identified as wise or foolish.
- The holiday of Purim commemorates the events of this story.

Purpose of the Book. The book of Esther is set in the Persian period (539–332 BCE), but it contains a narrative that is directed at the Jews who have become a part of the Hellenistic Empire after the conquests of Alexander of Macedon (after 320 BCE). The story provides an example of courage in the face of oppression to the Jews who are living in the lands of the Diaspora (cf. the stories in the first six chapters of Daniel). Like other hero and wisdom tales, the book of Esther delights an audience with quick-witted characters who manage to save the day by foiling despicable enemies. The storyteller provides real entertainment in scenes filled with comic irony, difficult dilemmas, and acts of extraordinary courage. In the end the point is made that by holding to their traditions and identity as a people, the Jews will eventually overcome their foes.

Much of the tale of Esther has an unreal character to it. Many of the principal characters are little more than stereotypes: the foolish king, the proud queen, the wise man, the unscrupulous villain, and the clever woman. They play their parts exactly according to the script, and the only truly realistic aspect of the story comes with Esther's selfless decision to reveal her true identity in an attempt to save her people. Such martyrdom, while also subject to becoming idealized, has a personal element with which the reader can easily identify.

This story has apparently gone through a number of different versions. One sign of this is that there are additions to the book found in the Apocryphal/Deuterocanonical books. However, the book of Esther is not among the scrolls discovered at Qumran, and that may indicate that it did not appeal to all of the Jewish sects. Opposition to the inclusion of the story in the canon may be based on its ties to the festival of **Purim** (Esther 9:28–32; Hebrew *pur* means "lot"). If Purim was originally a Babylonian or Persian festival that was later adopted by the Jews, it might well have been a source of contention among various Jewish groups in the Diaspora and in the Yehud community.

Date of the Book. The author of the book of Esther is unknown, and the date of its composition is uncertain. The reign of King Ahasuerus (Xerxes I) is from 486 to 465 BCE. However, there are a number of arguments against a fifth-century date for the book (see below). Most scholars place it in the second century BCE.

Arguments for Second-Century-BCE Date of Esther

- The earliest mention of Purim outside the book of Esther is in 2 Macc. 15:36, which dates to the first century BCE.
- Thirty-eight of the thirty-nine books of the OT/HB are contained in the Dead Sea Scrolls corpus at Qumran. Only Esther is not found there.
- There is no mention of Mordecai or Esther in the list of heroes of the faith found in the book of Ecclesiasticus (Wisdom of Jesus Ben Sira, or Sirach, ca. 180 BCE),

an apocryphal wisdom book very much like Ecclesiastes or Proverbs. Citing the absence of a reference to Esther in Ecclesiasticus is an argument from silence and must be used cautiously. On the one hand, it may mean that Esther was not known in the second century BCE. On the other hand, the writer of Ecclesiasticus may have excluded Esther because he did not have a high regard for women (none are mentioned in his list of famous persons [Sir. 44–49]).

- There is a mention of the dispersion of the Jews in Esther 3:8. That indicates the Jews are scattered all over the Persian Empire. Haman's charge includes a warning that these people strongly adhere to their own law code and traditions, suggesting that the Jewish Identity Movement has had time to mature.
- None of these arguments are entirely convincing in themselves. But collectively they suggest a late date for the book of Esther.

Summary. The book of Esther begins with a riotous scene involving the Persian king Ahasuerus (Xerxes) and his queen, Vashti. In the midst of a party, the king orders his queen to come out and show off her beauty for his drunken friends. Not wishing to humiliate herself in this manner, the proud queen refuses. As a result, the king demotes her and begins the search for a new queen. All the eligible young women are required to participate in a beauty contest that will select Vashti's replacement. Subsequently Esther wins the beauty contest and becomes the new queen (Esther 2:2–18). Unknown to the king, however, Esther is a Jew. This secret element plays into a plot to exterminate the Jewish people and serves as the basis for the remainder of the story. The audience also learns that Esther had been raised by her cousin (or uncle in some translations) Mordecai. At one point Mordecai is able to warn the king of an assassination attempt (Esther 2:21–23). Initially the king is grateful, but he does not adequately reward Mordecai until later in the story. His reward then becomes a comic catalyst that will drive the villain of

the story, Haman the Agagite, to formulate a plot to eliminate his rival for the king's favor. When Haman is forced to escort Mordecai, a man he hopes to hang from a magnificent gallows, through the streets while proclaiming him to be the man most honored by the king, the audience is both amused and given notice of action to come (6:1–13).

The stereotypical villain in the story of Esther is named Haman the Agagite. His diabolical nature is displayed when he plots to take revenge not only on Mordecai but also on all the Jews because Mordecai refuses to bow his head when Haman enters the palace gate. Once again a biblical author uses a character's name to let the audience know his true nature (see Nabal in 1 Sam. 25:2–3). The narrative cue is that Agag was a king of the Amalekites (1 Sam. 15:32), the traditional enemies of the Jewish people. Now a descendant of Agag will attempt to wreak vengeance on their ancient foes and exterminate all the Jews in the Persian Empire.

Haman's hatred is not just based on a social mistake. Mordecai's refusal to bow to Haman (Esther 3:2) also publicly humiliates this very vain man to whom all other persons are required to bow. Failure to acknowledge his authority sets the evil plot in motion. As the chief adviser to the king, Haman is able to convince him that the Jews are a dangerous element in the Persian Empire and that they must be exterminated (3:8–13). Mordecai, who sits beside the gate to the palace and hears all of the gossip, learns of the plot and goes to Queen Esther. He tells her that she now must take the side of Jews because they are going to be killed on the king's order (4:13–16). Esther is faced with a dilemma that forces her to choose between personal safety and the survival of her people. Eventually she decides that she has to

Figure 5.8. Cast from a palace doorway relief at Persepolis, Iran, showing a Persian king, probably Xerxes, and his attendant. (Baker Photo Archive, courtesy of the British Museum)

go to the king, reveal that she is a Jew, and explain to him that his decree will lead to her execution as well.

As part of her plan to save her people and herself, Esther invites Haman and her husband to a banquet in her chambers. Haman thinks this is a great privilege and a sign of favor to be invited to a private banquet with the king and his wife. Susceptible to flattery and filled with his own importance, Haman believes his influence and power are clearly on the rise. Like his inflated ego, the story is about to reach its climax.

The first dinner party is so successful that the king agrees to come a second time. But on the night before Haman and the king return to Esther's rooms for the second banquet, the king is troubled by a nagging memory. He orders his archivists to search the records for any official omission, and they find that the king has failed to reward Mordecai for saving his life (Esther 6:1–3). Haman, as the officer of the day, is summoned and instructed to parade Mordecai about the city and let him wear royal robes and a crown while Haman proclaims that Mordecai is

honored at the king's command (Esther 6:4–10). Haman, who expected that the king would reward Haman like this, had not planned for Mordecai to be honored in this manner. However, he cannot disobey the king's orders.

Smarting from this further humiliation, Haman contents himself with knowing that he will once again be dining with the royal couple and by the sounds of the construction of a massive gallows that he has ordered built for Mordecai's execution. In Esther 7:1–4 the king and Haman go to feast with Queen Esther for a second time. As they are drinking wine, the king offers to grant any request Esther wishes to make. Now, at last ready to make her appeal, Queen Esther answers:

If I have won your favor, O king, and if it pleases the king, let my life be given me—that is my petition—and the lives of my people—that is my request. For we have been sold, I and my people, to be destroyed, to be killed, and to be annihilated. If we had been sold merely as slaves, men and women, I would have held my peace; but no enemy can compensate for this damage to the king. (Esther 7:3–4)

Esther then tells the angry king that Haman is his enemy. Haman is terrified and falls prone before Esther. When the king sees this, he exclaims that Haman is trying to seduce his wife and has him arrested (Esther 7:8). Haman is hanged from the gallows he has built to execute Mordecai (7:9–10), and the king then issues a second decree that saves the Jews. They are given the right to defend themselves, and the Jews kill many thousands of their enemies (8:9–9:16). These events are subsequently commemorated in an annual festival named Purim (9:17–32).

Canonical Analysis. Why is Esther not found in the Dead Sea Scroll corpus? Was this book considered unworthy of inclusion in the canon at the time that the Dead Sea Scrolls were produced or just by the Essene community at Qumran (ca. 100 BCE–70 CE)? One possible reason why it eventually found its way into the Hebrew canon may be that the book shows the workings of God behind the scenes. Even though God is never explicitly mentioned by name, there is a sense within the story of the Jews' identity as God's people. Another reason for the omission of God's name may be suggested by the use of the phrase "the kingdom of heaven" in the Gospel of Matthew (Matt. 5:3, 10, 19) while other NT books use the expression "the kingdom of God" (Mark 1:5; 4:26; Luke 6:20). Matthew's Gospel, written for the early Jewish-Christian community, considers the name of God to be too sacred to mention and therefore mostly uses "kingdom of heaven" instead of "kingdom of God." Similarly, the book of Esther does not exclude God but excludes the name of God.

An example of this practice is found in the passage in which Mordecai and Esther are talking about Esther's going to the king and telling him about Haman's decree (Esther 4:5–17). The discussion includes the statement, "Perhaps you have come to royal dignity for just such a time as this" (4:14). This statement is an oblique reference to God and a divine plan for human actions. The statement is quoted to emphasize how Jews have survived persecution when they take the initiative to deal with danger (cf. the decision of the Hasidean rebels to fight on the Sabbath in 1 Macc. 2:39–41).

Among the other purposes for this book, it describes the origin of the festival of Purim, and it entertains with an interesting story. It has everything: two beautiful queens, love, romance, suspense, violence, and the death of the villain.

Historical Analysis. The book of Esther raises a number of historical questions.

The fifth-century-BCE Greek historian Herodotus states that the Persian king is required to marry only Persian women. In addition, no extrabiblical text mentions either Vashti or Esther as wives of the Persian king Xerxes (Ahasuerus).

The genealogy of Mordecai in Esther 2:5 ("Now there was a Jew in the citadel of Susa whose name was Mordecai, son of Jair son of Shimei son of Kish, a Benjaminite") raises some questions about Mordecai's age (over 118) if he is taken into captivity in 597 BCE. This issue has been resolved by some scholars who want to preserve the historicity of the book. They say it is not Mordecai who is taken captive in 597 BCE but one of his ancestors.

Would a Persian king allow Jews to kill Persian subjects? Generally kings want peaceful stability in their kingdoms because the more turmoil, the more likely it is that they will be overthrown. Yet, we do not know with certainty what kings would do.

Although some details in the book are consistent with Persian customs and culture, the story or the message is more important than the historicity of the characters. As we observed when we discussed the flood narratives, it is possible to communicate truth through nonhistorical events.

STUDY QUESTIONS

1. Discuss the various issues surrounding whether the book of Esther should be included in the biblical canon.
2. Discuss Esther's moral dilemma and provide other, similar biblical and nonbiblical examples.
3. Discuss the elements in the story that make it particularly entertaining.

4. Discuss Esther's strategy to save herself and her people (Esther 5:3–8; 8:1–15).

5. Compare and contrast the depiction of God in Esther with the depiction of God in Job and Jonah.

Wisdom Literature and Psalmody

Introduction

KEY POINTS

- Wisdom is part of the common literary milieu of the ancient Near East.
- Biblical narrative includes examples of both the wise and the foolish.
- Wisdom is found in many different literary genres, from jokes to longer treatises.

Having completed our historical survey of the postexilic prophetic books and postexilic narratives, we turn our attention to the Wisdom literature and psalmody of ancient Israel. To a great extent this is an arbitrary location for our discussion, since these literary traditions span the length of Israel's history. However, they are placed in a separate category in the Hebrew canon known as the Writings and thus fit together well as a unit. Having them gathered together also allows us to highlight the wisdom theme that is so much a part of ancient Near Eastern culture.

The traditional wisdom books in the Hebrew canon are Job, Proverbs, Ecclesiastes, and the Song of Songs. The book of Psalms also is a repository of wisdom sayings, but it will be treated separately in this chapter. Wisdom books in the Apocryphal/Deuterocanonical works, found in the Septuagint and the Catholic canon, include Sirach (Ecclesiasticus) and the Wisdom of Solomon.

Every culture produces its own store of wisdom. Wisdom may be expressed in the form of oral pronouncements or stories, or it may

Wisdom Theme

Examples of wisdom speech or admonition are found throughout the biblical text. Wisdom embodies both common sense and basic social values in antiquity. Ultimately all wisdom comes from God (see Prov. 3:5–8). The Wisdom theme includes the following:

1. wise behavior: no action taken hastily or without thinking (see Prov. 14:29);
2. wise speech: no word spoken that may injure someone else (Prov. 16:13);
3. wise person: one who walks in the "way/path" of Yahweh and who recognizes that wisdom may be acquired from persons of all ages, genders, and occupations (see Prov. 12:15; Eccles. 8:1).

blossom into major philosophical works that carefully explore questions that have troubled humanity since prehistory. Wisdom is also expressed in action, and thus it is possible to find numerous examples of wise action throughout the biblical narrative (see the wise woman of Abel in 2 Sam. 20:16–22). Wisdom may also be a source of false pride and therefore a catalyst for trouble when "craftiness" is mistaken for sound advice (Job 5:12–13; Isa. 5:21; 19:11). As a genre separate in theme and style from other biblical writing, Wisdom literature has these major characteristics: little concern with history, chronology, genealogy, or even place; strong emphasis on an established moral or social code of conduct; concern with the question of good and evil in the world; and a glorification of God as creator and source of all true knowledge.

In this section we will examine the various types of Wisdom literature produced by the ancient Israelites. A distinction will be made between passages that contain the wisdom theme and traditional works of wisdom literature. Comparisons also will be made between Israelite Wisdom literature and wisdom texts from other ancient Near Eastern cultures. In this way it will become possible to identify wisdom texts and wisdom sayings outside the traditional wisdom books.

Wisdom Is Where You Find It

The wisdom theme runs throughout the biblical text. It is woven into nearly every narrative and literally springs from the tongues of characters in scenes as varied as historical annals and private discussions. Here are several examples:

1. Eve's dialogue with the serpent in Gen. 3:1–6 is a typical wisdom piece. It examines a truism, "Do not eat of the fruit of the tree that is in the middle of the garden . . . or you will die," and tests its validity. In this tale, the serpent serves as a literary foil, posing the question that is to be analyzed and precipitating Eve's action by arousing her curiosity. Ultimately the story provides an etiological explanation for why humans are expelled from Eden, why free choice can lead to both personal accomplishment and great evil, and why death is the common fate of all mortals.

2. Jacob employs native wisdom when he places peeled rods in front of his flocks to ensure that they will produce the proper types of offspring (Gen. 30:37–43). While his action can be seen as a form of sympathetic magic (i.e., you obtain your goal by suggesting the result), it has the same ring to it as the modern wisdom employed by those who carry a rabbit's foot as a talisman to bring luck.

3. Joseph's response to Potiphar's wife when she attempts to seduce him is based on his understanding of right behavior. He is scandalized when she proposes that he steal the conjugal rights of his master and "sin against God" (Gen. 39:8–9). Betrayal of trust to fellow humans, whatever their status, is thereby equated with the fidelity owed to God, and

the warning is clear that this can lead only to trouble (Sir. 27:16–18).

4. Moses's father-in-law, Jethro, provides good advice on how best to administer the people. In explaining the value of appointing judges and thus delegating a portion of his authority, Jethro points out the truism that a leader can burn out if he tries to do every task himself. Moses learns that sharing the load is a more efficient method of leadership (Exod. 18:19–26). His lesson, like most wisdom accounts, can then benefit others when they find themselves in similar situations.

5. The wise and the foolish are graphically displayed in the story of Nabal (whose name in Hebrew means "fool") and Abigail, his wise wife. So much of ancient Near Eastern wisdom is predicated on the contrast between the wise and the foolish that this story immediately rings true to its audience. Nabal, who lacks all diplomatic or interpersonal skills, is grossly portrayed in his dealings with David (1 Sam. 25:2–11); his wife, who is forced to take on the male role of host and political ally, deftly repairs a potentially dangerous situation and is rewarded by becoming David's wife (25:12–42).

6. In attempting to protect her honor and that of her household, David's daughter Tamar urges her brother Amnon not to rape her and act "as one of the scoundrels in Israel" (2 Sam. 13:12–13). It is hard to imagine that in the face of her brother's lustful passion, Tamar could have tried to reason with him not to act the fool. More likely, the wisdom dialogue in this case stands outside the actual events. Its direct appeal to right behavior may have been intended more for the audience than for the foolish Amnon.

7. Solomon earns his reputation as a wise king by discerning the truth in the case brought

to him by two prostitutes (1 Kings 3:16–28). He is able to demonstrate that his reign will provide justice to all by personally judging such a case (cf. 2 Sam. 15:2–6). At the same time, it is made clear that it is the responsibility of the king, as God's civil representative and as the shepherd of the people, to provide fair and unbiased judgment. In this story, Solomon models the proper behavior of the truly wise king.

8. Although Daniel is portrayed as a wise man who interprets King Nebuchadnezzar's dreams when the "wise men of Babylon" fail to do so, he repeatedly makes the point that wisdom comes from God and is not a natural attribute of humanity: "Blessed be the name of God, . . . for wisdom and power are his. . . . He gives wisdom to the wise and knowledge to those who have understanding" (Dan. 2:20–21; cf. 2:26–28).

The wisdom theme is especially common in the prophetic literature and in books traditionally identified as Wisdom literature:

1. The prophets sometimes quote well-known proverbs to make a point in their message. Ezekiel 18:2–4 and Jer. 31:29–30 both quote the proverb, "The parents have eaten sour grapes, and the children's teeth are set on edge." In this way they can introduce a new theological principle by drawing on a well-known piece of traditional wisdom. The mixing of new wisdom with old makes the message more palatable.

2. The knowledge of God and right behavior are often paired. Samuel chides Saul for failing to be obedient: "Surely, to obey is better than sacrifice" (1 Sam. 15:22–23). Hosea points to the people's distress when he says, "My people are destroyed for lack of knowledge" (Hosea 4:6). The point is that it is impossible to obey the covenant if the people are not instructed in the law and the codes of right behavior.

3. The path to wisdom is found throughout the books of Psalms and Proverbs in statements like "The fear of the LORD is the beginning of wisdom" (Ps. 111:10; Prov. 1:7; 9:10). It is the task of education in the traditional society to instill these basic truths in the young so that there is continuity of belief and behavior. When a fuller explanation is necessary, then the biblical writers compose wisdom psalms, such as Ps. 1, which point to the proper course for the wise and the dangers of association with the foolish:

> Happy are those
>   who do not follow the advice of the
>   wicked,
> or take the path that sinners tread,
>   or sit in the seat of the scoffers;
> but their delight is in the law of the
>   LORD,
>   and on his law they meditate day and
>   night. (Ps. 1:1–2)

The Book of Proverbs

Solomon is often thought to be the fountainhead of wisdom and the author of Proverbs. This idea comes from the book itself (Prov. 1:1; 10:1; 25:1) and from 1 Kings 3:28. However, Prov. 30:1 refers also to the words of Agur, and Prov. 31:1 states that these are the words of King Lemuel that his mother taught him. Therefore it is better to think of the book of Proverbs as a collection of traditional wisdom sayings from throughout Israelite history. These sayings are generally short, although some, like Prov. 31:10–31, may run to considerable length on a single topic. Their purpose is to summarize the basic values of Israelite society in a form that can be remembered easily. These sayings are not unique to Israel because much of their wisdom is borrowed or recycled from older Near Eastern cultures.

Parallels within a Common Wisdom Heritage	
Biblical Texts	**Other Ancient Near Eastern Texts**

Prov. 6:25–29: Do not desire her beauty in your heart,
    and do not let her capture you with her eyelashes;
for a prostitute's fee is only a loaf of bread,
    but the wife of another stalks a man's very life.
Can fire be carried in the bosom
    without burning one's clothes?
Or can one walk on hot coals
    without scorching the feet?
So is he who sleeps with his neighbor's wife;
    no one who touches her will go unpunished.
	Teachings of Ankhsheshonq 23.6–7: A man who makes love to a married woman will be executed on her threshold. 8.12: Do not marry a wife whose husband is alive, unless you want to make an enemy. (*OTPar*[3], 311, 316)

Prov. 23:9: Do not speak in the hearing of a fool,
    who will only despise the wisdom of your words.
Sir. 21:14: The mind of a fool is like a broken jar;
    it can hold no knowledge.
Sir. 22:9: Whoever teaches a fool is like one
    who glues potsherds together,
    or who rouses a sleeper from deep slumber.
	Teachings of Ankhsheshonq 7.4–5: Do not instruct fools who hate you. Do not instruct those who do not learn from you. 10.6: Only a fool tells a teacher: "Don't treat me like a fool!" (*OTPar*[3], 310, 313)

Prov. 26:17: Like somebody who takes a passing dog by
    the ears
    is one who meddles in the affairs of another.
	Teachings of Ankhsheshonq 19.11–12: When two brothers quarrel, do not come between them. Anyone who comes between two brothers when they quarrel becomes their enemy when they make peace. (*OTPar*[3], 315)

Prov. 29:19: By mere words a servant is not disciplined, for though he understands, he will not give heed.	*Teachings of Ankhsheshonq* 7.18: Slaves who are not beaten become disobedient. (*OTPar*[3], 311)

Prov. 16:1: The plans of the mind belong to mortals,
    but the answer of the tongue is from the LORD.
Prov. 16:9: The human mind plans the way,
    but the LORD directs the steps.
	Teachings of Ankhsheshonq 26.14: Divine plans are one thing. Human desires are another. (*OTPar*[3], 317)

Prov. 2:3: If you indeed cry out for insight,
    and raise your voice for understanding,
if you seek it like silver,
    and search for it as for hidden treasures—
then you will understand the fear of the LORD
    and find the knowledge of God.
Prov. 19:20: Listen to advice and accept instruction,
    that you may gain wisdom for the future.
	Teachings of Ptah-Hotep 54–56: Seek advice from the powerless, as well as from the powerful. No one ever reaches one's full potential, there is always more to learn. Wisdom hides like emeralds, but it can be found even in a young woman grinding grain. (*OTPar*[3], 284)

Prov. 15:16–17: Better is a little with the fear of the LORD
    than great treasure and trouble with it.
Better is a dinner of vegetables where love is
    than a fatted ox and hatred with it.
	Instruction of Amenemope 8.19–20; 9.6–9: Better a single bushel from your divine patron, than five thousand stolen bushels. Better is a single loaf and a happy heart than all the riches in the world and sorrow. (*OTPar*[3], 297)

We do not mean for this to sound like a criticism. Wisdom, by its very nature, is universal and timeless. While its vocabulary or examples may occasionally need to be updated, the basic kernel of truth within the statements remains valid as it travels from one nation to another. Like law, wisdom is borrowed and refitted to new cultures.

Wisdom literature in the ancient Near East reflects a broad cultural milieu, not just isolated cultural pockets. As a result, direct connections exist between the Wisdom literature produced in ancient Egypt, Mesopotamia, and Israel. These literary and cultural links do not indicate that Israel is totally dependent on its neighbors. Rather, the wealth of available material is utilized and reworked to reflect regional, ethical, and chronological differences. Thus Prov. 22:20 can speak of "thirty" admonitions, perhaps in direct reference to the Egyptian Instruction of Amenemope, but that does not mean that all subsequent wisdom writers have to employ this strict literary framework.

A turn of phrase, a particular situation, or even direct borrowing of entire sayings therefore can be seen as acceptance of the validity of Wisdom literature in general, wherever it may have originated. The most commonly shared concepts in wisdom include the need for children (broadly defined as clients, slaves, apprentices, and offspring) to listen to and obey the commands of parents (broadly defined as employers, masters, and biological parents); a man's need to exercise discretion in dealing with women outside his immediate family; and the injunction that honesty is the best policy. In this case syncretism, so often maligned by the prophets, is countenanced because of these commonly held social principles and the real value to their culture procured by instilling them into the minds and behavior patterns of the people.

Ancient Near Eastern Wisdom literature strives to reinforce the idea that wisdom is a gift of the gods. Thus Prov. 8:22–31 celebrates wisdom as the first product of Yahweh's action in creation. Proverbs commonly identifies wisdom as female (Prov. 1:20; 8:1). The origin of this gender designation is most likely the fact that the mother is the first teacher of her children. Beyond keeping them safe and fed, it is her first responsibility to impress on them the basic values and social customs associated with Israelite culture and religion. It is therefore quite easy to imagine a mother's reciting of proverbial maxims: "A fool despises a parent's instruction" (15:5); "A stupid child is

---

Israelite Wisdom Ideals

Some biblical proverbs do reflect distinctive Israelite culture and thought. These sayings express both the character of Yahweh and the Israelite concept of justice.

The LORD by wisdom founded the earth;
by understanding he established the heavens;
by his knowledge the deeps broke open,
and the clouds drop down the dew.
(Prov. 3:19–20)

The LORD has made everything for its purpose,
even the wicked for the day of trouble.
All those who are arrogant are an abomination to the LORD;
be assured they will not go unpunished.
(Prov. 16:4–5)

The name of the LORD is a strong tower;
the righteous run into it and are safe.
(Prov. 18:10)

---

ruin to a father" (19:13); or "A wise child loves discipline" (13:1).

The Book of Ecclesiastes

Like Proverbs and Song of Songs, the book of Ecclesiastes (also called Qoheleth) has been traditionally ascribed to Solomon. This tradition is based on the first verse of the book, "The words of the Teacher, the son of David, king of Jerusalem." Yet other statements in the book raise questions about the authorship. Several verses (Eccles. 1:16; 2:7) imply that there were many kings over Jerusalem prior to the author's time, but only two preceded Solomon. Several other passages (8:2–9; 10:16–19) sound more like a common person speaking rather than a king. Like all Wisdom literature, it is impossible to determine the authorship conclusively, and the high percentage of Aramaic vocabulary and Persian loanwords in the text points to a date of composition in the late postexilic or early Hellenistic era. It is probably best to think of this work as an extended monologue discussing wisdom issues without trying to tie them to any particular person or time. The inclusion of what some scholars consider a very gloomy book in the biblical canon may be based on how it raises some of the universal questions that we have about our place in the universe and the value of human knowledge and achievement.

The primary theme of Ecclesiastes is the apparent absurdity of life (1:2) and the uselessness of human endeavor. In 6:10–11:6, the author repeatedly points out that it is impossible to know or to find out anything. Therefore nothing that a person accomplishes in this life has any lasting value. It is pointless to strive for power, knowledge, or property, since we all come to the same end. Unlike Gilgamesh, the hero of ancient Mesopotamian legend, the author of Ecclesiastes draws no consolation from his city's walls, even if they are apparently built to last forever.

Such a negative view of life is difficult for some modern readers to deal with. However, one way to explain it can be found by resorting to current postmodern thought, with its emphasis on the utility of knowledge as a way to acquire practical skills rather than a knowledge base for its own sake; a critique of the "grand narratives" or accomplishments of our culture; the meaninglessness of a world lacking much originality and based around millions of copies of the same music, the same movies, the same pieces of art, and the same books. In this

Gilgamesh's Consolation

Let us climb the walls of Uruk. Let us marvel at their magnificent foundations. Let us be grateful for their fired brickwork. Let us remember the seven sages who founded Uruk. Let us enjoy this great city with its orchards and pastures, rich with clay quarries and blessed by the House of Ishtar. (*OTPar*[3], 32)

system of thought, there does not seem to be any allowance for or even reason for the joy of accomplishment. It inspires few emotions whatsoever, except perhaps frustration, depression, and a realization that it is impossible to know and understand "all the work of God" (Eccles. 8:16–17).

As in most ancient Wisdom literature, the author of Ecclesiastes takes a realistic view of life and its uncertainties, providing a sevenfold admonition that it is best to enjoy the pleasures of life while it lasts (2:24–26; 3:12–13; 3:22; 5:17–19; 8:15; 9:7–10; 11:7–10). The Israelites, like the cultures of Mesopotamia, did not have a well-developed belief in a resurrection or afterlife. Death is the great equalizer, as well as the destroyer of all hopes and desires. There is a mention of *Sheol* ("abode of the dead" or "grave" but not "hell") as a repository for the spirits of all the dead (see 1 Sam. 28:11–19; Job 7:9), and archaeological investigations have revealed the inclusion of grave goods in Israelite burials. However, prior to the Hellenistic period (after 300 BCE), little is said in the biblical text about death other than how it is an end to life. The author of Ecclesiastes draws on this view of death to demolish the case that promotes human pride and foolishness (9:1–10). Once that is done, then the wisdom writer can lead the reader to recognize that it is contemplation of Yahweh's power and acceptance of God's purpose for the world and humankind that is of most value in life (12:13–14).

The author does not turn away from life or reject normal existence on earth. Nor does the author of this book advocate utter nihilism with its doctrine that nothing truly matters. Instead, he or she promotes balance, temperance of thought and word, and a more realistic understanding of humanity's place within the scheme of creation.

Death as the Destroyer

All go to one place; all are from the dust, and all turn to dust again. (Eccles. 3:20)

Remember that you fashioned me like clay;
  and will you turn me to dust again? (Job 10:9)

Baal and Anat 5.1.20–21: The dust of the grave devours its prey. Death eats whatever it wants with both hands. (*OTPar³*, 271)

STUDY QUESTIONS

1. Discuss how wisdom themes are expressed in the biblical narrative. How is a character in a story identified by the author as either a wise person or a fool?
2. Compare and contrast the proverbial statements in the Bible and those from the ancient Near East. What can they tell us about these ancient cultures, their values, and their concept of common sense?
3. Discuss ancient Israelite education and the ways in which the Proverbs and other wisdom genres were used to teach the young.
4. Discuss how Ecclesiastes' emphasis on recognizing the ephemeral nature of human accomplishment fits into ancient and modern understandings of the world.
5. Explain how wisdom is more than just common sense in ancient Israel.

The Book of Job

KEY POINTS

- The book of Job consists of two prose sections that enclose a larger poetic section.
- The wisdom theme in Job explores the relationship between right behavior and divine reward.
- Job and his friends debate the cause of human suffering.
- Job is confronted by God in a theophany and discovers the limits of human wisdom.

The message of the book of Job, as is the case with most Wisdom literature, addresses a timeless question: "Does Job fear God for nothing?" (Job 1:9). Although the book does not provide an entirely satisfactory answer to this question, especially for modern readers, it does function as a catalyst of critical thinking and an opportunity to explore the issue of human suffering. Arguments can be made for a tenth-century-BCE date of composition during the early monarchy period. But most scholars today argue for a date in the exilic or postexilic period based on linguistic evidence and references to officials (3:14–15) that suggest familiarity with Persian administrative practices. Given the fact that the hero of this book is an Edomite and other biblical books of the seventh to sixth centuries are blatantly anti-Edomite (see Joel 3:19; Jer. 49:7–22; Ezek. 25:12–16), it is probably best to suggest that composition took place over a long period rather than at one particular time. The author is also impossible to identify. All that can be said is that the author is one of the world's greatest psychological dramatists.

There are a number of ancient Near Eastern parallels to the book of Job. Generally in the form of a dialogue, they also explore the issues of suffering, justice, and the role of the gods in human existence.

Literary Analysis. The book of Job can be examined as a whole, but both the prologue (Job 1–2) and the epilogue (42:7–17) are written in a narrative prose style, while the remainder of the book (3:1–42:6) consists of poetic dialogue and monologue. This structure, also found in the wisdom teachings of the Assyrian sage Ahiqar, suggests that at least two separate stories have been joined together by the biblical editors. The character of Job in the two segments is also quite different. In the prose

---

Ancient Near Eastern Parallels to the Book of Job

Egyptian Sufferer: During the social and political upheaval in Egypt between 2258 and 2050 BCE, a dialogue is composed between a man and his soul over the advisability of suicide in order to end suffering. The man's arguments center on his life and his reputation:

> "My soul, do you really want me to go on living? When my life smells worse than bird drop on a hot day" and "when my reputation is worse than someone plotting to overthrow the government?" (OTpar³, 227)

Sumerian Job: The lament of this early second-millennium-BCE sufferer complains to his god about his loss of wealth, his health, and his reputation within the community:

> My righteous word has been turned into a lie. . . . You have doled out to me suffering ever anew. . . . My righteous shepherd [the king] has become angry. . . . My friend gives the lie to my righteous word. (ANET, 590)

Babylonian Job: This first-millennium-BCE sufferer complains to his friend about the suffering inflicted by the gods:

> "I am without resources, I am lost in the depths of despair. . . . As a young man, I sought the will of my divine patrons, I prayed and I fasted," but "the divine assembly decreed poverty for me. . . . Cripples and fools outran me. Sinners prospered. I failed." (OTpar³, 240–41)

God about the injustice of the situation. The dialogues contain three rounds in which a great deal of repetition occurs, but that is fairly common in wisdom material. The sequence is broken in Job 29–31, where Job leaves his friends and speaks directly to God. In these speeches or **soliloquies**, he details his former condition, his current affliction, and his plea of innocence (through an oath of clearance). When the other friends fall silent, one other person, Elihu, comes forward to sum up the arguments that they have made and to reiterate Job's need to repent (Job 32–37). The final segment of the poetic section then contains the theophany in which a frighteningly powerful Yahweh appears to Job, not to answer his questions but to demonstrate the gulf between human understanding and divine majesty (Job 38–41).

Figure 5.9. Assyrian tablet inscribed with "Ludlul bel Nemeqi," a poem describing a righteous sufferer, from Ashurbanipal's library (seventh century BCE). (Baker Photo Archive, courtesy of the Louvre)

sections, Job is long-suffering and totally faithful. He accepts his fate and never questions the justice of God (see 1:21). His attitude is quite different, however, in the poetic chapters. Here he cries out against the day he was born (3:11; 10:18), loathing his present condition and repeatedly proclaiming that "humans have a hard service on earth" (7:1) while their days pass "swifter than a runner" (9:25).

In the face of what he considers to be a clear case of injustice (Job 7:11), Job refutes all the charges of sin made against him by his three friends. There is an artificial character to these dialogues between Job and his friends. Each man makes his case for why Job has been afflicted. Job then answers their charges, sometimes indirectly, and then turns and speaks to

Story Summary. In the prologue to the book, we learn that there is a man named Job who lives in the land of Uz, which some have identified with the area of Edom. This man is said to be blameless and upright, one who fears God and continuously turns away from evil. And we are told that Job has many children and is quite wealthy.

After these initial statements, the scene shifts to the divine realm, where the heavenly beings gather to present themselves before the Lord (Job 1:6). These angels or heavenly beings are part of the divine assembly, which forms a royal court for God (cf. the use of "us" in the first Genesis creation story [Gen. 1:26]). A similar gathering is mentioned in 1 Kings 22:19–22, in the story of the prophet Micaiah. The angels appear before God. Among them is a being whose Hebrew title, *hasatan*, means "the adversary" (see this figure in Zech. 3:1–2).

Our modern conception of Satan or the devil is influenced by writings and art created long after the compilation of the OT/HB. These later images can cloud our understanding of the satan figure in Job. To think of the devil or Satan with horns and a tail and in some of the ways medieval people depict him, or even in the sense of the NT Satan (Matt. 4:10; Luke 10:18; Rom 16:20), is to miss the role and concept of this adversary in Job. The reason why we prefer to identify this character in Job as "the adversary" rather than as Satan is based on his role in the story and on linguistic grounds. Hebrew definitely implies that the term *hasatan* is not a proper name but a title.

The adversary is standing among the heavenly beings that come to the divine council. The Lord says to the adversary, "Where have you come from?" and the adversary answers, "From going to and fro on the earth and from walking up and down on it" (Job 1:7). In other

words, his inspection of creation has taken him all over the world. Having established his reason for being in God's presence, the next step is to have God ask the adversary the question that will set the story in motion: "Have you considered my servant Job?" (1:8). Job has already been introduced to the audience as blameless, a righteous and good man. It is reported how careful he is in giving strict attention to all the religious statutes and in praying for his children's sake (1:1–5). Now God throws out a sort of challenge by saying, "There is no one like him on the earth, a blameless and upright man, who fears God and turns away from evil."

Such a blatant assertion in wisdom tradition requires a test (cf. Gen. 3:1–5), and therefore the adversary takes his cue and answers the Lord:

> Does Job fear God for nothing? Have you not put a fence around him and his house and all that he has on every side? . . . But stretch out your hand now, and touch all he has, and he will curse you to your face. (Job 1:9–11)

The Lord agrees to a test and says to the adversary, "Very well, all that Job has is in your power; only do not stretch out your hand against him!" (Job 1:12). That is, don't touch his body. The adversary then departs, having been empowered by God to perform the test of righteousness. Job does not know that he is the object of a contest going on in heaven, a contest between God and the adversary.

Now the adversary, under Yahweh's orders, takes away everything that Job has. First his children are killed. Then his properties, his barns, and his houses are ruined in one kind of catastrophe after another. But after all this, Job rises, tears his robe, shaves his head, falls on the ground, and worships God without qualification. He says,

Naked I came from my mother's womb, and naked shall I return there; the LORD gave, and the LORD has taken away; blessed be the name of the LORD. (Job 1:20–21)

After demonstrating his piety and humility, Job passes this first test. A second dialogue then occurs between Yahweh and the adversary (Job 1:6–8 and 2:1–3 duplicate the introduction to each dialogue). Once again Yahweh extols Job's virtues, but the adversary responds, "Well, he still has his health; let me take away his health and then see if he still worships you." So God says, "All right, you can take away his health, but you can't kill him." The adversary then inflicts loathsome sores on Job, from the sole of his foot to the crown of his head (2:7). Job is in such distress that he takes a potsherd to scrape himself and sits among the ashes. Job's wife then becomes part of the test, urging her husband, "Do you still persist in your integrity? Curse God and die" (2:9).

What is the implication, from the ancient Israelite perspective, of saying "Curse God and die"? What happens to somebody who curses God? Recall the charge made against Naboth by the two lying witnesses when Ahab wanted to acquire his vineyard (1 Kings 21:13). Cursing God or the king is a capital offense. What Job's wife is saying to him is to commit suicide, for if one curses God, one will be killed. Job says to her, "You speak as any foolish woman would speak. Shall we receive the good at the hand of God and not receive the bad?" (Job 2:10). Job therefore passes the second test, refusing to sin with his lips even in the face of personal affliction. He also acknowledges that God alone is the power that provides both good and bad in life.

The major portion of the book then begins with the appearance of Job's three

so-called friends. Eliphaz the Temanite, Bildad the Shuhite, and Zophar the Naamathite hardly recognize the pitiful figure that Job has become. They raise their voices and weep aloud. They tear their robes and throw dust in the air upon their heads. These are typical ancient expressions of grief (see the inset "Ancient Israelite Grief Rituals" on p. 192). They then sit with Job on the ground for the traditional seven days and seven nights (see Lev. 13:2–8), and no one speaks a word to him because they see that his suffering is so great (Job 2:11–13).

We now begin to see a change in Job's character from the humble and accepting figure found in the prologue. In the poetic section, Job curses the day of his birth (3:1) and refuses to remain silent about the unfairness of his affliction (7:11). After Job completes his lament, each friend speaks in turn, trying to convince Job that he has committed some sin, perhaps a secret or forgotten one. They are convinced that this is the reason for his condition. In their persistence, they will argue in this fashion for more than thirty chapters. Job responds to their efforts by refuting their logic and even referring to them as "treacherous" companions (6:15). He repeatedly calls on God to provide an explanation for what he considers to be unjust suffering (10:2), even though he does not believe that he will necessarily get a fair hearing for his complaints (9:13–24).

After what seems like an endless barrage of moralizing, Job interrupts the statements of his three friends in Job 29 with a series of soliloquies, really private statements made to the audience, in which he turns and speaks directly to God. He details the happy condition in which he and his family once lived. He attributes this previous happiness to his piety and devotion

The Arguments Presented by Job's Friends

Job's friends present the sufferer with a series of arguments that represent the standard moral and legal viewpoints current in ancient Israel about suffering and punishment:

1. No mortal is perfect, and therefore all persons must expect that God will punish them for their transgressions (Eliphaz in Job 4:7–11, 17–21). This view is based on the doctrine of individual retribution.
2. The evidence of history proves that God is just (Bildad in Job 8:8–22). God does not reject the upright or take up the cause of the evildoer.
3. Self-righteousness is self-delusion (Zophar in Job 11:4–20). God's wisdom is beyond the understanding of any human (Elihu in 33:12–33). To deny the justice of affliction is to demonstrate a lack of desire to learn from the experience.

to Yahweh. In Job 30 he graphically describes his current pitiful state. Then, to complete his courtroom-like performance, Job takes an oath of clearance (Job 31) very similar to that found in the Egyptian Book of the Dead. He lists a series of sins (including adultery, abusing slaves, lack of charity to the poor, and greed) that might explain his afflictions and then denies that he has committed them.

Having given human wisdom an opportunity to make its arguments, the poet now shifts to a divine court. Job has asked for the opportunity to argue his case with the Almighty (Job 13:3), and now the transcendent and all-powerful God answers Job out of the whirlwind (38:1): "Who is this that darkens counsel by words without knowledge? Gird up your loins like a man, I will question you, and you shall declare to me." God's opening challenge is followed by question after unanswerable question.

> Where were you when I laid the foundation of the earth?
> Tell me, if you have understanding.

> Who determined its measurements—
> surely you know!
> Or who stretched the line upon it?
> On what were its bases sunk,
> or who laid its cornerstone
> when the morning stars sang together
> and all the heavenly beings shouted
> for joy? (Job 38:4–7)

What can Job's response be to these sixty to eighty rhetorical questions extending over a series of four chapters? Forced into a humble stance, a very frightened Job meekly answers the Lord:

> See, I am of small account; what shall I
> answer you?
> I lay my hand on my mouth.
> I have spoken once, and I will not
> answer;
> twice, but will proceed no further.
> (Job 40:4–5)

Even so, Job must submit to a second final exam, filled with even more pointed rhetorical questions, including, "Do you control the thunder, tornadoes, or the rain?" Of course Job certainly cannot answer such a question directly. Thoroughly beaten down by the volume of God's cross-examination, Job at last

The Egyptian Book of the Dead

I have not committed evil against men.
I have not mistreated cattle.
I have not committed sin in the place of truth.
I have not blasphemed a god.
I have not done violence to a poor man.
I have not made (anyone) sick.
I have not made (anyone) weep.
I have not killed.
I have given no order to a killer.
I have not caused anyone suffering.
I have not had sexual relations with a boy.
I have not defiled myself.
I am pure! (*ANET*, 34–35)

pleads his ignorance, and that gets to the heart of the matter. Job has repeatedly proclaimed that he knows God's purpose (Job 10:13) and that he knows as much as his tormentors (13:2). Now he is ready to admit that human knowledge cannot approach the mind of God.

> I know that you can do all things,
>> and that no purpose of yours can be thwarted. . . .
> Therefore I have uttered what I did not understand,
>> things too wonderful for me, which I did not know. (Job 42:2–3)

Job confesses that he has spoken about things he really did not understand and that God is far beyond what he ever envisioned: "I heard of you by the hearing of the ear, but now my eye sees you" (Job 42:5). He has had a new

Knowledge Theme

Many of the arguments in the book of Job center on what is true knowledge. There is the question of traditional knowledge and the question of whether Job can know why he is suffering. There is a corresponding set of statements about divine knowledge and whether it can be questioned. In the end, Job's final test may be to determine if he has the right to dispute his friends' statements or his physical condition based on the knowledge he possesses.

Job 8:8–9, Bildad: "For inquire now of bygone generations, and consider what their ancestors have found; for we are but of yesterday, and we know nothing, for our days on earth are but a shadow."

Job 11:7–8, Zohar: "Can you find out the deep things of God?
     Can you find out the limit of the Almighty?
   It is higher than heaven, . . .
     Deeper than Sheol—what can you know?"

Job 21:22, Job: "Will any teach God knowledge,
     seeing that he judges those that are on high?"

Job 34:35, Elihu: "Job speaks without knowledge,
     his words are without insight."

Job 37:16, Elihu: "Do you know the balancing of the clouds,
     the wondrous works of the one whose knowledge is perfect?"

experience, Job says, "therefore I despise myself and repent in dust and ashes" (42:6). In other words, Job has developed a new understanding of God, and he sees his own puniness and inadequacy in the face of God's awesomeness, sovereignty, power, and omniscience.

Wisdom Themes in Job. There are obviously several possible purposes for this book. One is to provide a theodicy that answers the question, How can God be righteous and allow righteous people to suffer? The arguments made by Job's friends in the poetic section of Job demonstrate that traditional wisdom has failed to address this question. Just as the book of Proverbs emphasizes that the righteous shall be rewarded and the wicked will be punished, it appears that the cosmic justice described in its wisdom sayings does not always appear to operate in daily life. We have all seen good people who suffer in our world (see Job 9:22). Job may have been written to explain or at least to analyze this phenomenon. One possible conclusion is that the book of Job is intended to show that righteous persons like Job suffer in order to gain a new understanding of God, particularly of God's power and greatness. That in turn might be compared with the role of the Suffering Servant in Isa. 52:13–53:12 who serves as part of Second Isaiah's theodicy of the exile.

Second, the book may be emphasizing that theological arguments about the relation between sin and suffering are useless. Persons in many ancient cultures believed that if people sinned, they would be punished: all sickness and misfortune are the result of sin. The same belief in the reciprocity of blessing for correct behavior and punishment for evil is expressed in the Deuteronomic legal tradition (Deut. 11:13–28), as well as in the book of Proverbs (22:22–23; 24:19–20). Psalm 1 also reiterates the belief frequently enunciated in Proverbs:

the wicked will be punished, and the righteous will be rewarded. In the face of this reliance on traditional wisdom, the books of Job and Ecclesiastes challenge the traditional forms of expressing this belief and call for a deeper understanding and reinterpretation of the causes of suffering.

Third, the book of Job suggests that readers should not complain or demand answers for these troubling issues. Like the book of Job, Wisdom literature often addresses fundamental problems of life with which we all wrestle and offers a variety of solutions. It is the task of wisdom to take difficult issues and to address them in a new or more in-depth way. In the book of Job, the ultimate resolution of the fundamental problem of suffering is unclear. The very lack of clarity, however, means that the author encourages the reader to leave the resolution of such problems in the hands of God rather than suffer even greater grief by obsessing on apparently senseless tragedies.

The fourth possible purpose of the book of Job is to argue that faith should not be based on the assumption that it will lead to material rewards. But if we take that approach, which certainly is the approach of the first couple of chapters in the argument between God and the adversary, then what about the end of the book of Job? There we learn the following: God says his wrath is kindled against Eliphaz and his two friends, for they have not spoken correctly. They are instructed to take seven bulls and seven rams to Job for him to offer up for their sakes as burnt offerings. God says that Job is to pray for them so that God will not deal harshly with them, "For you have not spoken of me what is right" (Job 42:7–9). God condemns the three comforters or friends for arguing that Job's misfortune is the result of his sins. Then in 42:10, the Lord restores the

fortunes of Job when he prays for his friends and gives Job twice as much as he had before. He lives a full life with this restored household. The blessing that Job receives because of his righteousness may function as a form of legal compensation for divine action. Although it is somewhat unsatisfactory to think that all Job had lost, property and children, can so easily be replaced, to this ancient culture such recompense may have been at least understandable within the bounds of legal practice.

One complicating factor to the book of Job as literature is that the opening two chapters and the last portion of the final chapter differ somewhat in literary character from the central portion of the book. The beginning and end of the book are more akin to prose than are the more poetic nature of the discourses of Job, his visitors, and God. If these central discourses are composed separately from a later prose introduction and conclusion, then the poetic section speaks quite clearly against the legal position taken in Deuteronomy that obedience is to be materially rewarded (11:1–17). The prose introduction and conclusion restore the prevailing Deuteronomic theology that proper living results in prosperity.

STUDY QUESTIONS

1. Discuss the role of the satan (adversary) in the prologue to the book of Job. Is this character independent of God?
2. Discuss the use of the knowledge theme in Job. Notice how knowledge is used as the basis for Job's test, as his defense, and as the basis for his repentance.
3. Compare and contrast the story of Job with the garden of Eden story in Genesis. How are the themes of knowledge and death developed in both of these books?

4. Describe the role of Job's three friends. What are their individual arguments? Note the pattern of argument and response that ties their statements together.

5. Discuss Job's use of the oath of clearance in Job 29–31, and compare it with the Egyptian Book of the Dead.

6. Are the questions posed to Job in the theophany (Job 38–41) directed at Job or an extended argument for God's sole power over creation?

7. Job repents in Job 42:4–6. Why does he do so? What is his sin?

8. Are the three friends right and Job wrong? Explain.

9. Why does God reward Job with riches, a new family, and a long life in the epilogue to this book? Could this have been added by a later editor? Why or why not?

The Book of Psalms

KEY POINTS

• The book of Psalms contains examples of every theme in Israelite tradition, from creation to wisdom to law and politics.

• The psalms were performed in the temple by professional choirs, and they contain technical language.

• The psalms express both joy and grief, thanksgiving and pleas for help.

The book of Psalms is a collection of hymns compiled over a long period of time, reflecting all the major traditions that developed in ancient Israel. Structurally, the book of Psalms is divided into five sections, but the psalms are not arranged within these sections according to any particular category or type. Ultimately the collection of psalms that appear in this book reflects nearly every period of Israelite history, and some are fairly easy to date because they describe a specific historical event (Ps. 137 makes reference to the fall of Jerusalem to the

Babylonians). Like any songbook associated with worship practices, some of the psalms can be identified with particular cultic events: coronation of a king (Pss. 2; 20; 45), covenant renewal (Pss. 78; 105), celebrations of creation (Pss. 19; 104; 139), sacrificial offerings (Ps. 100), the Sabbath (Ps. 92), or pilgrimages (Pss. 120–134). Many of the psalms can be categorized as pleas for help, hymns of general praise or thanksgiving, or laments.

Technical Aspects. Because these songs are originally designed to be used in both individual and corporate worship, many of them have rubrics (instructions) for orchestration, instrumentation, and tempo. The majority of these rubrics appear in the superscriptions, which appear at the beginning of about two-thirds of the psalms and were added by the editor(s) or musicians in charge of liturgical worship. Some are simple: "A psalm of David." Others commemorate a specific event in David's career (Pss. 51; 52; 56), though we should remember that such superscriptions may be traditional but not necessarily historically accurate. Still others describe the instruments and the tune to be used (Ps. 22) or mention persons who were apparently choirmasters (Pss. 73; 77; 78 [Asaph]; 84; 85; 88 [Korah]; see 1 Chron. 25:1–8 for their appointment).

What is clear from these rubrics is that there were trained musicians and organized choirs within the temple community whose responsibility was to perform the musical accompaniment to both major and minor cultic events (see Ps. 84). Given the importance of the priestly community after the restoration of the Jerusalem temple in 515 BCE, it seems likely that particular Levitical choirs developed strong identities as well as their own repertoire of music, which became traditional and exclusive to them. The detailed description of temple music found in the writings of the Chronicler indicates that the formal choirs were joined in the organization and performance of liturgical music by several other groups, including those associated with Chenaniah, "leader of the music of the singers" (1 Chron. 15:27), and Mattithiah and five other men, who were "to lead with lyres" (1 Chron. 15:21).

One aspect of the rubrics that prevents a total understanding of the musical performance of the psalms is that many of them contain words that appear only in Psalms. These are technical terms similar to those we use today (e.g., andante, allegretto), but they are now untranslatable. Some may refer to tone, tempo, or volume, but we do not know for sure. One that appears in the body of some of the psalms is the word *Selah* (Pss. 54; 55; 57; also in Hab. 3). It may be a signal to repeat a phrase, sing the chorus refrain, or to take a breath. It is possible that eventually some of these words will be discovered in texts outside the Bible and deciphered.

Archaeological discoveries, including Egyptian tomb paintings, have added to our knowledge of ancient forms of music and the methods musicians have used to play their instruments. A wide variety of instruments are depicted in these scenes, showing their development through time, and fragments of a few have survived, attesting to their manufacture and providing clues to musical intervals and notation. As one might expect, music changed and became more complex and institutionalized as ancient Israel's society evolved from a village-based culture into one that was dominated by an urban-based elite.

Authorship. In the superscription of seventy-three (almost half) of the psalms, there appears the Hebrew expression *l dwd*. The Hebrew word *l* is a preposition that indicates direction

> ### Superscriptions of Psalms
>
> - To the leader: According to "The Deer of the Dawn." A psalm of David. (Ps. 22)
> - To the leader: "Do Not Destroy." Of David. A *miktam*, when he fled from Saul, in the cave. (Ps. 56)
> - To the leader. Of David, for the memorial offering. (Ps. 70)
> - A song. A psalm of the Korahites. To the leader: According to *Mahalath Leannoth*. A *maskil* of Heman the Ezrahite. (Ps. 88)
> - A song of ascents. Of Solomon. (Ps. 127)

or relationship. In the superscription of a psalm, it may signify that the psalm is a psalm of David, a psalm from David, a psalm from David's time, or a psalm composed by David. It can also mean a psalm dedicated to David and honoring his role as king. All these translations are possible. The expression does not necessarily mean authorship by David. In religious circles, it is traditional to say that David wrote the book of Psalms. This is a popularization, both modern and ancient (see 2 Sam. 23:1; Amos 6:5; 4 Macc. 18:15; Luke 20:42; and a note attached to a psalms scroll found at Qumran, 11QPs[a] 27.2–11). David could have written some of the psalms, but probably they were composed by scribes during the monarchic and postexilic periods who wished to celebrate or commemorate David and his reign.

Another point regarding the authorship of the psalms is that the names of many persons are mentioned in the superscriptions (Asaph, Korah, Ethan, Heman, Solomon). One psalm is even attributed to Moses (Ps. 90). But many psalms are anonymous. The same is true of a church hymnal. In some cases the hymnal may identify the author of a hymn, and in other cases, it may state that the writer is unknown.

Content and Classification of the Psalms. Why is Psalms one of the most popular books in the OT/HB? One reason is that people find

Figure 5.10. Reproduction of a painting from the tomb of Nacht showing Egyptian musicians playing a flute, lyre, and harp. (The Yorck Project / Wikimedia Commons)

it much easier to relate to Psalms than to Leviticus or Deuteronomy. The psalms describe particular human feelings such as discouragement or joy. An individual's frustrations are voiced here, and arguments are made for worshiping God. These ancient songs are the closest thing we have to individual expressions of personal emotion and introspection in the biblical text.

The psalms were designed to be used for individual and collective worship. They formed Israel's ancient hymnal because they were probably sung or chanted. We do not have the music, but we do have the words. Modern Judaism uses cantors in worship who chant the psalms with a kind of musical intonation based on an ancient pattern. Attempts to recreate the music of the ancient Near East have been made, and it is possible that these ancient sounds may one day be heard again.

One of the most important contributors to modern Psalms studies is Herman Gunkel. As a form critic, Gunkel was the first modern scholar to group the Psalms by class or type. He bases his classification system on the use of the psalms in worship or on their setting in life (*Sitz im Leben*). Gunkel outlines six major types or classifications.

1. *Hymns.* Psalm 8 is an example of a hymn. The first and last verses of this psalm are exactly the same. A literary bracket formed in this way is called an inclusio. This device typically occurs in music but seldom characterizes speech except in dramatic contexts. Another common hymnic theme in the Psalms is the recitation of the creation story (Pss. 8; 19; 104; 139). The celebratory musical expressions found in these psalms are a poetic match for songs embedded into biblical narrative, such as the Song of the Sea and the Song of Miriam in Exod. 15. Similar expressions of joy and thanksgiving are found in the singing of pilgrim songs, such as the Songs of Ascent (Pss. 120–134), which extol the opportunity to go up to Jerusalem and worship in the sanctuary at Zion. These songs are probably associated with the three great agricultural festivals in the Israelite calendar (Exod. 23:17; Deut. 16:16).

2. *Royal psalms.* A royal psalm appears in Ps. 2. This psalm speaks about the role of the king as Yahweh's political agent. It originally may have been used at coronation ceremonies or on the anniversary of a king's coronation. A group of enthronement psalms (among them Pss. 2; 20; 72; 89; 101; 110; 144) reiterate the Davidic dynasty's right to rule and would be used in the autumnal festival commemorating its founding. The annual festival would include a grand procession, perhaps using Ps. 68, which exhorts the people: "Sing to God, sing praises to his name" (68:4) in its opening chant. Priests

and nobles, advisers and representatives of designated tribes would use the occasion to march through the streets of Jerusalem to the temple with "the singers in front, the minstrels last, between them girls playing tambourines" (68:25). Once there, sacrifices and speeches would be made, which, as in this psalm, would likely consist of a recitation of the mighty acts of God. Both Yahweh, "who rides upon the clouds" (Ps. 68:4—a title also given to Baal in the Ugaritic epics [COS 1:86, v. 121, 261]), and his chosen king were thus exalted.

3. *Communal laments.* The majority of the psalms are laments. Some, like Pss. 74 and 80, are communal laments intended to express the collective sorrow of the nation. Since they deal with the fall of Jerusalem and the destruction of the temple, these psalms were probably written sometime after 587 BCE. In Ps. 74, one can feel the frustration of the psalmist. God is entreated, "How long . . . is the foe to scoff?" (74:10) and "Why do you hold back your hand?" (74:11). The text goes on to mention the divine deliverance in the past and asks for the sake of the covenant that God deliver his people in the present (74:12–23). Human experience is filled with periods of frustration. In composing laments, the psalmist provides a means to express feelings of anger and despair.

4. *Individual laments.* One example in this category is Ps. 51. The writer of this psalm asks God to purify and cleanse him (51:2, 7). In exploring the nature of sin, the psalm resolutely relies on God's ability to forgive the penitent, literally "to put a new and right spirit within me" (51:10). The psalm also refers to the wisdom ideal that prefers right behavior to sacrifice (51:16–17; see 1 Sam. 15:22).

5. *Communal songs of thanksgiving and individual songs of thanksgiving.* Psalm 116 includes the words that the people utter when they are making their sacrifices in the temple in thanksgiving for recovery from an illness or other life-threatening events. The instructions for the ritual of the sacrifice of well-being are found in Lev. 7:11–16, and it is likely that Ps. 116 would have been performed or recited as part of this ritual. This chant promises to "pay my vows" to Yahweh for releasing one from the "pangs of *Sheol*" and "my soul from death" (116:3–8). With eyes filled with tears of thanks, the worshiper comes forward with the sacrifice in acknowledgment of the covenant in the presence of family and friends (116:17–18).

6. *Psalms of anger/wrath or imprecatory psalms.* In the face of personal or communal troubles it is not surprising to find among the psalms cries for revenge or retribution against enemies or evildoers. Like the distressed exiles in Ps. 137:7–9, the psalmists' pain causes them to consider horrific punishments for those who have wronged them. For example, in Ps. 35:4–10 the writer calls on God to disgrace and put to shame those "who seek my life." In other cases, the psalm contains a detailed curse. Psalm 109:6–20 contains a list of these curses, including "May his children be orphans and his wife a widow. May his children wander about and beg; may they be driven out of the ruins they inhabit" (109:9–10).

Songs, like legal pronouncements and wisdom sayings, are part of the store of literature common to the entire ancient Near East. Literary borrowing is quite common. The text of a song is often reshaped to fit individual cultures or religions while the theme remains the same. The Egyptian Hymn to the Aten, composed in the reign of Akhenaten (1379–1353 BCE), contains many themes and phrases resembling those in Ps. 104. Both are creation hymns, celebrating the creative and life-giving

Psalm 104 and the Hymn to the Aten

By the streams the birds of the air have their habitation;
they sing among the branches. (Ps. 104:12)

Birds fly to their nests, they spread their wings to praise your *Ka*. (Hymn to the Aten, *OTPar³*, 277)

These all look to you
to give them their food in due season;
when you give to them, they gather it up;
when you open your hand they are filled
with good things. (Ps. 104:27)

You assign each a place. You allot to each both needs and food, you count out to each the days of life. (Hymn to the Aten, *OTPar³*, 278)

When you hide your face, they are dismayed;
    when you take away their breath, they die
    and return to their dust.
When you send forth your spirit, they are created;
    and you renew the face of the ground. (Ps. 104:29–30)

When you rise, the Earth lives. When you set, the Earth dies. You are life itself, all live through you. (Hymn to the Aten, *OTPar³*, 279)

power of the Deity. The Egyptian song glorifies the Aten, the sun disc, while Ps. 104 praises Yahweh. The author of Ps. 104 probably drew on existing material, choosing to use statements that could extol Yahweh without regard to the original context of another culture's religious literature. It is also possible that the intent of the writer is to add the power of other gods to that of Yahweh. It was a common belief that when a god becomes a supreme power within the pantheon, lesser gods give their names and attributes to the chief of the gods. That is the case in the Babylonian story of creation, the *Enuma Elish*, when the gods meet in assembly and "proclaim his fifty names" (*COS* 1:111, VII.402). As Israel began to see its God as the one true power in the universe, it would have been natural to devalue other gods by using their literature and words of praise for Yahweh.

STUDY QUESTIONS

1. Discuss the authorship of the Psalms and the reasons for borrowing from ancient Near Eastern poetic models.
2. Discuss the different types of psalms and their intended audience.
3. Examine the superscriptions before nearly half of the Psalms and discuss how rubrics are a part of modern music and liturgical performance.
4. Discuss the various ways that the psalms are used as part of cultic celebrations, commemorations, and sacrificial rituals.
5. Consider the emotions that lead to the composition of imprecatory psalms.

The Song of Songs (Canticles)

KEY POINTS

- The Song of Songs provides insight into the emotions of physical attraction and love.
- The Song of Songs has been used as an allegory for God's relationship with the covenant people.

Examples of romantic love are rare in the biblical text (see Jacob's love for Rachel in Gen. 29:20 and Michal's love for David in 1 Sam. 18:20). Outside of marriage, the emotion expressed most often is lust or infatuation, such as Samson's desire for Delilah (Judg. 16:4) and Amnon's lovesickness for his half-sister Tamar (2 Sam. 13:1–4). Romantic love is rarely mentioned in the Bible because marriages usually were arranged between families. Personal relationships generally take second place to the desire for honor and the advancement of the household. This makes the Song of Songs (also known as Canticles and Song of Solomon) a unique set of romantic poems that clearly expresses the love of two people for each other.

It is probably best to refer to these poems as a collection rather than a unified composition.

Unlike victory hymns or chants (Exod. 15; 1 Sam. 18:7), the lack of a refrain or a determinable meter suggests that the poems in the Song of Songs are intended to be read, not sung. As a group, these poems are similar only in their common theme and some repetition of language, which may be standard to this literary type (cf. Song 2:6–7 with 8:3–4). Aside from the basic genre of love poetry, they contain subthemes of yearning, boasting, and admiration of physical charms. Given their disparate nature and the inclusion of loanwords and many *hapax legomena* (terms appearing only once in the OT/HB), the authorship and date of the book are uncertain. Tradition ascribing it solely to Solomon is doubtful and is based primarily on the references to Solomon in 3:9, 11; 8:11–12.

Basic to the dialogues is the passion that the lovers express for each other and the graphic descriptions of each other's physical attributes (see Song 4:1–7). All the senses are engaged in these erotic songs, capturing the intimacy of the lovers and their desire to share their persons and their lives with each other. The use of the term "sister" is synonymous with "bride" (see 5:1) and reflects both endearment and the granting of equal status with her husband, at least emotionally.

Direct comparison can be made between the erotic phrasing of these poems (Song 5:3–5) and those of Egyptian love songs from the eighteenth to the twentieth dynasties (1570–1197 BCE). Literary borrowing is possible since the Egyptian songs were originally composed for oral performance and traveled with merchants and soldiers from one region to another. However, the common experience of sexual interaction could also have produced similar phrasing and poetic themes.

The Song of Songs and Egyptian Love Songs

My cup is still not full from making love with you—my little jackal, you intoxicate me. I will not stop drinking your love, even if you beat me with sticks into the marsh. (Egyptian Love Songs, *OTPar*[3], 323)

How sweet is your love, my sister, my bride!
　How much better is your love than wine,
　and the fragrance of your oils than any spice!
　　(Song 4:10)

I come to my garden, my sister, my bride;
　I gather my myrrh with my spice,
I eat my honeycomb with my honey,
　I drink my wine with my milk. (Song 5:1)

Her head is a trap built from branches, . . . and I am the goose. Her hair is the bait in the trap . . . to ensnare me. (Egyptian Love Songs, *OTPar*[3], 323)

Your head crowns you like Carmel,
　and your flowing locks are like purple;
　a king is held captive in the tresses. (Song 7:5)

In addition to being seen as an example of romantic poetry, the Song of Songs has often been understood as symbolic of Yahweh's love for Israel. This would place it in the same metaphoric genre as Hosea's marriage to Gomer (Hosea 1–2) and the marriage between Yahweh and the abandoned child in Ezekiel (16:3–14). The emphasis on fidelity and personal devotion in Song of Songs (e.g., "My beloved is mine and I am his" [Song 2:16]) makes them useful to the religious establishment and to society in general.

Another interpretation of the Song of Songs is as an allegory for the search for wisdom. Wisdom is described as a woman who offers an ordered existence and maturity of thought

The Desire for Wisdom

I come to my garden, my sister, my bride;
　I gather my myrrh with my spice,
　I eat my honeycomb with my honey,
　I drink my wine with my milk.
Eat friends, drink,
　and be drunk with love. (Song 5:1)

in the book of Proverbs (8:1–9:6). This tradition is comparable to the desire expressed in Song of Songs for food and drink. Allegorical interpretations should not obscure what is most likely the original intent of the authors of these poems. They serve as examples of romantic feeling (perhaps to be recited during wedding celebrations; for wedding songs see Jer. 7:34; 16:9). They express emotions that are common even in a society of arranged marriages.

STUDY QUESTIONS

1. Compare and contrast the themes found in the love poetry in Song of Songs and those in Egyptian love songs.
2. Discuss possible interpretations of the Song of Songs and its use by the covenantal community.

THE HELLENISTIC PERIOD

Historical Overview

Alexander and the Diadochi

- Alexander's conquest of the Persian Empire pre-cipitates the development of Hellenistic culture in the Near East.
- Rivalries between Ptolemies and Seleucids continue the age-old struggle between Egypt and Mesopo-tamia for control of Syria-Palestine.
- The Maccabean Revolt leads to a short-lived, independent Jewish kingdom in Judea.
- Rome takes advantage of political infighting in Judea to oust the Hasmoneans and add Judea to the Roman province of Syria.

Figure 6.1. Coin with the head of Alexander the Great minted in Ephesus 306–281 BCE. (Baker Photo Archive, courtesy of the Art Institute of Chicago)

Alexander of Macedon (northern Greece) begins his attack on the Persian Empire in 333 BCE. After only two years of campaigning, he burns the Persian capital of Persepolis and breaks Persia's control over the Near East. His conquests and the mixing of cultures that result set the stage for the introduction of a new period in the region's history. Alexander believed in the creation of a world culture based on Greek philosophy, law, and political administration. The resulting **Hellenistic culture** develops from a synthesis of Greek ideas with the customs and traditions of the areas into which those ideas are introduced.

One sign of Alexander's determination to create such a synthesis of cultures can be seen in his inclusion of Greek scholars and scientists in his army. They introduce Greek as the principal language of culture as well as commerce and government in the conquered regions. These scholars also study local lan-guages and customs, popularizing some of them among the Greeks and thereby speed-ing the process of cultural blending. An even more far-reaching contribution to the spread of Greek culture is the founding of many new cities, such as the Egyptian Nile delta's port city of Alexandria. Over the course of their history, the Greeks had organized their society around the polis, the political community of the city-state. New immigrants to the Near East therefore expected that their lives would continue to revolve around the polis. As a result the polis and its architectural designs (gymnasium, public baths, public forum) become the major vehicle for the transmission of Greek culture to the rest of the ancient world.

The speed with which Alexander conquers the Near East reflects his own genius as a military commander as well as a general discontent with Persian rule, especially in Egypt and Syria-Palestine. Pacification of these conquered regions is made even easier when the Greeks choose to retain the old administrative structure. To establish political stability, Alexander and his successors keep officials in place who prove to be loyal to the new regime. The local economy is then stimulated by the introduction of Greek marketing techniques and fresh operating capital taken by plundering the Persian cities and the imperial treasury.

Following Alexander's untimely death in 323 BCE, his generals divide the empire among themselves. These successors, or **Diadochi**, complete the process of pacifying conquered regions and advance the introduction of Hellenistic culture. However, this rather sudden shift in leaders does mean that much of the administration of such a vast domain has to rely on Persian models. In many cases it also results in the return to the inefficient and corrupt management that has facilitated Alexander's conquest. Two of Alexander's generals quickly establish themselves as the rulers in the principal areas of the former Persian Empire. Ptolemy rules Egypt and Syria-Palestine; Seleucus gains control over the provinces of Asia (Mesopotamia and Persia) and Asia Minor. Their successors, the Ptolemies and the Seleucids, introduce elements of Greek culture: the

gymnasium, the theater, and social associations for professional, cultural, and religious groups. At the same time, these foreign rulers and their Greek subjects acclimate themselves to the patterns and traditions of their new environment, forming the hellenized culture that will dominate the area even during the Roman era, until the arrival of Islam in the seventh century CE.

Palestine under the Hellenistic Rulers

During the early years of Greek rule, the area that once held Judah and Israel and that will now be referred to as Palestine will see no drastic cultural changes. The Ptolemies exploit the economic resources of the region and put their economic and military imprint on the people. They introduce new coinage and draft Jews into the army (Josephus, *Jewish Antiquities* 12.8). They control commerce and keep an administrative presence throughout their domain by placing Egyptian agents in every town and village to collect taxes and facilitate trade interests. However, the Ptolemies, who quickly assimilate to Egyptian culture, do not attempt to impose Hellenistic ideas on the Jews. As long as the Jews pay their taxes and do not pose a threat of rebellion, then their temple worship and sacrificial system is allowed to continue unhindered. Furthermore, the high priest retains his authority over matters of religion, although the office does begin to become politicized when some officeholders attempt to curry favor with the Greeks. The writings of the Hellenistic historian Hecateus of Abdera (ca. 300 BCE) indicate just how important the high priest is as the nominal representative of the people of Judea to the Ptolemaic court. He also reports that priests take on the responsibility of local judicial officials.

Map 6.1. Roman World

For over a century after Alexander's conquest, hellenization is merely a choice rather than a requirement. Greek culture tends to become popular among Jews of the new generation after the conquest and among Jews who have regular contact with Greeks outside Palestine, such as those who live in the large Jewish communities in Antioch, Alexandria, and Damascus. Jewish merchants and administrators are especially open to hellenization because those who choose to adopt Greek language and manners tend to acquire financial and political advantages.

Competition between the Ptolemies and Seleucids for control of Syria-Palestine intensifies during the mid-third century BCE. Both sides will seek to create or maintain support for their rule among the power groups in the province. One of the most significant of the growing political conflicts occurs when the high priest Onias II takes a pro-Seleucid position and refuses to pay tribute to the Ptolemaic government in 245. Even members of the high priest's family chose sides. His nephew Joseph, the son of Tobias, remains loyal to the Egyptians and as a result obtains a post as chief tax collector of Syria and Palestine. Joseph's economic success persuades the Tobiads to become major advocates for hellenization, as noted in the writings of the Jewish historian Josephus (*Jewish Antiquities* 12.160–195).

The political loyalties of the Tobiads shift to the Seleucids after 200 BCE, when Antiochus III (223–187 BCE) wins the battle of Panion in the Upper Galilee region and gains control over Palestine and Jerusalem. This battle changes the political balance, leaving the Ptolemies bottled up in Egypt. The new high priest, Simon II, quickly transfers his allegiance to Antiochus III. Simon is the leader of a group that advocates strict adherence to

Jewish tradition with as little hellenization as possible. To obtain the support of this group, Antiochus makes a series of concessions to the leaders in Jerusalem. His decree forbids gentiles from entering the precincts of the Jewish temple. He also provides grants of financial assistance to the Jerusalem temple and authorizes an exemption from taxes for members of the priesthood and the council of elders, the **Sanhedrin** (Josephus, *Jewish Antiquities* 12.145–153; cf. Ezra 7:24).

These concessions and promises of religious freedom quickly evaporate as Antiochus III becomes embroiled in an international dispute with the Romans. He helps the Carthaginian general Hannibal and tries to aid the embattled Greeks of Asia Minor. Eventually, however, Roman territorial ambitions and military prowess are too much for both the Greeks and Antiochus. He is forced to sign a treaty in 188 BCE deeding his territories in Europe and Asia Minor to Rome. His nephew Demetrius is sent to Rome as a hostage, an event that later will help to destabilize the Seleucid monarchy. Antiochus is forced to abandon some of his previous policies because of the loss of revenues from areas taken by the Romans. He increases taxes and acquires additional revenues by plundering the temple of Bel in the Persian city of Susa. He is killed during this expedition in 187, and a brief struggle then ensues for the throne. The struggle for power ends when Antiochus IV, who surnames himself *Epiphanes* ("god appearing"), takes power in 175 by usurping the rights of Demetrius and several other legitimate claimants (see Dan. 7:1–8).

The rather chaotic position of the Seleucids sparks a new wave of political shifts in their satellite states. Onias III, Simon's successor as high priest, revives interest in a pro-Ptolemaic policy. The Tobiads, at least outwardly, continue to support Antiochus and respond to the Oniad party by taking advantage of Antiochus IV's desire for allies and additional revenues. The Tobiads purchase the office of high priest by offering to pay higher tribute to the Seleucid ruler. Antiochus IV then ousts Onias and replaces him with his pro-Seleucid brother Jason (2 Macc. 4:7–10). Onias flees to Transjordan, but his proximity to Jerusalem and his vocal opposition to the actions of the high priest eventually lead to his murder in 171 (2 Macc. 4:33–34).

As high priest, Jason attempts to improve his political position with Antiochus IV by transforming Jerusalem and the rest of Palestine into a hellenized state. His model for this policy is the capital of the Seleucid kingdom, Antioch in Syria. First Maccabees 1:11–15 describes Jason's role in carrying out Antiochus's policy of hellenization. The text describes a group of "lawless men" (Hellenizers) who willingly violate the covenant in order to please the Greek king. Opposition becomes increasingly vocal during the construction of gymnasia and because of the neglect of sacrifices (2 Macc. 4:10–15). Finally Jason is deposed after three years when a fellow Tobiad ally, Menelaus, wins the office of high priest from his rival

by outbidding him by a sum of three hundred talents of silver (2 Macc. 4:24).

Once installed as high priest, Menelaus only makes matters worse. He embezzles funds and steals sacred vessels from the temple treasury in order to pay his debts to Antiochus IV (2 Macc. 4:27–32). When Onias III denounces him for doing this, Menelaus orders that Onias be murdered (2 Macc. 4:33–34). A struggle for control of the office of high priest then ensues between Jason and Menelaus. Jason wins the contest by capturing the city of Jerusalem and driving out the Seleucid officials (2 Macc. 5:5–7).

These internal power struggles are interpreted by Antiochus IV as open rebellion against his administration. As a result, in 169 BCE he sends in Syrian troops, who subdue the province at the cost of tremendous loss of life. In addition to looting the temple treasury, Antiochus orders that a military garrison be left in Jerusalem (2 Macc. 5:11–16). In 167, probably on Menelaus's advice, Antiochus allows the Jerusalem temple to be dedicated to the Greek god Zeus (probably equated with Baal Shamem of the Syrians [1 Macc. 1:54–64]).

The admittedly biased account of these events in 1 Maccabees describes how Antiochus then institutes an anti-Jewish campaign designed to make all the subjects of the Seleucid realm one people. A series of decrees is issued to force the Jews to renounce their traditions and religious practices (1 Macc. 1:41–42). Antiochus's anger and his policies may have been sparked by the continued pressure placed on his kingdom by the Romans, but at their heart is the Seleucid king's need for money. He chooses to exercise a political rather than a purely religious policy to deal with Jerusalem and the Jews in Palestine. Still, the stipulations of his decree suggest that his plan will ultimately lead to a more complete hellenization of the Jews. Their shrines and altars are to be defiled, and swine are to be sacrificed in the temple. Other ritual acts associated with Jewish identity, such as circumcision, are prohibited (1 Macc. 1:45–48).

Temporary Independence: The Hasmonean Kingdom

The construction of an altar to the Greek god Zeus Olympios in the Jerusalem temple is often seen as the turning point in relations between Antiochus IV and the Jews (Dan. 11:31; 1 Macc. 1:54; Mark 13:14). This "abomination that makes desolate," combined with his other anti-Jewish measures, contributes to the revolt led by the priest Mattathias, of the house of Hasmon, and his sons. Such a provocative act may be a reflection of Antiochus's lack of good advice (cf. Rehoboam in 1 Kings 12:6–11). To be sure, his overdependence on Menelaus shows a lack of understanding of an ally whose motives are centered more on maintaining his position as high priest than on assisting Antiochus.

What eventually causes a shift from the infighting between the forces of Jason and Menelaus to an open revolt in Judea is unknown. However, it is likely that one factor in the revolt is the more conservative attitudes of the peasant population of the rural areas of Palestine. With their support, Mattathias, a member of a priestly family from the village of Modein, northwest of Jerusalem, refuses to obey the decree to sacrifice to idols and even kills the first Jew in Modein who attempts to obey this command. His act of rebellion signals that no further hellenization is acceptable. There is a precedent for the killing in the story of Aaron's grandson Phinehas, who kills an Israelite for marrying outside the congregation (Num. 25:6–8). In both cases the principles involved

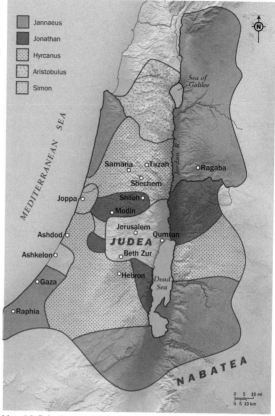

Map 6.2. Palestine under the Hasmoneans

are obedience to the covenant and maintaining the purity of the nation.

Following his act of defiance, Mattathias leads his five sons into the hill country, where they begin to wage a guerrilla war against the Seleucids and their supporters. The rebels, joined by the traditionalists called the *Hasideans* (holy ones), proclaim this war to be both a national struggle and a cultural one. Their strict adherence to the law, however, leads to terrible tragedy. A group of one thousand Jews refuse to defend themselves when they are attacked on the Sabbath, and the entire group is massacred (1 Macc. 2:29–38). More pragmatic interpretations prevail as the conflict continues, and reluctance to fight on the Sabbath is overcome by the spirit of holy war that sets aside legal restraints, at least temporarily (2:39–41).

By 164 BCE, Judas, Mattathias's oldest son, has recaptured most of Jerusalem (1 Macc. 3:1–9), thereby justifying his title *Maccabaeus* (the hammer). The title becomes the source for the name of the revolt and is sometimes applied to the rest of Judas's family (i.e., Maccabees). After Judas recaptures the temple, it is rededicated, and all restrictions on the practice of Judaism are removed. The rededication of the temple is still celebrated today as the feast of **Hanukkah**.

The final victory in this conflict is made possible by further disputes within the Seleucid royal house. After the death of Antiochus IV in 164 BCE, rival claimants attempt to outbid one another for the support of the provincial leaders. The Maccabees are also approached by some of these aspiring kings, and in return for their support they receive legitimization for their position as secular leaders of Judea. This process then goes a step further in 152, when Judas's successor, Jonathan, is appointed high priest by the Seleucid king Alexander Balas (1 Macc. 10:20).

After Jonathan's death, the people proclaim his brother Simon to be "their leader and high priest forever, until a trustworthy prophet should arise" (1 Macc. 14:41; Josephus, *Jewish Antiquities* 13.213). His appointment is particularly important since Simon is not of the Zadokite line and thus is not, according to tradition, legally entitled to hold the office of high priest (see 1 Kings 2:35). In his account of this confusing period, Josephus (*Jewish Antiquities* 16.163) notes that John Hyrcanus, Simon's successor, is given the even grander title of high priest of "God Most High." The

implication is that the Maccabees are attempting to justify their position as priests and civil leaders through a comparison with the ancestral period King Melchizedek, who is described as a ruler of Salem and the priest of "God Most High" (Gen. 14:18).

The Hasmoneans, as they are now called, take full advantage of Simon's dual authority. But a significant number of Jews dispute Maccabean claims to the high priesthood. Documents associated with the Essene community (*Rule of the Community* and the so-called *Damascus Document* from the Cairo Geniza) indicate that this is when the Essenes break from the Hasmonean party and create their own separatist group. The *Testament of Moses* (6:1), most likely a Pharisaic document dating to about 100 BCE, expresses growing discontent with the Hasmonean claims to both civil and religious authority.

Simon and his son John Hyrcanus continue to use the unsettled political situation in the Seleucid Empire to their advantage. Simon seeks out official recognition of his position from the Roman Senate in 138 BCE to add yet another dimension to his authority. The Seleucids then attempt to reassert their power at the beginning of John Hyrcanus's reign. However, according to Josephus (*Jewish Antiquities* 7.393), when Antiochus VII besieges Jerusalem, John succeeds in bribing him to leave with spoil taken from David's tomb. During the course of his long reign (135–104 BCE), John expands his area of control. Moving north, he conquers Samaria and destroys the Samaritan temple on Mount Gerizim. In the south, he forces the Idumeans, living in the area once known as Edom, to convert to Judaism and to be circumcised.

Despite these accomplishments, John is not popular with all segments of his people. His hellenized court and lifestyle are offensive to

262

the stricter elements of Jewish society. One group, known as the Pharisees, demands that he renounce the office of high priest and in one instance even accuses him of uncertain parentage, saying his mother had been a captive of Antiochus IV (Josephus, *Jewish Antiquities* 13.288–292). This does not prove to be a particularly damaging accusation, however, since John is able to rely on the support of the wealthier landowners and merchants. This group, known as the Sadducees, also controls membership in the priesthood during that time (Josephus, *Jewish Antiquities* 13.293–296). Both the Pharisees and the Sadducees eventually emerge as important elements in the political and religious history of the nation during the Roman period.

John Hyrcanus's son Aristobulus I is the first to bear the title of king of Judea (Josephus, *Jewish Antiquities* 13.301). He continues his father's expansionist policies in the north but is deposed after only one year by his brother Alexander Jannaeus (103 BCE). This man is a particularly cruel and ambitious ruler who uses the support of the Sadducees and a company of mercenary troops to impose his rule on the people. The Pharisees, however, are ardently opposed to his dual position as high priest and king. They ridicule him as he officiates at sacrifices (Josephus, *Jewish Antiquities* 13.372) and ally themselves with the Seleucid king Demetrius III with the hope of deposing him. After resisting a Seleucid invasion, Alexander manages to take a terrible revenge on his opponents. He systematically exterminates the leading families of the Pharisees, crucifying eight hundred of them and killing their wives and children during a banquet for his supporters (Josephus, *Jewish Antiquities* 13.380).

Alexander's troubling reign takes a toll on his health. On his deathbed, he advises his wife and successor, Salome Alexandra (76–67 BCE), to make peace with the Pharisees. When she appoints Alexander Jannaeus's older son, Hyrcanus II, as high priest, his more energetic brother Aristobulus II waits only until his mother's death to initiate a civil war to gain the throne.

Figure 6.2. Cave 4 at Qumran, the site near the Dead Sea of a religious sect that separated from the temple in Jerusalem. The Dead Sea Scrolls were found there. (Baker Photo Archive)

Throughout this period of political chaos, two new elements significantly influence Judean politics and have long-lasting consequences. The first is the emergence of Antipater of Idumea as a power broker in Judean affairs. He advises Hyrcanus II during his struggle against Aristobulus II and establishes himself as a man of influence in the conflict. The other new factor, however, proves to be the decisive element in the dispute between the brothers: the Mithridatic wars with Rome. These lengthy wars between Rome and Mithridates of Pontus (134–63 BCE) eventually herald the arrival in Jerusalem of Pompey, the Roman general. Rome has made alliances with the leaders of Judah as far back as Jonathan and Simon. Their interests in the Near East have been growing and are combined with their desire to prevent the Anatolian king Mithridates VI from setting up a rival kingdom that would block access to the Black Sea area. In 63, Pompey is sent to unseat him and protect the new Roman province of Syria. His success in this mission establishes Rome as the emerging power in the East.

Thus, when Pompey arrives in Damascus, he is met by representatives of many of the small kingdoms of the Near East, including Hyrcanus II and Aristobulus II of Judea. Pompey sides with Hyrcanus and takes Aristobulus captive to Rome, where he is displayed as part of Pompey's triumphal procession (Josephus, *Jewish Antiquities* 14.69–79). As a result of Pompey's intervention, Judea is added to the Roman province of Syria and is administered by Pompey's chief lieutenant, Gabinius. At that point the country is divided into five districts, each centered on a major population hub: Jerusalem, Jericho, Sepphoris in Galilee, Amathus (east of the Jordan River), and Gazara (Gezer). The Romans also claim all the cities

in the north and in Transjordan that once had been ruled by the Hasmoneans.

STUDY QUESTIONS

1. Discuss the changes Alexander and his immediate successors bring to the ancient Near East.
2. Consider how the fighting between the rival high priests contributes to the conflict over hellenization of the Jews, as well as to the political destabilization of the region.
3. Describe the actions of Antiochus IV (Epiphanes) that lead to the Maccabean Revolt and the formation of the Hasmonean kingdom.

The Book of Daniel

KEY POINTS

- The book of Daniel provides both heroic tales set in the exile period and apocalyptic visions of the end time.
- It is possible that Daniel is composed during the second century as a way to encourage the Jews during the Maccabean Revolt.
- Judaism is influenced by both Hellenistic and Zoroastrian ideas and begins to develop new beliefs and religious parties.

Although the book of Daniel is positioned right after the book of Ezekiel in the Christian canon, we have chosen to discuss it in this chapter because Daniel is probably not a prophet and the book associated with his name is most likely a Hellenistic work. The first half of the book contains a series of heroic tales that are set in the period of the exile (ca. 597–539 BCE). However, there are many similarities between the trials of Daniel and his three friends and challenges faced by the Jewish people during the Seleucid period.

Although these stories have cultural aspects that can be related to the anti-Jewish policies of Antiochus IV, there is no way to directly tie them to specific events in the Maccabean Revolt. Some of the traditions about Daniel may predate the Hellenistic period, but clearly the placing of Daniel in the Writings section of the Hebrew canon, its historical problems, and the use of late Hebrew and Aramaic words by the writer all point to a date of composition in the second century BCE.

Literary Analysis

The book of Daniel can be divided into two sections. Daniel 1–6 contains what could be called the Tales of the Young Men, that is, stories about Daniel and his three friends and their trials during the Babylonian exile. Written in narrative form centuries after the events that they depict (see the disparity over the dates in Dan. 1:1 and 2 Kings 24:8–12), these stories describe how these young men are brought to Babylon with the first group of exiles in 597 BCE. The tales depict their heroic efforts to champion their adherence to elements of the Jewish Identity Movement. In particular, they will maintain the necessity of strict obedience to the dietary laws and to a belief in Yahweh as the only god, a true monotheistic understanding of the covenant. In every way they resist being assimilated into Babylonian culture or accepting, even under threat of death, any changes in their religious practices. Daniel's ability to interpret dreams further reinforces the superiority of Yahweh over the gods of Mesopotamia and Persia.

The remaining chapters (Dan. 7–12) are apocalyptic visions. Apocalyptic literature can be defined as a special literary genre that contains secrets of the future or knowledge possessed

The Chronological Framework for the Book of Daniel

626–539 BCE	Neo-Babylonians
605–562	Nebuchadnezzar
550–332	Persians and Medes
332–63	Hellenistic Age in Palestine
301–198	Ptolemies (Egypt)
198–63	Seleucids (Asia)
175–164	Antiochus IV (Epiphanes)
	-tries to hellenize Jews
	-outlaws Judaism (167)
	-forces Jews to eat forbidden foods
	-forces Jews to sacrifice on pagan altars
	-sets up altar to Zeus in Jerusalem temple and sacrifices pigs on it
166–142	Maccabean Revolt
142	Hasmonean kingdom established

only by God and revealed only to the elect. The revelation is usually marked by bizarre imagery, cryptic numbers, and angelic interpreters. In the apocalyptic chapters, Daniel or an angel describes the visions, which deal with the eventual triumph of Yahweh over the kings, gods, and angelic armies of the Babylonians and Persians. These visions are difficult for modern readers to interpret because they are based on Israelite traditions and symbolism, and they

Characteristics of Apocalyptic Literature

Primary Characteristics
- Dualism (universe divided between two opposing forces of good and evil)
- Eschatology (study of last things, last times, last events)

Secondary Characteristics
- Visions
- Animal symbolism (sometimes with bizarrely shaped creatures)
- Numerology (mystical significance of numbers)
- Angelology and demonology

hinge on the political agenda of the writer at the time they are composed.

There is no direct relation between the earlier chapters and the apocalyptic visions other than the inclusion of Daniel in both sections. The chronology of events and the order of the kings are both different. For example, Dan. 7:1 refers to Belshazzar as the king ruling in Babylon, but Dan. 6:1 describes the accession of Darius the Mede after the death of Belshazzar. Linguistic differences further complicate the authorship problem: Dan. 1:1–2:4a and Dan. 8:1–12:13 are written in Hebrew, while Dan. 2:4b–7:28 is composed in Aramaic. There are a variety of theories regarding the appearance of the two languages in the book. Some scholars consider the Aramaic sections to be somewhat older traditions, while the Hebrew chapters may reflect the nationalistic fervor of the Jews during the Maccabean period. Based on this interpretation, it is possible that the Maccabees saw Hebrew as one of the hallmarks of their cultural identity even though it was no longer the commonly spoken language. It seems likely that the majority of the book is composed prior to 164 BCE. This conclusion is based on Dan. 11:45, which mistakenly prophesies the death of Antiochus IV in the land of Israel. The Seleucid ruler actually dies in late 164 while in Persia.

Because Daniel's visions are written in the form of apocalyptic literature, they have definite characteristics that differentiate them from prophetic visions (see inset). Particularly important here is the fact that prophets write and speak in their own names while apocalypticists use the authority attached to the name of an ancient hero or righteous person as their **pseudonym**. In addition, the sense of time is different between these two groups. Prophets believe God works within history while

> ### Differences between an Apocalypticist and a Prophet
>
> **Apocalypticist**
> - Is a writer and uses literary conventions
> - Uses a **pseudonym** instead of his own name
> - *Theme:* how to cope with this evil world
> - *Goal:* encourage people to hold on, until the end
> - Deliverance in next world
>
> **Prophet**
> - Speaks God's message
> - Uses own name
> - *Theme:* failure to obey the covenant
> - *Goal:* encourage people to repent and return to proper behavior
> - Deliverance in this world

apocalypticists believe this world is evil and that God's deliverance will come outside of history, at the time of a new creation.

Tales of the Young Men (Dan. 1–6)

After being forced into exile by the forces of the Babylonian king Nebuchadnezzar, Daniel and his friends are given Babylonian names: Belteshazzar, Shadrach, Meshach, and Abednego. This renaming process is only the first step in **acculturizing** these young men into adopting Babylonian customs. The eventual aim is to seduce them into the lifestyle of their captors, making them more loyal and sympathetic officials when they are sent back to Judah to serve as administrators. Acculturalization is a policy used by many of the empires in the ancient Near East. The conquerors assume that conquered peoples are less likely to revolt if they are administered by their own people (see Nehemiah's appointment as Yehud's governor in Neh. 2:1–8). To ensure the loyalty of these officials, at an early age they are brought to the capital of the empire, educated, and acculturized. The problem in these stories, however, is that Daniel and his friends refuse to be educated. Thus begins a recognized literary device, a court contest, designed to demonstrate these young men's heroic character, courage, and commitment to their Jewish identity. In each instance the Israelites proclaim that they will let Yahweh decide their fate rather than submit to the demand to assimilate. Like other contest motifs (see 1 Kings 18:20–40), the issue at hand is to determine who really is a god and can therefore protect the deity's worshipers from harm.

To distinguish the two story types in this section, we will first describe the tests of courage faced by Daniel and his companions (Dan. 1; 3; 6) and then discuss the chapters in which Daniel displays his ability to interpret visions and dreams (Dan. 2; 4; 5).

Dietary Laws Upheld. The new trainees are privileged to eat from the king's table. However, these meals are not prepared in a **kosher** manner, according to the dietary laws of the Jews, and may contain elements that are forbidden. Rather than allow themselves to be defiled, Daniel and his friends refuse to eat the king's food. Instead, they ask to be tested for ten days, during which they will consume only water and vegetables while other persons eat from the king's table (Dan. 1:8–14). At the conclusion of the test, Daniel and his companions are healthy and well nourished, and they are rewarded by God with wisdom and insight (1:15–17). Here and in the other stories, Nebuchadnezzar also rewards

them with positions of importance (1:18–20; 2:48–49). The courage and intelligence shown by Daniel and his friends would have been an inspiring example for the people during the oppression of Antiochus IV and the Maccabean Revolt. However, the kings in these stories (with the exception of Belshazzar in Dan. 6) are capable of learning from their mistakes and are portrayed as recognizing the power and majesty of Yahweh as the "God of gods" (2:47) and the "King of heaven" (4:37). So far there is no evidence that Antiochus IV ever reacted in this manner.

Idol Worship Rejected. In Dan. 3, Shadrach, Meshach, and Abednego refuse to obey Nebuchadnezzar's command to bow down and worship an idol (3:1–12; cf. 1 Macc. 2:15–28). Their punishment is to be thrown into a furnace, possibly an industrial-size brick kiln, to be consumed by the flames (Dan. 3:13–23). When they survive with the miraculous aid of an angelic being (3:25–26), Nebuchadnezzar responds to this miracle in a statement of faith in the "God of Shadrach, Meshach, and Abednego" that follows the pattern of other examples of the universalism theme found elsewhere in the OT/HB (Dan. 3:28–30; cf. 2 Kings 5:15–19 and Dan. 2:46–47).

In an episode very similar to the harrowing escape in Dan. 3, Daniel is placed in a den of hungry lions because he insists on praying to Yahweh in violation of the king's decree (6:13–17). Once again, divine intervention saves the life of a faithful person (6:19–22). There is also a comic twist in the story when the king, who has been tricked into sentencing Daniel to death, orders his unfaithful advisers to be cast into the lions' den (Dan. 6:24; cf. Haman's fate in Esther 7:5–10).

Dream Interpretation Motif. The stories of Daniel's ability to interpret dreams and

---

Kosher Regulations (Dietary Laws)

- "Sinew of the thigh" forbidden (Gen. 32:33)
- Passover regulations on paschal sacrifice and grain fermentation (leavened bread; Exod. 12:8–14)
- "Seething the kid in its mother's milk" forbidden (Exod. 23:19; 34:26; Deut. 14:21)
- Kosher animals (Lev. 11)

signs are found in Dan. 2; 4; and 5. Each story demonstrates the insight given to Daniel as a *khakam*, a wise man. Daniel's wisdom far exceeds that of the king or any of his advisers (cf. Joseph's interpretative ability that leads to his appointment as an Egyptian court official in Gen. 41:1–45). The first story involves the interpretation of Nebuchadnezzar's troubling dream. In his dream, the king sees a mighty statue that is divided into four separate sections of different metals: gold, silver, bronze, and a mixture of iron and clay (Dan. 2:31–35). When no one else can fathom the meaning of the dream, Daniel steps forward and proclaims that "God in heaven" has revealed the interpretation to him. Daniel explains that in Nebuchadnezzar's dream each layer of the statue represents one of the successive kingdoms that have conquered and ruled Israel or Judah. The destruction of the statue marks Yahweh's intervention and heralds the establishment of an eternal kingdom (2:36–45). Nebuchadnezzar is greatly impressed by Daniel's wisdom, and he promotes Daniel and praises the power of Daniel's God (2:47–49). Daniel supplies an interpretation similar to this one when he describes four monsters in the apocalyptic vision of Dan. 7.

Nebuchadnezzar's second troubling dream begins and ends much like the first. It involves a bounteous tree that, like the statue, is to be destroyed at the "decree of the Most High" (Dan. 4:10–17). The tree, which previously has brought great blessings to the creatures that inhabit its branches, is identified by Daniel as Nebuchadnezzar himself. Daniel states that the proud king will be humbled. He is doomed to a period of insanity, after which he will acknowledge the power of Yahweh above all else (4:24–37).

The final example of Daniel's interpretative ability is found in the story of Belshazzar's feast. Belshazzar is serving as the coregent in Babylon for his absent father, Nabonidus. The ruler arrogantly stages a feast and uses the sacred vessels from the Jerusalem temple to serve his guests. In response, a disembodied hand appears and writes a series of Aramaic words on the banquet room's wall: "*Mene, Mene, Tekel,* and *Parsin*" (Dan. 5:2–9, 25). At his queen's urging, Belshazzar summons Daniel to interpret the meaning of these words and is confronted with a prediction of the destruction of his kingdom, whose days have been numbered (*mene*), whose sins have been weighed on the scales of justice (*tekel*), and that will be "divided [*parsin*] and given to the Medes and Persians" (5:25–28). This story varies from the other two since it does not result in a statement of praise for Yahweh or in Daniel's personal advancement. However, Daniel's stature as a true seer is proved

Figure 6.3. Babylonian boundary stone. Babylon's powerful influence throughout the ancient world affected the telling of history years later, as the book of Daniel attests. (Kim Walton, courtesy of the British Museum)

when the events he describes occur (Dan. 5:30; compare 1 Kings 22:17–38).

Apocalyptic Visions (Dan. 7–12)

The apocalyptic visions in Daniel can be treated more as a body rather than as separate tales. They share the common eschatological theme that the present age is evil. All good things have been subverted, and evil seems to be triumphant everywhere. The righteous are oppressed and need encouragement to continue in their faith. The climactic intervention of God is the last hope of the righteous in the face of such disaster because this age cannot be expected to survive. When God does take action, a new age is in the making and significant change can be expected. However, great persecution, turbulence, and warfare will foretell the end days. The more intense the conflict, the more evident it is to the righteous that the end is fast approaching. An ancient Egyptian text, the Vision of Neferti, describes a similar disintegration of Egyptian society prior to the breakup of the Old Kingdom (1991–1786 BCE), and it contains the same gloomy appraisal of a world gone mad.

All these eschatological beliefs, as well as the appearance of angels as the leaders of Yahweh's forces, may have been influenced or at least reinforced by **Zoroastrianism**. This dualistic faith

---

The Vision of Neferti

I see a land of chaos,
What is happening should never have happened.
Ordinary people are at war with one another,
. . . .
They make copper arrows like soldiers,
They kill for bread.
People laugh at the misfortune of others.
No one weeps for the dying,
No one mourns and fasts,
People only look after their own welfare. (*OTPar*[3],
    337–38, lines 38–48)

---

is the principal religion of ancient Persia. Zoroastrianism may be one factor in some of the substantial changes that Judaism experiences during the Persian and Hellenistic periods, including the concept of resurrection: "Many of those who sleep in the dust of the earth shall awake, some to everlasting life, and some to shame and everlasting contempt" (Dan. 12:2).

Summary of the Visions

The visions found in the last six chapters of Daniel are filled with conflict and describe the eventual downfall of the kingdoms that have oppressed Israel. Daniel 7 contains a vision of deliverance illustrated by four fantastic beasts: a lion with eagle's wings, a bear with three ribs from its prey in its mouth, a leopard with four wings and four heads, and a terrible beast with iron teeth and ten horns (7:3–8). Like the multilayered statue in Dan. 2, each beast represents an oppressive kingdom, and the various wings, heads, and horns are symbolic of the number of kings who reigned during the time that they controlled Syria-Palestine. Various identifications have been made for these kingdoms in an attempt to establish a chronology for Daniel. The consensus today is that they run in this sequence: Babylonian (Chaldean), Medes, Persians, Seleucids (with Antiochus IV being the small horn in the fourth beast, who plucks out three other horns; 7:8, 23–25).

The reign of these kingdoms ends with the decree of the enthroned Ancient One, who appoints a messiah-like figure to have dominion over all peoples and nations forever (Dan. 7:9–14). Daniel also receives an explanation of the judgment of God over the fourth beast, which is the last to oppress Israel (7:23–28).

The vision in Dan. 8 has a similar explanation. Daniel sees a vision of a ram and a male goat, representing the Medes/Persians

Major Tenets of Zoroastrianism
• Dualistic universe, with the forces of light (good) led by Ahura-Mazda and the forces of darkness (evil) led by Ahriman
• Continual conflict between light and darkness expressed in battles fought between rival angel armies and with human supporters fighting for each side
• Eventual victory for light in a final battle
• Resurrection of the dead
• Judgment of the forces of darkness and their punishment in a lake of fire
• Eternal reward for the forces of light in a blissful afterlife

(the ram) and the successors of Alexander (the male goat). An angelic interpreter, Gabriel, is introduced to interpret the terrifying experience for Daniel (8:15–17). Gabriel's interpretation of the vision reaffirms the promise given in Daniel's earlier visions: The destructive efforts of evil leaders will be extinguished by the "Prince of princes" (8:23–25).

The vision of the seventy weeks, found in Dan. 9, provides an explanation for the length of time that Israel will be oppressed by foreign kingdoms. It is a lengthy interpretation of the meaning of Jeremiah's prophecy of a seventy-year exile (25:11–12; 29:10).

In Dan. 10–12 the last days are described for Daniel by the angel Michael (10:13–14). This description includes a historical outline that begins at the end of the Persian period, progresses through the Seleucid period, and concludes with events that the writer believes will occur in the immediate future, as viewed from his own point in time. The section includes a series of episodes, each prefaced with the statement "in those times" or "at the time of the end" (11:7, 14, 20, 29, 40). These visions are filled with descriptions of the disorder caused by uprisings and the overthrow of the Seleucid kings (11:2–45).

The culmination of these events is found in Dan. 12. Here the visionary is assured that despite the long periods of conflict, evil, and disorder, those who remain faithful will ultimately be delivered by God:

At that time Michael, the great prince, the protector of your people, shall arise. There shall be a time of anguish, such as has never occurred since nations first came into existence. But at that time your people shall be delivered, everyone who is found written in the book. (Dan. 12:1)

Happy are those who persevere and attain the one thousand three hundred thirty-five days. But you, go your way, and rest; you shall rise for your reward at the end of the days. (Dan. 12:12–13)

The injection of the resurrection of the dead in this passage suggests Zoroastrian influence and is a sign of new beliefs entering at least some strands of Judaism. In the NT period, resurrection is espoused by the Pharisees (Josephus, *Jewish Antiquities* 18.14–15; Acts 23:6–8) but rejected by the Sadducees (Josephus, *Jewish Antiquities* 18.16; Mark 12:18). Daniel's theodicy helps to explain how the Jews are able to continue to face oppression without succumbing to cultural extinction. Despite their differences on some matters of belief, these statements in Daniel do serve to encourage the Jews to remain faithful to their ancestral religion, even in the face of oppression or the allure of Hellenistic culture.

■■■■■■■ **STUDY QUESTIONS** ■■■■■■■

1. Discuss possible dates for the book of Daniel in the light of your knowledge of the Neo-Babylonian and the Hellenistic periods.

2. Explain the value of the book of Daniel to people who are being oppressed.

3. What purpose is served by the tales of the four heroic young men in Dan. 1–6?

4. Is Daniel's ability to interpret dreams a repetition of the story of Joseph's skills at the Egyptian court (Gen. 40–41; Dan. 2:1–45; 4:18–27)? Why or why not?

5. How are the basic characteristics of apocalyptic literature exemplified in Dan. 7?

6. Note the introduction of last judgment and resurrection of the dead in Dan. 12:1–3. This concept is a new development in ancient Israel. Is it likely that this belief is based on the influences of Zoroastrianism?

The Apocrypha or Deuterocanonical Books

KEY POINTS

- Although Hebrew tradition closes with Ezra, a number of Deuterocanonical books are composed during the Hellenistic period.
- In some cases, there are additions to canonical works, including to Daniel and to Esther.
- The theological concerns and fears of cultural assimilation are major themes in the Apocrypha.

There is a gap in Jewish tradition and history between the OT/HB and the NT writings. This space is partially filled by the books of the Apocrypha, which are also called the Deuterocanonical books. Because they can be counted in various ways (as individual pieces of literature or additions to previous books), the Apocrypha/Deuterocanonical books consist of seven to eighteen works. This collection includes both historical accounts and various genres of literature from the period encompassing 300 BCE to 70 CE (see "Historical Overview," at the start of ch. 6). There are continuations of some of the books in the Hebrew canon (Daniel and Esther) and additional examples of Wisdom literature and prophecy. Although the Deuterocanonical books are included in both the Septuagint and the Vulgate, they are not counted as part of the Hebrew canon, and they are not included in most of the Bible translations that are produced during the Protestant Reformation (sixteenth to seventeenth centuries CE). The result is that many modern Protestants have little or no familiarity with these books. Unlike Protestants or Jews, Roman Catholics use the term "Deuterocanon" and include all these books in their biblical canon.

The following section will provide brief descriptions and analysis of the books of the Apocrypha in the context of their time and will relate them to the rest of the canon. Many of these books were composed to entertain and encourage rather than to report on actual events. They contain numerous historical errors and anachronisms that may confuse the casual reader. The theological perspective of the authors is mostly that of the Hellenistic period, when Judaism is undergoing a transformation that affects its very roots. At that time Jews were debating the nature of life after death, the existence and function of guardian angels, and the role of the law in their lives.

Tobit

The book of Tobit is set during the period immediately after the people of the northern kingdom of Israel are deported by the Assyrians in 721 BCE. It is the only work purported to describe the lives of the people taken into exile by the Assyrians. The size and structure of Tobit classifies it as a **novella** (a literary form shorter than the novel, with a compact style and plot). It is similar in tone to the first

271

six chapters of Daniel. Tobit is probably composed sometime in the second century BCE. The book contains several literary genres in addition to the narrative: wisdom admonitions (4:5–19), laments (3:1–6, 11–15), and prayers of thanksgiving (11:14–15; 13:1–17). The story describes the trials of a devout Jew who suffers because he refuses to set aside his principles and chooses to uphold the religious traditions of his people. For his courage and devotion, Tobit is eventually rewarded by God.

The story begins with a description of Tobit's acts of charity, which include burying Jews who have been executed or murdered by the Assyrians (Tob. 1:17–18). When the Assyrian authorities discover what he is doing, they seize his property and leave him and his family destitute. Tobit's troubles are magnified when he goes blind (2:9–10). No longer able to work, Tobit and his household must be supported by his wife and his son, Tobias.

In this desperate situation, the only way that Tobit's family can survive is if Tobias can retrieve some money that his father has entrusted much earlier to a man in Ecbatana, the capital of Media in Persia (Tob. 1:14–15; 4:1–4). His journey ultimately brings Tobias into contact with another grieving Jewish family. This family has a daughter named Sarah who has been plagued by a demon, Asmodeus. The demon has killed seven of her bridegrooms on their wedding night (3:8). In her anguish, Sarah prays (3:11–15) in much the same way that Tobit has prayed for help from God (3:1–6).

Such devout behavior warrants God's attention. The angel Raphael is sent to help both Tobit and Sarah. Raphael brings Tobias and Sarah together, which fulfills Tobit's fatherly advice to uphold the principle of endogamy. His hope for the future is that Tobias will marry "a woman from among the descendants

of your ancestors" (Tob. 4:12–13). Disguised as an old man named Azariah, the angel accompanies Tobias and provides him with the advice needed to win Sarah as his wife (6:16–7:14). Raphael also instructs Tobias on how to defeat the demon. He is to use the odor of liver and heart of a fish as a protective charm (8:1–3).

When the young couple returns to Nineveh, the angel tells Tobias of a fish-based ointment that will cure Tobit's blindness (Tob. 11:7–15). After revealing his true identity, Raphael explains that the prayers of Tobit and Sarah and Tobit's previous acts of charity have brought the divine messenger to their aid (12:11–22). The positive outcome of the story is intended to encourage the Jews of the Diaspora to hold to their traditions and to trust that God will intervene on their behalf when they are in distress or danger.

Judith

The book of Judith is probably composed toward the end of the second century BCE. Evidence for this conclusion is based on many examples of historical problems in this short tale (e.g., Nebuchadnezzar is said to be the ruler of the Assyrians) and the author's familiarity with Palestinian Jewish religious practices. The tale fits into the same literary genre as a number of other stories that highlight how a woman steps forward to commit a heroic act on behalf of the people of God or to protect the rights of her household. These include the story of Judah and Tamar (Gen. 38), as well as the stories of Esther, Susanna, and Jael (in the Song of Deborah in Judg. 4–5). Judith's story mixes both historical and nonhistorical information as a backdrop to the heroic actions of this beautiful Jewish widow. She is described in glowing terms as pious and upright (Jdt. 8:4–8). Interestingly, she is also capable of coolly beheading the enemy of her people and carrying the grisly trophy out of the enemy camp in a basket in order to save her people from destruction.

The first section of the book details a military and political struggle that is threatening to divide the Assyrian Empire. The conflict begins in Persia and eventually spreads as far as the unknown Israelite town of Bethulia (Jdt. 1:1–7:32). This section of the book contains a brief recitation of the history of the Israelites, as told by Achior, the leader of the Ammonites (5:5–21). His speech provides the key to the book, citing the Deuteronomic maxim that "as long as they [the Jews] did not sin against their God they prospered, for the God who hates iniquity is with them" (5:17). In this way the audience is forewarned of the Israelites' continuous struggle to obey and trust God.

The Assyrian general's belligerent response in Jdt. 6:2 ("What god is there except Nebuchadnezzar?") sets the stage for another example of the contest-between-gods motif so common in the OT/HB (see the plague sequence in Exod. 5–12 and Elijah's Mount Carmel contest in 1 Kings 18:20–40). Once again the outcome of a war and the fate of the Jewish people are to be determined by the answer to the question, "Who truly is God?" Achior is handed over to the Israelites, and they rejoice to hear of Holofernes's "arrogance" and pray to God to protect "those who are consecrated to you" (Jdt. 6:19).

Prayers of thanksgiving, however, quickly turn to cries of fear when Holofernes's vast army is arrayed before the walls of the Israelite city of Bethulia. Faced with such impossible odds, the besieged people of Bethulia are about to surrender and bow down to the divine-king Nebuchadnezzar when they are convinced by

the elder Uzziah to give God five more days to save them (Jdt. 7:23–31). At this point Judith is introduced. She cautions the people that they should not put God to the test but should instead pray that God will give them the courage to continue to trust that their enemies would be defeated as in times past (Jdt. 8:11–27; cf. Isa. 7:3–17).

Realizing that she must also take direct action, Judith prays for success with her plan (Jdt. 9). She then transforms herself by removing her widow's garments (cf. Tamar in Gen. 38:14) and bathing and perfuming her body. The result is a startling beauty that enchants the Assyrian commander Holofernes and blinds him to any danger she may represent (Jdt. 11; cf. the Jael and Sisera episode in Judg. 4:18–21).

Figure 6.4. Judith beheads Holofernes by Gustave Doré. (Doré's English Bible/Wikimedia Commons)

After inviting her to his tent, where he hopes to seduce the beautiful widow, Holofernes overindulges and falls into a drunken stupor (Jdt. 12:10–20). Judith takes advantage of the opportunity and beheads the general (13:6–10). She returns to Bethulia with his head hidden in her food bag, and she exhorts the Israelites to use it to frighten the besieging army. The ensuing confusion caused by Holofernes's death leads to the defeat of the enemy (Jdt. 14:1–4; 14:11–15:7; cf. the story of Ehud in Judg. 3:12–30).

Perhaps the most significant event in the story of Judith for Jews in the Hellenistic period is Achior's conversion to Yahweh worship (Jdt. 14:5–10). His firm belief in God and submission to circumcision follow the pattern of the universalism theme as it appears elsewhere in the OT/HB. As in these previous cases, a non-Israelite is used to highlight the power of Yahweh (cf. Naaman in 2 Kings 5:15 and Ruth's conversion ritual in Ruth 1:16–17).

Judith functions as a trickster figure in this story, much as Jacob and Esther do in their stories. She stands as a model of proper behavior (wisdom theme), even though she lies and murders to save God's people, like Jael in Judg. 4:17–22 and Judg. 5:24. These themes and characters are very popular with Jews during the Hellenistic period.

Additions to Esther

The Greek version of the book of Esther (Add. Esther) dates to the period of the second or first century BCE and is considerably longer than the Hebrew version. In most of the chapters, one finds additions that clarify and elaborate on the narrative. These narrative details include copies of the king's letters (13:1–7; 16:1–24) and a description of Mordecai's dream (11:2–11). They may be added

to deal with theological concerns raised in the Hebrew version, such as the absence of any direct mention of God. A woman serving as the central figure in the story may also bother the male-dominated, Hellenistic Jewish community (cf. Sir. 26:6–18). That may explain why Mordecai is given a much more significant role in the Greek version. The desire for vengeance, so prominent in Esther 9:5, is also softened, and the number of enemies slain is drastically reduced (75,000 in Esther 9:16, compared with 15,000 in the Greek version, Add. Esther 9:16).

Wisdom of Solomon

The Wisdom of Solomon is composed between 30 BCE and 50 CE. It consists of a collection of wisdom sayings and admonitions that are compiled by the Jewish community in Alexandria, Egypt. It is written in a lyric Greek style, fiercely attacking pagan worship and the Egyptians (perhaps as a response to anti-Jewish riots in 38 CE). Its late date is also indicated by the theme of the immortality of the soul, which develops in Judaism only after the Hellenistic period (see Dan. 12:1–3).

As is common in Greek and Hebrew Wisdom literature (see Prov. 8:22–31), the central figure in these sayings is "Woman Wisdom" (Greek *sophia*), the manifestation of God's power and glory:

For she is a breath of the power of God,
and a pure emanation of the glory of
the Almighty;
therefore nothing defiled gains entrance
into her.
For she is a reflection of eternal light,
a spotless mirror of the working of
God,
and an image of his goodness. (Wis.
7:25–26)

Although other names are also used for wisdom (*logos*; Wis. 18:15), the concept remains essentially the same.

The author uses the theme of measure for measure as the basis for wise judgment and divine action. Comparison is also a device that is employed here, using seven separate antitheses to show how Egypt is punished and Israel is rewarded (see Wis. 11:1–14; 16:1–19:22). In each of these antitheses, the Egyptians are subjected to plagues (hunger, darkness, thunderstorms) while the Israelites are protected or provided for by God.

Throughout the book the author exhorts fellow Alexandrian Jews to take pride in their heritage and to hold fast to their faith despite the allure of Greek and Roman religions. The arguments for remaining in the faith are designed to offset anti-Jewish attacks and the fears of oppression faced by a minority people living in a foreign land.

Sirach

Unlike most biblical books, Sirach (Ecclesiasticus) is signed by its author, Jesus Ben Sira (Joshua son of Sirach [Sir. 50:27]). Ben Sira is a teacher in Jerusalem during the period 200 to 180 BCE. His book is completed prior to the Maccabean Revolt (167–142 BCE), during a turbulent time when the issue of hellenization is tearing the Jewish community apart. The cultural conflict is compounded by the political ambitions of the family of the high priest, which wishes to gain favor with the Ptolemaic and Seleucid rulers (see "Historical Overview" at the start of ch. 6). Ben Sira's task is to defend the basic elements of Jewish identity, defined as strict obedience to the law, and its traditional beliefs and practices.

Ben Sira attempts to do this by directing attention to the law and by emphasizing that it is equated with "the fear of the Lord." Awe of Yahweh's power will hold the believer to right action and right speech. The following are examples of his theme:

> Do not glorify yourself by dishonoring
> your father,
> for your father's dishonor is no glory
> to you.
> The glory of one's father is one's own
> glory,
> and it is a disgrace for children not
> to respect their mother. (Sir.
> 3:10–11)

> With all your soul fear the Lord,
> and revere his priests.
> With all your might love your Maker,
> and do not neglect his ministers. (Sir.
> 7:29–30)

> Whose offspring are worthy of honor?
> Human offspring.
> Whose offspring are worthy of honor?
> Those who fear the Lord.
> Whose offspring are unworthy of
> honor?
> Human offspring.
> Whose offspring are unworthy of
> honor?
> Those who break the commandments. (Sir. 10:19)

One particularly enlightening segment in Ben Sira's work is the prologue, which includes a mention of "the Law and the Prophets and the other books of our ancestors." The mention of these three collections of books suggests that the groupings of the canon are becoming more formalized by the second century BCE. During the course of his admonitions, Ben Sira mentions every book of the Hebrew canon except Ezra, Daniel, Esther, and Ruth.

Ancient Egyptian Wisdom: Denouncing Fools

Foolish dreamers become casualties of unwise actions. (Teachings of Ptah-hotep, *OTPar³*, 286)

Do not treat fools the way that fools treat you. (Instruction of Amenemope, *OTPar³*, 295)

The wise seek friends. Fools seek enemies. (Teachings of Ankhsheshonq, *OTPar³*, 313)

Their absence may be due to the fact that these books are not yet set in their final written form at the time that Ben Sira is active.

Because Ben Sira's aim is to pattern his work after other ancient wisdom pieces, his statements have close parallels to those found in the book of Proverbs and in Egyptian wisdom literature. Like many of these works, Sirach has little patience for "the fool" (8:17; 20:13).

Since Ben Sira wishes to focus the people's attention on the guidance provided by the law, his central theme is the requirement that members of the community be honorable and avoid shameful action. Much of his advice centers on right speech and thoughtful reflection before speaking (Sir. 20:7; 21:11; 23:7–15). The one who acts in an honorable manner is careful to observe proper discretion while still speaking out when the law demands it (11:7–9).

The book employs several typical styles of Wisdom literature (e.g., use of parallel lines) in much the same way they are used in the book of Proverbs. However, the structure of the book is too disjointed to allow for a coherent reading from beginning to end. Among its many notable features are the psalm to Wisdom in Sir. 1 and the hymn honoring famous men in Sir. 44–50, including figures from Enoch to Nehemiah. The choice of notable persons in this list is interesting, especially the obvious exclusion of important female figures, another clue to why there is also no reference to the books of Ruth and Esther. Ben Sira reflects a

Jewish androcentric society that places restrictions on the roles of its women.

Due to the varied nature of its contents, it is probably best to see this book as a reference work, with advice provided on individual items (e.g., physicians, death, women, and friends). Ben Sira's rather rigid views on other cultures reflect the Jewish struggle with Hellenistic influences during his time period.

Baruch

Although authorship of this short book is attributed to Baruch, the friend of Jeremiah, that is unlikely. The book of Jeremiah says that both Jeremiah and Baruch are taken to Egypt in about 586 BCE (Jer. 43:1–7), not Babylon, following the destruction of Jerusalem (contrast Bar. 1:1). In addition, the writing style and the apparent dependence on the book of Daniel are more suggestive of compositions in the second century BCE. Therefore, our conclusion is that Baruch's name is chosen to add greater authority to this work.

The book consists of three unconnected poems. They each have distinct vocabulary (e.g., each respectively uses "Lord," "God," and "Everlasting" for God) and are tied together by a narrative introduction. There is a

---

Hymn in Praise of Famous Men

Enoch pleased the Lord and was taken up. . . .
Abraham was the great father. . . .
Moses . . . [was] made . . . equal in glory to the
    holy ones. . . .
He exalted Aaron, a holy man like [Moses]. . . .
Phineas . . . ranks third in glory. . . .
Joshua son of Nun was mighty in war. . . .
As the fat is set apart from the offering of
    well-being,
    so David was set apart from the Israelites. . . .
Solomon reigned in an age of peace. . . .
Elijah arose, a prophet like fire. . . .
Josiah is like blended incense. (Sir. 44:16, 19;
    45:1–2, 6, 23; 46:1; 47:2, 13; 48:1; 49:1)

---

prose prayer (Bar. 1:15–3:8), a wisdom poem (3:9–4:4), and a poem of consolation (4:5–5:9). The prose poem contains a number of quotations taken from both Daniel and Jeremiah (cf. Bar. 1:15–2:19 with Dan. 9:4–19). The poem of consolation appears to be heavily influenced by the work of Second and Third Isaiah (Isa. 40–66), especially in Baruch's use of the Zion theme: "Take courage, O Jerusalem, for the one who named you will comfort you" (Bar. 4:40; see Isa. 40:1–2).

The metaphorical use of clothing in Baruch has interesting parallels with a passage in the apostle Paul's Letter to the Ephesians:

> Take off the garment of your sorrow
>   and affliction, O Jerusalem,
>   and put on forever the beauty of the
>   glory from God.
> Put on the robe of the righteousness
>   that comes from God;
>   put on your head the diadem of the
>   glory of the Everlasting;
> for God will show your splendor every-
>   where under heaven. (Bar. 5:1–3)

> Stand therefore, and fasten the belt of truth around your waist, and put on the breastplate of righteousness. As shoes for your feet put on whatever will make you ready to proclaim the gospel of peace. (Eph. 6:14–15)

These parallels suggest either a common theme throughout ancient literature or influences from the Apocryphal/Deuterocanonical books on the NT writers (see Isa. 11:5; Wis. 5:17–20; 2 Cor. 6:7; 1 Thess. 5:8).

The Letter of Jeremiah

Composed in the form of a letter (included as ch. 6 in Baruch in the Vulgate and in the KJV of the Apocrypha), the Letter of Jeremiah is almost unique in the writings attributed to the OT/HB period. The letter form is common in postexilic literature from the time of Ezra onward and later in the NT. This suggests a late date for the Letter of Jeremiah and perhaps an early influence on various NT works. The Letter of Jeremiah imitates the style found in Jer. 29:1–23 and purports to be addressed to the exiles in Babylon. Its primary purpose is to exhort the exiles not to worship foreign gods and images, and it uses several canonical texts to make its case (Deut. 4:27–28; Isa. 40:18–20; Jer. 10:2–16). Biting satire is employed to ridicule these idols as a way of challenging their divinity and arguing that Yahweh is the only true God (cf. Isa. 44:9–20; 46:1–7). Since it draws on these earlier works, it is usually dated to the Hellenistic period, most probably the early second century BCE.

The letter consists of ten warnings against idolatry. Statues of deities are denounced as mere human creations; they are not representations of the true God (compare Isa. 40:18–20). The style and content of the Letter of Jeremiah are not particularly original. The author is content to use the arguments of earlier writers.

Additions to Daniel

There are three additions to Daniel not found in the text of the OT/HB.

The Prayer of Azariah and the Song of the Three Jews. The Prayer of Azariah and the

---

The Futility of Idols

They are bought without regard to cost,
    but there is no breath in them. (Ep. Jer. 6:25)

Goldsmiths are all put to shame by their
    idols;
for their images are false,
    and there is no breath in them. (Jer. 10:14b;
    cf. Isa. 46:6)

Song of the Three Jews is an addition to the book of Daniel that is generally found inserted between Dan. 3:23 and Dan. 3:24 as part of the story of the survival of the three Jewish heroes Shadrach, Meshach, and Abednego in the fiery furnace. The insertion provides additional information on the episode, as well as unrelated theological reflections. For example, the Prayer of Azariah (vv. 1–22) is a national lament similar to those found in Pss. 44 and 80. Since the three young men in Daniel's version have not committed the sin of idolatry when they are ordered into the furnace by Nebuchadnezzar, this prayer of confession and repentance does not fit the character of the story. But it does have value, for the postexilic Jewish community is not always as faithful as these three heroes.

The second portion of this insertion (Pr. Azar. 23–27) provides a detailed description of the furnace and its fuel. The last section (Pr. Azar. 28–68) is a song of thanksgiving sung by the three young men, who have been miraculously saved from the flames. It is a litany, with the phrases "blessed are you" and "bless the Lord" at the beginning of each statement, followed by the antiphonal response "sing praise to him." The structure of the song can be compared with that found in Pss. 146–149.

Susanna. Susanna is considered to be chapter 13 of the Greek version of the book of Daniel and probably dates to the late second century or early first century BCE. This fictional addition provides yet another example of a righteous person who is faced with false accusations and then is vindicated (cf. Joseph in Gen. 37–50; Esther; the three young men in Dan. 3 and 6; Tobit). One unique aspect of the story is its setting in a local court of law rather than in a royal court. It has a detective-story quality, with the flavor of a courtroom drama added to make the story even more suspenseful and entertaining.

The principal theme in the tale of Susanna is false accusation. A beautiful married woman arouses the sexual desire of two of the elders who serve as judges in the exilic community in Babylon. They are overcome with lust, and when they have the opportunity, they propose that she give herself to them or they will denounce her as an adulteress (Sus. 15–21; cf. the seduction of Joseph by Potiphar's wife in Gen. 39:7–18). Their argument is strong, because she is caught with them alone and there are no witnesses to refute the claims of the elders. Rather than commit the same sin with which they threaten to accuse her, Susanna cries out for help (Sus. 22–27). Because her accusers are elders, Susanna is forced to go to trial, and initially she is condemned to death (34–41).

Susanna's prayers for help are heard by God, and at this point Daniel appears in the story as the inspired and fair judge. He separates the two elders. Variations in their testimony prove that they are lying (Sus. 47–59). Absolved of guilt, Susanna and her husband rejoice in a God who rises up men like Daniel to aid the people. In this way the exilic community reinforces its faith in God and in the protection afforded by the law.

Bel and the Dragon. Yet another addition to the book of Daniel (ch. 14 in the Greek version) is titled Bel and the Dragon. It includes two sections that denounce the worship of idols. Like Susanna, it is probably composed in the second century BCE. It contains a slightly more fantastic version of the lions' den episode than does the version found in Dan. 6, but it is truer to historical and political fact than Dan. 6 because Cyrus is listed as the Persian ruler rather than Darius the Mede.

The story describes Daniel's conflict with the priests of the god Bel. They denounce him for not worshiping their god. Daniel is able to prove to the king that the sacrificial meals fed to Bel have been eaten by his priests and their families (Bel. 19–20). He then kills the great dragon that they have been worshiping by feeding it a mixture of pitch, fat, and hair (Bel. 27). In this way, Daniel proves that Bel is not a god.

Despite Daniel's efforts to display the truth, the king is faced with public outcry over the destruction of the native cult and is even called a Jew himself (cf. Judg. 6:28–32). The frightened ruler is forced to throw Daniel into the lions' den. The prophet Habakkuk is suddenly thrust into the story to provide an additional miraculous element. An angel transports him by his hair (cf. Ezek. 8:3) to Babylon to feed Daniel during his imprisonment. As a result, the hero is able to survive for a week with the lions. The king acknowledges the power of Israel's God with the statement, "You are great, O Lord, the God of Daniel, and there is no other besides you!" This exclamation follows the pattern of similar statements made by Nebuchadnezzar in Dan. 3:28 and Dan. 4:3 and the pattern found in other examples of the universalism theme (Rahab in Josh. 2:11; Naaman in 2 Kings 5:15).

1 and 2 Maccabees

The books of the Maccabees are useful in reconstructing the history of the Hellenistic period (see our survey above). These books contain an enormous amount of data on the history of the period and of various developments within Judaism. But much of this material, like that in the books of Kings and Chronicles, must be used carefully in any historical reconstruction because of the strong propagandistic and theological slant of the writers.

> **The Decision of Mattathias**
>
> But Mattathias answered and said in a loud voice: "Even if all the nations that live under the rule of the king obey him, and have chosen to obey his commandments, everyone of them abandoning the religion of their ancestors, I and my sons and my brothers will continue to live by the covenant of our ancestors." (1 Macc. 2:19–20)

The book of 1 Maccabees is probably composed during the reign of John Hyrcanus (134–104 BCE). Its narrative traces the events from the conflicts leading up to the Maccabean Revolt and concludes with John Hyrcanus's accession to the high priesthood in 134. Like other documents of its time, the poems, speeches, and letters quoted in the text may well be free compositions by author(s) who wish to bolster the program and the rule of the Hasmonean kings (1 Macc. 3:3–9; 14:4–15; cf. 2 Macc. 8:18–20). The appearance of a number of quotations or paraphrases from the books of Samuel and Psalms in 1 Maccabees indicates the availability of these earlier biblical traditions and their use in later writings:

> The flesh of your faithful ones and their
> blood
>   they poured out all around
>   Jerusalem,
> and there was no one to bury them.
>   (1 Macc. 7:17; Ps. 79:2–3)

> How is the mighty fallen,
>   the savior of Israel! (1 Macc. 9:21;
>   2 Sam. 1:19)

1 Esdras (Latin Vulgate: 3 Esdras or Greek Ezra)

First Esdras is made up of a selection of parallel passages from Chronicles, Ezra, and Nehemiah, but this Greek work from the second century BCE serves as a slightly different version of the older material. The return from exile (cf. 1 Esd. 2:1–15 with 2 Chron. 36:22–23 and Ezra 1:1–3), the rebuilding of the temple and its community in Jerusalem (cf. 1 Esd. 5:47–55 with Ezra 3:1–7), and the expulsion of foreign wives by Ezra (cf. 1 Esd. 9:37–55 with Neh. 7:73b–8:13) dominate the narrative of 1 Esdras. Its emphasis on the roles of Ezra and Zerubbabel and its exclusion of Nehemiah suggest authorship by a group who saw Ezra and Zerubbabel as the truly important figures in their version of history. Josephus, the Jewish historian of the first century CE, uses 1 Esdras in compiling his *Jewish Antiquities*. Therefore it is likely that prior to the completion of the Hebrew canon, this version of events held equal weight with the Hebrew text and is therefore of interest to those who wish to compare the material and the time period.

A unique section of this book is the "debate of the three bodyguards" in 1 Esd. 3–4. Whiling away their shift, they argue over the relative strength of wine, kings, and women. The authors have modified the original story by appending truth to the statement regarding the power of women (3:12) and by naming Zerubbabel as the third young man (4:13). Zerubbabel wins the debate and is rewarded by King Darius. Having impressed the monarch and his court, Zerubbabel is able to ask the Persian king to fulfill Cyrus's vow to rebuild the temple in Jerusalem (4:42–62; cf. Joseph in Gen. 41:37–45 and Daniel in Dan. 5:10–29).

Which Is the Strongest?

"Let each of us state what one thing is strongest." . . . The first wrote, "Wine is strongest." The second wrote, "The king is strongest." The third wrote, "Women are strongest, but above all things truth is victor." (1 Esd. 3:5, 10–12)

---

2 Esdras (4, 5, 6 Ezra; Apocalypse of Ezra; Latin Vulgate: 4 Esdras)

Though the bulk of 2 Esdras is composed originally in Hebrew or Aramaic, the present form of the book derives from a Greek translation. That version has substantial additions incorporated into the text. Unfortunately, much of the original Greek text has survived only in later translations into Latin, Syriac, Coptic, Arabic, and Armenian works.

Second Esdras 3–14 is composed in about 100 CE. This part of 2 Esdras is a Jewish work that is usually referred to as *4 Ezra* in modern scholarship. Second Esdras 1–2 is a later Christian addition that is often called *5 Ezra*. Second Esdras 15–16 is an even later Christian addition now known as *6 Ezra*. Our discussion will be limited to the original Jewish document (*4 Ezra* = 2 Esd. 3–14).

The book of *4 Ezra* is the only book in the Apocrypha that is an **apocalypse** (a book containing symbolic visions and revelations concerning the end of time). It is comparable in form to Isa. 24–27; Dan. 7–12; and Zech. 9–14. As is the case in these earlier books, *4 Ezra* includes signs and premonitions:

Now concerning the signs: lo, the days are coming when those who inhabit the earth shall be seized with great terror, the way of truth shall be hidden, and the land shall be barren of faith. (2 Esd. 5:1)

At that time Michael, the great prince, the protector of your people, shall arise. There shall be a time of anguish, such as has never occurred since nations first came into existence. (Dan. 12:1)

See, a day is coming for the LORD, when the plunder taken from you will be divided in your midst. (Zech. 14:1)

Like other apocalyptic literature, *4 Ezra* speaks of both public and secret testimony. The latter should be revealed only "to the wise among your people. For in them is the spring of understanding, the fountain of wisdom, and the river of knowledge" (2 Esd. 14:46–47). The author of *4 Ezra* also attempts to establish a greater authority for the book by using Ezra as a pseudonym (a fictitious name derived from some great figure of the past, in this case Ezra).

The book of *4 Ezra* consists of seven revelations that are presented to the author by the angel Uriel (2 Esd. 3:1–5:20; 5:21–6:34; 6:35–9:25; 9:38–10:59; 11:1–12:51; 13:1–58; 14:1–48). These revelations are primarily concerned with the wickedness of Rome, symbolically named Babylon, just as in Rev. 14:8. Uriel reveals how to deal with the problems and concerns voiced by the Jewish community as an oppressed people within the Roman Empire. In particular, Uriel instructs the author on the issues of divine justice and the relative merits of human and divine knowledge (cf. Job 38:1–7; Wis. 9:16).

Prayer of Manasseh

The Prayer of Manasseh is composed in the first century BCE. It is a penitential prayer based on 2 Chron. 33:10–17 that provides the occasion for Manasseh's restoration to the throne in Jerusalem. The narrative in 2 Kings 21:10, unlike the Chronicles account, leaves Manasseh with the reputation as the most evil king in Judah's history. In this way, the Deuteronomistic Historian is able to contrast him with his righteous grandson Josiah. For the postexilic community, however, it was important for God to be both just and forgiving. Thus Manasseh's repentance, his prayer, and ultimately his restoration serve as a model for

> **Questions of a Seer**
>
> Then I said in my heart, Are the deeds of those who inhabit Babylon any better? Is that why it has gained dominion over Zion? For when I came here I saw ungodly deeds without number, and my soul has seen many sinners during these thirty years. And my heart failed me, because I have seen how you endure those who sin, and have spared those who act wickedly, and have destroyed your people, and protected your enemies, and have not shown to anyone how your way may be comprehended. Are the deeds of Babylon better than those of Zion? (2 Esd. 3:28–31)
>
> Then the angel that had been sent to me, whose name was Uriel, answered, ... "Your understanding has utterly failed regarding this world, and do you think you can comprehend the way of the Most High?" ... "I have been sent to show you three ways, and to put before you three problems." ... "Go, weigh for me the weight of fire, or measure for me a blast of wind, or call back for me the day that is past." (2 Esd. 4:1–3, 5)

the people. Based on this episode, Yahweh retains the image of a God of justice while maintaining the ability to be merciful in the face of true repentance.

> For the sins I have committed are more
> in number
> than the sand of the sea;
> my transgressions are multiplied,
> O Lord, they are multiplied!
> I am not worthy to look up and see the
> height of heaven
> because of the multitude of my iniquities. (Pr. Man. 9)

The belief in the redemption of even the worst offender can also be found in the story of Ahab's repentance when faced with Elijah's curse (1 Kings 21:25–29) or Manasseh's repentance in the Chronicler's account (2 Chron. 33:10–12). Clearly the theodicy of the exile can be explained in the portrayal of a just God who takes notice of the people's cleansing confession.

1. Explain how the Apocrypha, or Deutero-canonical books, differ from the books in the Hebrew canon, and discuss why they are not included in the Hebrew canon.

2. Discuss the ways in which the book of Tobit can be used to describe the exiles and the problems they faced.

3. Compare the book of Judith with the book of Susanna, the book of Esther, and the story of Jael in Judg. 4–5. In what ways do these women exemplify the basic values of their community?

4. Point out examples of how the book of Sirach compares and contrasts with the book of Proverbs. What is particularly distinctive about Sirach's view of his world?

5. Discuss the possible reasons for the additions to the book of Daniel and to the book of Esther. Do they substantially add to the story, or are they designed to reflect a later understanding of the meaning of these books?

6. Compare the books of Maccabees with the stories of the young men in Dan. 1–6. How do the events of the Maccabean Revolt compare with the trials faced by Daniel and his friends?

7

CONCLUDING REMARKS

Developing Traditions

Although the narrative of the OT/HB officially ends in the Persian period, the influence of these stories on Jewish culture continues to live on in the Apocryphal/Deuterocanonical books and in the NT writings. Since the people of the ancient world considered history to be a significant source of identity, it is only natural that they continue to study and use their literary and religious heritage. This is not to say that no change in their culture is possible, for Judaism does not remain static. The immediate inheritors of the biblical tradition of law and story, the Jews of the rabbinic period (first century BCE through seventh century CE) and the early Christian community, create new and vibrant religious movements that build on the foundation of the OT/HB and allow for the changes that are made necessary by life within the Roman Empire. They use their cultural heritage to shape dynamic and growing cultures that build on the past and lay the foundation for the future of their religions and their scattered people.

Evidence for the use of the material in the OT/HB can be found in the Jewish commentaries of the rabbinic period (ca. 70–500 CE). The teachings of prominent rabbis, among them Hillel and Shammai, are compiled in 200 CE into the Mishnah. The sections or tractates of this work of **halakah** (rules for human conduct) are arranged into topics such as religious feasts and festivals, matters concerning women, and holy objects. In the period between 400 and 600 CE, the Palestinian and Babylonian Talmuds are produced by rabbis to serve as commentaries on the Mishnah. These scholarly works quote portions of the Mishnah passages, sections of the HB, and then relevant and detailed comments by the rabbis. A reference work like this is referred to as **haggadah** and is designed to draw together the strands of tradition contained in Scripture, the Mishnah, and the commentaries. At a later stage in the history of interpretation, these early works are augmented by the comments and decisions laid down by the great medieval rabbis—Maimonides, Rashi, and Ibn Ezra. Mysticism and elaborate interpretations of the law develop side by side during this process. The richness of the text allows for multiple interpretations, contributing to the creation of new religious communities and inspiring a vast range of scholarly discussions on the relation between the Jewish people and their God.

In the Christian writings, it is easy to identify the use of the OT/HB in both thought and quotation. Nearly 10 percent of the NT alludes to the OT/HB, and about 4.5 percent is direct quotation. For instance, Paul quotes the OT/HB ninety-three times and makes many allusions to Hebrew Scriptures. The early church fathers (150–400 CE) employ typology and allegory when dealing with OT/HB stories, social customs, and characters. Their events are designed to illuminate Christian doctrine, such as the importance of the cross displayed by the setting up of the bronze serpent by Moses to redeem the people and cure them of snakebite (Num. 21:4–9; John 3:14). The use of allegorical interpretations of Scripture, however, sparks controversy in the early church, and eventually church councils are called (between 400 and 509) to deal with these issues and to establish a firm doctrinal base for the church as a whole. In particular, the work of the councils is designed to suppress heresy (unorthodox beliefs).

While it has become acceptable to downplay the importance of the OT/HB and to emphasize the gospel message since the time of the Protestant Reformation, this approach does not do justice to the immense importance of these earlier writings. The NT writers are steeped in the ancient traditions of the Israelites. It is inconceivable to think that both the NT writers and their audience would gloss over the material found in the OT/HB as unimportant. For those modern readers who wish to study the development of Christian tradition, it is misguided to do so.

The other religious descendant of Judaism and the writings of the OT/HB is Islam. Muhammad points to Abraham and Ishmael as the founders of the Arab tribes and accepts both Judaism and Christianity as "religions of the book" and precursors to his own revelation. In medieval tradition, Islam also shares an interest in the prophetic figure Elijah, who functions in mystical Judaism as an adviser to rabbis, instructing them on the secrets of the universe (Qur'an 6:89; 37:123–132). Muslim writers report a meeting between Elijah and Muhammad, and Sufi Muslims equate Elijah with the immortal prophet Khidr. As a result of these and other shared traditions, the third major Western religion, Islam, also emphasizes a monotheistic perspective common to Judaism and Christianity.

Relevance of Studying the Bible in Today's World

Perhaps the greatest relevance of the biblical materials for our own world can be found in the value attributed to biblical traditions in the writings produced by members of these three vibrant religions. They have chosen to formulate many aspects of their belief systems based on the ancient teachings found in the Bible. The followers of these major world religions constantly cite passages from the text and note that their ritual and traditions have their origin in events recounted by the biblical writers. Thus if we are to understand the most basic assumptions as well as the often-contentious issues that divide our modern society, in the United States and in other countries, then we must be aware of the roots of the beliefs and philosophies that govern our speech and thoughts. For instance, the conflicts that arise in our own culture over the interpretation of

Some of the Values of Studying the OT/HB

Obtain a clearer understanding of the basic traditions that shape human culture

- We do not live in Eden and must therefore learn to survive in this world while recognizing the need to conserve the resources placed in our charge (Gen. 3:16–19; Ps. 74:12–17).

- It is the responsibility of each generation to care for one another and faithfully teach those values that keep a society intact and free from anarchy (Exod. 20:12; Prov. 6:20–22).

- The world is a complex place, and those who understand how power, privilege, and authority operate have a better chance of survival

and of effecting change themselves (Deut. 8:17–20; Isa. 7:1–9).

- Justice is a goal that is not always achieved but is always worth striving for (Exod. 22:21–27; Amos 5:14–15).

Recognize how the OT/HB serves as a foundation for the NT

- The Shema (Deut. 6:4) provides the creedal statement of Jewish monotheism that undergirds both NT and Judaic theology.

- The Hebrew tradition of the righteous person who can "stand before the Lord" because of obedience to the Torah (cf. Ps. 24:3–6) is broadened in the parables of the NT (Luke 18:8–14). There is a recognition that failure to have a prayer heard may be based on the

degree of repentance (see Ahab's humbling acts in 1 Kings 21:27–29).

- Easy comparisons can be made between Jesus's career and the miracle stories of Elijah and Elisha (1 Kings 17–2 Kings 8; Matt. 15:32–38; 17:1–12) or the suffering of prophets like Isaiah and Jeremiah (Isa. 52:13–53:12; Jer. 20:7–18; Matt. 5:12; Luke 11:47–51).

- The socially and economically vulnerable (widows, slaves, the sick, and the poor) are attracted to Jesus's message and healing, and this is in line with OT/HB concerns for these weakest members of society (Exod. 22:22–24; Isa. 1:17; Mal. 3:5; Luke 4:39; 18:43; James 2:1–17).

- Jesus provides a strong affirmation of Torah (Matt. 5:17–18; 7:12).

the Bible; over the display of biblical materials (e.g., the Ten Commandments) in schools, courthouses, and other public buildings; and over the place of religion in public life—such conflicts dictate that we must be familiar with what the Bible says. If we are to understand the cultural complexities of our own multinational community and of the world community at large, then we must start with the religious values that have shaped these communities. Conflict and compromise or war and peace may well hinge on how well we do this.

We hope that every reader will continue to study the OT/HB so that its value will become more obvious. We conclude with additional resources to assist in that future study.

How to Evaluate Bible Translations

It is essential that the student find a biblical translation that will encourage careful reading and study. Many good translations are

available, and not one is superior for every purpose. The questions and explanations below can be used to help evaluate Bible translations.

Has the Best Text Been Used to Make This Translation? We do not possess the original manuscripts of any biblical writer. We only rarely have the original manuscript for any ancient text. The exceptions are inscriptions that have been carved in stone or on clay tablets. So what we have for the Bible are copies of originals made by scribes and monks over the centuries. Like other human copies, they are not always identical. Today we have hundreds, even thousands, of manuscripts and fragments written in many languages that are available to help us reconstruct the original words of the text. That reconstruction process is called textual criticism (or textual analysis, if "criticism" holds too many negative connotations), and the goal is to reconstruct as accurately as possible all of the words of the Bible. Scholars have to use the many different manuscripts to determine what might be the most likely original words. So no single ancient manuscript always has the best readings. The best text to use for translation is therefore an eclectic text. This means each variant in the ancient manuscripts has been evaluated separately to determine its proximity to the original.

It is obvious that all of us are greatly indebted to those scholars who labor diligently over ancient texts and variant readings to reconstruct as accurately as possible all the words of the Bible. Their work is never final because of the subjective nature of any reconstruction of the text and because additional manuscripts are being discovered and read. It should also be clear that the KJV, like other older versions, does not have the benefit of all of the new manuscripts discovered in the four hundred years since it was completed in 1611.

To decide whether a translation is based on the best text, check the introductory preface for specific statements. Does it say that this is an eclectic text or that each variant in the ancient manuscripts has been evaluated separately? Check key passages. Almost all modern translations indicate the questionable nature of certain passages in their footnotes. Determine whether they have been omitted, put in the footnotes or margins, put in the text, or set in brackets. The preferred approach is to put questionable words or passages in footnotes or to omit them.

How Accurate Is the Translation? Have the latest philological and linguistic insights been used? Is there a fidelity to seeking out the best approximation of the original meaning? Here the average student has no way of checking since he or she seldom knows Greek or Hebrew. Therefore, two general questions will test the accuracy of a translation.

Is it up to date? Check the copyright date. In general, the newer the translation, the more likely it is up to date. Try to determine if the translation is a revision of an earlier translation or a reprint of an earlier translation. There are several reprints with new names. Do not take the date of printing at face value.

Did the translation team consist of a cross-section of religious groups? No single individual can stay current with all the new scholarship that is necessary to make the best translation. Team translations are always preferable. Generally, the greater the diversity of the team, the better the translation will be.

Is the Translation Readable? Readability differs from one person to another, but some translations, in an effort to be comprehensive or amplified, are not very readable. Likewise, rigidly literal translations are often too hard for some students to read. There are three methods of translation: the concordant method or word-for-word translation tends to be the least readable; the free paraphrase tends to be the most readable; the equivalence method is based on the closest equivalents in two languages and tends to avoid awkward literalness on the one hand and inaccuracies on the other hand.

How Is the Translation Intended to Be Used? Is the translation for church or synagogue use? If so, then it should be more formal and dignified. Paraphrased translations use more colloquial and slang expressions, which would not be appropriate for formal religious use. Is the translation for private reading, especially for those who seldom read the Bible or for those who frequently do and are looking for some new expression or insight? Here is where the colloquial or slang expression of a paraphrased translation is more appropriate. Is it readable and intelligible to the average person?

Is the translation intended for study purposes? If so, then the translation should preserve the ambiguity of the original and the distance between the ancient and modern worlds. A careful student wants to know what the text says and draw out the relevance on his or her own. In general, the paraphrases and idiomatic translations are least satisfactory for careful study.

What Kind of Information Is in the Annotations and Notes? Check to see if the annotations are slanted to defend a particular religious approach. Are the notes helpful or distracting? Since the average person tends to accept the notes on the same level as the biblical text itself, we recommend a Bible with as few notes as possible for the beginning student. Nevertheless, consumers are demanding Bibles specifically targeted for women, men, athletes, young people, and so on. Study Bibles are very popular, but they must be used cautiously since these notations may be mistaken to be inspired or canonical.

What Is the General Format Like? Is the text reader-friendly? Are there illustrations, and do you need them? Are there paragraph divisions? Divisions do not appear in the original text. Are there paragraph headings? Remember these are also not in the original text. How are the verses laid out? Is poetry put in a different format? Special formatting is not always used by ancient authors to distinguish poetry from prose.

Is Inclusive Language Used? Inclusive language attempts to avoid sexist language and to include both women and men where it is clear that both genders are being addressed (e.g., he or she, humankind, people). Some translations are rightfully gender-inclusive but go further and make God female. In this textbook, we try to include women wherever the text does not specify males, but we do not stray from the original languages in our discussion. We do not treat God as exclusively male or female. There are biblical passages in which God is described as a female (Isa. 42:14) and other instances in which God has both male and female characteristics (Hosea 11:1–7).

No translation is best for every purpose. Since there are hundreds of English versions now available, individuals have to decide what is best for them. We hope each person will take the time to ask the necessary questions. Most of the Bible translations in the last forty to fifty years are far superior to those made earlier. For instance, despite its literary beauty and long-standing use in the church, we cannot recommend the KJV because it contains archaic language and reflects out-of-date scholarship. It is necessary to realize that some translations are much better than others for modern use. We recommend the following:

- Revised Standard Version (RSV)
- New Revised Standard Version (NRSV)
- New International Version (NIV)
- New American Bible (NAB)
- *Tanakh:* A New Translation of the Holy Scriptures according to the Traditional Hebrew Text (NJPS)
- Revised English Bible (REB)
- New Jerusalem Bible (NJB)
- Contemporary English Version (CEV)

How to Find Answers to Your Questions: Additional Resources

A serious study of the OT/HB raises many questions for both new students and seasoned scholars. Some of these questions have been raised in the past and discussed for centuries while remaining unresolved. To assist students with further study, we have provided below an annotated list of additional resources that may provide some of the answers to your questions. In some cases these works may also point out the difficulty of answering a particular question. As one can imagine, over the course of more than twenty centuries, there has been a great deal of careful thought given to understanding the Bible, and whole libraries are dedicated to these studies. The short guide we provide is arranged in categories of reference works to assist students to obtain several levels of information, from the simplest to the most complex. A reference librarian will also be able to provide additional help.

Study Bible. Suppose a student would like to have a limited but helpful resource that is always available when he or she is reading the Bible. The study Bible is a good solution.

Several study Bibles have come on the market. These are a useful resource, especially for studying a particular book in the Bible, because the notes on each page provide quick insights and philological and historical data. We recommend *The HarperCollins Study Bible* (NRSV; HarperOne, 2006); *The Catholic Study Bible* (NAB; Oxford, 1990); *Oxford Study Bible* (REB; Oxford, 1992); *New Oxford Annotated NRSV Bible with Apocrypha* (3rd ed.; Oxford, 2001); *The Jewish Study Bible* (NJPS; Oxford, 2004); or *New Interpreter's Study Bible* (Abingdon, 2003).

Bible Atlas. Suppose a student wants more information on a place name or region that is mentioned in the Bible. A good resource for this is a Bible atlas.

One of the least understood aspects of biblical studies is the spatial and environmental character of Syria-Palestine and the ancient Mediterranean world. Bible atlases can fill this void; they come in all price ranges and are available in electronic form. For instance, *Hammond Atlas of the Bible Lands* (Hammond, 2008) and the *Bible Atlas and Companion* (Barbour, 2008) are inexpensive but serviceable

atlases. Slightly more expensive, but also in paperback, is the *Oxford Bible Atlas* (4th ed.; Oxford, 2009). The model for most modern reference atlases is Y. Aharoni, M. Avi–Yonah, and A. Rainey, *The Macmillan Bible Atlas* (3rd ed.; Macmillan, 1993). Several atlases, like *The Harper Atlas of the Bible* (HarperOne, 2008); C. Rasmussen, *Zondervan Atlas of the Bible* (Zondervan, 2009); and A. Rainey and R. S. Notley, *The Sacred Bridge* (Carta, 2006), have spectacular color pictures and excellent discussions of geography. However, they are all fairly expensive, and this expense must be weighed against the need to purchase other resources. Bible dictionaries and commentaries do deal at least somewhat with biblical geography and usually contain a set of color maps.

One-Volume Bible Dictionary. Suppose a student wants to have more information on a lesser known character such as Rahab. He or she could check a one-volume Bible dictionary.

The most important resource for students other than the Bible is a one-volume Bible dictionary. This aid is affordable for personal collections, and it allows for quick reference to all the persons, places, and major concepts of the Bible. There are four one-volume Bible dictionaries on the market that we recommend. The *HarperCollins Bible Dictionary* (rev. ed.; HarperOne, 1996) is the best Bible dictionary currently available. *Eerdmans Dictionary of the Bible* (Eerdmans, 2000) is also excellent and a little more recent. The *New Bible Dictionary* (rev. ed.; InterVarsity Press, 1996) and the *Holman Illustrated Bible Dictionary* (Holman, 2003) are more conservative in orientation. A somewhat different volume is the *Mercer Dictionary of the Bible* (Mercer, 1998). It is designed as a textbook and therefore does not have as many minor articles as do other dictionaries. Still, it is highly recommended.

Multivolume Dictionary. Suppose a student wants a detailed explanation of a term used in the Bible, such as the ark of the covenant. He or she could find an in-depth treatment of the topic in a multivolume Bible dictionary.

Two excellent multivolume dictionaries are on the market. The first is *The Anchor Bible Dictionary* (abbreviated *ABD*) in six volumes (Doubleday, 1992). With some exceptions, it has balanced and complete treatments of textual, theological, and archaeological data. More balanced and significantly updated is *The New Interpreter's Dictionary of the Bible* (NIDB; 5 vols.; Abingdon, 2006–9), although the price for either multivolume Bible dictionary may be somewhat prohibitive. (Both are also available on CD.) Most student questions can be answered by using either of these dictionaries. Bibliographies at the ends of most articles will be especially helpful to students who are writing term papers.

Bible Handbook. Suppose a student wants information on social customs or life in biblical times. One possible resource would be a Bible handbook.

This is a much abused category of biblical resources. It has been dominated in the past by such works as *Halley's Bible Handbook* (Zondervan, 1959). This book has not been revised and is badly out of date. We are reluctant to recommend any of the volumes in this general category because they tend to be abbreviated versions of one-volume commentaries, are often superficial, and in many cases are apologetic or very limited in their perspective and treatment of the Bible. Instead, we suggest the purchase of a volume dealing with the social world of the Bible. Philip King and Lawrence Stager, *Life in Biblical Israel* (Westminster John Knox, 2001); Victor H. Matthews, *Manners and Customs in the Bible* (3rd ed.;

Hendrickson, 2006); and Oded Borowski, *Daily Life in Biblical Times* (SBL, 2003) all provide historical summaries of each of the biblical periods from the time of Abraham through the NT. Among the topics discussed are marriage customs, clothing styles, diet, economic life, warfare, architecture, and burial customs.

Books on Archaeology. Suppose a student has an interest in archaeology. Several books can be recommended to help illuminate the values and limitations of archaeology.

For those students who wish to know more about archaeological methods and the results of excavations in biblical lands during the last century, there are a number of reference works and monographs to choose from. For the beginner, we recommend the following: Don C. Benjamin, *Stones and Stories: An Introduction to Archaeology and the Bible* (Fortress, 2009); A. Ben Tor, *The Archaeology of Ancient Israel* (Yale University Press, 1994); and J. Laughlin, *Archaeology and the Bible* (Routledge, 1999). For the more advanced student or scholar, we recommend A. Mazar, *Archaeology of the Land of the Bible, 10,000–586 BCE* (Doubleday, 1990); and Ephraim Stern, *Archaeology of the Land of the Bible*, vol. 2; *The Assyrian, Babylonian, and Persian Periods* (Doubleday, 2001). All these studies provide good, readable coverage. For a more comprehensive reference work, consult T. E. Levy, ed., *The Archaeology of Society in the Holy Land* (Continuum, 1998); or the multivolume work of Eric Meyers, ed., *Oxford Encyclopedia of Archaeology in the Near East* (Oxford, 1997); or Ephraim Stern, ed., *The New Encyclopedia of Archaeological Excavations in the Holy Land* (Carta, 1993).

Commentary. Suppose a student needs more information on a difficult biblical passage or verse (such as Exod. 4:24–26) and wants help understanding various interpretations. He or she might turn to either a multivolume or a one-volume Bible commentary.

Since the 1950s, the multivolume Bible commentary category has been dominated by the twelve-volume *Interpreter's Bible* (Abingdon, 1952). This set was the first real attempt to provide a scholarly treatment of the biblical text for ministers. An updated and thoroughly revised edition has been released in twelve volumes called the *New Interpreter's Bible* (Abingdon, 1994–2002).

In the category of the one-volume Bible commentary, *The New Jerome Biblical Commentary* (Prentice Hall, 1990) is the best of this genre on the market. Produced by Roman Catholic clerical and lay scholars, it provides an amazing depth of theological, textual, and archaeological discussion. Additional volumes in this category are the *HarperCollins Bible Commentary* (HarperOne, 2000) and the *Eerdmans Commentary on the Bible* (Eerdmans, 2003). *The IVP Bible Background Commentary: Old Testament* (InterVarsity Press, 2000) describes everyday life and offers cultural and historical background to the entire OT/HB. A more specialized volume, *The Women's Bible Commentary* (2nd ed.; Westminster John Knox, 1998), provides a feminist perspective on the text, including the Deuterocanonical books.

Bible Abstracts and Biblical Journals. Suppose a student wants to examine what scholars have to say about the Bible and about particular themes or narratives. One place to start would be with Bible abstracts and popularly written journals. For more advanced study, more technical journals can be consulted.

Since a student will not always have access to scholarly publications, one way to keep up is to regularly check *New Testament Abstracts* and *Old Testament Abstracts*. These very helpful quarterly publications provide brief summaries of hundreds of articles and books published each year.

While a student's interests may vary, three popular journals currently available by subscription will be useful to all. They are *Near Eastern Archaeology*, *Biblical Archaeology Review*, and *The Bible Today*. The first two deal primarily with developments in archaeology, while the last one is concerned with current developments and theological issues in biblical studies. They are an inexpensive way to stay current on modern theological discussions and archaeological discoveries.

More technical discussions of biblical issues in both Testaments can be found in *Interpretation*, the *Journal of Biblical Literature*, the *Catholic Biblical Quarterly*, and *Biblical Theology Bulletin*.

Collections of Ancient Near Eastern Texts in Translation. Suppose a student wants to read an extrabiblical source that will shed light on the biblical text (e.g., flood story). There are several translations to choose from.

Since our textbook contains excerpts from many ancient Near Eastern texts, some students may wish to examine collections of the texts in translation. V. H. Matthews and D. C. Benjamin, *Old Testament Parallels: Laws and Stories from the Ancient Near East* (3rd ed.; Paulist Press, 2006) contains colloquial, student-friendly translations of texts from throughout the Near East. Smaller collections include M. Coogan, *Stories from Ancient Canaan* (Westminster, 1978); and S. Dalley, *Myths from Mesopotamia* (Oxford, 2009). For scholarly translations, we recommend W. W. Hallo and K. Lawson Younger Jr., eds., *The Context of Scripture* (3 vols.; Brill, 1997–2002); or J. Pritchard, *Ancient Near Eastern Texts Relating to the Old Testament* (3rd ed.; Princeton University Press, 1969).

GLOSSARY OF TERMS AND CONCEPTS

Aaronide priesthood: that portion of the Israelite priestly community that traces its origins directly back to Aaron through Zadok, high priest in Solomon's time (1 Kings 2:35; 4:2).

acculturizing: to cause a people to adopt the culture of another people through close social contact, economic coercion, or political decree.

acrophonic: shaping the letters in a writing system based on sound and meaning.

acrostic: a literary device in which each line or stanza begins with a consecutive letter of the alphabet (see Ps. 119).

anachronism: a detail or word in a story that does not fit the time period of the story itself but often reflects the time in which the story is composed (see Gen. 11:28; Exod. 13:17).

annunciation: the announcement or declaration of the birth of a child by a representative of God (e.g., angel, priest, prophet).

anthropomorphism: attributing to a god the characteristics of a human, specifically human physical form (see Gen. 8:21).

apocalypse: a book containing symbolic visions and revelations concerning the end of the world (see *4 Ezra*).

apocalyptic: a type of literature dealing with end things, characterized by word or number symbols, monstrous visions, and predictions of final battles (see Dan. 7–12).

Apocrypha: *See* Deuterocanonical books.

apodictic: a type of legal statement that is in the form of a command given without supporting explanation (e.g., "You shall not steal").

apology: a literary defense of a character or idea such as the apology of David in 2 Sam. 9–20.

apostasy: any action that allows or condones false worship (see Solomon in 1 Kings 11:1–8).

ark of the covenant: the gold-covered box created to house the Ten Commandments. It is carried by the Levites and is kept in the holy of holies of the tabernacle during the wilderness period.

Asherim: cult objects (e.g., wooden poles) symbolizing the fertility goddess Asherah.

assimilation ritual: a set of ceremonial words and actions designed to induct an outsider as a member of a group (see Ruth 1:16–17).

autograph: the original copy of any manuscript. No autographs of any biblical text have survived. Only later handwritten copies are available for study.

barren-wife motif: the theme of childlessness principally found in the ancestral narratives. This theme is used to add dramatic tension to the search for the covenantal heir in each generation.

baulks: walls of earth left unexcavated at an archaeological dig used to divide the excavated squares, primarily allowing a clear record of the stratigraphy as well as providing walkways around the dig site.

call narrative: the event in which a person is called to become a prophet (see Isa. 6).

canon: those books designated by a faith community as Scripture and as the written standard for faith and practice.

canonical: items such as clothing, ritual practices, or books or writings that conform to a general rule of religious orthodoxy.

carbon 14: dating of organic remains using the computation of the atomic half-life of an isotope of carbon.

casting his mantle: an action designed to designate someone as a person's successor (see 1 Kings 19:19).

casuistic: a conditional form of law that is based on an "if . . . then" structure.

chronicler: unknown author of the books of Chronicles during the fifth century BCE. He draws material, such as genealogies, from Genesis and apparently has access to the text of the books of Samuel and Kings. The Chronicler's use of these sources is selective in what appears to be an attempt to promote a pro-Davidic agenda.

city-states: ancient political units comprising an urban center and its immediate environs and villages.

clean/cleanness: the desirable ritual or ceremonial status that results from following the rules established by a society. The opposite is to be unclean. *See* ritual purity.

codices: a book manuscript with individual pages. This innovation in book binding replaces scrolls and makes references to anything in the codex much easier to find quickly.

cognitive dissonance: a mental state resulting from a situation in which two completely credible statements are made, both of which may appear true although one of them is false. The dissonance is caused in the decision-making process (see 1 Kings 22:19–28).

colophon: a statement or phrase placed at the end of a document that may serve as a summary or simply an end marker (see Hosea 14:9).

concubine: a secondary wife who may have come to the marriage without a dowry (often as a slave) and whose children usually do not inherit from their father unless he publicly declares them his heirs.

corporate identity: a legal principle that rewards or punishes an entire household for the righteousness or the sins of the head of the household (see Noah in Gen. 6–9 or Achan in Josh. 7).

cosmopolitan: having an attitude of cultural openness and sophistication that allows for the quick acceptance of new ideas, fashions, or beliefs.

covenant: any contractual agreement, but within the Bible especially a contractual agreement between Yahweh and the chosen people that promises them land and progeny in exchange for their exclusive worship and obedience.

Covenant Code: one of the seven bodies of Israelite law (Exod. 20:18–23:33) and considered to be the oldest. It contains both casuistic and apodictic forms of legal pronouncement.

covenant-renewal ceremony: a ritual mentioned as occurring several times and led by Israelite leaders to reinforce the importance of the people's covenant with Yahweh (see Exod. 24:1–8; Josh. 24:1–28).

culling process: the method of eliminating the worthless from the valuable. Used with reference to God's removing the unfaithful worshipers from the faithful during the wilderness period (see Num. 16).

cultic sites: locations where religious activity takes place (e.g., high place, temple).

cuneiform: the wedge-shaped script pressed into wet clay with a reed and invented by the Sumerians. It is used by every subsequent civilization in Mesopotamia until the coming of the Greeks. Cuneiform is a syllabic (e.g., la, ba, ku, a, lum) script rather than an alphabetic script such as later used by the Hebrews and Greeks (e.g., b, c, d; later including vowels, e.g., a, e). Ugaritic is unusual in that it was written in an alphabetic cuneiform script.

Dead Sea Scrolls: the scrolls discovered in the caves near Qumran on the northwestern shore of the Dead Sea beginning in 1947. These scrolls include the oldest copies of the OT/HB books that have been found to date. They are dated from the second century BCE to the first century CE.

Decalogue: the Ten Commandments (Exod. 20:1–17; Deut. 5:6–21).

demythologize: to use a story from another culture without ascribing any powers to the gods in those stories.

Deuterocanonical books, or Apocrypha: the seven to fifteen books (e.g., 1 and 2 Maccabees, Judith, Baruch) written between 300 BCE and 100 CE that are contained in the Septuagint and the Vulgate and are accepted as authoritative by Roman Catholics and the Eastern Orthodox but not by Protestants and Jews.

Deuteronomic Code: a late-seventh-century-BCE law code (Deut. 12–26) that updates some of the legal stipulations found in the earlier Covenant Code and may be associated with Josiah's reform movement.

Deuteronomist/Deuteronomistic Historian: the name given to the unknown author(s) or editor(s) of the long and complex history found in Deuteronomy through 2 Kings, called the Deuteronomistic History. It is characterized by a strict moralism and a view of Israelite history in which the people continually fail to obey the covenant and therefore deserve Yahweh's punishment.

Diadochi: the generals of Alexander the Great who succeed him as rulers in the territories they had conquered together. Among the most important are Ptolemy in Egypt and Seleucus in Mesopotamia.

Diaspora: the scattering of the people of Israel and Judah throughout the countries and regions of the Near East following the destruction of Samaria (721 BCE) and Jerusalem (587 BCE). The term has subsequently been applied to the scattering of the Jews throughout the Roman Empire following the destruction of Jerusalem in 135 CE.

diasporic Judaism: the life and practice of Jews outside Palestine. The major impetus for the development of the Diaspora is the Babylonian exile. Diasporic Judaism finds continued vitality among Jews who remain in the lands of the exile or who emigrate from Palestine in the centuries following the exile. This diasporic Judaism also accompanies those who return to Judah (later Israel) from exile.

disqualification stories: a set of stories designed to eliminate a person or a family from succession to the throne of Israel or from inheriting the covenantal promise (see the negative narrative of Saul in 1 Sam. 13–15).

dittography: a scribal error created when a scribe accidentally writes the same word or phrase twice. *See* haplography.

divine assembly: the divine company that serves Yahweh in the form of messengers and is portrayed surrounding the enthroned Yahweh (e.g., Job 1:6).

Divine Warrior: Yahweh depicted in the role of a combatant in human warfare.

documentary hypothesis: the literary theory voiced most cogently by Julius Wellhausen (late nineteenth century) that identifies four strands of editing in the Pentateuch, signified respectively by the letters J, E, D, and P (designating the Yahwist [Jahwist in German], Elohist, Deuteronomist, and Priestly sources).

D-source: according to the documentary hypothesis, the layer of the editing of the biblical text dated to about 600 BCE and associated primarily with the book of Deuteronomy and the historical narrative found in Joshua through 2 Kings. *See* Deuteronomistic Historian.

egalitarianism: a social system in which all persons have equal status before the law.

egalitarian ideal: as expressed by the prophets, this ideal of society considers every member of the covenant community equal under the law. However, this does not discount the reality of social divisions based on wealth and status.

eisegesis: reading into a passage an interpretation based on one's own ideas, often creating a misinterpretation. *See* exegesis.

Elohim: one of the names for the Israelite God in the Bible. Associated with the E-source, it usually is translated as "God" in English translations of the Bible.

emendation: a suggested alternative reading of the original text that makes better sense in the context (see inset on Amos 4:3 in ch. 4).

emic: an insider's understanding of a person's actions and symbolic gestures that allows the enacted prophecy to convey a message without a long explanation to its original audience.

enacted prophecy: a prophecy that includes an action by the prophet designed to attract attention and reinforce the message.

endogamy: the practice and policy of marrying only within one's own identifiable group.

eponym/eponymous ancestor: heroic characters considered to be the founding fathers of a tribe or nation.

eschatology: the study of last things or events just prior to the end of the world.

E-source: according to the documentary hypothesis, the layer of editing of the biblical text dated to about 850 BCE that reflects a northern or Israelite viewpoint from the period after the division of the kingdom.

Essenes: a Jewish sect described by Josephus, commonly thought to have built the Dead Sea community at Qumran and to have produced the Dead Sea Scrolls. They withdraw from active participation in the Jerusalem cult to protest the Hasmoneans' usurpation of the high priesthood in 152 BCE.

etic: an outsider's viewpoint or understanding of another's actions and symbolic gestures that makes it somewhat more difficult to understand their full significance.

etiologies: stories that are designed to explain the origin of an event, the background of a place name, or the basis for a tradition.

everlasting covenant: a pledge made by God to David in which Yahweh promises that there will always be a king of the line of David ruling in Jerusalem (2 Sam. 7:7–17).

execration: the act of cursing someone or something (see Jer. 19).

execration ritual: a series of ceremonial actions that curse a person or place.

exegesis: the process of careful study of biblical passages, ideally in their original ancient languages, with the intent to produce useful interpretations of these texts. *See* eisegesis.

framework story: a narrative with an outline structure that can be applied whenever a similar set of events occur or that can be used as the basis for a drama (see Gen. 1:1–2:4a).

genealogies: the listing of the familial histories of several generations of a family, people, clan, or profession (e.g., priests).

glory: in the Hebrew Bible the word used is *kabod* ("weighty") and thus of great importance. When applied to God, it refers to the Deity's powerful manifestation in a theophany, physical events, or in visions.

glosses: scribal additions to the text.

haggadah: a form of Jewish scholarship designed to draw together the strands of tradition contained in Scripture, the Mishnah, and the commentaries.

halakah: originally spoken rules for conduct formulated by the rabbis of the period from 200 to 400 CE, which were compiled in the Mishnah.

Hanukkah: the festival that commemorates the rededication of the temple in 165 BCE after the initial victory of the Maccabees over the Seleucid Greeks during the Maccabean Revolt.

hapax legomenon: single occurrence of a word, which cannot be translated with certainty based on either context or comparison with other texts.

haplography: a scribal error created when a scribe accidentally deletes a word or a phrase. *See* dittography.

Hasmonean: independent Jewish kingdom founded in 142 BCE by Jonathan, brother of Judas Maccabeus. It lasts several tumultuous generations until the Roman general Pompey absorbs Judea into the Roman Empire in 63 BCE.

Hebrew canon: the set of thirty-nine books commonly accepted by Jews and Protestants as holy Scripture. It does not include the Apocrypha (Deuterocanonical books).

hegemony: a political situation in which a powerful nation or empire exercises extensive influence over the policies and actions of neighboring states.

Hellenistic culture: following Alexander (the Great) of Macedon's conquest of the Near East, Greek cultural ideas, architecture, and philosophy are introduced in these regions, creating a synthesis that contains aspects of both Greek and Near Eastern culture.

henotheism: belief in the existence of many gods conjoined with the choice to worship only one of them.

heresy: originally the designation of a sect, but in later usage the term applies to those religious beliefs that deviate from the accepted or orthodox teachings of the dominant group.

high place: *bamah* (pl. *bamot*) in Hebrew; a hilltop used as a local shrine.

Holiness Code: a portion of the Priestly source (P-source; Lev. 17–26), probably dating to the fifth century BCE, that reiterates the command to "be holy" and is concerned with matters of ritual purity.

holy: a term employed in the biblical text for the sacredness and otherworldliness of God to distinguish the divine from human. The opposite is profane. The word is also used to modify other words (war, words, places).

The central concept is to be set apart for service to the Deity.

holy of holies: that most holy portion of the tabernacle, and later the Jerusalem temple, that houses the ark of the covenant. Only the high priest is allowed to enter this sacred precinct.

immanent: the quality of being present within this world and also affected by it (e.g., get wet when it rains). The opposite is being transcendent.

impurity: *See* Uncleanness and its opposite, Ritual purity.

inclusio: a literary device in which the same element occurs at the beginning and at the end (e.g., ABCB'A').

inclusive language: words that express the inclusion of both male and female in a statement (e.g., in the place of "sons of God," the use of "children of God").

infrastructure: the public-works projects that aid communication, travel, and economic activity (e.g., roads, bridges, irrigation canals, and dams).

Jeroboam's sin: the actions taken by King Jeroboam I to establish a separate identity for the northern kingdom. They were used by the biblical writers as the hallmark of the evil king (see 1 Kings 12:25–33).

Jewish Identity Movement: theology of the postexilic era characterized by emphasis on Sabbath worship, use of Hebrew in liturgy, development of a canon of Scriptures, ritual purity and dietary laws, and endogamous marriage practice.

J-source: according to the documentary hypothesis, the first layer of editing of the biblical text, dated to about 900–850 BCE; containing a narrative style, and reflecting the political boundaries of David's kingdom.

khabiru ('apiru): a term used in Mesopotamian and Egyptian texts for stateless persons. Sometimes Hebrew is identified with *khabiru,* but this is unlikely.

kherem: an element of holy war in Israelite warfare that requires the destruction of all persons, animals, and property as a dedicatory sacrifice to Yahweh.

khesed: "everlasting love," a covenantal term that is used as the basis for Yahweh's willingness to make a covenant with the people of Israel and Judah.

khirbet: small rural settlement with a limited number of occupational strata. Contrast this with the tell of a city or town, which has many strata.

kosher: a term used for "clean" (i.e., ritually pure) food.

Law: *See* Torah.

legend: a story that centers on human heroes or founders of nations and that includes superhuman feats or dealings with gods.

levir: the brother or nearest male relative who has the obligation to impregnate the childless widow of his deceased brother or relative so that she will have a child to continue the line of her late husband and to provide for her needs.

levirate obligation: a legal arrangement based on the obligation of the brother or nearest male relative to provide a deceased kinsman with an heir (see Gen. 38:1–11). The brother or relative is required to impregnate the widow and to provide for her needs. The resulting child is legally considered the child of the dead man. Procreation is required, but an actual marriage tie is not necessary.

lex talionis: the legal principle of retaliation in kind or measure that is epitomized in the phrase "an eye for an eye."

liturgy: the outline, body of material recited or sung, and stages of a worship service.

Maccabees/Maccabean: based on the name of its leader, Judas Maccabeus, the name applied to the Hasmonean rebels who revolted against Seleucid rule in Judea in the second century BCE.

Masoretes: Jewish scholars who in about 500 CE add a vowel-pointing system to the Hebrew text of the Bible in order to facilitate its pronunciation. They also develop procedures to detect and prevent as many scribal errors as possible as they copy the manuscripts of the Hebrew text.

Mesha Stele: a monumental inscription commissioned by King Mesha of Moab in about 850 BCE. It contains a parallel version of the story in 2 Kings 3 of the revolt led by Mesha against Ahab of Israel.

messenger formula: a standard phrase used by a prophet to make it clear that these are the words of the Deity: "Thus says the LORD [Yahweh]" (see Mic. 2:3; Jer. 5:14).

Messiah: an English derivative of the Hebrew word for "anointed" applied to individuals chosen by Yahweh for leadership positions.

monotheistic: the belief that only a single, all-powerful God exists.

motif: a repeated story element in a narrative.

murmuring motif: a recurrent theme in the wilderness period consisting of complaints by the Israelites about their needs for food and water or rebellion against Moses's leadership and the resulting punishment by God (see Exod. 16). The murmuring motif is paired with a culling process designed to eliminate the unfaithful.

Mushite priesthood: that portion of the Israelite priesthood that traces its origins back to Moses and through the line of priests housed at Shiloh and Nob (e.g., Abiathar during the early monarchy). They are exiled to Anathoth in Solomon's reign (1 Kings 2:26–27).

myth: a story that centers on the origin of events or things (*See* etiologies) and usually involves the activities of gods.

Nazirite: an Israelite, either male or female, who takes an oath to refrain from consuming any product of the grape, from coming in contact with the dead, and from cutting his or her hair (see Num. 6).

nepotism: the hiring of one's relatives.

novella: a literary form for a story shorter than the novel, with a compact style and plot.

onomatopoeic: a word designed to express deep emotions like anger, grief, and fear by imitating the involuntary sounds uttered by a person who is experiencing those emotions.

oracle: a prophetic speech.

ostracon (pl., ostraca): broken piece of pottery used to record a message or inscription.

pantheon: all of the gods in a religious system.

pastoralism/pastoral nomadism: a form of human activity based on seasonal movement of flocks of sheep and goats from one pasture area to another. This lifestyle is described in the ancestral narratives.

Pentateuch: the first five books of the OT/HB (i.e., Genesis through Deuteronomy). *See* Torah.

Pharisees: a Jewish sect described by Josephus and known for belief in an afterlife and the acceptance of both oral tradition and the canonical Scriptures as authoritative.

philology: the study of language used in literature, particularly as it informs one about human culture.

polytheistic: the belief in the existence of many gods.

prophetic immunity: protection given to prophets when they speak in God's name that prevents people from killing the messenger for delivering a negative message. This protection does not prevent persecution or torture (see Jer. 20).

pseudonym: a pen name or fictitious name chosen by the author of a literary work that is frequently the borrowed name of some revered figure of the past.

P-source: according to the documentary hypothesis, the final layer of editing of the biblical text, dated to about 500 BCE, which reflects priestly concern for matters of religious ritual and purity after the exilic period. Some portions of the Priestly source may date to the eighth century BCE.

Purim: Hebrew word for "lot" (akin to "dice"). The Festival of Purim commemorates a major victory of the Jews in the Diaspora over oppression and is recounted in the book of Esther. Purim takes place on the fourteenth and fifteenth days of Adar, the twelfth month of the Jewish calendar (usually in present-day March).

purity: *See* clean/cleanness, ritual purity.

Qumran: a settlement at the northwestern end of the Dead Sea believed to have been established by Essenes and closely associated with the Dead Sea Scrolls.

redaction: a revision of a text by a later editor.

remnant: the righteous portion of the community who will, according to the prophets, survive God's wrath and rebuild the nation.

retribalization: the process of moving from an urban existence to a seminomadic existence, which requires the formation of tribal loyalties and a cautious attitude to strangers.

ritual purity: the steps taken to transform persons or objects into a clean or pure religious state. Impurity can be caused by contact with the dead or the diseased, bodily emissions, or through eating certain forbidden foods. Some individuals, like the high priest, must maintain an even higher level of ritual purity in order to carry out sacred duties.

rubrics: instructions that are usually placed in margins or as footnotes in a text.

Sabbath: the celebration of Yahweh as the creator God and the commemoration of the creation event by ceasing work one day each week.

Sadducees: a Jewish sect described by Josephus that dominates the ritual activity of the Jerusalem temple during the period from 200 BCE to 70 CE. They do not believe in an afterlife and accept only the canonical Scriptures as authoritative.

Sanhedrin: the supreme council in Jerusalem, made up of the most powerful and influential leaders and active during the first century CE.

Sea Peoples: a term used for groups of invaders who, in about 1200 BCE, attacked many of the population centers along the eastern Mediterranean coast, weakening both the Egyptian and Hittite empires and destroying the port of Ugarit. Some, later known as the Philistines, settled along the southern coastal plain of Canaan.

search-for-heir motif: a theme in ancestral narratives in which the patriarch seeks to assure the continuation of the family through an heir designated as successor by a formal blessing.

second temple: the period in Jewish history following the construction of the second temple in Jerusalem (515 BCE) until the destruction of Herod's temple in Jerusalem (70 CE) by the Romans.

Seleucids: rulers of the successor kingdoms of Asia, including Mesopotamia, Syria, and, after 200 BCE, Judea. They were successors of Seleucus, one of Alexander of Macedon's generals. *See* Diadochi.

Septuagint: the Greek translation of the HB by the Jews of Alexandria, Egypt, in the fourth through second centuries BCE, which contains the Apocrypha (Deuterocanonical books) and is abbreviated LXX.

seraphim (seraphs): supernatural attendants or fiery guardians who surround God's holy throne, analogous to other angelic beings such as the cherubim (Isa. 6:1–7).

seventy elders: that group of men selected to help administer the Israelites and who represent them at major events.

Shema: the statement of faith of the Israelites found in Deut. 6:4 declaring that there is only one God, Yahweh.

Sheol: Hebrew word meaning "pit," the abode of the dead. According to the OT/HB, both the righteous and the wicked go there after death. There is no indication in the Hebrew tradition of punishment or reward and little indication of anything that happens in Sheol. Older translations of the Bible often translate "Sheol" as "hell," but that is incorrect.

Shephelah: the low hills in western Canaan separating the coastal plains from the central hill country to the east.

soliloquies: private statements made for the benefit of the audience, such as those in Job 29–31.

sons of the prophets: apprentice prophets who serve Elijah and Elisha as a support group and as messengers.

stele: inscribed monument usually carved on a stone or pillar and erected to commemorate a military victory or other important event.

stratigraphy: in archaeology, the succession of occupation layers revealed by excavations, which can be used for dating artifacts.

stratum: a distinct layer of occupation within the mound of a tell.

superscription: the rubrics of instruction found at the beginning of many of the psalms.

syncretism/syncretistic: the mixing together of cultural and religious ideas and traits borrowed from neighboring peoples.

tell(s): an English word derived from Arabic. An artificial hill that is created by the successive layers or strata of occupation on a site. Extensive layers suggest an ancient town or even a city rather than a rural village. *See* khirbet.

teraphim: the image of a household god or patron spirit representing the good fortune of the household and to be inherited by the heir.

theodicy: an explanation for God's actions most often found in the words of the prophets.

theophany: the appearance of God to a human being.

Torah: Hebrew word for "Law," a term used for the first five books of the OT/HB. These books are also called the Pentateuch.

transcendent: a characteristic of a deity who is separate from the creation and is not affected by the forces of nature.

trickster: a character who constantly struggles to outwit other characters and generally ends up being tricked.

uncleanness: the undesirable ritual or ceremonial status that results when the rules of the society are broken. *See* ritual purity.

universalism: a theme in biblical narrative trying to demonstrate that Yahweh is God over the whole of humanity and the creation, rather than a deity localized to or interested in Israel alone.

Vulgate: the Latin translation of the OT/HB and the NT made by Jerome in the fourth century CE. It includes the Apocrypha (Deuterocanonical books).

wife-sister motif: a theme in the ancestral narratives that appears three times (Gen. 12; 20; 26) and in which the patriarch describes his wife as his sister in order to deceive a local ruler.

wisdom: the body of literature and tradition that comprises a culture's understanding of its basic values and honorable behavior.

Wisdom literature: a type of literature that concentrates on how one should live and the basic values and common sense of a culture.

wise woman: a female elder (e.g., the woman from Tekoa mentioned in 2 Sam. 14:1–24).

xenophobic: fearing strangers or anything that is different.

Yahweh: one of the names for the Israelite God in the Bible that is sometimes anglicized into Jehovah. This name is associated with the J-source. In English translations of the Bible, Yahweh is usually translated as LORD.

Zealots: a militant, nationalistic Jewish sect described by Josephus that opposed Roman occupation of Judea.

Zoroastrianism: a dualistic religion found in ancient Persia that is characterized by the belief in a constant struggle between the forces of light and darkness, a final battle, and the resurrection and judgment of the dead.

Index of Names and Subjects

INDEX OF ANCIENT SOURCES

321